CHILDREN AND CROSS

In 2009, Stephen Barker was convicted of rape on the evidence of a little girl who was four-and-a-half years old at the trial, and about three-and-a-half when first interviewed by the police. The high point of the proceedings was the child's appearance as a live witness in order for Barker's counsel to attempt a cross-examination.

This case focused attention on the need, imposed by current English law, for even tiny children to come to court for a live cross-examination.

In 1989, the Pigot Committee proposed a scheme under which the whole of a young child's evidence, including cross-examination, would be obtained out of court and in advance of trial. In 1999 a provision designed to give effect to this was included in the Youth Justice and Criminal Evidence Act, but it has not yet been brought into force.

The full Pigot proposal was implemented, however, in Western Australia, and similar schemes operate in a number of European jurisdictions. This book of essays examines a number of these schemes, and argues the case for further reforms in the UK.

Children and Cross-Examination

Time to Change the Rules?

Edited by

John R Spencer
and
Michael E Lamb

OXFORD AND PORTLAND, OREGON
2012

Published in the United Kingdom by Hart Publishing Ltd
16C Worcester Place, Oxford, OX1 2JW
Telephone: +44 (0)1865 517530
Fax: +44 (0)1865 510710
E-mail: mail@hartpub.co.uk
Website: http://www.hartpub.co.uk

Published in North America (US and Canada) by
Hart Publishing
c/o International Specialized Book Services
920 NE 58th Avenue, Suite 300
Portland, OR 97213-3786
USA
Tel: +1 503 287 3093 or toll-free: (1) 800 944 6190
Fax: +1 503 280 8832
E-mail: orders@isbs.com
Website: http://www.isbs.com

British Library Cataloguing in Publication Data
Data Available

ISBN: 978-1-84946-307-2

Typeset by Compuscript Ltd, Shannon
Printed and bound by
CPI Group (UK) Ltd, Croydon, CR0 4YY

CONTRIBUTORS

John R Spencer is a Professor of Law at the University of Cambridge. His areas of expertise include criminal law, criminal evidence, comparative criminal procedure and EU criminal law. One of his particular interests has long been the evidence of children, on which he wrote, with Rhona Flin, a pioneering book *The Evidence of Children, the Law and the Psychology* (2nd edn 1993). In 2000–01 he was a consultant to Lord Justice Auld's Review of the Criminal Courts. He is a QC (*honoris causa*), an Academic Bencher of the Inner Temple, and holds an honorary degree from the University of Poitiers. In 2008 the University of Cambridge awarded him an LLD.

Michael E Lamb is Professor of Psychology at the University of Cambridge. He has authored or edited about 45 books, including *Investigative Interviews of Children* (1998), *Child Sexual Abuse: Disclosure, Delay and Denial* (2007), *Tell Me What Happened: Structured Investigative Interviews of Children* (2008) and *Children's Testimony* (2011) as well as about 600 professional publications. He received the James McKeen Cattell Award from the Association for Psychological Science for Lifetime Contributions to Applied Psychological Research (2004) and edits the journal *Psychology, Public Policy, and Law.*

Joyce Plotnikoff has a law degree from the University of Bristol and a diploma in social and administrative studies (distinction) from the University of Oxford. She was admitted to the Bar in the USA, was awarded a Judicial Fellowship by the US Supreme Court and worked in the US federal court system for 10 years. She subsequently worked as a research fellow at the Universities of Oxford and Birmingham and as a children's guardian in care proceedings.

Richard Woolfson studied mathematics at the University of Glasgow and took his doctorate at the University of Oxford. He became an academic and then joined the information systems industry. Richard has been a lay magistrate, a Courts Board chair and is currently facilitator of the CPS Hate Crime Scrutiny Panel for Hertfordshire and Bedfordshire. Richard and Joyce began working together in 1991. Their company, Lexicon Limited, conducts research in the criminal, civil and family jurisdictions. Their research concerning children includes *Prosecuting Child Abuse* (1995), *Reporting to Court under the Children Act* (1996), *Evaluating Young Witness Support* (2007), *The 'Go Between': Evaluation of Intermediary Pathfinder Projects* (2007) and *Measuring Up? Evaluating Government Commitments to Young Witnesses in Criminal Proceedings* (2009). They coordinated *A Case for Balance* (1997), the first judicial training video demonstrating good practice in managing young witness cases.

Emily Henderson is a barrister with a strong interest in the treatment of vulnerable witnesses by the criminal court and in the ethics and practice of cross-examination generally. In 2001 she was awarded a PhD from Cambridge University, supervised by Professor John R Spencer, for a thesis entitled 'Cross-examination—a Critical Examination'. Recently she co-authored a review of the situation of child witnesses in New Zealand and of a study into options for developing an intermediary system for New Zealand. She is an honorary research fellow of Auckland University. She practises as a Crown Prosecutor in the far north of New Zealand where she lives with her husband and four children.

Hal Jackson was a Judge of the District Court of Western Australia between 1986 and 2006. Prior to his appointment he had served on the Law Reform Commission of Western Australia and had been President of the Law Society. Between 1989 and 1993 he was the inaugural President of the reconstituted Children's Court of that State. He has been involved with the implementation and monitoring of various changes in the handling of children's evidence in Western Australia, both legislative and technological, and with the operation of child witness services. He has also been involved in a number of community areas concerning children and from 2003 to 2008 was the chairman of the Western Australian Ministerial Advisory Council on Child Protection. He holds the degrees of BA, LLB (UWA) and LLM (London).

Annie Cossins is an Associate Professor in the Law School at the University of New South Wales. She is the pre-eminent Australian expert on legal reform in the area of sexual assault and a scholar in theoretical criminology. She has been involved with a number of Australian government committees and taskforces whose brief has been reform of sexual assault laws. A number of legal reforms in the area of sexual assault in Australia have come about as a result of her academic publications and lobbying of governments, including a sexual assault communications privilege, reforms to the hearsay rule to enable evidence to be given of a child's first report of sexual abuse and reforms to discriminatory judicial warnings in sexual assault trials.

Verena Murschetz is a Professor at the Criminal Law Department at the Leopold Franzens University in Innsbruck, Austria. She has published extensively in the fields of juvenile law, criminal law and procedure, as well as European and international criminal law. After completing her law studies at the Leopold Franzens University, she obtained an LLM from the University of California at Los Angeles, and her PhD *summa cum laude* as well as her *Habilitation* from the Leopold Franzens University. Since 2003 she has been joining Victoria University of Wellington, New Zealand on a regular basis as a teaching fellow.

While serving as a police officer, **Trond Myklebust** gained his bachelor's degree from the University of Oslo and an MSc in investigative psychology from the University of Liverpool. In 2009 he became the first police officer in Norway to obtain a PhD (Department of Psychology, University of Oslo). He has specialised in tactical investigation both in Norway and abroad. Having both theoretical and practical experience in forensic psychology and police work, he holds a position as Detective Chief Superintendent at the Norwegian Police University College. He also holds an honorary lectureship at Teesside University in England, and is one of the founding members of the 'International Investigative Interviewing Research Group' (iIIRG). He has published his research in various peer-reviewed journals and has presented at various national and international conferences. Myklebust was decorated in 2009 with the Norwegian Police Service Medal with Laurel Branch for his merits in the development of investigative interviewing and investigative procedures in Norway.

CONTENTS

TABLE OF CASES

TABLE OF LEGISLATION

EU

International

National

United Kingdom

Other Jurisdictions

Australia

Austria

Canada

France

Ireland

Israel

New Zealand

South Africa

United States

1

Introduction

JR SPENCER

Until a quarter of a century ago, a combination of legal rules made it very difficult for the evidence of a young child to be heard in a criminal court in England and Wales—and where it was heard, to be acted on. Specifically, the *competency requirement* made it impossible for young children to give oral testimony, and the *hearsay rule* usually made it impossible for their evidence to be delivered to the court by any other means—for example, by an adult's account of what the child had said to them, or even by an audio or videotape of the child actually saying it. Where children were old and mature enough to satisfy the competency requirement, and could come to court to testify as live witnesses, a collection of sub-rules which can be collectively called *the adversarial package* then made it difficult for them to communicate their evidence when they got there. The contents of this 'adversarial package' included the rule that required witnesses to tell the whole of their tale in court, right from the beginning, without incorporating or referring back to statements they had previously made; the rule that required prosecution witnesses to give their evidence in the physical presence of the defendant; and the rule that witnesses are 'examined adversarially'—meaning that, having first been questioned by someone who wants them to say one thing, they are then cross-examined by another person who wants to make them say the opposite. Finally, in those cases where the child had managed to testify orally, and in the course of it say anything that was coherent, the *corroboration requirement* required the judge in jury trials to warn the jury, in effect, not to believe it (and in summary trials, required the magistrates, at least in theory, to issue a similar warning to themselves).

During the 1980s this state of affairs was increasingly criticised. Police officers, social workers, paediatricians, child psychiatrists, psychologists, judges, academic lawyers and even a number of practising lawyers raised their voices to say that rules needed to be changed. Prominent public figures pressing for reform included Professor Glanville Williams and Baroness Lucy Faithfull, both regrettably now dead, and Esther Rantzen, happily still very much alive. Organisations concerned with children's welfare also took an active part—led, of course, by the National Society for the Prevention of Cruelty to Children (NSPCC). This combined pressure produced important legislative changes. Some initial ones were introduced by the Criminal Justice Act of 1988, and further more important ones by the

Criminal Justice Act of 1991, a piece of legislation which implemented some (though unfortunately not all) of the recommendations of the Pigot Committee in 1989. Eight years later came the report called *Speaking up for Justice*,[1] which recommended further reforms to the law of evidence, this time for the benefit of vulnerable witnesses generally. This led to further important reforms in the Youth Justice and Criminal Evidence Act 1999.

As one who was involved in the movement for reform myself,[2] a backward glance over the developments of the last 25 years fills me with mixed feelings. One part of me is astonished at how much has been achieved, but another part is disappointed at how regularly the complaints that were made 25 years ago about the way child witnesses are treated by the criminal courts are still heard today. Much of the criticism centres around the fact that child witnesses, like adult witnesses, are still required to come to court to undergo a live cross-examination, and about the way they are treated when they get there. This book of essays is the product of a conference, held in Cambridge in April 2011, which was intended to confront this issue: in particular, by hearing presentations from speakers in other jurisdictions in which the evidence of child witnesses is tested without the live in-court cross-examination which English law still routinely requires. The papers they gave are the basis of chapters three to eight.

The rest of this introductory chapter sets the scene by reviewing those changes that have been made in England and Wales over the last 25 years in respect of the evidence of children, by explaining how it is that we still subject them to live cross-examination, and by explaining the practical consequences of this. In order to end this introductory chapter at a point which leads on to the issue of cross-examination, the topics are not discussed in the sequence listed in the first paragraph above, and are instead treated as follows: (i) corroboration; (ii) hearsay; (iii) competency; and (iv) the 'adversarial package'.

Corroboration

In its unreformed state, English law sought to limit the impact of children's evidence by a three-pronged approach. By statute, there was a total ban on convictions based on the evidence of a child who gave evidence unsworn. This was supplemented by a judicial duty to warn juries that it was 'dangerous' to convict on the uncorroborated evidence of a child, whether giving unsworn evidence or evidence on oath. And where (as often) the child was the complainant in a sex case, this duty was reinforced by a further judicial duty to warn juries that it was 'dangerous' to convict on the uncorroborated evidence of a sexual complainant.

[1] *Speaking up for Justice, Report of the Interdepartmental Working Group on the Treatment of Vulnerable or Intimidated Witnesses in the Criminal Justice System* (London, Home Office, 1998).

[2] JR Spencer and R Flin, *The Evidence of Children—the Law and the Psychology* (London, Blackstone Press, 1st edn 1989, 2nd edn 1993).

(As previously mentioned, at summary trials, where there are no juries, a magistrate or bench of magistrates were required to 'warn themselves'—in other words, legally required to proceed with caution.)

The statutory ban on convictions based on the unsworn evidence of a child derived from section 38 of the Children and Young Persons Act 1933, the provision which made it possible for children insufficiently mature to understand the nature of an oath to give their evidence unsworn, a provision which reenacted an earlier and similar provision dating from the end of the nineteenth century.[3] Having set out the terms on which children were permitted to give evidence unsworn, this went on to say:

> Provided that where evidence admitted by virtue of this section is given on behalf of the prosecution the accused shall not be liable to be convicted of the offence unless that evidence is corroborated by some other material evidence in support thereof implicating him.

The teeth of the provision were sharpened by a judicial gloss to the effect that the corroboration had to consist of something other than further unsworn evidence from different children: so one unsworn child witness could not corroborate another.[4] The effect of this, of course, was particularly bad for justice, because it meant that a person could indecently assault a series of young children, or a collection of them each in the presence of the others, and do so with impunity if they were all too young to take the oath.

The two supplementary 'judicial duties to warn' were created by the judges. At the beginning of the twentieth century the judges, worried about innocent men being falsely accused of sex offences, invented a rule requiring judges to warn juries of the danger of convicting on the uncorroborated word of a sexual complainant. The early cases involved complainants who were young,[5] and in the course of the following decades those cases spawned two separate rules: (i) judges must warn juries of the danger of believing the evidence of children, whatever the nature of the case and (ii) judges must warn juries of the danger of believing sexual complainants, whether young or old.

Over the years these rules sprouted a luxurious growth of legal technicalities. This included detailed rules about what types of evidence were capable, in law, of amounting to 'corroboration', detailed requirements about the precise words a 'corroboration warning' must contain, and a particularly obtuse rule requiring judges to warn juries about the danger of acting on uncorroborated evidence not only in cases where the evidence of the complainant stood alone, but even where it was amply supported by corroboration. Needless to say, the resulting body of law was a fertile ground for defence lawyers seeking possible grounds of appeal in cases where, despite these impediments to conviction, a conviction had occurred.

[3] Criminal Law Amendment Act 1884, s 4.
[4] *DPP v Hester* [1973] AC 296.
[5] *Graham* (1910) 4 Cr App R 218; *Brown* (1910) 6 Cr App R 24.

In 1987, when a Criminal Justice Bill was before Parliament, a group of peers moved an amendment to alter the corroboration rule in cases involving children. The government responded by ordering a review of recent psychological research bearing on the reliability of children's evidence,[6] on the basis of which it introduced a clause which later became section 34 of the Criminal Justice Act 1988. This repealed the statutory provision forbidding courts to convict on the uncorroborated evidence of unsworn children, abolished the judge-made requirement for judicial warnings against believing children's evidence, and, for good measure, also made it clear that the evidence of one child giving unworn evidence could corroborate that of another.

The effect of this provision was initially limited, because judges were still obliged to warn juries of the danger of believing sexual complainants—including, of course, those who happened to be children. Three years later, in 1991, the Law Commission recommended that the remaining corroboration requirements should be abolished. Pressure for further reform in this area grew when Lord Taylor, the Lord Chief Justice, publicly criticised this area of the law as 'arcane, technical and difficult to convey'.[7] And finally, after three more years had passed, Parliament abolished the duty to warn of the danger of believing complainants in sex cases by enacting section 32 of the Criminal Justice and Public Order Act 1994.

The impact of the abolition of the corroboration rules relating to children's evidence has been significant. When taken together with the reform of the competency rules described in the next section, the abolition has made it possible for persons who abuse young children to be convicted in situations where previously they would undoubtedly have got away with their misdeeds. A conviction in a case like *Barker*[8] for example—a case discussed in detail below—would have been out of the question.

(Interestingly, Scots law, unlike English law, has a general requirement of 'corroborated proof'. Apart from a few minor exceptions established by statute, no accused person may be convicted of any offence on one single piece of evidence, however credible. There must always be two pieces of evidence that point towards his guilt. Needless to say, a side-effect of this rule is to add to the difficulties prosecuting people for sexual offences against children—and indeed sexual offences generally. Yet at the time when public pressure led to the abolition of the more limited corroboration rules in England and Wales there was little discontent about the broader rule in Scotland. The position has now changed, however, and its possible abolition is under public discussion.[9])

[6] C Hedderman, *Children's Evidence: The Need for Corroboration*, Home Office Research and Planning Unit Paper 41 (London, Home Office, 1987).

[7] *Cheema* [1994] 1 WLR 147. This case concerned accomplice evidence—another category of evidence for which a corroboration warning was required.

[8] *Barker* [2010] EWCA Crim 4, [2011] *Crim LR* 233.

[9] At the time of writing it is one of the topics under examination by Lord Carloway, who is conducting an official review of aspects of criminal procedure in Scotland: www.scotland.gov.uk/About/CarlowayReview. And see F Crowe, 'A Case for the Abolition of Corroboration in Criminal Cases?' 2011 *Scottish Law Times* (News) 179.

The Hearsay Rule[10]

In essence, the hearsay rule provides that a disputed fact may not be established by calling X, who did not see or hear it, to tell that court that he or she heard Y, who did, describe it; either Y must be called as a live witness, or the fact must be established by other means; and if no other means are available, then in law the fact cannot be proved. So stated, the rule is obviously wide—but in fact it is even more restrictive than it first appears, because in principle it renders inadmissible much more than 'hearsay' in the colloquial sense, which is where X repeats what he claims to have heard, by word of mouth, from Y. Thus it also renders inadmissible attempts by Y to communicate directly with the court, if done by means other than using words uttered orally in the witness box. So, for example, the law regards as hearsay, and hence inadmissible, a letter that Y had written in which the matter is described, and even an audio- or videotape of Y actually describing it.

A particular application of the hearsay rule in its classic form is that, where a young child will not or cannot give oral evidence about what happened, the court is not permitted to hear what he or she said about the incident to anyone else—a parent, doctor, social worker or police officer, for example. This restrictive rule was sometimes defended as necessary to protect persons from accusations that are false; but paradoxically, in the leading case the accused, a white man who was prosecuted for assaulting a little girl of three, was prohibited from calling evidence that, just after the incident, the child had described her attacker as black.[11]

Over the years the hearsay rule was increasingly criticised. In response to this, the government referred it in 1994 to the Law Commission, which in due course produced a discussion paper, and then in 1997 a Report[12] containing proposals for reform. The Law Commission's proposals were accepted by the government and, six years later, they were enacted—with certain fairly minor changes—in Chapter 2 of Part 11 of the Criminal Justice Act 2003.

Under the reformed law, the hearsay rule is essentially retained for the purpose of criminal proceedings,[13] but made subject to a statutory list of exceptions, which are more general and wider than the limited range of exceptions that were applicable before. One of these, set out in section 116 of the Act, potentially operates where the original maker of the statement is 'unavailable' for any of a list of specified reasons. These are death; where the person in question is 'unfit to be a witness because of his bodily or mental condition'; where he is outside the UK and it is 'not reasonably practicable to secure his attendance'; where he cannot be found, though efforts have been made to find him; and lastly, where he does

[10] For an account of the reformed law, see JR Spencer, *Hearsay Evidence in Criminal Proceedings* (Oxford, Hart Publishing, 2008).

[11] *Sparks v R* [1964] AC 964.

[12] *Evidence in Criminal Proceedings: Hearsay and Related Topics* (Law Com No 245, 1997).

[13] Though not for civil proceedings, in respect of which it was completely abolished by the Civil Evidence Act 1995.

not give evidence 'through fear'. In the first four of these five cases the hearsay evidence is automatically admissible, unless it is prosecution evidence and the court rules that admitting it would render the proceedings 'unfair'.[14] In the last case—unavailability through fear—the hearsay evidence is admissible only where, having weighed up a list of factors,[15] the court gives leave.

The list of specific exceptions set out in the Act was supplemented by a general 'inclusionary discretion' under which the court may admit a piece of hearsay evidence that falls outside the explicit exceptions where the court 'is satisfied that it is in the interests of justice for it to be admissible'. This 'safety-valve provision', as it is sometimes called, is set out in section 114(1)(d) of the 2003 Act. In deciding to admit hearsay evidence under this provision, the court must 'have regard to' the list of nine factors set out in section 112(2) and, for good measure, 'any others it considers relevant'.

Though worded in language that looks extremely cautious, this reform of the hearsay rule was potentially important for child abuse cases, especially those involving children who were very young. In 2009 this was dramatically demonstrated by the case of *J (S)*.[16] The defendant, 'Sid', was accused of a grave sexual assault on his partner's baby daughter, who was aged two-and-a-half at the time. While she lay in bed, someone entered the room and penetrated her vagina, causing extensive cuts and bruises which required internal stitches under a general anaesthetic to repair. At the time this happened, the only people who had ready access to the room were the mother and the defendant (who at the time was drunk); though it was possible, but unlikely, that a random intruder could have entered and assaulted the child. In the days after the incident several people asked her what had happened and she told them that the person who had hurt her was Sid. The trial judge ruled this evidence admissible under the 'inclusionary discretion' contained in section 114(1)(d), and the Court of Appeal upheld the resulting conviction. Giving judgment, Lord Justice Hooper said 'We have no doubt that the judge was right to rule the evidence in.'

Competency

Originally, child witnesses, like adult ones, could only give evidence on oath; and in order to take the oath the court would have to be satisfied that that they 'understood the nature of an oath'. Originally, 'understanding the nature of an oath' meant saying that you believed you would burn in hell for ever if you lied; and where children tendered as witnesses appeared not to understand this, judges

[14] In which case the court will exclude it under its general power to exclude prosecution evidence, conferred by s 78 of the Police and Criminal Evidence Act 1984.

[15] Set out in s 116(4).

[16] *J (S)* [2009] EWCA Crim 1869.

would sometimes adjourn the proceedings for the child to receive religious instruction—a practice which, astonishingly, lingered on until, in 1976, the Court of Appeal decided that nowadays the test was satisfied where the witness 'has a sufficient appreciation of the solemnity of the occasion, and the added responsibility to tell the truth, which is involved in taking an oath, over and above the duty to tell the truth which is an ordinary duty of normal social conduct'.[17] Meanwhile much earlier, in 1885 Parliament, responding to pressure from the NSPCC, had enacted a provision enabling children who were too immature to 'understand the nature of an oath' to give their evidence unsworn: a provision which was re-enacted at intervals, eventually to become section 38 of the Children and Young Persons Act 1933. However, this provision also contained a competency requirement, albeit an attenuated one. To allow a child to give unsworn evidence, the court had to be satisfied that he or she 'is possessed of sufficient intelligence to justify the reception of the evidence, and understands the duty of speaking the truth'.

In 1958, this provision was given a restrictive judicial gloss in *Wallwork*,[18] a case in which a father appealed against his conviction for incest with his daughter, a little girl of five. At trial the prosecution had tried to call her as a witness but, predictably enough, had been unable to persuade her to communicate. Commenting on the unsuccessful attempt to use her as a witness, Lord Goddard CJ said:

> The court deprecates the calling of a child of this age as a witness ... The jury could not attach any value to the evidence of a child of five: it is ridiculous to suppose that they could ... in any circumstances to call a little child of the age of five seems to us to be most undesirable, and I hope it will not occur again.

These remarks were taken on board by the legal profession, making lawyers very diffident about even attempting to call young children as witnesses.

During the 1980s the rules on competency, like the rules on corroboration, were increasingly attacked. Against them critics made the following four simple points. First, the practical effect of the competency requirement—particularly when taken together with the hearsay rule—was to confer impunity on many child abusers, particularly those who chose victims who were very young. Secondly, little children were usually able to provide reliable information about events they had experienced well before they had the mental and verbal capability required to articulate the difference between truth and falsehood and to explain why it is important to tell the truth, as the rules about competency required. Thirdly, the ability to satisfy the competency requirement was in reality no guarantee that, having done so, the child's evidence would actually be truthful. And fourthly, and more fundamentally, the immaturity of a witness and his or her ability to understand (and explain) the difference between truth and falsehood was something

[17] *Hayes* (1976) 64 Cr App R 194; for a late example of the earlier practice being followed, see *Fawcett*, The Times, 20 November 1976.

[18] *Wallwork* (1958) 42 Cr App R 153.

which, in principle, ought to go to the weight the court is prepared to place upon the evidence, not whether it will listen to it or not.

In 1989 these arguments convinced the Pigot Committee, which recommended that all children who are capable of communicating intelligibly should be competent to give evidence, and that all witnesses under the age of 14 should do so unsworn.[19] A few months later, the Court of Appeal disavowed the decision in *Wallwork*, insofar as it purported to impose a minimum age for giving evidence.[20] Then just after this, the government accepted the Pigot Committee's recommendation and introduced legislation[21] designed to abolish the existing competency requirement. Unfortunately the resulting provision was ineptly and obscurely drafted;[22] but the courts, with some difficulty, managed to find that it had produced the desired effect.[23]

Then in 1999 Parliament put the matter beyond doubt by enacting new and clearer provisions in part 2 of the Youth Justice and Criminal Evidence Act. The key provision is section 53, of which the relevant parts are as follows:

> (1) At every stage in criminal proceedings all persons are (whatever their age) competent to give evidence.
> (2) Subsection (1) has effect subject to subsection (3)…
> (3) A person is not competent to give evidence in criminal proceedings if it appears to the court that he is not a person who is able to—
>   (a) understand questions put to him as a witness and
>   (b) give answers to them which can be understood.

This basic rule is elaborated in the four sections that follow, one of which—section 55(2)—provides that all children under the age of 14 shall give evidence unsworn.

In *Barker*,[24] the Court of Appeal—following what had already been said in several previous cases[25]—held that this provision means exactly what it says. It is not, they said, to be read subject to any gloss to the effect that the witness must understand the special importance of telling the truth in court, or that he or she must be able to understand each and every question put. And it added that

> [39] … whenever the competency question is addressed, what is required is not the exercise of a discretion by the making of a judgement, that is whether the witness fulfils the statutory criteria. In short, it is not open to the judge to create or impose some additional but non-statutory criteria based on the approach of earlier generations to the evidence of small children.

The approach of earlier generations, said the court, was based on 'accreted suspicions and misunderstandings about children, and their capacity to understand

19 Pigot Report, reprinted as chapter 10 below, §5.14 and §5.15, and recommendations 17 and 18.
20 *Z* [1990] 2 QB 335.
21 Criminal Justice Act 1991, s 52.
22 The unhappy tale is set out in Spencer and Flin (n 2), 62–63.
23 *Hampshire* [1996] QB 1; *DPP v M* [1997] 2 Cr App R 70.
24 *Barker* [2010] EWCA Crim 4, [2011] *Crim LR* 233.
25 *MacPherson* [2005] EWCA Crim 3605, [2006] 1 Cr App R 30; *Powell* [2006] EWCA Crim 3, [2006] 1 Cr App R 31.

the nature and purpose of an oath and to give truthful and accurate information at trial', which have now been swept away.

In this case, the defendant had been accused of the anal rape of a little girl, virtually the only evidence of its commission being what she had told various people about it afterwards. After making several unprompted disclosures, she was video-interviewed by a woman police officer and a social worker with a view to criminal proceedings, when she was aged three-and-a-half. A year later, when the case finally came to trial, the tape of the interview was played as her evidence-in-chief, after which she underwent a live cross-examination, conducted through a live video link. On this evidence a jury at the Old Bailey convicted.

On appeal, the defence sought to persuade the Court of Appeal that the child was not competent as a witness—without success, as we have seen. One of the fall-back arguments was, in effect, 'But if she was competent, surely a conviction cannot be safe if it is founded on such evidence as this?' In the days when the law forbad courts to convict on the unsworn evidence of children unless corroborated, this argument would necessarily have succeeded. But as we have seen, the corroboration requirement has been abolished. Thus the defendant's fall-back argument also failed, and his conviction was affirmed.

The 'Adversarial Package'

By the 'adversarial package' I mean, as previously mentioned, a combination of the following traditional rules. First, that witnesses must tell their tale in open court, in the physical presence of the defendant; secondly, that the whole of their tale must be told under these conditions: they must tell the whole of their story in open court, from the beginning to the end, and must do so without incorporating or referring back to statements they have previously made; and thirdly, having so given their account, they must then submit to an adversarial cross-examination by someone whose agenda is to persuade the court that their account is incomplete, or that they are lying or mistaken.

Giving evidence under these conditions can be a distressing experience even for an adult. For children, particularly young ones, these conditions often used to make it impossible for them to deliver their evidence at all. From the report in *Wallwork*, discussed above, we learn that when the little girl was called upon to give her evidence she was tongue-tied and unable to speak. And here from the same epoch is an even more dramatic account:

> In a recent case when an accused exercised his right to question a small girl she appeared to realise his presence in the court for the first time, and dived screaming under the clerk's desk where she remained for the rest of the proceedings.[26]

[26] Magistrates' Association, *Memorandum on criminal procedure and child victims of sexual offences* (1962).

Since the 1980s, the first two of these elements have been modified to make allowances for children and indeed other vulnerable witnesses. But as we shall see, much less has been done to modify the third element—adversarial cross-examination.

'Open Court'

Modifications to the first element—'open court'—began many years ago. The explicit power of judges and magistrates to clear the court when children give evidence in sex cases dates back to 1908[27] and allowing child witnesses to be shielded from the defendant's gaze by screens or by permitting them to testify from out of the courtroom via a live TV link are developments of the 1980s.[28] Today, however, the relevant law is to be found in the 'special measures' provisions of the Youth Justice and Criminal Evidence Act of 1999. Section 23 allows the court to direct that persons under 18, and certain other vulnerable witnesses, be screened from the gaze of the accused when giving evidence, and section 24 allows the court to direct that such persons be allowed to give evidence by means of a 'live link', meaning a live television link or other link enabling the witness to communicate with the persons asking questions, and to be seen by persons in the courtroom. Section 25 enables the court to be cleared of the general public when children and other vulnerable witnesses are giving evidence. And as a further measure to prevent contact between the accused and children and other vulnerable witnesses, sections 34–40 prohibit accused persons who are conducting their own defence from cross-examining such witnesses in person. (Where the accused is unrepresented, the court appoints a lawyer to conduct the cross-examination.)

No Evidential Use of Previous Statements

The rule requiring witnesses to give the entirety of their evidence orally and without any reference to their previous statements was effectively gutted as regards child witnesses in 1991, when an Act of Parliament allowed the live evidence-in-chief of a child witness to be replaced by a videotape of a previous interview.[29] This provision was designed for what were then called 'Memorandum interviews', and are now called 'ABE[30] interviews': interviews conducted by the police and social services following the guidance contained in official documents published

[27] Children Act 1908, s 114; it was then replicated in the Children and Young Persons Act 1933, s 37.

[28] The live TV link was introduced by s 32 of the Criminal Justice Act 1988. Screens were introduced at the initiative of the judges: see Spencer and Flin (n 2), 99–100.

[29] Criminal Justice Act 1988, s 32A, inserted into that Act by s 54 of the Criminal Justice Act 1991.

[30] 'ABE' stands for 'Achieving Best Evidence'—see the next note.

by the government.[31] Where one of these video-interviews has been conducted, this will now nearly always be played at trial, so relieving the child of the need to rehearse the whole unhappy story from the beginning in the courtroom. In practice, this makes it possible for the court to hear evidence from very young children which it would never have been able to hear before, even had they been deemed competent witnesses. (It was by this means, of course, that the court heard the evidence-in-chief of the little girl in *Barker.*)

However, the third element in the 'adversarial package'—submission to an adversarial cross-examination—continues to cause grave difficulties for child witness. In essence, the problems it creates are two. One arises from the time at which this cross-examination currently takes place, and the other from the manner in which it is often done.

Cross-examination: The 'Timing Issue'

As regards the 'timing issue', the problem is that, as the law currently stands, the cross-examination must be conducted by the viva voce examination of the witness, live, at the defendant's eventual trial; and this is so, however young and however vulnerable the child may be, however distressing the evidence, and no matter how long after the initial video-interview the trial takes place.

This state of affairs has three grave disadvantages, each of which is accentuated in a case like *Barker*, where the child is very young.

The first disadvantage is that justice fails when trials are abandoned before the issue of guilt or innocence can be determined on the basis of the evidence. Though it proved possible—surprisingly enough—to persuade the small girl in *Barker* to communicate with defence counsel under these conditions, meaningful communication often proves impossible, particularly with little children. Sometimes they cannot be persuaded to say anything intelligible, even though they managed to communicate intelligibly during the video-interview that has now taken the place of their live evidence-in-chief. Sometimes they are able to communicate intelligibly, but cannot be cross-examined to any useful purpose because by the time of trial they have forgotten all about the incident. And sometimes they cannot be cross-examined because they are scared out of their wits and unable to communicate at all: like a little girl in a case I once watched at Snaresbrook Crown Court, who got up from her chair as soon as the cross-examination started and just ran away.

Where the attempt to cross-examine the child fails, and (as often) the child's evidence is central to the prosecution case and there is little other evidence, the judge will usually be obliged to stop the case, because it is considered to be a

[31] The first document was the *Memorandum of Good Practice on Video Recorded Interviews with Child Witnesses for Criminal Proceedings*, published by the Home Office and the Department of Health in 1992. This was later replaced by a document entitled *Achieving Best Evidence in Criminal Proceedings; Guidance on Interviewing Victims and Witnesses, and Guidance on Using Special Measures*, published by the Ministry of Justice, with input from other Departments; current version, 2011.

fundamental rule of criminal procedure that a defendant must not be convicted on the word of an accuser whose evidence he has not been able to challenge by putting questions.[32] The result will then be that the defendant is acquitted: and not because the evidence leaves the tribunal of fact in doubt about his guilt, but simply because the evidence, though available, cannot be tested as the law requires. He will be acquitted because justice has failed, in other words, rather than because justice has weighed the evidence and found it wanting. That this particular problem is currently a real one is demonstrated by the fact that it is a central feature in a number of unhappy cases that have reached the law reports.[33]

The second disadvantage of holding a cross-examination at this stage in the proceedings is that it is particularly burdensome for the child. The cross-examination of a child (or any other) complainant in a sex case will inevitably be a painful experience; but to hold it at the eventual trial is bound to add to the stress and pain. It means that, if the incident really happened, the child is forced to relive it at a time when she or he ought to be forgetting about it and getting on with life. It also means that the child has to undergo the stressful experience of coming to court, and probably waiting around, in a strange and hostile environment, getting increasingly tired and increasingly nervous.

This is vividly and painfully illustrated by what happened in the *Barker* case.[34] When the little girl had to be cross-examined she was brought to court for the beginning of the sitting on a Monday morning—a trip that required her carers to get her up at 6 am—only to find that the court was not ready for her. Having spent the whole of that day waiting around the Old Bailey she was then sent home unheard. With great difficulty she was persuaded to come back the next morning, only for the same thing to happen again. When the cross-examination finally took place in the afternoon of that day, she was exhausted and at the end of her tether, to the point where she was barely able to engage with the process of cross-examination at all.[35] Surely it is monstrous for the legal system to inflict an ordeal like this on a child of four if it is possible to avoid it.

The third disadvantage of a live cross-examination at the trial is that, where a little child can be induced to engage with the cross-examiner, any exchange is likely to be rudimentary, and to provide little real probing or testing of the child's evidence-in-chief. And whereas the two disadvantages previously examined operate to the benefit of the guilty, this one works to the detriment of the innocent.

Back in 1989, the Pigot Committee produced a scheme under which the whole of a child's evidence—cross-examination and all—would be taken ahead of trial. When the suspected offence came to light the child would first be interviewed by trained examiners, this interview being video-recorded. If this interview

[32] This point is elaborated in ch 9 below.

[33] *MacPherson* [2005] EWCA 3605, [2006] 1 Cr App R 30; *Powell* [2006] EWCA Crim 3, [2006] 1 Cr App R 31; *M* [2008] EWCA Crim 2751; *Malicki* [2009] EWCA Crim 365.

[34] This information comes by word of mouth from the police officers in the case who accompanied her.

[35] Information from the police officers involved in the case.

confirmed the commission of an offence the tape would be shown to the defence, who could then request a further interview at which they could put their questions to the child, in the presence of a judge. At the eventual trial, should there be one, the first video-interview would replace the child's live evidence-in-chief, the second video-interview would replace the child's live cross-examination, and the child would drop out of the proceedings. About the merits of this scheme, however, opinion was divided; and instead of the full Pigot scheme, the government of the day decided in 1990 to put forward the legislation that gave us the 'half-Pigot' scheme that is in force in England and Wales today: with all the disadvantages that have just been described.[36]

Pressure for the 'full Pigot' continued, and in response to this, Parliament—going further than the government had originally intended—inserted a section of the Youth Justice and Criminal Evidence Act 1999 that added pre-trial cross-examination to the list of 'special measures' provided for vulnerable witnesses by part II of that Act. This provision is section 28, the text of which is set out as an appendix to this chapter. But predictably, the government of the day, which had not wanted it, then did not implement it;[37] and to date, its successors have followed its example. For the best part of a decade the government—meaning in reality the relevant parts of the Civil Service—adhered to the position that it was out of the question even to hold an experiment.[38]

The main argument[39] that has been used against implementing pre-trial cross-examination is related to the issue of *disclosure*. The defence, it is said, would not be able to cross-examine the child effectively unless and until it had received full disclosure of all the evidence the prosecution had collected, including any 'unused material'. Under the statutory regime for disclosure,[40] this is likely to take place long after the initial video-interview, and perhaps only a relatively short time before the trial. A pre-trial cross-examination held at this late stage, it is said, would carry most of the disadvantages of a cross-examination at the trial—and as such it would add a further complication to cases with young witnesses without yielding any real benefits in return.

This may be a valid objection to conducting a pre-trial cross-examination in certain cases, but it is not a convincing reason for refusing to change the law to make it possible in all of them. Although there are cases where the issues are

[36] See n 29 above.

[37] Technically, the status of s 28 is that it is in force, but only for the limited purpose of making Rules and Regulations governing its operation, should it ever be properly in force. For an explanation of the labyrinthine process of implementation see JR Spencer, 'Special Measures and Unusual Muddles' (2008) 6 *Archbold News* 7–9.

[38] The story is told by Laura Hoyano, 'Coroners and Justice Act 2009: (3) Special Measures Directions Take Two: Entrenching Unequal Access to Justice?' [2010] *Crim LR* 345, 348–49.

[39] At one time a further objection was that a pre-trial cross-examination would oblige the defendant to reveal the nature of his defence ahead of trial, thereby infringing his right of silence. But this argument was forgotten once the Criminal Procedure and Investigations Act 1996 imposed a statutory duty on the defendants to disclose the nature of their defence in cases that are to be tried on indictment.

[40] Under the Criminal Procedure and Investigations Act 1996.

complex and the unused material voluminous, there are many others where there is no unused material to disclose, the issues in dispute are simple, and the questions the defence need to put to the child are obvious from the outset. Indeed, this was the situation in a number of cases in the law reports where the attempt to cross-examine a young child witness at the trial failed, the judge allowed the case to continue and the Court of Appeal then felt obliged to quash the resulting conviction.[41] In such cases, surely, an early pre-trial cross-examination could be done without any injustice to the defence: and indeed, to the benefit of the defendant, if he is innocent. So having pre-trial cross-examination available as an option, surely, would be an improvement, even if it were not a panacea. The fact that a reform will not solve every problem is not a sensible reason to reject a reform that would solve at least some of them. Furthermore, this (and other) objections to the implementation of section 28 are weakened by the knowledge that versions of the 'full Pigot' scheme have been introduced in a number of other countries. These include not only countries in continental Europe, but certain others in the common law world as well, headed by Western Australia—as readers will discover when reading the later chapters of this book.

A further argument for implementing section 28 is that a system of pre-trial cross-examination appears to be required in order to comply with European Union law. In 2001, the EU adopted a Framework Decision on the Rights of Victims,[42] which required all EU Member States to put in place various protections for the victims of crime—including, for vulnerable ones, mechanisms to enable their evidence to be given without having to appear in open court. According to Article 8(4):

> Each Member State shall ensure that, where there is a need to protect victims—particularly those most vulnerable—from the effects of giving evidence in open court, victims may, by decision taken in open court, be entitled to testify in a manner which will enable this objective to be achieved, by any appropriate means compatible with its basic legal principles.

A Mrs Pupino, a teacher at an infant school in Italy, was accused of acts of cruelty to the children in her care. As Italian criminal procedure then stood, for the children's evidence to be received in this type of case it was necessary for them to attend court and give evidence orally. In 2005, the Court of Justice of the European Communities held this state of affairs to be inconsistent with the obligations imposed by the Framework Decision.[43]

In the spring of 2012, as this book goes to press, there are now signs that—a mere 12 years after it was enacted—section 28 of the Youth Justice and Criminal

[41] *Powell*, and *Malicki* (n 33).

[42] Council Framework Decision of 15 March 2001 on the standing of victims in criminal proceedings OJ L 82, 22 March 2001.

[43] Case C-105/03 *Criminal Proceedings Against Pupino* [2005] ECR I-5285; [2006] QB 83; noted (2005) 64 *Cambridge Law Journal* 569.

Evidence Act may eventually be implemented. In 2008 the Ministry of Justice[44] set up a working group to consider the practical issues of implementing the provision, and serious consultations are now taking place. It seems possible that an experiment, at least, will result.

Cross-examination—The 'Style Issue'

For child witnesses, the 'style issue' in connection with adversarial cross-examination is a combination of two things. First, where the party which has called the child (in practice, usually the prosecution) claims that he or she has told the truth, the cross-examiner will suggest to the child that she or he is lying or mistaken. Even adults who are mature enough to understand the reason why the suggestion must be made do not relish the experience of being publicly called liars, especially when they have told the truth; and for children who do not understand the reason the experience can be devastating.[45] Secondly, during cross-examination, a lawyer is allowed (and indeed encouraged) to put suggestive questions. Where a witness is suggestible, or inclined to be compliant with authority figures, suggestive questions are likely to produce answers that conform to the suggestion, whether or not they represent the truth. And obviously, child witnesses, particularly young ones, are more likely to be both suggestible and compliant than adults.

All this of this, of course, is part and parcel of an adversarial examination, the basic idea of which is that the witness is examined by a person who has an agenda, which is to get the witness to tell a story that fits with the theory of the case that the questioner already has in mind; and it is to be contrasted with the notion of an 'inquisitorial examination', where the witness is questioned by a person operating from a neutral standpoint, whose aim is to get the witness to tell the truth, however comfortable or uncomfortable it may be. Both methods have their advantages and their disadvantages: even the 'inquisitorial method', which tends to miscarry when the supposedly neutral questioner has an unconscious agenda of which she or he is unaware—with damaging results where the examiner is also the person who has to make the final decision in the case. But in the context of child witnesses, particularly those who are very young or highly vulnerable, the advantages of the inquisitorial method are widely thought to prevail over the disadvantages. And so it was that, in 1989, a majority of the Pigot Committee recommended that 'the court should have discretion to order exceptionally that questions advocates wish to put to a child should be relayed through a person approved by the court who enjoys the child's confidence'.[46]

[44] Which was created in 2007, and took over responsibility for reforms in criminal procedure from the Home Office.

[45] J Quas, G Goodman, S Ghetti, K Alexander, R Edelstein, A Redlich, I Cordon and DPH Jones, 'Childhood Sexual Assault Victims: Long-term Outcomes After Testifying in Criminal Court', *Monographs of the Society for Research in Child Development* 70, serial no 280, vii–145 (2005).

[46] Recommendation 6; see pp 254–255 below.

A similar recommendation was made nine years later in the official report *Speaking up for Justice*,[47] and shortly afterwards this led to the enactment of section 29 of the Youth Justice and Criminal Evidence Act 1989, which makes it possible for the court to order 'any examination of the witness (however and wherever conducted) to be conducted through an interpreter or other person approved by the court for the purposes of this section ('an intermediary')'. Readers will find the full text of this provision in the appendix to this chapter.

The wording of this provision contains what is sometimes called a 'constructive ambiguity': a form of words, capable of widely different interpretations, enabling a political purpose to be advanced by enabling both sides of a debate to believe that they have won. An 'intermediary' as so defined could be a person to whom is given, by the opposing sides, a list of issues to explore with the child in the manner that person considers most likely to bring out the truth. Or it could be someone more like an interpreter, whose role is limited to helping the usual team of adversarial questioners to put their questions in language that the child can understand. When, after an eight-year delay, section 29 was eventually implemented nationally,[48] it was the more limited type of intermediary who emerged from pages of the official manuals that the government produced, and who now operates in the courts of England and Wales. In consequence, the intermediaries that are currently in use are not a means by which child witnesses can be questioned inquisitorially rather than adversarially. They can improve on the situation as it used to be by ensuring child witnesses understand the questions that are put to them in cross-examination. But if the questioning is inappropriate in substance as well as form, they are not usually in a position to rectify this fundamental problem.

How far, if at all, adversarial cross-examination is a satisfactory method for testing the evidence of children is a complicated issue on which there is a great deal more to be said. It is the theme to which we shall return in the final chapter of this book.

The scheme of the rest of this book is as follows. In chapter two, Joyce Plotnikoff and Richard Woolfson, researchers with enormous practical experience, describe the problems that the traditional methods of cross-examination still cause for child witnesses, even after the reforms that have been carried out to date. The case they make for change could hardly be more compelling.

In chapter three, Emily Henderson reviews attempts to deal with these problems in a number of other criminal justice systems which, like England and Wales, follow the common law adversarial tradition as regards the examination of witnesses. One recurrent problem is delay: the long period that frequently elapses between the incident in relation to which the evidence of children is required and the date on which they are expected to give evidence about it live in court. In some places attempts have been made to deal with the problem by reducing these

[47] Note 1 above, at para 8.47.

[48] Joyce Plotnikoff and Richard Woolfson, 'Making Best Use of the Intermediary Special Measure at Trial [2008] *Crim LR* 91.

delays, in others to avoid their impact by taking the evidence of children ahead of trial. She also describes attempts to reduce the distress that cross-examination can cause to children, and the confusion that it can produce. A means currently employed to this end in England and Wales is the use of intermediaries. Dr Henderson describes how different types of intermediaries are used in South Africa, Israel and parts of the United States.

Among the countries where the adversarial tradition reigns there is one which, unlike England and Wales, immediately adopted the proposal of the Pigot Committee that the cross-examination of child witnesses should take place ahead of trial. This was Western Australia. In chapter four, Hal Jackson, a retired judge from Western Australia, describes how the system works in that jurisdiction. As readers will discover, the account he gives is a story of success. The author of chapter five, Annie Cossins, is an Australian academic who has been heavily involved in law reform in relation to sexual offences, and through that, the law of evidence. The theme of her chapter is that, on the basis of the Australian experience, pre-trial cross-examination is only part of the solution to a bigger problem, which is the nature of adversarial cross-examination itself. She concludes her chapter with practical suggestions as to how its abuses might be controlled. In chapter six, Emily Henderson then describes the movement to improve the position of child witnesses in her native land, New Zealand, where the government has recently announced its intention to promote reforms which are inspired in part by current practices in continental Europe.

In continental Europe, adversarial examination is not the usual method by which the evidence of witnesses is delivered to the court. Instead, they are usually examined by the presiding judge, with prosecution and defence being allowed to put supplementary questions afterwards. In many parts of Europe it used to be common for child witnesses to be examined ahead of trial, in private, in sessions during which the defence were given no opportunity to put their questions. If good for children, who were spared cross-examination, this system was obviously bad for defendants. It was also incompatible with Article 6(3)(d) of the European Convention on Human Rights, which—inspired by the traditions of the common law[49]—guarantees the right of the defendant to 'examine or have examined witnesses against him'. In the light of all this, a number of continental countries have reformed their criminal procedure to give the defence a chance to put questions to child witnesses where this was previously impossible. The scheme adopted is for the child witness to be examined ahead of trial, as heretofore, but for the defence to be given an opportunity to have their questions put to the child during that examination. The result is something rather similar to what the Pigot Committee proposed—though reached by a journey that started from the opposite end of the road. In chapters seven and eight we learn how the examination of child witnesses

[49] As indeed is much of the rest of the Convention: a fact that is frequently forgotten in public discussion. On this see Jack Straw, 'Human Rights in the Twenty-First Century' (2007–08) *Cambridge Yearbook of European Legal Studies*, ch 16.

is now conducted in two countries which have followed the road this way to reach the Pigot destination: Austria, described for us by Verena Murschetz, of the Criminal Law Department at the Leopold Franzens University, Innsbruck, and Norway, described for us by Trond Myklebust, of the Norwegian Police University College.

In chapter nine John Spencer, one of the editors of this book, attempts to draw the threads of the previous discussion together. And the final chapter sets out the text of the Pigot Report—so making available to readers an important document which, though for many years an inspiration for reform, has for many years also been out of print.

Appendix

Youth Justice and Criminal Evidence Act 1999 (c.23)

28.— Video recorded cross-examination or re-examination.

(1) Where a special measures direction provides for a video recording to be admitted under section 27 as evidence in chief of the witness, the direction may also provide—
   (a) for any cross-examination of the witness, and any re-examination, to be recorded by means of a video recording; and
   (b) for such a recording to be admitted, so far as it relates to any such cross-examination or re-examination, as evidence of the witness under cross-examination or on re-examination, as the case may be.

(2) Such a recording must be made in the presence of such persons as Criminal Procedure Rules or the direction may provide and in the absence of the accused, but in circumstances in which—
   (a) the judge or justices (or both) and legal representatives acting in the proceedings are able to see and hear the examination of the witness and to communicate with the persons in whose presence the recording is being made, and
   (b) the accused is able to see and hear any such examination and to communicate with any legal representative acting for him.

(3) Where two or more legal representatives are acting for a party to the proceedings, subsection (2)(a) and (b) are to be regarded as satisfied in relation to those representatives if at all material times they are satisfied in relation to at least one of them.

(4) Where a special measures direction provides for a recording to be admitted under this section, the court may nevertheless subsequently direct that it is not to be so admitted if any requirement of subsection (2) or Criminal Procedure Rules or the direction has not been complied with to the satisfaction of the court.

(5) Where in pursuance of subsection (1) a recording has been made of any examination of the witness, the witness may not be subsequently cross-examined or re-examined in respect of any evidence given by the witness in the proceedings (whether in any recording admissible under section 27 or this section or otherwise than in such a recording) unless the court gives a further special measures direction making such provision as is mentioned in subsection (1)(a) and (b) in relation to any subsequent cross-examination, and re-examination, of the witness.

(6) The court may only give such a further direction if it appears to the court—
   (a) that the proposed cross-examination is sought by a party to the proceedings as a result of that party having become aware, since the time when the original recording was made in pursuance of subsection (1), of a matter which that party could not with reasonable diligence have ascertained by then, or
   (b) that for any other reason it is in the interests of justice to give the further direction.

(7) Nothing in this section shall be read as applying in relation to any cross-examination of the witness by the accused in person (in a case where the accused is to be able to conduct any such cross-examination).

29.— Examination of witness through intermediary.

(1) A special measures direction may provide for any examination of the witness (however and wherever conducted) to be conducted through an interpreter or other person approved by the court for the purposes of this section ('an intermediary').

(2) The function of an intermediary is to communicate—
(a) to the witness, questions put to the witness, and
(b) to any person asking such questions, the answers given by the witness in reply to them,

and to explain such questions or answers so far as necessary to enable them to be understood by the witness or person in question.

(3) Any examination of the witness in pursuance of subsection (1) must take place in the presence of such persons as Criminal Procedure Rules or the direction may provide, but in circumstances in which—
(a) the judge or justices (or both) and legal representatives acting in the proceedings are able to see and hear the examination of the witness and to communicate with the intermediary, and
(b) (except in the case of a video recorded examination) the jury (if there is one) are able to see and hear the examination of the witness.

(4) Where two or more legal representatives are acting for a party to the proceedings, subsection (3)(a) is to be regarded as satisfied in relation to those representatives if at all material times it is satisfied in relation to at least one of them.

(5) A person may not act as an intermediary in a particular case except after making a declaration, in such form as may be prescribed by Criminal Procedure Rules, that he will faithfully perform his function as intermediary.

(6) Subsection (1) does not apply to an interview of the witness which is recorded by means of a video recording with a view to its admission as evidence in chief of the witness; but a special measures direction may provide for such a recording to be admitted under section 27 if the interview was conducted through an intermediary and—
(a) that person complied with subsection (5) before the interview began, and
(b) the court's approval for the purposes of this section is given before the direction is given.

(7) Section 1 of the Perjury Act 1911 (perjury) shall apply in relation to a person acting as an intermediary as it applies in relation to a person lawfully sworn as an interpreter in a judicial proceeding; and for this purpose, where a person acts as an intermediary in any proceeding which is not a judicial proceeding for the purposes of that section, that proceeding shall be taken to be part of the judicial proceeding in which the witness's evidence is given.

2

'Kicking and Screaming': The Slow Road to Best Evidence

JOYCE PLOTNIKOFF AND RICHARD WOOLFSON

> Where child witnesses are concerned the existing process is quite fundamentally flawed (section 2.15, Pigot Report, 1989)[1]

> You simply do not see unreasonable cross-examination of children. I cannot think of a single case (Barrister, 2007)[2]

> We've achieved the worst of all possible worlds. The current system [of children's cross-examination] is absolutely absurd (QC, 2010)[3]

> Outraged members of the Bar claimed never to have been so insulted in all their lives: 'been doing the job this way for 30 years, don't need someone to check how I am doing it now' (Chairman of the Bar, 2011)[4]

Introduction

It has been over 20 years since publication of the visionary Pigot Report in 1989.[5] Most of its recommendations have been implemented. However, there has been little progress on two of its principal concerns: that children's evidence should be disposed of 'as rapidly as is consonant with the interests of justice'; and that children should give evidence in 'circumstances which do not intimidate or overawe them' (section 2.14). The Coalition Government is considering implementation

[1] *Report of the Advisory Group on Video Evidence* (1989) London, Home Office, reproduced as the final section of this book.

[2] J Plotnikoff and R Woolfson (2007) *The 'Go-Between': Evaluation of the Intermediary Special Measure.* London, Ministry of Justice. www.lexiconlimited.co.uk/PDF%20files/Intermediaries_study_report.pdf.

[3] J Plotnikoff and R Woolfson (2011) *Young Witnesses in Criminal Proceedings: A Progress Report on 'Measuring Up?'.* London, NSPCC and Nuffield Foundation. www.nspcc.org.uk/measuringup.

[4] P Lodder QC (2011) 'Why Fear the Assessment of Advocacy?' Issue 50, Spring 2011, *The Middle Templar*, 20.

[5] *Report of the Advisory Group on Video Evidence*, above (n 1).

of section 28, Youth Justice and Criminal Evidence Act 1999, the only special measure to facilitate the evidence of vulnerable witnesses yet to be implemented. This takes forward a Pigot recommendation by allowing cross-examination to be recorded on video at a pre-trial hearing for use at trial. Special measures provisions have been extended to young witnesses under 18,[6] but any section 28 pilot seems likely to apply to younger witnesses only.

There is a fundamental conflict between the aims of cross-examination and criminal justice policy objectives concerning the questioning of children. Government policy focuses on facilitating the child's 'best evidence', whereas cross-examination aims not at accuracy or best evidence but at persuading witnesses to adopt an alternative version of events or discrediting their evidence. When children are cross-examined, methods used often contravene principles for obtaining complete and accurate reports from children and may actually exploit their developmental limitations. This strategy was summed up by a barrister who said 'You're looking … to make sure they make mistakes … Some counsel … give double negatives to kids. And the kids get it wrong … But that is a valid technique that is used by very senior counsel and very successfully.'[7]

Pigot accepted that 'cross-examination is essential' but concluded that changes were necessary 'in the interests of justice' (sections 2.18, 2.22). This chapter revisits outstanding issues from Pigot's recommendations and considers the implications for implementation of section 28. As Annie Cossins states in chapter five below, experience in Australia suggests that pre-recording 'does not tackle the endemic problems' of cross-examination: 'rather than being a method for uncovering the untruthful child witness, empirical evidence shows that it is a process that manufactures inaccurate evidence'. We argue that the benefits of pre-recording will not be fully achieved unless the system also addresses questioning that actively hinders children from giving their best evidence. A fresh approach is needed.

The chapter draws on our young witness research since 1995; in particular, on interviews with 182 young witnesses in the 2009 study *Measuring Up?*[8]; and on discussion at the June 2010 Nuffield Foundation–NSPCC seminar *Questioning Young Witnesses and Incorporating Good Practice into Advocacy Training*, chaired by Lord Justice Hooper.[9]

[6] Sections 16(1)(a) and 21 Youth Justice and Criminal Evidence Act 1999, amended to this effect by s 98 Coroners and Justice Act 2009.

[7] E Henderson (2002) 'Persuading and Controlling: The Theory of Cross-examination in Relation to Children' in H Westcott et al (eds), *Children's Testimony: A Handbook of Psychological Research and Forensic Practice.* Chichester, Wiley.

[8] J Plotnikoff and R Woolfson (2009) *Measuring Up? Evaluating Implementation of Government Commitments to Young Witnesses in Criminal Proceedings.* London, NSPCC and Nuffield Foundation. www.nspcc.org.uk/measuringup.

[9] Plotnikoff and Woolfson (n 3).

Delay

The Pigot Committee recommended that judges should be able to schedule the cross-examination of 'very young or very disturbed children' at a preliminary hearing because of 'quite unacceptable delays' before young witness cases come to court (sections 1.20, 2.32). Pigot was concerned not just about the potential impact on children's testimony but the effect on children themselves:

> the sense of insecurity and uncertainty induced by delays make this a harmful, oppressive and often traumatic experience ... most children are disturbed to a greater or lesser extent by giving evidence in court ... the effects are generally agreed to be peculiarly injurious and very often long-lasting (section 2.10).

Measuring Up? found that, before the trial, most young witnesses were anxious and 52 per cent experienced stress symptoms ranging from sleep and eating problems and depression to bed-wetting and self-harming. More than a third said their school studies or attendance were affected in the run-up to the trial: some had changed schools due to intimidation or dropped out altogether. Around one-fifth were still worried, upset or scared when interviewed weeks after the trial. No research here has examined the impact of the witness role on children years after court. However, a study in the USA followed up over 200 young victims of sexual assault 12 years after trial.[10] It found that the extent of distress while waiting to testify and while actually testifying predicted poor psychological adjustment in later life, especially in those who were adolescents at trial.

In 1988, around the time the Pigot Committee was convened, Home Office Minister John Patten announced guidance to ensure 'speedy progress' for child abuse cases.[11] This policy has been restated by successive governments so that it now applies to all young witnesses.[12] The commitment is also part of the statutory *Victims Code* requiring a designated staff member to 'liaise with the judge and the court staff to make sure that the [young victim's] case comes to court as soon as possible'.[13] Despite the 'priority' policy being in place for almost a quarter of a century, no government has ever monitored whether it works. The only available statistics come from occasional independent young witness studies. In 2004, the decision not to implement section 28 was based in part on an indication that 'case processing [of young witness cases] has dramatically changed in recent years ... apparently proving effective in bringing serious offences to trial within months'.[14]

[10] J Quas et al (2005) 'Childhood Sexual Assault Victims: Long-Term Outcomes After Testifying in Criminal Court'. *Monographs of the Society for Research in Child Development* 280: 70–72.

[11] *Child Abuse Cases to Get Greater Priority* (18 February 1988). Home Office news release.

[12] For example, *Adult Criminal Case Management Framework* (2008). London, CJS, Annex A (Section 16, Crown Court Manual), 2(b).

[13] *Code of Practice for Victims of Crime* (2005). London, Home Office. The Code was established under the authority of s 32 Domestic Violence, Crime and Victims Act 2004.

[14] D Birch and R Powell (2004) *Meeting the Challenges of Pigot: Pre-trial Cross-examination Under s.28 of the Youth Justice and Criminal Evidence Act 1999* (unpublished).

However, no research was invoked in support of this claim and closer scrutiny suggests that young witness cases have been dealt with more quickly only because disposition times for all cases have also fallen. Over the years, comparisons of young witness studies (*Measuring Up?* and other studies[15]) with national statistics show that the average times to trial in young witness cases remain consistently longer (across youth/magistrates' court and Crown Court) than for all criminal cases. *Measuring Up?* found this was true even for trials involving young victims covered by the statutory *Victims Code.*[16]

In magistrates' or youth court, *Measuring Up?* found that the average time between the defendant's first court appearance and trial was three months, with the longest being 16 months. In the Crown Court, the average was around eight months, with the longest being 30 months. Trials involving over one-third of the children were rescheduled up to three times; one was rescheduled nine times. Some courts are still unable to expedite trials even for the youngest children. An increasing number of three- and four-year-old children are entering the criminal justice process.[17] At the time of writing, some are due to testify in trials listed to take place a year or more after the alleged offence.[18]

Children's ability to give their best evidence is also affected by the length of time they wait to give evidence at trial. *Measuring Up?* found that this routinely exceeded policy targets.[19] At magistrates' or youth court, the target waiting time is no more than one hour: 92 per cent of the children waited longer. At Crown Court, the target waiting time is no more than two hours: 73 per cent waited longer. In all, children waited on average 5.8 hours at Crown Court and 3.5 hours at magistrates' or youth court. Only 67 per cent completed their evidence on the first day of court attendance.

Pigot's Concerns about Cross-examination

Coupled with the recommendation about cross-examination at a pre-trial hearing, the Committee proposed that it should be possible to have the advocate's questions 'relayed by a person approved by the court who enjoys the child's confidence' (Recommendation 6 and section 2.32). The use of an interlocutor would be justified in situations 'where it is absolutely impossible for counsel to

[15] Two of the earliest were J Plotnikoff and R Woolfson (1995) *Prosecuting Child Abuse.* London, Blackstone; and G Davis et al (1999) *An Assessment of the Admissibility and Sufficiency of Evidence in Child Abuse Prosecutions.* London, Home Office.

[16] *Code of Practice for Victims of Crime* (n 13).

[17] In a 14-month period, children aged five and under were assessed by a Registered Intermediary in 114 cases (it is not known how many were involved in a trial). Plotnikoff and Woolfson (n 3).

[18] Communications to the authors from Registered Intermediaries.

[19] Standard 24, *The Witness Charter* (2008). London, CJS.

communicate successfully with a child' (section 2.33). The one dissenting member of the Committee, a barrister, believed that any difficulty 'should be overcome by allowing greater opportunities for counsel to establish rapport with a witness before the hearing takes place' (section 2.34). Pigot does not explore underlying reasons why communication may fail or why cross-examination might 'intimidate or overawe' the child, concluding only that informal surroundings might improve the quality of evidence: 'the formality and solemnity of the courtroom context ... may actually have a deleterious effect on the fullness and accuracy of children's testimony' (sections 2.14, 2.17, 2.18).

Section 24 of the Youth Justice and Criminal Evidence Act 1999 permits eligible witnesses to give evidence by live link from outside the courtroom. This normally means somewhere else in the same building, which children do not see as 'informal surroundings'. Many young witnesses in *Measuring Up?* described court facilities as unpleasant, stuffy, cramped and noisy, accessed through locked doors ('like Fort Knox'); 45 per cent saw the defendant in or around the building. Section 24 also permits live-link evidence from other court buildings or non-court locations. A 2007 survey found that members of the judiciary and lawyers favoured locating remote links at witness support organisations.[20] However, this option is available in just a few areas, and only 7 per cent of children interviewed for *Measuring Up?* gave evidence this way. Remote links included those hosted by the NSPCC Devon and Cornwall Young Witness Service in Truro, Plymouth and Exeter where it is the norm for young witnesses not to attend court. The Ministry of Justice had considered this area for inclusion in the section 28 pilot but it has been informed that these remote links are being withdrawn due to closure of the NSPCC scheme.

It is revealing that the Pigot Committee stopped short of criticising cross-examination practice in seeking to justify the specialist interlocutor role. The only adverse comment about cross-examination was relegated to a discussion of training, which stressed the need for lawyers to be aware of 'the consequences of misleading or oppressive questioning' (section 7.9). The rest of this chapter examines cross-examination in light of research findings unavailable to Pigot, and considers the challenges faced by the judiciary and legal professions in confronting the conflicting objectives of cross-examination and children's 'best evidence'.

[20] This was favoured by 69% of circuit judges, 85% of magistrates and district judges and 56% of barristers and solicitors. J Plotnikoff and R Woolfson (2007) *Evaluation of Young Witness Support: Examining the Impact on Witnesses and the Criminal Justice System.* London, Ministry of Justice. www.lexiconlimited.co.uk/PDF%20files/Young_Witness_Study_Report.pdf.

Is Cross-examination of Children 'Fit for Purpose'?

Is a failure rate of 50 per cent acceptable in any profession? In studies conducted in 2001,[21] 2004,[22] 2007[23] and 2009,[24] we interviewed a total of 394 young witnesses around the country. In each project, at least half of the children said they did not understand some of the questions they were asked at court: and these were just the ones capable of identifying that they did not understand.[25] In the general population, around half the socio-economically disadvantaged children have speech and language skills that are significantly lower than those of other children of the same age;[26] 10 per cent of children have a clinically recognisable mental disorder;[27] and rates of childhood autism are around 1 per cent, far higher than previous estimates.[28] More than a million children in this country suffer from speech, language and communication difficulties, with an increase of 58 per cent of young school children identified with the problem in the past five years: a growing number are reported not to know their own name when starting school.[29]

The prevalence of communication difficulties among children generally goes some way towards explaining the problems with cross-examination they report at court. However, poor 'communicative competence' on the part of some court practitioners mean that even children with normal communication skills may be thwarted from giving their best evidence. *Measuring Up?* found that 65 per cent of young witnesses reported problems of comprehension, complexity, pace of questioning (too fast) or being interrupted before they had finished their answers. Difficulties were more common at the Crown Court. Problems of comprehension occurred across all age groups (teenagers are at particular risk of miscommunication because of unrealistic expectations of their abilities):

> She was using all her lawyerly language—they get taught to speak like that and we don't. They don't realise they're talking to young people. (16-year-old)

[21] J Plotnikoff and R Woolfson (2001) *An Evaluation of Young Witness Support.* Scottish Executive Central Research Unit, Edinburgh, Scottish Executive.

[22] J Plotnikoff and R Woolfson (2004) *In Their Own Words: The Experiences of 50 Young Witnesses in Criminal Proceedings.* London, NSPCC.

[23] Plotnikoff and Woolfson (n 20).

[24] Plotnikoff and Woolfson (n 8).

[25] Similar findings were reported in D Hayes et al (2011) *The Experiences of Young Witnesses in Criminal Proceedings in Northern Ireland.* Northern Ireland, Department of Justice.

[26] Department for Children, Schools and Families (2008) *The Bercow Report: A Review of Services for Children and Young People (0–19) with Speech, Language and Communication Needs.* London, Department for Children, Schools and Families.

[27] Office for National Statistics (2004) *Survey of the Mental Health of Children and Young People in Great Britain.* London, Office for National Statistics.

[28] G Baird et al (2006) 'Prevalence of Disorders of the Autistic Spectrum in a Population Cohort of Children in South Thames' *The Lancet* 368 (9531) 210–15.

[29] www.telegraph.co.uk/education/educationnews/8668117/Growing-number-of-children-dont-know-their-own-name-when-starting-school.html.

> Some words were too complicated—too adult. (12-year-old)

> I didn't understand all he said. He should speak a bit nicer and simpler. (7-year-old)

Judges and lawyers are encouraged to explain that children should say if they do not understand[30] but more than half of the young witnesses who recognised that they had a problem did not tell the court even though they had been advised they could do so. Again, this occurred across all age groups. Questions that violated good practice principles included compound questions; those requiring understanding of complex concepts, especially time; figures of speech likely to be interpreted literally (particularly problematic for those with autism eg 'Let me paint you a picture'); and questions that were repetitive (which may cause children to change the answer, believing that the first response must be wrong), jumped around in time or were paced too fast (a problem seldom recognised at court).

The questioner's tone and approach are the subject of guidance[31] but in practice often caused difficulties. While 28 per cent of young prosecution witnesses described defence lawyers as 'polite', half of the group as a whole said they were 'sarcastic', 'rude', 'aggressive' or 'cross'. Terms used included 'bullying', 'badgering', 'intimidating', 'degrading', 'disrespectful', 'snappy', 'pushy', 'loud', 'relentless', 'abrupt' and 'snotty'. A 15-year-old said:

> When I was answering questions, I felt completely white and my throat was dry. The defence lawyer was trying to trip me up. He deliberately made the questions complicated and he was trying to be intimidating—his tone of voice, body language—he was very aggressive.

The defence case may be that the child is lying. This accusation can cause a child to give inaccurate answers or to agree with the suggestion that they are lying simply to bring questioning to an end.[32] *Measuring Up?* found that 57 per cent of the young witnesses recalled being accused of lying, and of these, 70 per cent said it happened more than once.

Children are particularly susceptible to questions suggesting the answer.[33] Sometimes these are reinforced by physical cues from the questioner (for example a nodding advocate who seeks an answer in the affirmative). Tag questions make a statement and then add a short question inviting corroboration of its truth ('He didn't do it, *did he*?'). They are 'one of the most powerfully suggestive forms of speech that we have in the English language. For that reason, and because in effect they allow the questioner to do the testifying, tag questions are the weapons of

[30] *Equal Treatment Bench Book* (2009) London, Judicial Studies Board, section 4.1.3.

[31] *Achieving Best Evidence in Criminal Proceedings: Guidance on Interviewing Victims and Witnesses, and Guidance on Using Special Measures* (2011) London, Ministry of Justice, section 5.17.

[32] J Schuman et al (1999) 'Developmentally Appropriate Questions for Child Witnesses' *Queen's Law Journal* 25, 251–304.

[33] R Zajac (2009) 'Investigative Interviewing in the Courtroom: Child Witnesses under Cross-Examination' in R Bull et al (eds), *Handbook of Psychology of Interviewing: Current Developments and Future Directions*. Chichester, Wiley.

choice in cross-examination. They are also surprisingly complex linguistically.'[34] Nevertheless, tag questions are routinely used to cross-examine even the youngest children (see the case of *Barker*, discussed below).

Leading questions also require the ability to resist psychological pressure from a powerful questioner. Many young witnesses interviewed for *Measuring Up?* experienced leading questions as oppressive. More than half said the other side's lawyer tried to make them say something they did not mean or put words in their mouth. One 12-year-old reported, 'He was trying to get me to say wrong things; that made me feel upset and angry.'

Decades of research have established methods for obtaining the most complete and accurate accounts from children. These include asking open-ended questions (for example, 'Tell me more about that') and avoiding asking the witness to confirm information supplied by the questioner. In contrast, studies have demonstrated that cross-examination techniques used with children are evidentially unsafe.[35] For example, in a series of studies psychologist Rachel Zajac has interviewed children about staged events and then cross-examined them months later, to compare their answers with what actually happened and what they said in interview. Her 2009 study design was intended to rule out memory impairment as the cause of inaccuracies.[36] She found that when 9- and 10-year-olds were cross-examined, they changed 43 per cent of their previously correct responses; 85 per cent of the younger children changed at least one interview answer with a 'significant decrease' in accuracy. Zajac concluded that 'cross-examination-style questioning appears to exert an overall negative effect on children's accuracy'.

It has proved difficult for the legal profession to take such findings on board, particularly in relation to leading questions. An Advocacy Training Council[37] working group suggested that leading questions are acceptable provided they are short and simple: 'there can be no objection to the use of leading questions which are an important tool in cross-examination *per se*, but if leading questions put to a vulnerable witness or defendant are not short and straightforward, they can be unfair'.[38] However, case law now acknowledges that, for some witnesses, a

[34] A Graffam Walker (1999) *Handbook on Questioning Children—A Linguistic Perspective.* Washington DC, American Bar Association Center on Children and the Law.

[35] See eg K Hanna et al (2010) *Child Witnesses in the New Zealand Criminal Courts: A Review of Practice and Implications for Policy.* Institute of Public Policy, AUT University; L Ellison (2001) *The Adversarial Process and the Vulnerable Witness.* Oxford, OUP; K Saywitz (2002) *Developmental Underpinnings of Children's Testimony* in H Westcott et al (eds) *Children's Testimony: A Handbook of Psychological Research and Forensic Practice* Chichester, Wiley; and Henderson (n 7).

[36] Zajac (n 33).

[37] The Advocacy Training Council coordinates the delivery and monitoring of advocacy teacher training to members of the Bar. Membership is drawn from the Inns of Court and the Circuits of the Bar of England and Wales with representatives from the Bar Council, Specialist Bar Associations and employed barristers. See www.advocacytrainingcouncil.org/index.php?option=com_content&view=article&id=80&catid=34.

[38] Recommendation 19 for practitioners: Advocacy Training Council Working Group on Vulnerable Witness Handling (2011) *Raising the Bar: The Handling of Vulnerable Witnesses, Victims and Defendants at Court.* London, Advocacy Training Council.

suggestive question—however short and simple—may not be permissible at all. In 2010, the Court of Appeal in *R v W and M*[39] upheld a conviction even though the eight-year-old complainant retracted much of her account in cross-examination. The judgment stressed that children's answers to leading questions may be of limited evidential value because of the child's wish to please or simply to bring questioning to an end. The court recognised that 'particularly with child witnesses short and untagged questions are best at eliciting the evidence. By untagged we mean questions that do not contain a statement of the answer that is sought.'

In *Fairness in Courts and Tribunals* (2010), the Judicial College (formerly Judicial Studies Board) recommended that judges control the use of tag questions:[40]

> 'Tag' questions e.g. 'He didn't touch you (with his willy) did he?' take at least seven stages of reasoning to answer and should be avoided with children. Children need more time to process questions (for younger children, almost twice as much). A more direct question should therefore be put to the child e.g. 'Did he touch you? How did he touch you?' However, rather than use the term 'he', it is better that the name of the alleged perpetrator is used, as children may not always immediately connect 'he' with a question previously put about a person.

The 'seven stages of reasoning' to which the Judicial College refers are drawn from American Bar Association guidance which recommends that 'Tag questions of all kinds should be avoided with children' because, in order to answer a tag question correctly, they would have to be able to perform at least seven 'extraordinarily complex' operations.[41] These include the following (not an exhaustive list):

- judging whether the statement part of the question is true or not;
- translating the tag from its elliptical form to a full form and understanding that the word 'it' in the tag is a substitute for the entire original question;
- tracking what pronouns in the question and in the tag refer to ('*She* looks nice, doesn't *she*?');
- learning that a positive statement takes a negative tag ('It *is* raining, *isn't* it?') and vice versa ('It *isn't* raining, *is* it?');
- learning that the negative in a tag does not affect the main clause ('It is raining, *isn't* it/ is it *not*?' does not mean that it is not raining);
- understanding that the tag expresses the point of view of the speaker, and does not necessarily mean that the statement is true; and finally,
- learning how to meet or counter that point of view. Children cannot be expected to resist both the psychological and linguistic pressure which a tag question exerts in a court setting where the questioner is a powerful authority figure.

[39] *R v W and M* [2010] EWCA 1926.

[40] *Fairness in Courts and Tribunals—A Summary of the Equal Treatment Bench Book* (2010) London, Judicial College.

[41] Graffam Walker (n 34).

In 2010, the landmark Court of Appeal judgment in *R v Barker*[42] upheld a conviction based primarily on the evidence of a four-year-old witness and set new standards for questioning very young children. The QCs involved did not use an intermediary to facilitate communication with the young child. Questions posed to her included the following:

> She [the police officer] touched down here and said, 'Did you ever get touched by Stephen there?' You shook your head, did you not? That is right, is it not?
>
> He did not touch you with his willy, did he? Did he, [child's name]? I have to ask you one more time, please: he did not touch you with his willy, did he?

The Lord Chief Justice described the purpose of the trial as identifying 'the evidence which is reliable and that which is not, whether it comes from an adult or a child'. Children's evidence should be placed on the same level as that of all other witnesses. However, the advocate's cross-examination techniques must be adapted 'to enable the child to give the best evidence of which he or she is capable' while ensuring the defendant's right to a fair trial. When the issue is whether the child is lying or mistaken, the advocate should ask 'short, simple' questions putting the essential elements of the defendant's case. 'Aspects of evidence which undermine … the child's credibility must, of course, be revealed to the jury, but it is not necessarily appropriate for them to form the subject matter of detailed cross-examination of the child.'

Impact of the Intermediary Special Measure

As noted above, Pigot recommended that, in certain cases, the advocate's questions should be relayed by a specialist interlocutor (Recommendation 6 and section 2.32). The Youth Justice and Criminal Evidence Act 1999 provides that an intermediary may facilitate communication at interview and trial with a young witness (some vulnerable adult witnesses are also eligible, but defendants are excluded). If any child witness seems unlikely to be able to recognise a problematic question or tell the questioner that he or she has not understood, then assessment by an intermediary should be considered.[43] Section 29(2) of the Youth Justice and Criminal Evidence Act, 1999 describes the function of an intermediary as communicating, to the witness, questions put to the witness; and to any person asking such questions, the answers given by the witness in reply. In practice, intermediaries do not relay all questions or answers unless this is required by the needs of the individual witness. Questioners are expected to adapt their questions, informed by recommendations based on the intermediary's prior

[42] *R v Barker* [2010] EWCA Crim 4.
[43] Box 2.1, p 23, *Achieving Best Evidence* (n 31).

assessment of the witness. At trial, the intermediary generally intervenes only to flag up potential miscommunication.

The Witness Intermediary Scheme was created when the special measure was rolled out nationally in 2008. Best practice is set out in the Registered Intermediary Procedural Guidance Manual.[44] Registered Intermediaries are independent officers of the court, not expert witnesses. Around 100 provide criminal courts with professional expertise from different communication disciplines, principally speech and language therapy; about 100 appointments are made monthly for assessment of adult and child witnesses.[45] The Ministry of Justice oversees the registration process which involves screening; training by barristers at the City Law School, City University, London; examination; and finally assessment by a retired judge. To remain on the register, they must meet Continuing Professional Development requirements. Requests for a Registered Intermediary are handled by the National Policing Improvement Agency which appoints someone from the register with skills matching the needs of the witness.

Evaluation of pilot intermediary areas identified initial resistance from some judges and lawyers who overestimated the competence of questioners to ask children questions and underestimated the risks of potential miscommunication.[46] For example, a judge said: 'I would not allow this special measure for a child of five because it would be hard to test their evidence. We do trials with witnesses with minor learning difficulties day-in day-out.' A common view was that intermediaries were unnecessary because witnesses were advised to say if they did not understand. This failed to take account of vulnerable witnesses who were incapable of identifying questions they did not understand or lacked the confidence to say so at court.

The evaluation of the intermediary scheme saw a sea-change in attitude among judges and advocates after their first experience of using Registered Intermediaries. For example, a barrister commented, 'A defence advocate is naturally suspicious of doing anything like this. As it was, I ended up being the one who was surprised—by the extreme difficulty the complainant had in understanding what I thought were the simplest questions.'[47] A judge concluded:[48]

> The intermediary has an important function in the interests of justice. The intermediary can assist counsel to phrase their questions appropriately and if counsel cannot do this, then the intermediary can put the question in a way that is understood. The intermediary did that several times, each time achieving an answer where counsel had failed. That revealed that it is difficult for counsel to comprehend or effect the right approach to such a witness.

[44] *Registered Intermediary Procedural Guidance Manual* (2012) London, Ministry of Justice.

[45] Email (5 September 2011) Victims and Witnesses Unit, Justice Policy Group, Ministry of Justice.

[46] Plotnikoff and Woolfson (n 2).

[47] Ibid.

[48] Ibid.

The Registered Intermediary's primary responsibility is to enable complete and accurate communication with the witness.[49] Based on their assessment of a particular witness's understanding, they may conclude that the witness's compliance with suggestive questions is likely to produce unreliable answers and that, in the interests of a fair hearing, alternative questioning styles should be used. A 2010 survey of Registered Intermediaries found that they recommended avoiding leading questions in around three-quarters of the trials for which they were appointed.[50] Their recommendations must be discussed at a ground rules hearing (discussed further in the next section) attended by the intermediary, judge and advocates. Such discussions are vital, not least because advocates and intermediaries do not share a common understanding about what constitutes a 'leading' question. The divergence in perspectives is graphically illustrated in a study by psychologist Sarah Krähenbühl.[51] She asked small groups of Registered Intermediaries and advocates to comment on the transcript of the interview and cross-examination of a six-year-old. The intermediaries highlighted many more leading questions than the advocates. Tag questions were the greatest area of difference: none of the advocates flagged these as leading, while most intermediaries did so.

The Registered Intermediaries were also much more likely than the advocates to identify as leading those questions beginning 'I suggest to you that …' and questions in the form of statements of fact. Judges may also fail to see questions as statements as leading and therefore potentially problematic. The Judicial Studies Board's 2009 *Serious Sex Offences Seminar* DVD included a series of suggestive statements as questions demonstrating good cross-examination practice, for example: 'He never touched your breast area' and 'You're not telling the truth, you just wanted Kevin out of your life'. Children and other vulnerable witnesses may not recognise these statements as a question at all. A 14-year-old interviewed for *Measuring Up?* said: 'He [the defence advocate] said "I suggest to you that you picked the wrong person." I didn't know this was a question.' This prosecution rested on identification evidence and it failed when the witness did not contradict the advocate's assertion.

Registered Intermediaries have rapidly gained the confidence of most criminal justice practitioners with whom they have interacted, raising awareness about risks of miscommunication in cross-examination practice and how to remedy them. The Lord Chief Justice considers that 'the use of intermediaries has

[49] Registered Intermediaries Code of Practice and Code of Ethics, Part 3, *Registered Intermediary Procedural Guidance Manual* (2012). London, Ministry of Justice. The 'quality of evidence' test (section 16(5) Youth Justice and Criminal Evidence Act 1999 used in deciding whether special measures, including an intermediary, should be granted) encompasses 'completeness, coherence and accuracy'.

[50] P Cooper (2011) *Registered Intermediary Survey 2010 'Tell Me What's Happening'*. City Law School, City University, London. www.city.ac.uk/__data/assets/pdf_file/0006/92499/Tell-Me-Whats-Happening-2-RI-Survey-2010-FINAL-VERSION-14062011.pdf.

[51] S Krähenbühl (2011) 'Effective and Appropriate Communication with Children in Legal Proceedings According to Lawyers and Intermediaries' *Child Abuse Review*, Vol 20 Issue 6, Nov/Dec 2011, 407–20.

introduced fresh insights into the criminal justice process'.[52] The Court of Appeal has described intermediaries as 'an integral part of the structure of the special measures regime'[53] and a recent report found that 'Remarkably, every professional with whom we spoke described working with intermediaries as educative, if not "revelatory".'[54] Judges in family courts (not covered by the legislative provision) have occasionally used their inherent discretion to appoint an intermediary. In *Re W (Children)* (2010),[55] the Supreme Court removed the presumption that children will not give live evidence in family proceedings. Guidelines on taking children's evidence were approved by the Family Justice Council in 2011, and the President of the Family Division has been asked to recommend issuing them as Practice Guidance.[56] They include use of an intermediary to relay questions directly, as envisaged by Pigot and raised as an option by the Supreme Court in *Re W*.

Judicial Control of Children's Cross-examination

In 1989, the Pigot Committee proposed that judges 'should control cross-examination with special care' (section 2.29). In 2011, the Lord Chief Justice called for 'active positive case management' in which judges are 'increasingly alert to all the nuances of over cross-examination and unfair cross-examination'.[57]

The 'Overriding Objective' that cases be dealt with 'justly' (Criminal Procedure Rule 1 (2011)) has been interpreted as meaning 'in essence, that judges and magistrates are both bound and entitled to intervene to check a cross-examination which appears to be hindering the court from reaching a truthful outcome, rather than helping it to do so'.[58] *Achieving Best Evidence* (2011) states:[59]

> The responsibilities of judges and magistrates also extend to the prevention of improper or inappropriate questioning ... An advocate may be asked to rephrase a question if it is in a form or manner likely to lead to misunderstanding on the part of the witness ... Judges and magistrates should be alert to the possibility that a witness might be experiencing difficulty in understanding a question which, if not corrected, might lead to the giving of evidence that is not of the best quality that the witness could provide.

[52] Lord Judge, Lord Chief Justice (7 September 2011) *Vulnerable Witnesses in the Administration of Criminal Justice*, Australasian Institute of Judicial Administration Criminal Justice Conference. www.judiciary.gov.uk/Resources/JCO/Documents/Speeches/lcj-speech-vulnerable-witnesses-in-admin-of-criminal-justice-29092011.pdf.

[53] *R v Watts* [2010] EWCA Crim 1824.

[54] Hanna et al (n 35).

[55] *Re W (Children)* [2010] UKSC 12.

[56] Email from Private Office of the President of the Family Division (20 July 2011) concerning *Guidelines in Relation to Children giving Evidence in Family Proceedings*, forthcoming.

[57] Lord Judge (n 52).

[58] J Spencer (2010) *Evidence and Cross-Examination* in M Lamb et al (eds), *Children's Testimony: A Handbook of Psychological Research and Forensic Practice* 2nd edn. Chichester, Wiley.

[59] Section 5.11, *Achieving Best Evidence* (n 31).

The *Equal Treatment Bench Book* emphasises that:[60]

> If a child does not understand a question, they may be tempted to give the answer that they think the questioner wants, rather than the true answer. The child may also be afraid to disagree with a powerful adult figure. Judicial vigilance is always necessary.

Judicial policies also extend these principles to pre-trial planning. The *Equal Treatment Bench Book* encourages the use of judicial orders governing the way the child should be questioned:[61]

> Orders will generally deal with agreement by all parties on use of language—some terms may need to be agreed. At trial, the judge should check at an early stage that all directions are in place and all special needs are catered for. This may include ascertaining that advocates are sensitive to the child's vulnerability and that any special arrangements are made concerning the child's disability, language, race or culture. Issues may include areas of agreement and any areas on which the child might be led; and the tenor, tone, language and duration of questioning and cross-examination.

Ground rules are particularly important in setting the parameters of appropriate questioning: too often, by the time inappropriate questioning is recognised and challenged in the heat of cross-examination, it is too late for the witness. Unfortunately, the guidance on advance planning seems to be honoured in the breach: such meetings to discuss how the witness will be questioned are not held routinely even when they are required. When an intermediary is appointed, ground rules discussions *must* be held between the judge, counsel and the intermediary before the witness testifies.[62] However, a survey of Registered Intermediaries in 2010 revealed that these occurred in only 61 per cent of their trials,[63] usually just before the witness's testimony. One QC has stressed that an advocate cannot properly tailor questions to the needs of the witness if ground rules are only discussed at the last minute.[64] Half of the intermediaries surveyed said that their recommendation to avoid leading questions was always agreed by the judge at the ground rules hearing. Where the intermediary is appointed for a prosecution witness, ideally the defence follows ground rules discussed beforehand, relieving the intermediary of the need to intervene at all. However, most of the intermediaries surveyed reported that ground rules were contravened at trial, and they usually had to point out the contravention before the judge corrected the advocate. A few said the judge sometimes allowed the leading question even after the intermediary pointed it out. Professor Penny Cooper, author of the survey report, concluded:

> A 'Ground Rules are made to be broken' attitude may be prevalent amongst cross-examining counsel and if so it undermines the purpose of the Ground Rules hearing.

60 Section 4.43, *Equal Treatment Bench Book* (n 30).

61 Sections 4.4.2, 4.4.3, ibid. See also page 106, *Crown Court Bench Book—Directing the Jury* (2010) London, Judicial Studies Board.

62 Special Measures Application Form, Section F1, CrimPRC(10)02(a).

63 Cooper (n 50).

64 J Cutts QC (9 February 2011) Registered Intermediary Continuing Professional Development Day, Ryton.

> The survey suggests that generally judges could be more proactive in enforcing the Ground Rules that they have put in place.

Policy makes clear that the judge never relinquishes responsibility for controlling questions: 'The use of an intermediary does not reduce the responsibility of the judge or magistrates, or of the legal representative, to ensure that the questions put to a witness are proper and appropriate to the level of understanding of the witness.'[65] There is nevertheless some confusion about this. An Advocacy Training Council working group thought that use of an intermediary allowed the judge 'to retain a distance from the arena … thus ensuring that [judicial] interventions are as limited as possible'.[66] This perspective does not take account of questions that may be inappropriate for reasons not relating to communication (falling outside the intermediary's terms of reference), another reason why primary responsibility for intervention must remain with the judge.

Judicial control of cross-examination has increased in recent years but is still uneven. Many developmentally or otherwise inappropriate questions go unchallenged. Sometimes this is due to the judge not recognising the difficulty, but even where they are aware of the problem, they may still not intervene. At the 2010 Nuffield Foundation–NSPCC young witness seminar, some judges acknowledged constraints on how far they could go when faced with an advocate unable to modify his or her language, or who resolutely declines to do so. One said: 'I did intervene quite a lot but it's very difficult. The defence could argue I was interfering.' Another voiced his frustration, explaining:

> You can only interrupt or send the jury out so many times. If I interrupt four out of seven questions, I can't do it again … [and even if poor practice is brought to the attention of the head of chambers] they come back and do it in exactly the same way. Their role is to get the client off and they will.[67]

The seminar noted that it is impossible to make a formal complaint about a barrister's inappropriate cross-examination of a child as this does not constitute a specific transgression of the *Code of Conduct*.[68]

Can Training Achieve a 'Cultural Change'?

In 1989, the Pigot Committee called for 'a fundamental change of attitude towards children in the legal context' (section 7.9):

> The professional training of judges and lawyers could usefully address some issues in child psychology and cognitive development. Lawyers should understand how to

[65] Section B.9.32, *Achieving Best Evidence* (n 31).
[66] Section 17.8, *Raising the Bar* (n 38).
[67] Plotnikoff and Woolfson (n 3).
[68] www.barstandardsboard.org.uk/regulatory-requirements/the-code-of-conduct/.

speak to children and should appreciate the consequences of misleading or oppressive questioning.

The first Judicial Studies Board child abuse seminars did not begin until 1996. The judge who was course director said: 'It became immediately apparent how much practice varied at different courts. That surprised both those organising the seminars and those attending.'[69] The 1997 video *A case for balance: Demonstrating good practice when children are witnesses* was introduced by Lord Justice Judge (as he then was) and addressed judicial control of cross-examination, among other matters.[70] It was used to promote discussion at judicial training courses for several years.

In 2009, Lord Justice Thomas, Vice-President of the Queen's Bench Division and Deputy Head of Criminal Justice, called for a 'cultural change' to ensure that young witness policy 'operates in practice'.[71] This was taken forward by the Judicial Studies Board (now Judicial College) training, where research findings about communication difficulties have been addressed on serious sex offences courses, criminal continuation courses and training for district judges.[72] Participants are asked to make a 'cultural change' to control children's questioning, including avoiding 'tag' questions.

The judiciary is in advance of the legal professions in integrating research findings about children's communication into its training and guidance.[73] The position of the professions is complicated by the number of bodies involved in delivery of advocacy training and differences in course content. There are, however, more fundamental difficulties. The advocate's poor communication style can unfairly advantage his case by confusing, inhibiting or intimidating the other side's witness. Training routinely encourages advocates to 'tell, don't ask' and 'lead, lead, lead'[74]; and to control witnesses in a way that may not permit them to give a full response.[75] A quarter of the children interviewed for *Measuring Up?* complained that their answers were interrupted.

Proposals to reform advocacy practice in relation to children have involved accreditation, appraisal and specialist training but all three have proved controversial. Judicial support for accreditation was expressed at the 2010 Nuffield

[69] P Crane (1999) Child abuse procedures in practice. *Judicial Studies Board Journal*, 7.

[70] Funded by the NSPCC, Home Office, ChildLine, Crown Prosecution Service, Department of Health, General Council of the Bar, Law Society, Lord Chancellor's Department, NCH Action for Children and Nuffield Foundation. Project coordinators J Plotnikoff and R Woolfson.

[71] Introduction, Plotnikoff and Woolfson (n 8).

[72] HHJ S Cahill QC, Vulnerable Victim and Witness judge (25 February 2010) Area Witness Champion Conference, Ryton.

[73] Eg J Plotnikoff and R Woolfson (2012) *Judicial College Bench Checklist: Young Witness Cases*. www.judiciary.gov.uk/publications-and-reports/guidance/2012/jc-bench-checklist-young-wit-cases.

[74] P Cooper (9 February 2011) Registered Intermediary Continuing Professional Development Conference, Ryton.

[75] Advocacy Training Council (undated) *Report to BVC Providers on the Common Errors Made by Pupils in Advocacy Training Sessions*. 'Lack of control. Allowing the witness to give a full answer' appeared among the 'common errors' listed on this website report but was removed when drawn to the attention of the ATC.

Foundation–NSPCC advocacy seminar. One judge said that 'We won't get this right until defence counsel are ticketed [accredited]. Some shouldn't be doing it.' Another agreed: 'Until the Bar accept the need for specialisation the situation won't improve.' However, in 2009 a proposal to set up accredited panels of young witness practitioners was rejected by the Crown Prosecution Service, Law Society, Criminal Bar Association and Council for Circuit Judges, which favoured 'education not accreditation'.[76] Even so, barristers rejected the need for further training or assessment in respect of dealing with children in a further consultation in 2010[77] and Bar training that year on juveniles continued to omit any mention of child development or communication issues.[78] A judge at the Nuffield Foundation–NSPCC seminar in 2010 acknowledged: 'Barristers don't have the remotest idea about children's development—and judges only have a little.'

In 2010, we asked the Inns of Court, Bar Circuits and some other providers of advocacy training[79] whether their courses addressed 'dealing appropriately with vulnerable witnesses', one of the first profession-wide quality assurance standards proposed in a 2009 consultation.[80] Only one of the four Inns and three of the six Bar Circuits dealt with vulnerable witnesses in training for pupils. None of the Inns and only one circuit held relevant training for new practitioners. One circuit said:

> We don't include specific training in respect of vulnerable witnesses in our pupil or new practitioner courses. So far as we're aware, this hasn't been required or recommended by the Advocacy Training Council, nor is it included in Inns of Court courses, upon which our training is based.

In 2011, the Advocacy Training Council published *Raising the Bar*, a report from its vulnerable witness working group.[81] This identified 'a clear and pressing need' for specialist training, beginning in pupillage and extending throughout the advocate's career. It also proposed that two of the annual requirement of 12 Continuing Professional Development points be ring-fenced for this area of competence (sections 2.6 and 5.3). The working group also recommended

> training leading to certification, with no counsel having conduct of cases involving vulnerable witnesses or offenders unless certified. A system by which only advocates certified or 'ticketed' to take cases involving vulnerable witnesses—akin to the system

[76] Ministry of Justice (2009) *Government Response to the Improving the Criminal Trial Process for Young Witnesses Consultation.* London, Ministry of Justice.

[77] Paras 3.7.3–4, Joint Advocacy Group (2010) *Quality Assurance for Advocates.* This referred to a previous consultation on 'the necessity within a QAA framework for additional specialist training or assessment for particular types of work (such as cases involving juveniles ...). The response to this question was overwhelmingly against the inclusion of further training or assessment for particular types of cases.'

[78] Eg section F (Juveniles and the Criminal Courts), *Bar Vocational Course* (2010) expected the student 'to be able to demonstrate a sound understanding' of legal and procedural matters.

[79] Unpublished survey conducted for the NSPCC–Nuffield Foundation advocacy seminar (June 2010).

[80] B3(2), Advocacy Standards in Joint Advocacy Group (2009) *Consultation on Standards for Criminal Advocates at Trial.* www.ilex.org.uk/pdf/IPScon%20Advocacy%20Standards.pdf.

[81] *Raising the Bar* (n 38).

for those qualified to prosecute or adjudicate on serious sexual offence cases—would allow for greater clarity and assure standards. It would also provide a clear indication to wider society that the Bar takes this topic very seriously—so much so that a higher level of professional training is required to deal with such cases (section 22.4).

Conclusion

'Whenever smart people cling to an outlandishly incorrect idea despite substantial evidence to the contrary, something interesting is at work … a convergence of multiple forces, all coming together to prop up a theory that should have died out decades before.'[82] Something of this sort has preserved perverse strategies for questioning children at trial. If used at the investigative interview, these same strategies would result in the case being thrown out. History tells us to expect a long learning curve—with resistance along the way—when professions are forced to shift direction. But how long is too long on the road to best evidence? As recently as 2010, a QC acknowledged that some advocates still fail to accept their limitations in questioning vulnerable witnesses due to 'ignorance, arrogance or misconceptions'.[83] Also in 2010, a senior barrister responsible for advocacy training admitted that: 'Advocates only learn when they're under threat.' It is hard to envisage the stick or carrot that will induce some practitioners to relinquish tag questions and other 'impoverished … conventional instruments'[84] of cross-examination when questioning children.

There is not much 'stick' by way of incentive to abandon bad habits. As noted above, judicial control of poor practice is increasing but remains uneven and there is no formal complaints procedure for cross-examination that repeatedly crosses the line in the face of judicial intervention. Registered Intermediaries are helping to raise awareness of communication problems, but only a minority of advocates have worked with them and intermediaries are not routinely consulted as trainers. Recent Court of Appeal judgments, while helpfully highlighting what constitute inappropriate forms of questioning, nevertheless decline to criticise the questioners.[85]

Do proposals to quality assure criminal advocacy constitute a 'carrot' to motivate cultural change? The origins of the scheme date back to 2006 when Lord Carter identified the need for a scheme to quality-assure the standards of advocacy.[86] In July 2011, the Joint Advocacy Group—which brings together the regulatory

[82] S Johnson (2006) *The Ghost Map*. New York, Riverhead Books.

[83] J Cutts QC (n 64).

[84] E Loftus (2006) 'General Review of the Psychology of Witness Testimony' in A Heaton-Armstrong et al (eds) *Witness Testimony: Psychological, Investigative and Evidential Perspectives*. Oxford, OUP.

[85] D Wurtzel 'Advocacy Focus' *Counsel*, January 2011, 40–42.

[86] Lord Carter (2006) *Legal Aid: A Market-based Approach to Reform*. London, Department for Constitutional Affairs and Legal Services Commission.

authorities for the Bar (Bar Standards Board), solicitors (Solicitors Regulation Authority) and legal executives (Institute of Legal Executives Professional Standards)—submitted its Quality Assurance Scheme for Advocates to the Legal Services Board.[87] It proposed that all advocates in criminal cases be assessed against standards leading to accreditation at one of four levels, with Level One applying to advocates in the magistrates' court and Level Four to those undertaking the most serious Crown Court cases. A Generic Standard expects everyone to handle vulnerable witnesses 'appropriately' and comply with all relevant obligations and 'good practice guidance in respect of victims and witnesses'.[88] The scheme was scheduled to be introduced in stages from the end of 2011 but has been delayed and is subject to changes.[89] At present, it is hard to envisage these provisions encouraging the necessary shift of approach across the professions.

Advocates—and those who are to assess them—may struggle to identify relevant obligations and guidance referred to in the Generic Standard. *Measuring Up?* drew on over 40 young witness policies, not including guidance concerning vulnerable adults. Practitioners need ready access to authoritative guidance bringing together relevant and updated material. There is also a need for a 'gold standard' checklist or code on questioning young witnesses, endorsed by the necessary bodies, as called for by participants at the 2010 Nuffield Foundation–NSPCC advocacy seminar. Guidance on questioning children produced alongside *Measuring Up?* was seen as a useful starting point.[90] Seminar participants also saw a need for an online training video: viewing could be made compulsory for those who want to be deemed competent on this subject. The Criminal Bar Association and NSPCC have convened a group to develop such material.

The legal profession's recent acceptance of the need for advocacy training on vulnerable witness issues is welcomed, but 'training the trainers' exercises are essential to ensure that messages are delivered in a consistent and unequivocal manner. Role-play cross-examination is a common training technique, but during 'vulnerable witness' exercises we have seen teachers conveying conflicting messages (eg 'tag questions are undesirable' vs 'tag questions are essential'). Delivery should be in the hands of those familiar with good practice guidance and who are also 'signed up' to the messages. Training content must go beyond suggesting that questions be simplified. It should encompass how to make best use of a Registered Intermediary and the ground rules hearing, the limitations on 'putting your case' as proposed in *Barker* and how to test the witness's evidence without leading, if this is required by a judicial direction based on the communication needs of the witness.

[87] Joint Advocacy Group (2011) *Quality Assurance Scheme for Advocates (Crime) Application of the Joint Advocacy Group.*

[88] Generic Standard B3, ibid.

[89] For example, see C Baksi (14 October 2011) *Quality Assurance Scheme to Go Ahead from April* Law Society Gazette http://www.lawgazette.co.uk/news/quality-assurance-scheme-go-ahead-april.

[90] J Plotnikoff and R Woolfson (2009) *Good Practice Guidance in Managing Young Witness Cases and Questioning Children.* NSPCC and Nuffield Foundation. www.nspcc.org.uk/measuringup.

Effective implementation of section 28 will require rigorous timetabling and case management. Monitoring is needed to check that taking children's evidence at a pre-trial hearing indeed reduces the amount of time that elapses before the child's evidence is completed. However, even if section 28 is brought into effect, this will still not constitute what is known as 'full Pigot'. The risk remains that developmentally inappropriate cross-examination is simply brought forward to a pre-trial stage.

Pigot recognised that sometimes 'it is absolutely impossible for counsel to communicate successfully with a child' (section 3.33). Current practice provides no adequate response to this situation: even when a Registered Intermediary is appointed, the norm is for the judge to ask the intermediary to rephrase a question only after two failed attempts by the advocate.[91] When communication breaks down after a series of problematic questions, some judges have considered requiring counsel to write out their questions for judicial scrutiny or even posing the questions themselves. As yet, accepted practice does not include the final element of 'full Pigot': permitting the advocate's questions to be 'relayed by a person approved by the court who enjoys the child's confidence' (Recommendation 6, section 2.32). Following discussion about the scope of questioning at a ground rules hearing, an intermediary using an earpiece could relay the advocate's questions. The wording of section 29 of the Youth Justice and Criminal Evidence Act (the intermediary provision) allows for this. The Lord Chief Justice feels that the justice system has not yet 'arrived at our final destination on the use of intermediaries'.[92] We believe that use of the intermediary as interlocutor (as is done in South Africa) is a necessary part of the court's arsenal of special measures: an option to be planned for as indicated by the needs of the witness, not merely invoked once communication has broken down. Based on their assessment, Registered Intermediaries could identify witnesses for whom the assistance of an interlocutor is appropriate, and in particular, those for whom any breakdown in communication at court is likely to be irrecoverable.

In recent years, more robust prosecution policy has triggered a 60 per cent increase in the numbers of young witnesses being called to court,[93] with more very young children entering the system. Over 20 years ago, Pigot called for 'quite radical changes … if the courts are to treat children in a humane and acceptable way'. In 2011, the Lord Chief Justice called on lawyers to abandon unfair cross-examination of children and other vulnerable witnesses or defendants and get rid of 'strait jacketed' ideas about how this should be conducted: 'The testing of

[91] The advocate asks a question, the Registered Intermediary flags up a problem to the judge, who gives the advocate a second attempt. Only if this fails do most judges invite the Registered Intermediary to rephrase.

[92] Lord Judge (n 52).

[93] Different sources indicate that around 48,000 were called to court in 2008/9, compared to around 30,000 in 2006/7. There are no official figures for those who actually give evidence. Plotnikoff and Woolfson (n 3).

the evidence—which is legitimate, whether of the defendant or the prosecution witnesses—must be fair in that broadest possible sense.'[94]

The shocking court experience of the four-year-old in *Barker*[95] shows that the objective of fair questioning 'in the broadest possible sense' is still out of reach, at least for some children. A fresh approach must be grounded in messages from research about how they understand and process language. Otherwise, we are failing to meet the Overriding Objective set out in Criminal Procedure Rule 1 (2011), that cases be dealt with 'justly'.

94 Lord Judge (n 52).
95 See ch 1 above.

3

Alternative Routes: Other Accusatorial Jurisdictions on the Slow Road to Best Evidence

EMILY HENDERSON

Introduction

Over the last 30 years since this subject was first widely discussed in the United Kingdom and all across the common law world, great strides have been made towards creating a better process for the taking of children's evidence. So great has been the distance travelled and so difficult the journey that it is hard not to want to believe that we have come far enough.

However, professional experience and research both show that there are still major problems with the way in which we approach child witnesses. The two most significant problems appear to be, first, that children in many of these countries still face significant delays before trial and second, that there are still widespread and significant problems with the language and techniques of cross-examination.

This chapter discusses the ways in which five common law countries, namely South Africa, Israel, Northern Ireland, Scotland[1] and the United States have attempted to deal with those issues, focusing particularly upon the issue of cross-examination. The chapter attempts to place these countries in context with the others discussed more fully in this book, especially England and Wales, New Zealand and Western Australia, and attempts to draw some conclusions as to the direction in which their successes and failures might point those of us seeking to design better systems.

[1] I am very grateful to Joyce Plotnikoff, Lexicon Ltd, for her comments upon my descriptions of the Scottish and Northern Irish systems. All mistakes are of course my own.

Delay

Delay before trial creates significant problems for children both in terms of their psychological welfare and in terms of the quality of the evidence they are able to give. Time erodes children's memories even more quickly than it does adults' memories.[2] Meanwhile the waiting also causes a great deal of stress,[3] especially as many children fear the trial and cross-examination in particular.[4] Stress in its turn may further erode memory.[5]

Concern with delay is a feature of commentary and research across all the jurisdictions under discussion in this chapter. In New Zealand, as described in chapter six, one recent study found that, on average, children waited 15 months from committal to trial. If time was measured from the police investigation through to trial then the average delay was 20 months.

Research in 2009 and 2011 suggested that children in Northern Ireland suffer similar delays before trial. The average delay between reporting the offence to police and trial in the Crown Court was 18.1 months and the average to trial in the magistrates' or youth courts was 12.9 months.[6]

As Plotnikoff and Woolfson state elsewhere in this book, the average time for cases involving children from reporting offences to trial in the English Crown Court is around 13 months and around eight months from the defendant's first appearance to trial.[7] Whilst the figures in England and Wales are an improvement upon New Zealand's, these are still long periods for children to wait.

[2] L Molloy and J Quas 'Children's Suggestibility: Areas of Consensus and Controversy' in K Kuehnle and M Connell (eds), *The Evaluation of Child Sexual Abuse Allegations: A Comprehensive Guide to Assessment and Testimony* Hoboken, NJ, Wiley, 2009.

[3] J R Spencer and R Flin *The Evidence of Children: The Law and the Psychology* London, Blackstone Press 1993, 366, cite research as at 1993; J Plotnikoff and R Woolfson *Measuring Up? Evaluating Implementation of Government Committments to Young Witnesses in Criminal Proceedings* London, NSPCC/Nuffield Foundation 2009, 32–33; K Hanna, E Davies, E Henderson, C Crothers and C Rotherham *Child Witnesses in the Criminal Courts: A Review of Practice and Implications for Policy* Auckland, The New Zealand Law Foundation, 2010, 26; Plotnikoff and Woolfson, ch 2.

[4] J A Quas, G S Goodman, G S Ghetti, K W Alexander, R Edelstein, A D Redlich and DPH Jones *Childhood Sexual Assault Victims: Long-Term Outcomes After Testifying in Criminal Court* (2005) vol 70(2) Boston, Blackwell Publishing; N Troxel, C Ogle, I Cordon, M Lawler, G S Goodman 'Child Witnesses in Criminal Court' in B Bottoms and G S Goodman (eds), *Child Victims, Child Offenders: Psychology and the Law* New York, Guilford Press, 2009, 5–6.

[5] Molloy and Quas (n 2).

[6] D Hayes, L Bunting, A Lazenbatt, N Carr and J Duffy *The Experiences of Young Witnesses in Criminal Proceedings in Northern Ireland: A Report for the Department of Justice (NI)* NSPCC(NI) May 2011, 24.

[7] Plotnikoff and Woolfson, ch 2.

There are also some comments from South Africa[8] and the United States[9] suggesting that child witnesses in each of those jurisdictions face long delays, too.

There is an irony to the fact that the longest delays are suffered by those least able to withstand them.

Solutions

For many years, various countries have attempted to encourage judges to case-manage delays out of existence. As Plotnikoff and Woolfson note, since 1988 it has been the policy of successive governments to give priority when scheduling to trials involving child witnesses in England and Wales (though no one has ever evaluated whether this is effective).[10] Similarly in New Zealand, the Chief Justice first issued fast-tracking directions in 1992.[11] Yet, by the present day, as already discussed, delays in New Zealand have increased considerably.

Similar failures have been reported in the specialist court pilot in New South Wales, where part of the aim was to fast-track children's cases but in fact increased demand for the special facilities and a lack of resources has increased the backlog.[12]

Throughout most of the 2000s Western Australia, too, was dogged by particularly long delays in child witness cases. In 2002 cases involving child witnesses in Western Australia took an average of 17.5 months from committal to trial[13] whilst by 2005 they waited 18 months.[14] However, as Judge Jackson reports in chapter four, due to their practice of fully pre-recording almost all children's evidence these delays were of far less significance than they would have been in other jurisdictions. Nonetheless, case management was also attempted to reduce waiting times. Until 2008 this approach was unsuccessful. In 2008, however, Western Australia managed to overcome its delays with the aid of a significant injection of

[8] G Jonker and R Swanzen 'Intermediary Services for Child Witnesses Testifying in South African Criminal Courts' (2007) 3 *SUR International Journal of Human Rights*, 18.

[9] M Sawicki 'The *Crawford v Washington* Decision—Five Years Later: Implications for Child Abuse Prosecutors' (2009) 21 (9) and (10) *National Center for Prosecution of Child Abuse Update* 1, describes delays of a year or more between the accused's being charged and trial as occurring 'often'.

[10] Plotnikoff and Woolfson ch 2. See also Hayes et al (n 6), which also mentions the failure of directives to prioritise children's cases in Northern Ireland.

[11] See Henderson, ch 6. L Hoyano and C Keenan *Child Abuse: Law and Policy Across Boundaries* Oxford, Oxford University Press, 2010, 652, report that the US Congress and 27 states have all legislated to prioritise cases involving child witnesses.

[12] J Cashmore, L Trimboli et al *An Evaluation of the NSW Child Sexual Assault Specialist Jurisdiction Pilot* Sydney, NSW Bureau of Crime Statistics and Research, 2005.

[13] C Eastwood and W Patton *The Experiences of Child Complainants of Sexual Abuse in the Criminal Justice System*, 2002, retrieved from www.criminologyresearchcouncil.gov.au/reports/eastwood.pdf, 49, 114.

[14] Australian Federal Police & Prosecutions *Responding to Sexual Assault: The Challenge of Change* Canberra, ACT: Australian Federal Police, Australian Capital Territory Office of the Director of Public Prosecutions, 2005, 144.

cash for new courts and new judges[15] and significant efforts to coordinate all of the agencies involved. In 2011 the Western Australian District Court Judge Kevin Sleight, Commissioner of the Supreme Court of Western Australia, described the work done to manage a crisis in the court system caused by a sudden influx of cases of child abuse from mid 2007 to early 2009, the result of inquiries in remote communities in the state.[16] The courts created a special high-level taskforce to manage the caseload to avoid 'causing a blowout of the District Court's normal listings'.[17] They obtained special government funding to resource the courts and brought in additional judges and lawyers to undertake the work, as well as making special arrangements with witness support and, for sentencing purposes, probation services.[18] Judge Sleight commented:

> What the taskforce operation in Western Australia demonstrated was that the management of charges involving alleged sexual offences requires adequate funding and resources to ensure that all stages of the process are dealt with efficiently and expeditiously.[19]

What is also evident in the judge's description is that the taskforce would not have succeeded without committed leadership from the senior judiciary and other senior members of the justice system and government. Equal determination and investment might go some way towards obviating delays in other systems. However, thus far there is little evidence of a similar convergence of will and resourcing elsewhere.[20]

One alternative is, as already mentioned, to pre-record children's entire evidence—in-chief and cross—at a pre-trial hearing well in advance of the actual trial. Many countries in the common law world of course already pre-record the child's evidence-in-chief,[21] but (as in England) children still have to come back to court at the actual trial to be cross-examined and so must still cope with the effects of long waiting times.

With full pre-recording, on the other hand, the child may still give evidence-in-chief via a video interview but will return to court for a pre-trial hearing at which they give the rest of their evidence as if at the trial proper. The hearing is recorded and later edited of inadmissible and prejudicial material. At trial the recording is replayed to the jury. The child need not attend unless he or she is recalled to testify about some new matter. I refer to this process as 'full pre-recording' in this chapter.

[15] Hanna et al (n 3): confirmed in personal communications with Judge Jackson.

[16] K Sleight *Managing Trials for Sexual Offences—A Western Australian Perspective* AIJA Conference, Sydney, 2011, 22.

[17] Ibid, 23. This taskforce included the chief judges from each of the district, youth and magistrates' courts together with the Director of Public Prosecutions, the Aboriginal Legal Services and the Police.

[18] Sleight (n 16), 23.

[19] Sleight (n 16) 24.

[20] Although in Auckland, New Zealand the District Court is attempting to cut delays for children from 15 months to under 6: it is too early to tell whether this initiative is likely to succeed.

[21] Excepting South Africa and, mostly, the US.

The advantage of pre-recording a child's entire evidence is that it has the potential to circumvent at least some pre-trial delay since once the child's evidence is recorded it matters very little, at least to the child, when the actual trial takes place. Meanwhile, the evidence could, in theory, be taken while it is still relatively fresh. The child can move on with his or her life without the stress of waiting for trial. Although it must be possible to recall children to give evidence at trial where new issues arise, experience suggests that this happens only very exceptionally.[22]

The pros and cons of pre-recording are discussed in detail by Professor Spencer in the introductory chapter and Judge Jackson gives a detailed description of its use in Western Australia. The following is a brief overview of other jurisdictions with provision for full pre-recording.

States with but not using Pre-recording

United Kingdom

England and Wales

As we saw in chapter one, England and Wales have had legislation allowing full pre-recording since 1999, following the recommendations of the Pigot Committee. However, whilst it has the legislation it has not so far brought it into force,[23] although at the time of writing there is renewed discussion in government as to whether to bring the provision into force.[24]

This is not the first time this situation has arisen in England and Wales. In 1894 it enacted the legislation allowing children's evidence to be pre-recorded by written deposition where appearing in court would seriously endanger his or her 'life and health', provided the defence could cross-examine wherever the deposition was taken. However, this provision appears to have been rarely if ever used.[25] Nevertheless, it was still technically in force when in the 1990s efforts to resuscitate and update it to include video-taping were defeated in the House of Lords. As a dead letter, it is still in principle in force today.[26] This was despite academic advocacy of videoing complainants' interviews from the 1960s onwards[27] and a clear precedent in the use of full pre-recording in parts of the United States during

[22] See Jackson, ch 4.

[23] See Spencer, chs 1 and 9.

[24] See Spencer, ch 1.

[25] The Prevention of Cruelty to Children (Amendment) Act 1894. The provision continues in ss 42 and 43 Children and Young Persons Act 1933. Spencer and Flin (n 3) 90.

[26] Spencer and Flin (n 3).

[27] Glanville Williams first advocated pre-recording in the 1960s, but it was in the 1980s that debate took off: See, eg, G Williams 'Videotaping Children's Evidence' (1986) 137 *New Law Journal*; G Williams 'More About Videotaping Children' (1987) 137 *New Law Journal*; JR Spencer 'Child Witnesses, Video Technology and the Law of Evidence' (1987) *Criminal Law Review* 76; see also Spencer and Flin (n 3) 83–86, 165–73.

the 1970s and 1980s.[28] England is not unusual in having enacted legislation to permit full pre-recording, only to then ignore it.

Northern Ireland

A long-lasting legacy of the 'Troubles' is that laws in relation to criminal justice matters in Northern Ireland are made not locally, but by Orders issued by the executive in London. Accordingly, in 1999 an Order was made for Northern Ireland replicating the special measures provisions made for England and Wales by the Youth Justice and Criminal Evidence Act 1999, including a provision permitting full pre-recording.[29] However, as in England and Wales, these pre-recording provisions have not been implemented.

As Northern Ireland also failed to bring into force the provisions allowing intermediaries included in the 1999 Order[30] (see discussion below), children there are restricted to using their ABE (Achieving Best Evidence) interviews as their evidence-in-chief[31] and to using live link[32] or screens[33] for cross- and re-examination.

Scotland

Scotland also enacted full pre-recording provisions in 1993 and again in 2004, a process known as 'taking evidence by a commissioner'. The Scottish situation is different from that in the rest of the United Kingdom in that the legislature has brought the provisions into force. However, criminal justice practitioners there are largely ignoring their ability to pre-record children's evidence.[34] Nonetheless, despite this reluctance amongst practitioners, the Scottish Executive has outlined in detail how it expects its system to work and has given some encouragement to practitioners to begin pre-recording.[35]

Children under 16 in Scotland are automatically entitled to use the 'standard special measures'[36] of screens, live link and a supporter once an application is made.[37] The court may also permit 'further available measures', the use of prior

[28] Spencer and Flin (n 3) 166–68; Anon 'The Testimony of Child Victims in Sex Abuse Prosecutions: Two Legislative Innovations' (1985) 98 *Harvard Law Review* 806; C Stiver 'Video-Tape Trials: A Practical Evaluation and a Legal Analysis' [1974] *Stanford Law Review* 26; J Armstrong 'The Criminal Videotape Trial: Serious Constitutional Questions' [1976] *Oregon Law Review* 567; J Humphrey 'Preparing the World for the Child: California's New Child Sexual Abuse Law' (1986) 23 *California Western Law Review* 52, 56–57, 69.

[29] Art 16 Criminal Evidence (Northern Ireland) Order 1999.

[30] See, eg, Government of Northern Ireland *Achieving Best Evidence in Criminal Proceedings (NI) Guidance for Vulnerable or Intimidated Witnesses including Children* www.nio.gov.uk.

[31] Art 15 Criminal Evidence (Northern Ireland) Order 1999.

[32] Art 12 Criminal Evidence (Northern Ireland) Order 1999.

[33] Art 11 Criminal Evidence (Northern Ireland) Order 1999.

[34] For the earlier situation see Spencer and Flin (n 3) 172–73; for the current one see Hoyano and Keenan (n 11) 650–51.

[35] See, eg, Scottish Executive *Special Measures for Vulnerable Adult and Child Witnesses: A Guidance Pack* Edinburgh, Scottish Executive, 2005, updated 2008.

[36] s 271A(14) Criminal Procedure (Scotland) Act 1995.

[37] s 271A(2)(a) Criminal Procedure (Scotland) Act 1995.

statements as evidence-in-chief (although apparently children's initial interviews are not often videoed, thus making the use of videos as evidence-in-chief also a rare occurrence) and, as aforesaid, the 'taking of evidence by a commissioner',[38] provided the court considers the child's views and is satisfied that the measure will not significantly prejudice the accused's right to a fair trial.[39]

The legislation sets out that the taking of evidence by a commissioner (a High Court judge or sheriff[40]) must be recorded on video[41] and may involve either the child testifying via live link or the child testifying in the courtroom.[42] The accused should not normally be present in any room with the child, but shall be able to watch and listen.[43]

The Scottish Executive has expanded upon this outline, suggesting two approaches (although admitting others are possible): first, that the child be examined via live link whilst the judge, both counsel and the accused are present in court and second, 'exceptionally', that the child, judge and counsel sit together at a table in the well of the court whilst the accused observes via live link.[44] Afterwards the recording would be edited of inadmissible material.[45] There is no guidance in the legislation or elsewhere as to when evidence should be taken.[46] The advice in relation to its earlier incarnation in legislation in 1993 was to conduct the examination close to the time of trial to ensure the defence had received full disclosure and completed its inquiries.[47] However, now the Scottish Executive appears to envisage taking the evidence earlier in order to avoid the deleterious effects of delay on children's evidence and well-being.[48]

The Scottish Executive encourages the use of this provision, stating that it can see 'no routine disadvantages'[49] and listing as benefits not only the avoidance of delay but also the ability to accommodate the child's needs for breaks etc and to hold the examination 'in an atmosphere more commensurate with their needs'.[50] However, just as few children's initial disclosure interviews are recorded, it appears that very few children have as yet had their evidence taken by a commissioner. By 2006 *no* child had used the procedure.[51] However, since then there has been at least one

[38] s 271I Criminal Procedure (Scotland) Act 1995, inserted by part 1 of the Vulnerable Witnesses (Scotland) Act 2004.
[39] s 271A(10) Criminal Procedure (Scotland) Act 1995.
[40] s 271I(7) and (8) Criminal Procedure (Scotland) Act 1995: whether a judge or sheriff depends upon whether the case is to be tried in the sheriff court or High Court.
[41] s 271I(2) Criminal Procedure (Scotland) Act 1995.
[42] s 271I(1A) Criminal Procedure (Scotland) Act 1995.
[43] s 271I(3) Criminal Procedure (Scotland) Act 1995. See also Scottish Executive *Special Measures* (2008) 7.
[44] Ibid, Scottish Executive, 9–10.
[45] Scottish Executive, 9–10 (n 35), 15–16.
[46] Scottish Executive, 9–10 (n 35) 13.
[47] Hoyano and Keenan (n 11) 650–51.
[48] Scottish Executive *Special Measures* (2008) (n 35) 5–6.
[49] Ibid, 6.
[50] Scottish Executive *Special Measures* (2008) (n 35) 6.
[51] Hoyano and Keenan (n 11) 651.

instance of its use: On 24 January 2008 Faisal Younas was convicted of battering his baby daughter to death after trial at Glasgow High Court where the evidence had included the evidence of his four-year-old son taken in advance of trial by the trial judge, Lord Hardie, as commissioner. It is not clear what process was used during its taking. The prosecution reportedly relied heavily upon the video evidence.[52]

Hoyano and Keenan ascribe the failure to make significant use of evidence by the commissioner to the fact that the legislation allows judges a wide discretion as to whether to allow the measure and to the 'deeply adversarial nature of the Scottish legal system', and the engrained conservatism of its practitioners.[53]

Moreover, despite the various special measures, guidance from the Executive that children should not be called upon to give evidence unless it is necessary[54] and long-standing criticism, child witnesses in Scotland are still subject to 'precognition'—whereby they may be interviewed in advance of the trial by agents of all parties—so exposing children to repeated questioning.[55] Thus, despite good legislation, the situation of child witnesses in Scotland remains extremely difficult on many levels.

New Zealand

In 1989 the New Zealand legislature enacted a provision allowing full pre-recording. However, the provision foundered because practitioners ignored it, as is now the case in Scotland. In 2006 any explicit mention of full pre-recording was removed from the legislation, although the new legislation was drafted quite broadly.[56] In 2010 Auckland prosecutors made a determined effort to begin pre-recording children's entire evidence, exploiting the broadness of the existing legislation. This attempt was repelled by the New Zealand Court of Appeal. The government has since indicated it will legislate for a presumption of pre-recording.[57]

Since New Zealand also failed to give effect to its provision allowing intermediaries (see discussion below),[58] help for children is restricted to using their ABE interviews as their evidence-in-chief[59] and to using live link[60] or screens[61] for cross- and re-examination.

[52] 'Baby Killer Found Guilty After Evidence of Boy Aged Four', www.news.scotsman.com, 25 January 2008; 'Four Year Old Gives Evidence As Experts Disagree' www.xproexperts.co.uk, 26 January 2008; *Younas v HM Advocate* [2011] HCJAC 48, which does not, however, discuss the commission process.

[53] Hoyano and Keenan (n 11) 651.

[54] Scottish Executive *Guidance on the Questioning of Children* Edinburgh, Scottish Executive, 2003, 4.

[55] See J Plotnikoff and R Woolfson *An Evaluation of Child Witness Support in Scotland* Edinburgh, Scottish Executive Central Research Unit, 2001, 69; Hoyano and Keenan (n 11) 651.

[56] See Henderson, ch 6 for a full discussion.

[57] Ibid.

[58] Ibid.

[59] s 105 Evidence Act 2006 (NZ).

[60] Ibid.

[61] Ibid.

United States

Any review of countries with, but not entirely utilising, full pre-recording must also make reference to the United States. Many US states have had legislation permitting full pre-recording for many years, and that legislation continues to be in force. In the 1970s several states began to record the entire evidence of adult witnesses in order to speed up the trial process and reduce costs.[62] As concerns rose about child sexual abuse and the difficulties of taking children through the courts, various US states introduced new legislation to fully pre-record children's evidence too, the first being Montana in 1977.[63] Hoyano and Keenan in their review note that Congress[64] and 38 states have legislation allowing children's evidence to be fully prerecorded.[65] However, there are difficulties that impede its use.

Unlike in Western Australia, where the pre-recording hearing is technically the beginning of the trial proper,[66] pre-recorded evidence in the United States constitutes hearsay, even if recorded at a pre-trial hearing. Because of the importance placed on face-to-face confrontation between accused and witnesses and the resultant evidence of the parties' demeanour, the admission of hearsay is strictly controlled in the United States, although various exceptions to the rule can encompass children's out-of-court statements.[67]

The Sixth Amendment to the US Constitution provides that 'in all criminal prosecutions the accused shall enjoy the right … to be confronted with the witnesses against him'. Such is the importance placed upon confrontation that in 1988 the Supreme Court rejected the use of screens to protect a child complainant on the basis that: '[T]here is something deep in human nature that regards face-to-face confrontation between accused and accuser as "essential to a fair trial in a criminal prosecution."'[68]

However, two years later, whilst acknowledging that confrontation serves a 'strong symbolic purpose', in 1990 in *Maryland v Craig*[69] the Supreme Court declared that despite the confrontation requirement, a child could testify via live link provided that evidence showed that the child would be unable to testify in the presence of the accused or in open court. Whilst this continues to be the leading authority on the matter[70] such is the importance placed on personal confrontation

[62] Stiver (n 28); Armstrong (n 28); Anon (n 28); Spencer and Flin (n 3) 166–68.

[63] Anon (n 28); Spencer and Flin (n 3) 166.

[64] s 3509 of the Federal Rules of Evidence permits full pre-recording of a child's evidence.

[65] Hoyano and Keenan (n 11) 652.

[66] Jackson, ch 4.

[67] See J Myers 'Children's Disclosure Statements as Evidence in the United States Legal System' in M Lamb, D La Rooy, L Malloy, C Katz (eds), *Children's Testimony: A Handbook of Psychological Research and Forensic Practice* Chichester, Wiley, 2011, 309, for a review.

[68] *Coy v Iowa* (1988), 865–66.

[69] *Maryland v Craig* (1990) 111 L Ed 2d 675 (US SC), 679.

[70] But see *US v Bordeaux* 400 F 3d 548, 554–56; Hoyano and Keenan (n 11) 653, fn 358.

that in some states the live-link room where the child sits must have a screen showing the accused's face.[71]

Considerable case law suggested that confrontation was not important in itself but as a prerequisite for the accused having adequate opportunity to investigate the evidence. It was seen as a necessary part of a number of investigation procedures,[72] including cross-examination,[73] taking the oath[74] and the jury's ability to observe the witness's demeanour.[75]

The strict interpretation of the confrontation clause appeared to be further undermined when, two years after *Maryland v Craig*, the Supreme Court in *White v Illinois*[76] allowed a conviction where the child was unable to testify on the basis of hearsay statements admissible under various exceptions to the rule excluding hearsay. Since the exceptions were all made upon the basis of the reliability of such statements there was no need for cross-examination. The practice of 'victimless prosecutions' for domestic violence and child abuse cases, often relying on ABE-equivalent video interviews and the like, became popular.[77] However, in 2004 in *Crawford v Washington*[78] the Supreme Court differentiated between hearsay statements recorded specifically for later use in a trial (or 'testimonial purposes') and statements such as 'excited utterances' or comments to a doctor which are made without contemplating their use later in court.[79] The Court declared that admitting 'testimonial' hearsay statements violated the confrontation clause unless the accused had the opportunity to cross-examine the witness.[80]

Whilst this makes the use of ABE-type video interviews difficult, as Hoyano and Keenan point out it should still be possible to use fully pre-recorded evidence in many US states provided the situation of the pre-recording is 'functionally equivalent' to testimony at trial and the accused is given sufficient opportunity to cross-examine the witness.[81] The Supreme Court has said that the confrontation

[71] M Brancatelli 'Facilitating Children's Testimony: Closed Circuit Television' (2009) 21(11) *NCPCA Update* 1 lists 11 states as requiring the child to have a monitor showing the courtroom including the accused; the Federal Rules of Evidence require a screen showing the accused to the child: s 3509(2)(B)(4).

[72] See Spencer and Flin (n 3) 277–79, challenging this belief.

[73] *Dutton v Evans* (1970) 400 US 74; *Ohio v Roberts* (1980); 448 US 56, 100 S Ct 2531, 65 L Ed 2d 597; *State v Thomas* (1989) 150 Wis 2d 374, 442 NW 2d 10 (1989), *Maryland v Craig* (1990) 497 US 836, 110 S Ct 3157, 111 L.Ed 2d 666 (1990); *California v Green* (1970) 399 US 149.

[74] *State of California v Green* (1970); *State v Thomas (No 1)* (1989).

[75] *Coy v Iowa* (1988) 487 US 1012; *Maryland v Craig* (1990): see also Hoyano and Keenan (2010), 653.

[76] *White v Illinois* (1992) 116 St C L Ed 2nd 851.

[77] M Sawicki 'The *Crawford v Washington* Decision—Five Years Later: Implications for Child Abuse Prosecutors'(2009) 21 (9) & (10) *National Center for Prosecution of Child Abuse Update* 1.

[78] *Crawford v Washington* (2004) 541 US 36.

[79] J Myers' 'Children's Disclosure Statements as Evidence in the united States Legal System' in M Lamb, D La Rooy, L Malloy, C Katz (eds) *Children's Testimony: A Handbook of Psychological research and Forensic Practice* (Chichester, Wiley, 2011) 309, 318–20; Sawicki (n 81) 2–5.

[80] Sawicki (n 81); T Harbinson 'When a Child "Freezes" in Court—Part One: Prevention' (2005) 2(2) *Reasonable Efforts* 1; T Harbinson 'When a Child "Freezes" in Court—Part Two: Strategies When Prevention Fails' (2005) 2(3) *Reasonable Efforts* 1.

[81] Hoyano and Keenan (n 11) 656.

amendment 'guarantees an *opportunity* for effective cross-examination, not cross-examination that is in whatever way, and to whatever extent, the defendant might wish'.[82] In fact, several state courts have ruled that much lesser opportunities for confrontation than conventional cross-examination will be sufficient to admit a hearsay statement not otherwise falling under one of the exceptions.[83] This issue has not been ruled on by the Supreme Court since *Crawford*.

Nonetheless, full pre-recording appears rarely used, with evidence that its use was tapering off even in the mid 1980s.[84] While there is a considerable volume of case law regarding applications for full pre-recording, currently it appears that prosecutors many view it as something of a 'last resort'.[85] Part of the reason for this may be that, even without questions of hearsay, there is a strong belief in the significance of demeanour evidence and wariness of the impact of screens on the jury's appraisal of a child's evidence.[86]

Moreover, although *Maryland v Craig* confirmed the door remains open to special measures, it set a high threshold for their admission. The court must be satisfied that there is sufficient evidence that the child is likely to be unavailable for testimony at trial, whether because of some disability or because the child is likely to be too afraid to testify in front of the accused and defence counsel or in open court generally.[87] Further, at trial before admitting pre-recorded evidence the trial judge must rule that the child continues to be unavailable for the same reasons.[88] In Hoyano and Keenan's words: 'The necessity for a "harm hearing" is a strong disincentive to prosecutors using innovative measures to protect the child whilst testifying.'[89]

Countries Fully Utilising Pre-recording

However, although some countries have found full pre-recording difficult, others have used it successfully over many years, and have found it to have many significant advantages beyond even overcoming delays.[90]

[82] *Delaware v Fensterer* (1985) 474 US 15, 20; *Kentucky v Stincer* (1987) 482 US 730, 739.

[83] See review of case law in Hoyano and Keenan (n 11) 655–56; Sawicki (n 81) 6.

[84] D Whitcomb 'Prosecuting Child Sexual Abuse: New Approaches' J Armstrong 'The Criminal Videotape Trial: Serious Constitutional Questions' (1976) 55 *Oregon Law Review*, 567 (1986) 2 *National Institute of Justice Report*, 4; Spencer and Flin (n 3) 167–69, 399.

[85] Hoyano and Keenan (n 11) 656 reviews case law; for example, the American Prosecutor's Research Institute recommends it only be used as a last resort and of two senior prosecutors writing in recent years for other prosecutors, Sawicki in 2009 and Harbinson in 2005 (n 80), Sawicki very briefly mentions pre-recording as a possibility not prevented by *Crawford* while Harbinson's list of options and special measures for children does not include pre-recording at all.

[86] *Coy v Iowa* (n 72) 866; *Maryland v Craig* (n 73) 679; see also Hoyano and Keenan (n 11) 653.

[87] s 3509 Federal Rules of Evidence (1996); Hoyano and Keenan (n 11) 652.

[88] Hoyano and Keenan (n 11).

[89] Ibid, 653.

[90] Jackson ch 4.

Full pre-recording is the norm in systems following the inquisitorial tradition where the evidence is traditionally taken in advance of trial. However, it is also used successfully in common law jurisdictions.

Israel

The first country with an accusatorial-style trial system to introduce and use pre-recording was Israel, which in 1956 provided for certain child complainants to have their evidence entirely recorded in writing by specialist Youth Investigators who would then present the child's evidence in court. Nowadays in Israel their evidence is presented at trial via a video recording of their forensic interview by the Investigator. Israel's system is described in greater detail later in this chapter.

Western Australia

The closest system to that in the United Kingdom which allows pre-recording on any regular basis is Western Australia. The specifics of the Western Australian model and its benefits are discussed by Judge Jackson in chapter four below.

The fact that, as Cossins details, the success of the Western Australian experience with pre-recording is such that five of the other Australian states have followed suit is of great significance.[91]

In the absence of well-resourced and systematically applied case management, the Australian experience strongly suggests that pre-recording is a natural and obvious solution to delays before trial. Even where courts control their lists adequately, pre-recording remains valuable as an option for unusually delayed cases or those where a simpler and more relaxed hearing process will better facilitate a particular witness to speak. As Jackson states, although Western Australia has largely managed to control its court list it continues to use pre-recording frequently because of its many auxiliary benefits.[92]

However, as is clear from the earlier recitation of the various common law countries that have failed to use their prerecording provisions, merely having legislation in force is insufficient to ensure pre-recording's success. Not only is proper resourcing necessary but practitioners must make use of the option. One way to see this is done is to make pre-recording mandatory or, more realistically, to put in place a presumption in its favour. This was the response in Queensland, when its original pre-recording legislation[93] went ignored for several years,[94] although there are still some indications that the Queensland judiciary are

[91] Cossins, ch 5, 2.

[92] See Jackson, ch 4 for a review of the many other benefits; see also Sleight (n 16) and E Henderson, K Hanna and E Davies 'Prerecording Children's Evidence: The Western Australian Experience' [2012] *Criminal Law Review* 3.

[93] C Eastwood and W Patton *The Experiences of Child Complainants of Sexual Abuse in the Criminal Justice System* Brisbane, Queensland University of Technology, 2002.

[94] s 21AK Evidence Act 1977 (Queensland) states that '[t]he affected child's evidence must be taken and video-taped at a hearing under this section.'

slow to allow any available measures where they have a discretion to refuse.[95] The New Zealand government has recently announced its intention to enact a presumption that children under 12 years have their evidence fully prerecorded,[96] although recent reports suggest concerns about funding are causing delays in implementation.[97]

Lawyers' Language: Cross-examination

The other outstanding problem with the criminal justice system in many accusatorial countries is the language and questioning techniques of cross-examination. Pre-recording may deal with delay before trial and on the day of hearing and even introduce some flexibility to the process of testifying, but, as Cossins says in her chapter, it does not have any effect on the questions asked in cross-examination.[98]

Developmentally inappropriate and confusing or misleading cross-examination was one of the earliest identified problems with the criminal trial for child witnesses, becoming a subject of general debate in the 1980s.[99] That the problems are ongoing is widely acknowledged across the accusatorial world. England and Wales,[100] New Zealand[101] and Australia[102] have reasonably recent empirical research showing cause for concern. Elsewhere in this book I also describe a recent study in New Zealand which found cross-examination is characterised by high levels of confusing, suggestive and misleading language.[103] As Plotnikoff and Woolfson remark in their chapter, recent research in England and Wales suggests cross-examination is a practice with a 'failure rate of 50%'.[104] Although there is no comparable empirical research in South Africa there are consistent enough criticisms by commentators, stakeholder groups and even the judiciary

[95] J Oliver 'The Legislation Changed, What About The Reality?' (2006) 6 *Queensland University of Technology Law and Justice Journal* 55.

[96] See Henderson, ch 6.

[97] D Cheng 'Child Witness Reforms Stalled By Lack of Funding' *New Zealand Herald* 2 Feb 2012.

[98] See Cossins, ch 5.

[99] And far earlier: see Spencer and Flin (n 3) 275–76.

[100] Eg M Kebbell, C Hatton et al 'Witnesses with Intellectual Disabilities in Court: What Questions Are Asked and What Influence Do They Have?' (2004) 9(1) *Legal and Criminological Psychology* 13; B Hamlyn, A Phelps et al *Are Special Measures Working? Evidence from Vulnerable and Intimidated Witnesses* London, Home Office Research, Development and Statistics Directorate 2004, 55–56; C O'Kelly, M Kebbell et al 'Judicial Intervention in Court Cases Involving Witnesses With and Without Learning Disabilities' (2003) 8(2) *Legal and Criminological Psychology* 12; J Plotnikoff and R Woolfson *In Their Own Words: The Experiences of 50 Young Witnesses in Criminal Proceedings* NSPCC and Victim Support (2006) 48–50, 73–74; Plotnikoff and Woolfson (n 3) 107–2.

[101] Henderson, ch 6.

[102] Eg Eastwood and Patton, (n 13) Cashmore and Trimboli (n 12).

[103] See Henderson, ch 6, describing Hanna, ch 2. See also E Davies, E Henderson, K Hanna 'Facilitating Children to Give Best Evidence: Are There Better Ways to Challenge Children's Testimony?' (2010) 34 *Criminal Law Journal* 347.

[104] Plotnikoff and Woolfson ch 2.

to indicate serious problems, especially with aggressive cross-examination.[105] Western Australia is also dogged by continuing issues, leading directly to the introduction of guidelines for advocates cross-examining children in 2011.[106]

The remainder of this discussion addresses three different possible methods of ameliorating poor cross-examination namely, legal education; increased judicial intervention; and the practice of inserting a third party intermediary to control the problem.

Legal Education

For many years the hope has been that it would be possible to educate advocates to cross-examine in developmentally appropriate ways.[107] Since the mid 1980s there have been streams of practitioner-orientated articles and books and numerous courses on the particular vulnerabilities of children. However, the various recent empirical studies already cited showing ongoing poor practice strongly suggest that this material has had little effect on practitioner behaviour.[108]

One of the aims of the New Zealand court transcript analysis mentioned earlier was to compare current standards of cross-examination with those found in an earlier study in 1996. There was no improvement in cross-examination practice over that period, although there were some changes in the particular types of language found to be used poorly.

In 2003 the NSW government piloted a specialist court for sexual offences in Parramatta in Sydney. Part of the project involved giving the judges and lawyers working in the court specialist training regarding child witnesses. When the project was evaluated by Cashmore and Trimboli in 2005, however, it was found that the training had made no difference to the standard of cross-examination.[109]

[105] Eg *Klink v Regional Court Magistrate* [1996] 1 All SA 191 (SE); *S v Mokoena, S v Phaswane* (2008) 2 SACR 216 (T); Hoyano and Keenan (n 11) 665; Centre for Child Law (University of Pretoria) and Childline *Written Submissions to the High Court in the case of Phaswane and Mokoena* Pretoria, The Centre For Child Law, University of Pretoria, 2007, para 70, downloaded from www.childlinesa.org.za/component/option,com_docman/.../gid,60/, last accessed 28 February 2012; South African Law Commission *Sexual Offences: Process and Procedure* Discussion Paper 102, Project 107, 2002, vol 3 para 38.3.1–9.

[106] Sleight (n 16).

[107] Eg Home Office *Report of the Advisory Group on Video Evidence* London, Home Office, 1989 ('The Pigot Report'), s 7.9; Australian Law Reform Commission *Seen and Heard: Priority for Children in the Legal Process Report No 84* Australian Law Reform Commission, 1997; J Plotnikoff and R Woolfson *The Go-Between: An Evaluation of the Intermediary Pathfinder Projects* Lexicon Limited/ Ministry of Justice UK, 2007, 67; Queensland Law Reform Commission *The Receipt of Evidence by Queensland Courts: The Evidence of Children Report 55* Queensland Law Reform Commission, 2000.

[108] See, eg, review by Plotnikoff and Woolfson in ch 2, 13.

[109] Cashmore and Trimboli (n 12). See also Australian Federal Police & Prosecutions (n 14) 157; Eastwood and Patton (n 13); Plotnikoff and Woolfson (n 108) 68.

The consensus amongst these and other researchers[110] is that legal education on examining child witnesses fails for two reasons:

First, best practice in questioning children is a massive subject and massively complex. The training on offer, whilst useful,[111] has never been extensive enough and, moreover, it cannot be much extended because lawyers do not have the time to spare.[112] In England and Wales[113] and in New Zealand[114] there is a new willingness amongst lawyers to accept the importance of specialist training. In neither case, however, has a sanction or mechanism for enforcing good practice been suggested and, as Plotnikoff and Woolfson comment in their chapter, the content of the training will need careful consideration.

Secondly, as Plotnikoff and Woolfson also point out in chapter two and Cossins points out in chapter five, ignorance is only part of the problem. The culture of the Bar and philosophy of accusatorial advocacy are fundamentally opposed to making many of the necessary changes. Lawyers respond poorly to education about how to communicate clearly and non-suggestively because their agenda is not about clear and non-suggestive communication. Cross-examination is not an interview to elicit facts in the same way as is an evidential interview or even direct examination. It is conceived of as an opportunity to present the case to the fact-finders both by persuading the witness to make certain responses and by blatant rhetoric. Convention states that obfuscation, obstruction and suggestion are all legitimate, indeed integral, aspects of cross-examination.[115] This is why all the techniques researchers revile appear so prominently in advocacy handbooks for young lawyers. It is not that lawyers do not know that such tactics are suggestive. It is that suggestion is seen as desirable.

Accordingly, advocates frequently deliberately ignore the common law restrictions on cross-examination questions[116] and they will also deliberately ignore statutory prohibitions (such as those restricting questions about a rape complainant's prior sexual history)[117] where they believe such questions are effective. Recent research into the 'ground rules' hearings in England suggests even advocates

[110] Australian Federal Police & Prosecutions (n 14); Cashmore and Trimboli (n 12); Eastwood and Patton (n 13); Plotnikoff and Woolfson (n 108).

[111] Although see Plotnikoff and Woolfson, ch 2.

[112] Australian Federal Police & Prosecutions (n 14) 157; Plotnikoff and Woolfson (n 108) 68.

[113] Advocacy Training Council *Raising the Bar* 2011. But see discussion in Plotnikoff and Woolfson, ch 2.

[114] NZ Law Society *Submission in Response to Issues Paper* February 2011.

[115] Spencer and Flin (n 3); E Henderson 'Mapping the Theory of Cross-examination in Relation to Children' in H Westcott, G Davies and R Bull (eds), *Children's Testimony: Psychological research and Forensic Practice* West Sussex, Wiley, 2002, 426; E Henderson 'Psychological Research and Lawyers' Perceptions of Child Witnesses in Sexual Abuse Trials' in R Bull and D Carson (eds), *Handbook of Psychology in Legal Contexts* Chichester, Wiley, 2003; P Hobbs '"You Must Say It For Him": Reformulating a Witness's Testimony on Cross-examination at Trial' (2003) 23(4) *Text*, 34.

[116] E Henderson *Cross-examination: A Critical Examination.* unpublished PhD Dissertation, University of Cambridge 2011; Henderson, 2003, n 116.

[117] J Temkin 'Prosecuting and Defending Rape: Perspectives from the Bar' (2000) 27 *Journal of Law and Science* 219.

who are given firm instructions as to the type of questions which are permissible before the trial are prepared to break the rules.[118]

Unless education can refocus lawyers' theory of the purpose of cross-examination it is likely to be of very little use.[119] Even if such education can begin it is a very long term project. It is likely to take years—and a leadership commitment—for advocates to change the culture of the profession. The current proposals in England and Wales fall short of giving an assurance that they will be sufficient to address these issues.[120] More is needed to show that the new agenda for legal education is more than a means of deflecting criticism.

Judicial Interventions

One obvious solution which has been tried in various countries is to increase the policing of cross-examination by judges. There is no doubt that the common law rules of cross-examination contain sufficient authority to enable judges to control improper questioning. Several jurisdictions now encourage greater judicial intervention,[121] and there are some signs of a slight increase in some jurisdictions.[122] However, even those increases are still far too low to deal with the overwhelming extent of the problem.[123] The New Zealand researchers concluded: 'The greater attention by some judges to complex questions is encouraging. However, there were many, many more complex questions which were *not* challenged.'[124] Recently, however, appellate courts in England and Wales have begun to give robust guidance as to how to cross-examine children, including restrictions on many of the types of questions research identifies as problematic.[125] This new body of case law supports trial judges in their efforts to prevent poor cross-examination practice.

[118] Cooper cited in Plotnikoff and Woolfson, ch 2.

[119] The need for a 'cultural change' is well recognised. See eg Pigot Report (1989) s 7.9; D Birch 'A Better Deal for Vulnerable Witnesses' [2000] *Criminal Law Review* 223; Temkin (n 118); L Ellison *The Adversarial Process and the Vulnerable Witness* Oxford, Oxford University Press, 2001; Henderson (2002) (n 116); Plotnikoff and Woolfson (n 108), 68–9; Plotnikoff and Woolfson ch 2.

[120] Plotnikoff and Woolfson, ch 2.

[121] Both Queensland and the Northern Territories have legislative provisions setting standards for the treatment of child witnesses created when it was realised that previous legislation to control cross-examination was ineffective: Hoyano and Keenan (n 11) 670. In New Zealand the Evidence Act 2006 included an expanded provision restating the judiciary's common law powers to prohibit questions which are misleading, repetitive, unintelligible or otherwise unfair (s 85 Evidence Act 2006 (NZ)).

[122] Research in England shows a slight increase: see Plotnikoff and Woolfson ch 2 at 12; Kebbell et al (n 101); O'Kelly et al (n 101). In New Zealand Hanna et al (n 3) found a slight increase in 2008–09 compared to 1996: 88; Conversely, Cashmore and Trimboli (n 12) found no increase in interventions at the Parramatta specialist court despite judges having had special encouragement to take greater control of inappropriate cross-examination; see Cossins, ch 5.

[123] Plotnikoff and Woolfson (n 108) 67–68; Hanna et al (n 3) 91.

[124] Hanna et al (n 3).

[125] *R v Barker* [2010] EWCA 4; *R v W & M* [2010] EWCA 1926; *Re W* (Children) [2010] UKSC 12; *R v Wills* [2011] EWCA Crim 1938; *R v Edwards* [2011] All ER(D) 108; Plotnikoff and Woolfson, ch 2.

Many judges are concerned that too many interventions will give the appearance of unfairness or bias against the party whose counsel is criticised.[126] As one Western Australian judge commented recently: 'If a judge frequently interrupts cross-examination then the process can become disjointed, confrontational between the judge and counsel and often add to the trauma of the complainant giving evidence.'[127] Accordingly the Western Australian judiciary intends its guidelines as a partial substitution for intervention: to 'reduce confrontation between a judge and counsel during a trial'.[128]

In reality, although judges have wide powers to control cross-examination they may not themselves recognise problems when they occur and, in any case, their ability to exercise their powers is restricted by the need to appear fair.[129] The scale of the problem of cross-examination is beyond individual judges' powers to correct.

Intermediaries

The third option for controlling problematic cross-examination is to appoint a third party or 'intermediary' to assist counsel and child to communicate. The role the intermediary plays can vary from court advisor to a sort of straightforward translator to proxy examiner, depending on the particular country and its particular driving concern.

Most systems which more closely follow the inquisitorial tradition of justice use experts to question children as proxies for the pre-trial investigating magistrate. The magistrate instructs a psychologist or specialist interviewer to examine the child and to test his or her evidence, and the defendant has rights to observe the interview and have input into the topics covered.[130]

Some common law countries also have their own versions of intermediaries including the United States, Israel, South Africa and England and Wales. Others have legislation allowing intermediaries but have more or less entirely failed to make use of it, whether because the legislature has failed to bring the provisions into force, as in Northern Ireland,[131] or because practitioners have ignored the provisions, as in New Zealand,[132] Western Australia and the Republic of Ireland.[133]

[126] Eg J Plotnikoff and R Woolfson *Young Witnesses in Criminal Proceedings: A Progress Report on 'Measuring Up?'* London, NSPCC, 2011; Plotnikoff and Woolfson ch 2, 12.

[127] Sleight (n 16) 20.

[128] Ibid, 22.

[129] Plotnikoff and Woolfson (n 128); Plotnikoff and Woolfson, ch 2.

[130] Spencer and Flin (n 3) 394–96; see also M Delmas-Marty and J R Spencer (eds) *European Criminal Procedures* Cambridge, Cambridge University Press, 2005; Henderson 'Innovative Practices' in Hanna et al (n 3) 153–58.

[131] Art 17 Criminal Evidence (Northern Ireland) Order 1999.

[132] See Henderson, ch 6.

[133] s 106F Evidence Act 1906 (WA). The Republic of Ireland also enacted a provision allowing intermediaries in 1992 and brought it into force in 1997 (s 14 Criminal Evidence Act 1992) but does not apparently make use of it, although the reason is not clear: personal communications, October

The next section of this chapter describes the intermediary systems in the United States, Israel and South Africa. England and Wales's intermediary system is described in Plotnikoff and Woolfson's chapter. However, it is necessary to outline the English system briefly as it will be referred to in the final discussion.

Israel: Intermediaries at the Extreme[134]

The oldest intermediary system in the accusatorial world is that of Israel, where an extreme form of intermediary was introduced as part of its reforms in 1956. The Israeli legal system is a mixed system, derived from a number of sources including continental inquisitorial and English accusatorial models. However, its trial system and its evidence law are largely based upon British models, albeit without a jury component.[135]

The driving force behind Israel's scheme for child witnesses was, and continues to be, concern that child witnesses may be harmed by their involvement in trials, especially by what is perceived to be a culture of aggressive cross-examination[136] and especially where they testify against parents. It was also believed that a less traumatic process for child complainants would overcome the public's reluctance to report abuse.[137] As one judge put it:

> The *Protection of Children Act* was meant to balance between three interests: the social interest of bringing offenders to court and punishing them, the social and the private interest to protect children from causing them additional mental damage as a result of the exposure to the legal processes and in general their being cross-examined, and the common interest of the defendant and society in the existence of a fair process and revealing the truth.[138]

While children under 14 are eligible to testify (provided they understand the duty to tell the truth),[139] Specialist social workers called 'Youth Investigators' effectively take total charge of any child complainant or child witness under the age of 14 where the offence charged is sexual, or relates to the parent's or guardian's cruelty

2011, from Joyce Plotnikoff and Professor John Jackson; Scottish Executive *Consultation Paper on the Use of Intermediaries for Vulnerable Witnesses in Scotland* Edinburgh, Scottish Executive, 2007 para 11: 'in practice this provision is never used and does not feature in the Public Information Materials on special measures issued in Ireland'.

[134] My thanks to those who reviewed this section including Dr Dana Pugach and Dr Irit Hershkowitz. Any mistakes are my sole responsibility.

[135] R Levush *A Guide to the Israeli Legal System* www.llrx.com/authors/220, 15 January 2001; D Pugach 'Are We Over-Protective? A Comparative Critique of the Israeli Criminal Justice Approach to Child Witnesses and the Rights of the Child' conference paper delivered at *World Congress on Family Law and Rights of Children* (Bath, UK, 2001) 24.

[136] E Harnon 'Children's Evidence in the Israeli Criminal Justice system with Special Emphasis on Sexual Offences' in JR Spencer, G Nicholson , R Flin and R Bull (eds) *Children's Evidence in Legal Proceedings: An International Perspective* (Cambridge, Cambridge University Press, 1990) 81; Sternberg et al, 'Child Sexual Abuse Investigation in Israel: Evaluating Innovative Practices' in BL Bottoms and GS Goodman (eds) *International Perspectives on Child Abuse and Children's Testimony: Psychological Research and Law* (Newbury Park, CA, Sage Publications, 1996) 63.

[137] Sternberg et al (n 139) 63; Pugach (n 138) 7, 29.

[138] *Mizrahi v the State Of Israel* (CA 3904/96) PD51(1) 385, 395 cited in Pugach (n 138) 8.

[139] s 55 Evidence Ordinance.

or neglect, or is one of several specific offences of serious violence, and also of any child under 14 who is suspected of having committed any of the relevant offences.[140]

The Investigator interviews the child and records his or her evidence on video,[141] theoretically within days of the report of an offence. At the same time the Investigator assesses the child's credibility. The Investigator then decides whether it is appropriate for the child to appear in court. The Investigator may also make it a condition of the child appearing to testify that certain special measures are made available.[142]

Whilst the legislation gives little guidance in this respect, it is accepted that the basis for the Investigator's decision is the likelihood that testifying will cause the child trauma or that the child would not be a competent witness. Investigators cite both secondary trauma caused by appearing in court and the trauma of revisiting events after a lengthy delay.[143] Investigators also sometimes consider whether the child is likely to remember events sufficiently at a trial some months away.[144] Where the child is competent to express a preference the Investigator will also consult the child as to whether he or she wishes to testify in court.[145]

If the Investigator decides that harm is likely he or she can refuse to allow the child to testify.[146] The Investigator's discretion is absolute: neither the court nor the parties may impose any conditions on its exercise.[147] Instead the Investigator's report and conclusions as to the child's credibility replace the child's evidence, together with the video of the interview.[148] The Investigator's report and conclusions about the child's evidence are also admissible when the child testifies[149] and when the child is 14 at the time of trial.[150]

Where a child under 14 is not permitted to testify in court there is a statutory requirement that their evidence be corroborated.[151] A different, lesser, requirement

[140] s 9 Law of Evidence Revision (Protection of Children) Law 1955. This has now been extended to include certain vulnerable adult witnesses. See Pugach (n 138) 10–11.

[141] s 5A Law of Evidence Revision (Protection of Children) Law 1955 (amended in 1999); Pugach (n 138) 43. Previously the interview would be audio-recorded or written down.

[142] Pugach (n 138) 42.

[143] H David 'The Role of the Youth Interrogator' in Spencer, Nicholson and Flin et al *Children's Evidence in Legal Proceedings: An International Perspective* (1990), 106–07; United Nations Committee on the Rights of the Child (2001) 'Consideration of Reports Submitted by States Parties Under Article 44 of the Convention: Periodic Reports of States Parties Due in 1993' 1439; Pugach (n 137) 18.

[144] David (n 146) 106; Pugach (n 138) 47.

[145] Personal communication, Pugach 25 October 2011. cf Pugach (n 138) 18.

[146] s 2 Law of Evidence Revision (Protection of Children) Law 1955.

[147] See Israeli Supreme Court: *State of Israel v Plony* Criminal Appeal 1880/91 per Shamgar CJ and see also discussion in Pugach (n 138) 17 and UN Committee on the Rights of the Child (n 145) para 1431.

[148] s 9 Law of Evidence Revision (Protection of Children) Law 1955; David (n 146); Harnon (n 139); Pugach (n 138) 15–16.

[149] Pugach (n 138) 16, reviews case law.

[150] Criminal Appeal 1421/71 *Mimran v Israel* PD26(1) 281; UN Committee on the Rights of the Child (n 145) para 1442.

[151] s 11 Law of Evidence Revision (Protection of Children) Law 1955. See also Pugach (n 138) 24–28.

of corroboration applies to the evidence of children under 12 who are permitted to testify in court.[152]

Investigators permit very few children to testify, although there is a suggestion that they are more prepared to allow children approaching the cut-off age of 14.[153] It has been said that whereas in most of the common law world the assumption is that children will testify in criminal proceedings, in Israel the assumption is that they will not.[154] Statistics are hard to come by but in 1984 Investigators allowed 28 per cent of children into court compared to only 6.8 per cent in 1993[155] and 15 per cent in 1998.[156] One judge stated a decade ago that out of a substantial number of cases only two children had ever testified in front of him.[157] The court and the parties have little power over the Investigator's decision to allow or disallow a child to appear, although the court can ask the Investigator to reconsider his or her determination.[158]

At court, the way in which a child testifies depends upon the crime charged and the child's age and status as complainant or witness. Since 2001 all child witnesses and complainants are eligible to apply to testify in the judge's chambers, and lawyers and judges may remove their formal robes. Children are also entitled to a support person while they give evidence.[159] In addition, children under 18 testifying regarding a sex offence allegedly committed by a parent[160] and (since 1995) child victims of sexual and some violent offences[161] may apply to testify in such a way that the witness cannot see the accused, whether from outside the court via live link 'or some other way',[162] including screening the accused from the child's view by a curtain.[163] The court may also be closed to the public where the witness is the complainant in a sex case or to protect a child's welfare.[164]

In cases where the charge is one of sexual or serious violence or parental neglect it is also possible for children to testify as soon as the indictment is laid or an

[152] s 55 Law of Evidence Revision (Protection of Children) Law 1955.

[153] Pugach (n 138) 16.

[154] Ibid, 6.

[155] Sternberg et al (n 139) 65.

[156] UN Committee on the Rights of the Child (n 1450 para 1439, citing the percentage of children allowed to testify of those for whom an application was made that they testify in court.

[157] Pugach (n 138).

[158] Ibid, 19–20.

[159] Victim's Rights Act 2001.

[160] s 2A Law of Evidence Revision (Protection of Children) Law 1955.

[161] s 2B Criminal Procedure Revision (Examination of Witnesses) Law 1957. This applies to all complainants of sexual offences.

[162] s 2B Criminal Procedure Revision (Examination of Witnesses) Law 1957; Regulation 4 Questioning of Witness Regulations KT, 5801 1997, 275.

[163] Law of Procedures (Witness Examination) (amended) 1952 Law of Evidence Revision (Protection of Children) Law 1955.

[164] The Courts Law 1984; s 2(b) Law of Evidence Revision (Protection of Children) Law 1955: child to testify in presence of judge, prosecutor, accused and defence counsel, interrogator and anyone else the court permits.

inquiry begun, subject to the Investigator's permission.[165] The Investigator will still be as heavily involved in this early hearing as he or she would otherwise be at a normal hearing.[166]

Where a child witness who is under the Investigator's supervision appears in court, the usual practice is for the Investigator to be in court whilst the child testifies. The Investigator may request to be allowed to act as an intermediary or translator, intercepting the cross-examination questions via earphone and putting them to the child, rephrasing as necessary.[167] The Investigator monitors the examination and can ask the court to stop the examination at any point if he or she believes the child is being caused emotional harm.[168] If the proceedings are stopped, the court can then ask the investigator to re-interview the child but the decision as to whether to re-interview and as to what questions to put at any re-interview rest with the Investigator.[169] Nor can the Investigator be used as a proxy examiner for the parties, as when a judge sought to have the Investigator investigate a list of topics agreed by the parties.[170]

Where the Investigator appears to present his or her report and assessment of the child's credibility, the court examines his or her evidence and need not accept his or her conclusions and may criticise his or her interview technique.[171] However, the Investigator's assessment nonetheless often has great weight, especially when the court has little else to go on.[172]

Following serious criticism of the quality of interviews and of the infrequency of prosecutions and infringement of the accused's rights in the late 1980s, efforts were made to improve Investigators' practices and to ensure the interview methodology used is congruent with the most recent research.[173] A legislative requirement was introduced that interviews be, first, in 1988, audio-recorded and then, in 1999, video-recorded,[174] making the process more transparent.[175]

It seems that many cases involving a child witness are still settled outside the criminal courts by plea-bargaining and through parallel investigations in the welfare system.[176] Whilst this spares children potentially traumatic involvement

[165] s 117A Penal Procedures Act, amended in 1995; Pugach (n 138) 47; UN Committee on the Rights of the Child (n 145) para 1436.

[166] s 118 Penal Procedures Act; Pugach (n 138) 47.

[167] My thanks to Irit Hershkowitz for this information.

[168] s 2(c) Law of Evidence Revision (Protection of Children) Law 1955.

[169] s 10 Law of Evidence Revision (Protection of Children) Law 1955; David (n 146) 107–8; UN Committee on the Rights of the Child (n 145) paras 1437–38; Pugach (n 138) 17.

[170] *State of Israel v Plony* Criminal Appeal 1880/91 per Shamgar CJ cited in Pugach (n 138) 17; UN Committee on the Rights of the Child (n 145) para 1431.

[171] Pugach (n 138) 9–10.

[172] Ibid, 16–17; personal communication Pugach, October 2011.

[173] Sternberg et al (n 139) 65–69; M Lamb, Y Orbach, I Hershkowitz, D Horowitz and C Abbott 'Does the Type of Prompt Affect the Accuracy of Information Provided by Alleged Victims of Abuse in Forensic Interviews?' (2007) 21 *Applied Cognitive Psychology* 13, 19–20.

[174] s 5A Protection of Children Act.

[175] Pugach (n 138) 43–44.

[176] I Hershkowitz, personal communication, 13 August 2009; C Katz, personal communication, 8 June 2009; David (n 146) 101. Today's figures are unknown but in 1996 it was estimated that only

in criminal trials, it has the disadvantage that offenders are able to avoid sanction by the criminal courts.

There have been some calls for the Investigator system to be amended.[177] The system still attracts some criticism for its alleged failure to protect the defendant's right to test the child's evidence and because it prevents judges from having an opportunity to assess the child directly.[178] However, the corroboration requirement, which weighs more heavily on children who use the Investigator system than on those who do not,[179] is present as a protection for the defence. It has been described by the courts as a necessary consequence of the Investigator system and the court's inability to itself assess the child and see him or her cross-examined:

> A reliance on a child's evidence collected by a children's interviewer, where the court had no opportunity to get a direct impression of the child and his evidence, and where the defendant was not given the opportunity to cross-examine the child, impinges substantially the defendant's rights. The corroboration required in section 11 of the Protection of Children Act, is intended to mitigate the damage, and to insure the existence of a due process.[180]

However, concerns as to the judge's inability to assess the witness have reportedly diminished following the introduction of video-recordings of the interviews into court[181] and public confidence in the Investigator system is apparently steady.[182]

The Israeli system is, for those witnesses to whom it applies, a very complete form of protection from the difficulties of testifying. However, it is also somewhat unbalanced. The system both lacks adequate opportunity for the accused to test the evidence of any child not allowed to testify and simultaneously sets too high an evidential threshold for the prosecution of cases reliant on a child's evidence.

The main issue with the Israeli Investigator system as a model for development is that it is unlikely many common law countries would accept a process wherein the accused has so little opportunity to test the evidence.

Although standards amongst Investigators are reportedly high enough to provide a considerable assurance of the safety of the evidence they elicit, where the child does not appear in court the accused can only test the child's evidence

10% of allegations investigated were tried, although the majority were believed credible: Sternberg et al (n 139) 65.

177 Pugach (n 138) 11–14 reviews criticism; I Cordon, G Goodman, S Anderson 'Children in Court' in P v Koppen and S Penrod (eds) *Adversarial versus Inquisitorial Justice: Psychological Perspectives on Criminal Justice Systems* (New York, Kluwer Academic 2003) 167, 185; D Horowitz 'The Silence of Abused Children in Israel: Policy Implications' in M Pipe, M Lamb, Y Orbach and A Cederborg *Child Sexual Abuse: Disclosure, Delay and Denial* (Mahwah, NJ, Lawrence Erlbaum, 2007) 281, 282.

178 Pugach (n 138) 8; see also Judge Strashnov quoted at 12 criticising the court's inability to assess the child for itself.

179 Personal communication, Pugach, 25 October 2011.

180 Criminal Appeal 4596/98 *Plonit v The State of Israel* PD 54 vol 1, 145.

181 Personal communication, Pugach, October 2011.

182 UN Committee on the Rights of the Child (2001).

by challenging the Investigator's assessment of the child's credibility[183] or the interview methodology, since the court may acquit if it considers the interview suspect.[184] Otherwise the defence must hope that the Investigator might accede to a request that he or she re-interview the child.[185]

It seems unlikely that a process similar to that in Israel, wherein the child is completely sequestered from any challenge directed by the accused would be found to comply with Article 6 of the European Convention on Human Rights (ECHR).

The other glaring issue with the Israeli system from an outsider's perspective is its requirement that children's evidence be corroborated. This appears to be at least partly intended to redress the accused's inability to test the child's evidence. However, corroboration is a very blunt instrument indeed. Other jurisdictions have generally concluded that requiring corroboration of children's evidence of abuse is unrealistic and presents an unfair barrier to any such prosecution.[186]

Unlike the Israeli system, the intermediary systems chosen by the other accusatorial jurisdictions under discussion in this chapter all reflect an anxiety to interfere in conventional trial practices and the rights of the defendant as little as possible. In each system the intermediary operates or is embedded within the conventional court process rather than having any separate standing as do Israeli investigators.

United States of America: Intermediaries as Megaphones

At the far end of the spectrum from Israel lies the United States. Courts in some US states have extended legislative provision for translators to cases where children's language is incomprehensible or they have been too nervous to speak loudly enough or at all. Accordingly theirs is sometimes known as the 'megaphone model'.

In such cases interpreters can only relay the questions and answers verbatim. They cannot translate questions into developmentally appropriate language.[187] Generally a parent or the child's social worker has been sworn in as interpreter.[188] The limited nature of the model is illustrated by the following advice to prosecutors in situations where a child has 'frozen' in court: 'Ask the child if he could answer your questions if he could whisper his answers in someone's ear. Have

[183] David (n 146) 107.

[184] See Pugach (n 138) 9–10.

[185] Harnon (n 139) 84, 92.

[186] The following countries have abolished the requirement that the evidence of a child be corroborated purely on the basis of age alone: England and Wales (s 34 Criminal Justice Act 1988); Australia (Commonwealth of Australia: s 164 Evidence Act 1995 (Commonwealth of Australia); Victoria: s 23(2A) Evidence Act 1958; Northern Territories: s 9C Evidence Act 1939; Queensland: s 632 Evidence Act 1899; Western Australia s 106D Evidence Act 1906; Tasmania: s 164(1) Evidence Act 2001 (cf South Australia s 12A Evidence Act 1929 where children's unsworn evidence must be corroborated); Canada: Act to Amend the Criminal Code of Canada and the Canada Evidence Act SC 1987 c24 s 15; New Zealand s 125(1) Evidence Act 2006; US: see Hoyano and Keenan (n 11) 695–96; Republic of Ireland: s 28 Criminal Evidence Act 1992.

[187] J Myers *Evidence in Child Abuse and Neglect Cases* vol 1, 225–28; Hoyano and Keenan (n 11) 666.

[188] Harbinson Part two (n 80); Troxel, Ogle et al (n 4).

that person sworn in as a translator for the child.'[189] However, even this restricted procedure appears to be rarely used.[190] Prosecutors prefer to try the child on the stand in open court before applying for any special measure, the approach taken in the advice quoted above.

As discussed in the section above on pre-recording in the United States, part of the reason for this appears to be the disincentive to apply for special measures offered by the Supreme Court's adherence to a strict interpretation of the US constitutional guarantee of confrontation and the high threshold set by its requirement that the child be proven likely to be too traumatised to communicate at trial before such measures are permitted.[191]

Accordingly, the approach appears to be that the child will be asked to testify in the normal way in open court.[192] An application for a special measure will usually only be made if the child completely breaks down or becomes mute while testifying.[193] Even then, prosecutors are enjoined to try a range of other options, including taking a break, closing the court, and even sitting the child on a support person's lap.[194]

Conversely, South Africa and England and Wales have both developed systems which sit further along what might be called the interventionist continuum from the United States, without approaching the Israeli end of the spectrum.

England and Wales: the Monitor Model

English intermediaries are highly qualified communication specialists who may be involved in any or all of three stages in the criminal process: First, they assess the child's communicative competence and needs early in the police investigation and may assist with communication at the police interview if necessary. Secondly, they produce a written report which is then used by the court and counsel to make decisions as to the necessary special measures at trial and to inform judicial rulings about questioning (the 'ground rules' hearing). Thirdly, they may also appear at trial with the witness to monitor the questioning and advise the court of any problems that arise (intermediaries convey questions and/or answers directly only where this is necessitated by the witness's communication problem).[195]

[189] Harbinson (n 80).

[190] Hoyano and Keenan (n 11) 656.

[191] *Maryland v Craig* (n 73); Brancatelli (n 75); Harbinson, Parts 1 and 2 (n 80); Hoyano and Keenan (n 11) 652–53.

[192] Troxel, Ogle et al (n 4) 3.

[193] Harbinson, Part two (n 80); Brancatelli (n 75); Troxel, Ogle et al (n 4).

[194] Harbinson, Part 2 para. 7 (n 80); Troxel, Ogle et al (n 4).

[195] Plotnikoff and Woolfson, ch 2; see also Plotnikoff and Woolfson (n 108); Henderson in Hanna et al (n 3) 129–43; Hoyano and Keenan (n 11) 663–71.

South Africa: Intermediaries as Translators[196]

The South African intermediary operates in a different way from the English intermediary. While they have no role before trial, their role at court is more central. The South African intermediary is essentially a full-time interlocutor or go-between.

South Africa enacted provision for intermediaries in 1993 and seems to have begun using them almost immediately. The motivation in introducing the system was, as in Israel, the desire to minimise trauma to the child, particularly from what is perceived to be a very aggressive advocacy culture.[197]

Accordingly, as in the United States,[198] in order to access the system there must be a finding that the child will be traumatised by the experience of testifying.[199] However, unlike those in the United States, South African courts have recently held that almost every child testifying about abuse will find testifying in court stressful enough to make an intermediary necessary.[200]

South African intermediaries operate at trial only. Their role is similar to the (rarely used) process in the United States in that every question and answer must pass through them. However, they are free to translate any question into developmentally appropriate language, subject to the judge's power to direct them to put questions exactly as counsel has phrased them.[201]

The South African intermediary sits with the child in a live link room listening to the court proceedings through earphones. The defendant, counsel, and the judge and jury (if any—most cases are decided in lower-level courts) hear and see everything on their monitors in the courtroom.[202] The child will never hear anyone except the intermediary unless the judge wishes to speak directly to the child.[203]

While South African intermediaries may translate the lawyers' questions into developmentally appropriate language,[204] they must not alter the meaning of the question or the reply—even if it makes no sense. They cannot comment upon

[196] This section is drawn from research undertaken for Hanna et al (2010) which involved both a literature review and also a small number of interviews with South African practitioners and academics.

[197] *Klink* (n 106); *S v Mokoena* (n 107); Hoyano and Keenan (n 11) 665; Jonker and Swanzen (n 8) 5–17.

[198] Discussed in section on US above.

[199] s 170A(1) Criminal Procedure Act 1977.

[200] *Director of Public Prosecutions, Transvaal v Minister for Justice and Constitutional Development and Others* (CCT 36/08) [2009] ZACC 8; 2009 (4) SA 222 (CC); 2009 (2) SACR 130 (CC); 2009 (7) BCLR 637 (CC) (1 April 2009), para 108, 114; K Muller and K Hollely *Introducing the Child Witness* (Port Elizabeth, Printrite, 2009) 20–21.

[201] *Klink* (n 106); Australian Federal Police and Prosecutions (n 14) 154.

[202] *Klink* (n 106); Australian Federal Police and Prosecutions (n 14).

[203] s 170A(2)(b) Criminal Procedure Act 1977; *Klink* (n 106) 411I–J; Jonker and Swanzen (n 8) 5; Muller and Hollely (n 203) 39–41; F Schutte 'Child Witnesses in the Criminal Justice System in South Africa: An Overview of Proposals for Reform' *4th World Congress on Family Law and Children's Rights* Cape Town, South Africa, 2005, 11, 13.

[204] *Klink* (n 106) para 4111I–J; Schutte (n 206) 13.

issues with question sequencing, such as repetitive questioning, or on the child's comprehension.[205]

Moreover, South African intermediaries are not required to have the professional qualifications expected of their English counterparts and may not understand the need to simplify questions. To be appointed, intermediaries need merely be a member of one of several professions assumed to be familiar with children. There is no further formal training, accreditation,[206] or state support for intermediaries (although there are university and privately run training programmes[207]), a situation that attracts considerable criticism within South Africa.[208]

There is little empirical research on the South African intermediary system as of yet.[209] However, it appears widely accepted amongst South African commentators that the use of intermediaries markedly reduces children's stress,[210] increases the quality of their evidence[211] and some argue that it may increase conviction rates.[212] Intermediaries are also believed to make it far easier to bring pre-schoolers to the court as witnesses.[213]

There is some empirical evidence that the use of intermediaries may affect the number of guilty pleas.[214] Jonker and Swanzen studied 384 cases using intermediaries who were trained and supported by an independent agency. 'Not guilty' pleas accounted for 7 per cent of the sample, 56 per cent pleaded guilty, and 37 per cent had charges withdrawn. There were no mistrials. Conversely, police statistics available from before 2000 for the same age of witness and type of crime where no intermediary was used show that 58 per cent of offenders pleaded not guilty, only 9 per cent pleaded guilty and 18 per cent had charges withdrawn.[215]

The courts are very supportive of intermediaries. In 2009 the highest court, the Constitutional Court, called for greater use to be made of them.[216] The Court

[205] *S v Mokoena* (n 107) 34; Muller and Hollely (n 203) 43, 48.

[206] s 170A(4)(a) Criminal Procedure Act 1977.

[207] Eg Jonker and Swanzen (n 8); Muller and Hollely (n 203).

[208] S Coughlin and R Jarman 'Can the Intermediary System Work for Child Victims of Sexual Abuse?' (2002) 83 (5–6) *Families in Society* 54; Schutte (n 206) 16; Jonker and Swanzen (n 199) 21–22; Centre for Child Law and Childline (n 107) para 130; Muller and Hollely (n 203) 46.

[209] Jonker and Swanzen (n 8) 7.

[210] *S v Mokoena* (n 107) 21; Centre for Child Law and Childline (n 107) para 147; Schutte (n 206) 4, 16; Muller and Hollely (n 203) 28; Open Society Foundation for South Africa *Minutes of Meeting on Models for the Management of Sexual Offences* Johannesburg, SA, 2006, para 3.2.1.

[211] Centre for Child Law and Childline (n 107) para 147; Schutte (n 206) 9.

[212] *S v Mokoena* (n 107) 21; Schutte (n 206) 9.

[213] K Muller, *Baseline Success Indicators for Training of Social Workers Involved with Children in the Criminal Justice System*, UNESCO, 2002; K Muller and K Hollely *The Hidden Benefits of Court Preparation for Young Witnesses* (unpublished paper) 2003; Jonker and Swanzen (n 8). Plotnikoff and Woolfson in ch 2 note that pre-schoolers are increasingly being interviewed as witnesses in England and Wales as well.

[214] Jonker and Swanzen (n 8) 7.

[215] Ibid.

[216] *The Director of Public Prosecutions, Transvaal v the Minister of Justice and Constitutional Development and Others (the Centre for Child Law; Childline South Africa, Resources aimed at the Prevention of Child Abuse and Neglect, Operation Bobbi Bear, Children First, People Opposing Women Abuse and The Cape Mental Health Society as amici curiae) (2009)* CCT 36/08, Constitutional Court 8.

stated that the benefits of the intermediary to the witness are such that they outweigh any concerns that the defendant might be disadvantaged by the process.[217] However, the South African constitution gives priority to the best interests of the child in any proceeding and this affects the court's readiness to allow protective measures.[218]

Nevertheless, although the Constitutional Court lowered the harm threshold by holding that all children testifying about abuse are likely to be traumatised in court, the statutory eligibility criteria are criticised as too high,[219] since only children who are complainants are eligible[220] and then only on the grounds of trauma, so that a communication difficulty alone is an insufficient basis on which to obtain assistance.[221] Further, there are too few intermediaries nationally and few courts with intermediaries appointed to them.[222] Although theoretically there are various special measures available to all child witnesses, including dedicated sexual offence courts,[223] live link and screens,[224] the vast majority of child witnesses and complainants testify in open court without any special protections. There are simply not the resources to provide them.[225] There are also other legal hurdles faced by children in South African courts: case law requires judges to be cautious about convicting on the uncorroborated evidence of a child or a sexual assault complainant.[226]

Discussion

In summary, there are two problems which dog the criminal trial process across accusatorial jurisdictions. One is delay; the other is cross-examination. The purpose of this chapter has been to explore the systems created in several accusatorial jurisdictions to alleviate these problems.

[217] Ibid.

[218] s 28(2) South African Constitution; *Klink* (n 106); *S v Mokoena* (n 107); Muller and Hollely (n 202); *DPP v Transvaal* (n 219).

[219] *S v Mokoena* (n 107) 29–30; Centre for Child Law and Childline (n 107) para 130; Muller and Hollely (n 203) 24; Schutte (n 206).

[220] Muller and Hollely (n 203) 25.

[221] *S v Mokoena* (n 107) 29; K Muller and A Tait 'Little Witnesses: A Suggestion for Improving the Lot of Children in Court' (1999) 62 *Journal of Contemporary Roman-Dutch Law* (*THRHR*) 241, 247–48; Schutte (n 206) 6.

[222] Coughlin and Jarman (n 210); Open Society (n 212) para 3; Jonker and Swanzen (n 8) 17; Centre for Child Law and Childline (n 107) para 130; *S v Mokoena* (n 107) 32.

[223] Amici Curia Brief (n 106) para 10; Henderson in Hanna et al (n 3) 119.

[224] s 153(3) and (5) Criminal Procedure Act 1977.

[225] Centre for Child Law and Childline (n 107) para 63; *S v Mokoena* (n 107).

[226] This requirement has been repeatedly criticised: see SALC Issues Paper 10 (Project 108) (1997); Schutte (n 206) 22; South African Law Commission Issue Paper 26 (Project 126) *Review of the Law of Evidence* 2008 para 3.1.5.

In relation to delay it appears that the Australian practice of leapfrogging the problem by pre-recording children's evidence early is well worth adopting. However, despite more than 20 years of reform, no accusatorial jurisdiction has really managed to craft a solution which will overcome the problems riddling cross-examination. Accordingly, when children come to court, suggestive questioning and miscommunication are still major issues and witnesses are still likely to end up needlessly embarrassed and distressed, thereby increasing the likelihood of further memory deterioration. In the current situation, there is a significant risk that fact-finders may assess child witnesses' credibility and accuracy wrongly.

Experience internationally suggests that cross-examination is unlikely to be corrected by greater judicial policing of trials alone. It is also suggested that lawyers are unlikely to change their practices on their own initiative. Most hope is offered by systems that insert specialist intermediaries into the criminal process to, variously, advise on, monitor and translate lawyers' language for children. However, there are two aspects to safe questioning: the need to ensure that the child is facilitated to speak and the need to ensure that the evidence the child gives is adequately tested. None of the systems discussed in this chapter have yet achieved a clear balance between those objectives.

Each of the jurisdictions discussed in this chapter has issues either in its social circumstances or in its particular constitutional restrictions or other law (such as the requirement of corroboration in South Africa and Israel) that affect the effectiveness of its intermediary system and its processes for child witnesses generally. This section leaves those issues aside and concentrates purely upon the intermediary system in each jurisdiction.

As a method of dealing with the problems of cross-examination, the Israeli Investigator clearly offers the most comprehensive protection of the systems discussed. Conversely, the US megaphone model offers only minimal protection, being really only a system to assist the court in hearing the child's answers and not to assist the child in understanding the lawyer or the court. However, the Israeli intermediary system's failure to provide the defendant with an adequate opportunity to test the child's evidence is a significant flaw.

The South African translator and the English monitor models offer far more assurance to the accused than does the Israeli system, whilst also offering considerable (if not equal) assistance to the child and the court. However, even at their best it is questionable that they make enough of a difference.

The South African system, although it erects a total barrier between child and lawyer, does not focus on communication problems and its intermediaries may not have the necessary expertise to maximise communication. However, even were the South African intermediaries to have sufficient skills to translate every inappropriate question, they could not deal with the full extent of the problem, as South African commentators have noted.[227] Although translators can correct problems with individual questions, they cannot deal with the use of sequences and strings

[227] *S v Mokoena* (n 107) 34; Muller and Hollely (n 202) 48.

of questions to manipulate witnesses, such as repetitive questioning, sudden changes between subjects, closed questions which deliberately prevent the witness giving information that might qualify an apparent admission, or the illicit, but highly popular, technique of comment.[228] 'Big picture' issues like these are quite beyond their scope. However, big picture issues are very important to the question of whether cross-examination is actually a safe way to test a child's evidence.

The English system allows intermediaries to deal with a wider range of issues, including addressing problematic question sequences and some other techniques likely to cause a child difficulty provided they can be framed as impeding effective communication. However, there are still issues.

The English judiciary and advocates are highly supportive of the system. On one level this is very reassuring. On another level, the extent of that approval is disquieting. That lawyers do not consider intermediaries a serious imposition suggests intermediaries do not challenge much of what lawyers do in court. Since it is clear that a significant proportion of lawyers' questioning of children, especially in cross-examination, is highly suspect, a lack of challenge of the status quo does not seem right.

One possibility is that intermediaries do not interrupt because the combination of access to the assessment report and the pre-trial ground rules are sufficient in most cases to forestall any problem examination. In other words, they do not interrupt because they have no reason to do so. Unfortunately there is some suggestion that this is not so.

The evidence discussed by Plotnikoff and Woolfson in chapter two suggests that the ground rules are frequently ignored by counsel and insufficiently enforced by the judiciary.[229] Even Plotnikoff and Woolfson's original highly favourable evaluation of the pilot programme noted that observers reported intermediaries failed to address all unacceptable questions.[230] Some intermediaries have acknowledged that they cannot address the extent of the problems with cross-examination.[231]

Two possible reasons for this are, first, that it is actually very hard to interrupt a lawyer in mid-flow.[232] As one experienced intermediary commented, it is difficult 'as the questioning [becomes] faster and more probing, … to monitor whether [a witness is] … being suggestible and processing the questions before answering, and therefore whether [to] … intervene'.[233] Intermediaries in court are clearly in a potentially intimidating position. They must work in a notably formal and often highly charged environment, unfamiliar to themselves and dominated by other professionals accustomed to controlling that space and confident in their abilities. The intermediary is required to interrupt these people and

228 Spencer and Flin (n 3) 270–76; Henderson (n 116) 426.

229 Plotnikoff and Woolfson, ch 2, 12.

230 Plotnikoffand Woolfson (n 108).

231 J Jones 'Working with Defendants' *National Roll-Out and Beyond: Intermediaries Shaping the Future. Fourth National Registered Intermediary Conference* London, OCJR, 2007.

232 Plotnikoff and Woolfson (n 108) 54–55.

233 Jones (n 233).

criticise their performances publically. These are issues of which those running the intermediary training programmes are very aware. While they strive to inoculate their intermediaries against intimidation,[234] it is unsurprising that they do not meet with complete success.

Moreover, it is not as if the intermediary merely has to catch counsel's eye to intervene. The standard directions require that the intermediary must first catch the judge's attention (not simple when the intermediary is in the live link room with the witness and can see only the questioner on screen, not the judge). The judge then interrupts counsel. Counsel then has an opportunity to rephrase the question, at which point, if it is still inadequate, the intermediary must again get the judge's attention and get him or her to interrupt counsel again so that the intermediary can proffer an alternative phrasing. This complicated process seems de facto to create a situation where interruptions are more likely to be exceptional and to deal only with the most egregious instances of inappropriate questioning. They will not be able to deal with the real extent of the problems.

If the lawyer persists in using problematic language the intermediary's interruptions could very soon dominate the examination process. It is hard to see any intermediary having the stomach to continually intervene nor any counsel or judge being prepared to tolerate them doing so, particularly in front of a jury which may have been given little explanation of the intermediary's role. The potential for frequent interruptions to create the appearance that the intermediary is persecuting counsel (something, as said earlier, judges give as a reason for not intervening often) or to fatally undermine confidence in counsel's competence or to simply bring the cross-examination to a standstill is obvious. Although halting cross-examination might be a sensible response to a lawyer who cannot or will not question appropriately, it is problematic for the smooth running of a trial.

These issues suggest that the monitor intermediary is not a complete answer to the problem of policing cross-examination any more than is the translator intermediary. Even a race of 'super' intermediaries capable of simultaneously interpreting individual questions and monitoring sequences could not solve the problems of cross-examination. It is, as discussed earlier, neither fair nor feasible to expect lawyers to conduct a cross-examination where they are going to be pulled up frequently for inappropriate language and also then have to backtrack entirely when the intermediary realises that the last several questions were building into a sequence which was too suggestive. Such a system would be slow, unwieldy and would produce examinations which would be extremely hard for the watching jury to comprehend.

Perhaps part of the reason embedded intermediary systems cannot correct the problems for lawyers is that in their focus on compensating for the witness's incompetence (whether emotional or linguistic), these intermediary

[234] Henderson in Hanna et al (n 3) 137.

systems ignore the problems created by the lawyers' agenda in cross-examination. Obviously the fact that children's language abilities are still in development disadvantages them in dealing with adults. Equally obviously, many lawyers often do not have the linguistic competence to understand or cope with children's developmental language issues. An intermediary on the translator or monitor model is suited to correcting these problems. However, the 'big picture issues' described above do not arise from either incompetence or ignorance but from the lawyers' intention of manipulating the witness. Whilst the lawyer controls the questioning these bigger issues will continue to arise.

The question becomes whether there is more we can do or whether these systems represent the full extent of possibilities for reforming cross-examination in a common law system. The answer lies in an examination of what it is about cross-examination that is so crucial to a fair trial. We need to step back and examine our assumptions about the necessity of our current procedures and decide what is in fact fundamental. Once we are clear about those essentials we can decide what methodologies might achieve those ends most efficiently and fairly.

Cross-examination is considered by many lawyers to be the essence and paradigm of the accusatorial trial. However, it might be possible to envisage a process for testing witnesses within an accusatorial trial which did not rely upon lawyers to act as examiner.

What is essential to a fair trial is that the evidence of all witnesses be fairly and thoroughly tested. As the UK Supreme Court has concluded in its judgment considering the impact of Article 6 of the ECHR on processes for the examination of children in the English Family Court, '[t]he important thing is that the questions which challenge the child's account are fairly put, not that counsel should be able to cross-examine her directly.'[235] Cross-examination by counsel is a methodology adopted to meet a necessity—but it is not in itself fundamental.

Cross-examination as a methodology has many flaws, the root of which may be that the examiner is also an advocate. Allowing a partisan advocate to examine adverse witnesses produces, first, a desire to adopt questioning techniques which enable the advocate to produce evidence favourable to the client and, secondly, a strong desire to utilise the examination as part of his or her case presentation. Thus a partisan examiner will seek to suggest answers to the witness and a persuasive examiner will seek to use the questions to communicate with the jury.[236]

However, a highly partial examiner does at least bring one benefit. A good system for testing evidence will ensure that the examiner is sufficiently motivated to investigate all the issues thoroughly, and is prepared to investigate issues which may seem distasteful, such as the possibility that a child is lying. Partisanship does

[235] *Re W* (n 125) at [28].
[236] Henderson (2002), (2003) (n 116).

at least ensure the lawyer has the necessary motivation to investigate unpleasant ideas with zeal.

Some inquisitorial or semi-inquisitorial continental European systems, often under the imperative of the ECHR, balance the issues of safety and zeal by using specialist examiners to question children according to their best professional judgement but by also giving defence counsel the ability to direct the examiner to explore issues of concern to the defence. Two such countries, Norway and Austria, are discussed in this book. Clearly, it is not possible to export either country's system into that of another wholesale. They might, however, function as inspirations and help us to reconsider what might be possible in our own systems.[237]

[237] In October 2011 the New Zealand government announced its intention to develop an intermediary system apparently drawing inspiration from Austrian and Norwegian models: see Cabinet Domestic Policy Committee *Minute of Decision* DOM Min (11) 10/1; S Power *Alternative Court Processes for Child Witnesses* Press Release 5 October 2011, media release, www.beehive.govt.nz. Various models have been work-shopped: E Davies, K Hanna, E Henderson and L Hand *Questioning Child Witnesses: Exploring the Risks and Benefits of Intermediary Models* Institute of Public Policy, AUT University, 2011. See Henderson, ch 6 for further discussion.

4

Children's Evidence in Legal Proceedings—The Position in Western Australia

HAL JACKSON

When Australia's colonies federated in 1901 the six colonies each retained jurisdiction in all areas of law except those ceded to the Commonwealth. Since then the Australian Capital Territory and the Northern Territory have been created. The result, shortly put, is that the six States and two Territories make and control their own criminal, child protection and evidentiary laws and procedures, and the courts and administrative bodies relating to them, subject only to appeals to the High Court of Australia's rulings as to their meaning and effect. The result is a complex web of differences and similarities. My comments relate only to one State—Western Australia. The State is very large physically, about eight times the British Isles. But it has a tiny population of about 2.5 million, living mainly in Perth and to a lesser extent the south-west region, with a vastly separated number of small, remote communities in the remainder. The capital city, Perth, is a long way from the rest of Australia. CCTV and pre-recording are ideal tools to service such an area.

The court structure is similar to those elsewhere in Australia, with an ultimate right of appeal to the High Court of Australia.[1] It involves a Court of Appeal, a Supreme Court (of general jurisdiction), a District Court (equivalent to the English Crown Court and County Court), and Magistrates Courts.[2] At present the District Court in effect hears almost all indictable cases, that is all jury cases, involving children. Magistrates handle domestic and family violence applications and some other minor matters involving children. The Children's Court deals with offences allegedly committed by children, and care and protection matters.

In Australia, as in England, the period prior to the 1990s saw much criticism of existing laws and practices concerning victims of sexual and other abuse. The

[1] The federal courts structure is separate to that of the various States and Territories and may here be ignored.

[2] Magistrates Courts deal with the vast bulk of civil and criminal matters mainly of a lesser significance and also a range of other jurisdictions. Magistrates are all qualified and experienced lawyers. The State has a fused profession with common admission for all lawyers. Some practise as barristers only, many as solicitors only and a goodly number as both.

need for corroboration and the law as to a corroboration warning were both changed in 1988.[3]

In 1992, in Western Australia, following a report by a government-appointed Child Sexual Abuse Task Force in 1987,[4] which raised a range of social and administrative as well as legal issues, and then a report in 1991 by the Law Reform Commission of Western Australia,[5] dealing in detail with an even wider range of issues, widespread changes were legislated for in this area. One specific set of provisions dealt with the use of the then-emerging video technology. Apart from provisions enabling the use of CCTV to deliver evidence, recommendations to pre-record children's evidence were included, drawing on the United Kingdom Pigot Report. This chapter primarily focuses on this.

As a result the Evidence Act 1906, since 1992, has allowed the child's entire evidence (including examination-in-chief, cross-examination and re-examination) to be taken at a special hearing and recorded on videotape. The videotape can later be presented as the child's evidence at trial so that the child need not be present then. The aim is to enable children to give evidence early and as free from external pressures and stresses as possible. A policy decision was made to restrict the application of those new protective measures (and some of the others mentioned below) to those cases that were considered to be the most difficult for children, that is offences of or involving a sexual nature or physical violence alleged against relatives, carers etc. The restriction was considered necessary because, at that time, the amendments were innovative; the technology in its infancy, somewhat mistrusted, and the facilities scarce.[6] These restrictions, however, are offset by provision being made for applications by other persons, including children not within those limits, to be declared 'special witnesses' to whom the same protections essentially apply. As will appear, the provisions have been extended by subsequent legislation.

Since 1992 we have used live CCTV evidence at trial both for adults and children. It is an alternative to pre-recording for children.[7] Children rarely give evidence in open court before juries, although they can ask to do so. Although in legal terms there remain four possibilities—live CCTV, pre-recording, protection by screens, or open court—in practice for children only the first two are ever used.

[3] In this and other areas there has been extensive case law and debate about the use of judicial comment and warnings to juries. This chapter avoids those issues.

[4] Child Sexual Abuse Task Force, Department of the Premier and Cabinet (WA), *Child Sexual Abuse: A Report to the Government of Western Australia* (1987).

[5] Law Reform Commission of Western Australia, *Evidence of Children and Other Vulnerable Witnesses*, Project No 87 (1991).

[6] The new provisions were included in the Evidence Act 1906 and are mainly but not exclusively found in sections 106A to 106T. The Act can be found at www.slp.wa.gov.uk, as can other legislation mentioned herein. Whilst I hope this chapter will be useful, the original paper on which it is based was written for an audience I assume to be uninterested in the minutiae of exact dates, section numbers and case references from a far-off land. I have also avoided the intricacies of the legislation which grew like Topsy as the system developed. It needs simplification.

[7] There are still provisions in the legislation permitting screens to be used as a last resort. They are now never used in superior courts and would only be used rarely in remote Magistrates' Courts.

The 1992 changes not only introduced the use of CCTV evidence and pre-recording of children's evidence, they strengthened general definitions of consent and of jury directions in relation to delay in complaint and reformed the admissibility of evidence about sexual reputation, disposition and experience. Further, the Act made provision for the child to have a support person, not to be cross-examined directly by an unrepresented person,[8] for evidence of a representation made by a child about a relevant matter to be admissible despite the rule against hearsay, and for the use of child 'interpreters' or 'communicators'.[9]

Other amendments have followed. For example, in 2004 the Criminal Law Amendment (Sexual Assault and Other Matters) Act very significantly strengthened the rules for joinder of complaints and also made very significant changes to the law concerning similar fact, propensity and relationship evidence.[10] These are aimed at avoiding multiple trials involving the same offender where possible. The legislation also introduced provisions dealing with disallowance of cross-examination, as to which see further below, and widened the right to support persons, child communicators and prevention of cross-examination by an unrepresented accused. Sexual communications privilege provisions were introduced.

Over time various provisions have extended the special protection measures available to persons declared to be 'special witnesses'. These persons are not only children but may be, for example, adult victims of sexual offences. Some of the measures available to children have been specifically extended to persons suffering mental disability. To a degree these changes have coincided with the extension of available CCTV and pre-recording facilities and of the Child Witness Service discussed below.

In 2008 the legislation (inter alia) introduced provisions enabling the calling of expert evidence of child behaviour and development in sexual matters; and enabled a child under 12 or a person with a mental impairment to give evidence unsworn if the court considers them able to give an intelligible account of events observed or experienced by them. Such persons may give sworn evidence on oath or affirmation if the court finds they understand that giving evidence is a serious matter and that they have an obligation to tell the truth. Persons aged 12 or more always give sworn evidence or affirm.

Abolition of preliminary (or committal) hearings from 2002 added to child witness benefits. Previously very strict limits on calling children to give oral evidence in such hearings existed but it remained possible though rare. Instead of having committal proceedings, the position is now to require early and full disclosure in writing of the prosecution case to the defence.

Other protective legislation includes the Children and Community Services Act dealing with child protection matters in the Children's Court. In protection

[8] The latter rarely happens because no doubt the legal aid bodies do what they can to avoid it by granting aid but there will always be a small number of accused who think they can do the job best.

[9] This provision has been little used.

[10] Comment on these is set out in Appendix I.

proceedings a child may only be compelled to give evidence or be cross-examined with the leave of the Court. The Court must not grant such leave unless the Court is satisfied that the child is unlikely

(a) to suffer emotional trauma as a result of giving evidence or being cross-examined; or
(b) to be so intimidated or distressed as to be unable to give evidence or be cross-examined; or to give evidence or be cross-examined satisfactorily.

In that court there are no jury, wigs or robes, and the child's evidence is given by CCTV. However, more usually a written statement by the child or others is tendered.

In domestic or family violence cases before a magistrate in the Magistrates' Court a child is not to be summonsed to the hearing of an application unless a court makes an order allowing the child to be summonsed; or the hearing is to be held in the Children's Court. The court is not to make such an order unless the court is satisfied that exceptional circumstances exist which, in the interests of justice, justify summonsing the child.

General reforms that not only apply where children are involved include measures to minimise the number of trials not being taken to completion by:

— permitting a verdict of at least 10 jurors;
— permitting the use of reserve jurors to cope with juror illness or other absence; and
— provision for trial of indictable matters by judge alone at the court's discretion and provided the accused consents.

The Process and Legal Position of Pre-recordings

To return to the use of pre-recording children's evidence:

A common but not necessarily inevitable course of events leading to a jury trial in the District Court is that charges laid by police will follow an interview and the videotaping of the child's interview by a police and welfare unit set up for the purpose, equivalent to the English ABE (Achieving Best Evidence) interview. We were late in that.[11] The tape of that interview is made admissible as evidence by legislation.

When an indictable offence is charged the matter is referred to the independent statutory office of the Director of Public Prosecutions, which performs functions similar to those of the English Crown Prosecution Service. The Director files an indictment in the District Court. Unless the child chooses to give evidence in open

[11] This system was not the 1992 situation but was developed subsequently. Regulations were also made governing the making of visual recording of such interviews for use in court proceedings as part of that development.

court, in jury trials the choice is between giving live evidence for trial by CCTV and pre-recording. Let us focus on that latter course.

The prosecutor makes an application to pre-record the child's evidence, usually done at the accused's first arraignment. The accused is entitled to be heard on the application but so common are they, usually does not. The Child Witness Service may be asked to comment on the application. The Service may also advise the judge, and of course counsel, of the child's special needs, such as family circumstances or learning difficulties. Let us assume the court orders pre-recording. The judge hearing the application makes a number of standard directions for the pre-recording and a date is fixed. The basic provisions are set out in Appendix II at the end of this chapter.

The arrangements are flexible. For example, if the child lives in a different area from that where a trial will later occur, the pre-recording may be made at the more convenient place.

No person is allowed to be present in the remote room when the child's evidence is being taken unless authorised by the judge. This is usually limited to the court officer and the support person.

During pre-recording the judge, prosecutor, defence counsel, clerk of arraigns and usher remain in the courtroom with the accused and any security officers. The accused views the child's evidence on CCTV in the same way as he or she would do at trial. No attempt is made to ensure that the same judge who sits to pre-record evidence sits at the trial, so that often the pre-recording judge is a different judge from the trial judge. That will be evident to the jury who at trial hear the disembodied voice of the judge on the pre-recording. The same applies to counsel. Judges and counsel wear their usual court robes. The Child Witness Service has explained and shown the child this earlier so that the child knows who in the system has what role.

The judge commences the 'special hearing' (the pre-recording) usually by introducing himself or herself and following a standard format.[12]

This may be along these lines:

> This is a pre-recording of the evidence of the child X on the trial of the accused Y. I am Judge Z. There may well be a different judge at the trial. The evidence of the child will be taken and recorded on videotape today the [date]. This videotape will be available for use in the trial of the accused to be held later in the District Court.
>
> The procedure of pre-recording evidence is standard procedure for the taking of the evidence of children in this State. No inference as to the accused man's guilt or otherwise should be drawn from the manner in which the evidence is taken. It is a normal procedure.

[12] Judges in Western Australia have become familiar both with the special procedures and with the special needs of children. Information comes periodically in seminars and papers and in 'Guidelines for the Use of Closed Circuit Television, Videotapes and Other Means for the Giving of the Evidence of Children and Special Witnesses' prepared and revised from time to time by the Child Witness Service Reference Group and agreed by the judges.

In court today with me are the State prosecutor Mr/Ms A, the defence Mr/Ms B and the accused Y.

In the remote room are the child X along with a support person and a court officer. We will now identify the child and proceed with the recording.

During pre-recording the child sits facing a camera and two screens.[13] One screen always displays an image of the judge. The other screen, when appropriate, displays the image of the counsel who is questioning the child. The video cameras are carefully positioned in the courtroom for the child to see the judge and counsel and to avoid the accused. No portion of the dock is visible in the background. The clerk of arraigns is responsible for turning on the equipment and operating it during the hearing. It is standard practice for the clerk of arraigns to test the equipment immediately prior to the hearing. At that time adjustments can be made to the court cameras to take account of the height and position of counsel at the bar table, etc.

The only image recorded on the videotape is that of the child entering the remote room, or already being seated at the table, and attaching a lapel microphone, and then of the child giving evidence. A support person who has been approved is well behind the child in the remote room. The court officer is also present. Sometimes they are asked to identify themselves. In any event their presence is noted.

The judge speaks to the child to ensure he or she can see and hear the judge. If the child is below the age of 12 the judge then questions the child to determine competency to give sworn or unsworn evidence. Before the evidence commences, the judge usually tells the child to listen carefully to the questions and not to answer if the questions are confusing and to indicate to the child that if he or she needs to take a break at any time to let the judge know. Competency for children under 12 is determined before the jury and thus is pre-recorded. No further inquiry as to competency can be made at the subsequent trial. This reflects the general view which is that the pre-recording is a normal part of the trial and where normal rules apply. The judge then calls on the prosecutor to begin the evidence-in-chief.

At trial the initial interview recorded by police on videotape usually is played to the jury as evidence, as permitted by legislation. The practice which has developed is for the child to view this tape out of court shortly before the pre-recording is fixed for hearing. The child does not watch the police interview in court.

At the pre-recording the child is asked in examination-in-chief about it and about any other matters the prosecution wishes to put. In other words, he or she will be asked to confirm the interview and answer any supplementary questions. Cross-examination and re-examination follow. At the commencement of the

[13] I liked to have the child brought to the chair in the CCTV room by the court officer in the way analogous to an adult witness in open court so that jurors could assess for themselves the size and physical maturity of the child.

cross-examination and re-examination the judge checks with the child to ensure the child can see and hear counsel. At any time in the hearing, if the child becomes distraught, or if the child shows signs of being too tired (a clear sign of tiredness is when the child begins to repeatedly say 'I don't remember') they may adjourn briefly to allow the child to compose and refresh himself or herself. At the end of the pre-recording the videotape should always be checked before the child leaves the remote room to ensure that the proceedings were recorded.

Legal Issues

A pre-recording is not an exhibit. It is regarded as the child's direct evidence at trial. There is the legislative possibility of a child in such a case being required to be called again at the trial but the matter has hardly ever been raised. On the two occasions known to me, one such application succeeded but the following one failed. There is legislative, previously judicial, authority also that the prosecution may file a new indictment after the child's evidence has been pre-recorded eg, where the child does not come up to proof. This, if done, clarifies the issues at trial. There is provision for a child to come into court to physically identify an accused if identity is in issue. It hardly ever is. At least I know of no case of this happening. There is also provision for admission into evidence of a child's written deposition provided the accused has been given a copy and the child is available for cross-examination. Again it is rarely used. Because the pre-recording can be edited prior to the remainder of the trial legal interruptions and argument are minimal. They can usually wait until after the pre-recording has been made.

Benefits and Costs

The benefits to children clearly include the early hearing of their evidence, both with all that that achieves in the quality of memory and reduction of stress, but also:

- avoidance, or at least minimisation, of waiting about for jury selection, other witnesses to finish, legal argument etc—they are given fixed appointments which are kept; and
- not having to return to court on another day where an earlier case runs late, or other matters delay a trial.

However, in my view the benefits of pre-recording the child's evidence go far beyond a more expeditious examination and cross-examination of the witness. The benefits to the witness derive also from:

- he or she having time between giving evidence and the trial outcome to process the experience;
- family members being better able to focus on the child's needs—particularly if they are also to give evidence;

— a reduced likelihood of media attention; and
— reduced chances of feuding for families, as people are generally unaware this process is taking place.

More broadly, other benefits which may be considered to accrue to the justice system include:

— clarity prior to trial about the charges which will be proceeded with and what evidence by the witness is admissible; and
— the fact that court time and jury time can be saved by the use of edited tapes—in particular reducing the time for the jury to be asked to leave while argument is to take place about aspects of the evidence.

Further, by a provision introduced in 2000 the pre-recording can be reused at a retrial and/or appeal. To back this up it is now mandatory to record all children's evidence given in such matters either by pre-recording or by live CCTV.

Extension of the system

The procedure of pre-recording the child's entire evidence at a special hearing is extensively used in Western Australia. It is now regarded as normal. It has been extended beyond children to persons declared as special witnesses such as persons suffering mental disability, and adult sexual assault victims.

Cross-examination

The issue of the nature of adversarial cross-examination is raised in Professor Spencer's chapter one of this book. In part, this issue may be regarded as one simply inherent in the common law tradition. It may also, however, have to be regarded as part of the 'legal culture', which may vary from place to place or over time. Judicial culture may be involved as may statutory provisions. The Western Australian Evidence Act 1906, by section 26, presently provides:

(1) The court may disallow a question put to a witness in cross-examination, or inform the witness that it need not be answered, if the question is—
 (a) misleading; or
 (b) unduly annoying, harassing, intimidating, offensive, oppressive or repetitive.

(2) Subsection (1) extends to a question that is otherwise proper if the putting of the question is unduly annoying, harassing, intimidating, offensive or oppressive.

(3) Without limiting the matters that the court may take into account for the purposes of subsection (1), it is to take into account—
   (a) any relevant condition or characteristic of the witness, including age, language, personality and education; and
   (b) any mental, intellectual or physical disability to which the witness is or appears to be subject.

The District Court judges have, in addition, recently published 'Guidelines for Cross-examination of Children and Persons Suffering a Mental Disability'.[14] These are set out in Appendix III of this chapter.

It is of course hoped that thereby the position of such vulnerable witnesses will be ameliorated so that their evidence will be given under as little stress as possible. In my view the problems in Western Australia are often not so much deliberately caused, as the result of inadvertence or carelessness as to the real needs of the witnesses concerned in understanding questions and giving proper interpretation to their answers. That is often a matter requiring judicial vigilance and, if necessary, intervention and judicial clarification. The Guidelines supplement and expand the statutory provisions and enable judicial intervention. Other authors in this book address this issue in greater detail.

Technology for Court

Besides focusing on the operation of the statutory provisions and the legal issues involved, it is appropriate to discuss some critical issues which are perhaps sometimes overlooked—that of the equipment and facilities both in and out of the court and that of the preparation of children as witnesses.

Before either the use of CCTV evidence or the pre-recording provisions could be used the courts needed the relevant equipment. In the beginning, the equipment was missing from our courts as was the knowledge of how to instal and use it. The world moves on and pre-recording and the use of CCTV are now commonplace events in daily life and commerce. The good news is that the equipment is multipurpose. Prisoners in custody can be remanded, chamber conferences and applications heard, all by CCTV from remote locations. CCTV can be used to take evidence from live witnesses in ordinary civil and other cases. The system is also used many times daily to show jurors the evidence of pre-recorded police interviews with suspects, house and vehicle searches etc. Pre-recording also is familiar to everyone. Adding pre-recording of cross-examination and re-examination adds not much as far as technology is concerned.

[14] Circular to Practitioners: CRIM 2010/1, 8 September 2010.

Just a few points though and they are important. Get the best equipment—if possible make it uniform in every court, get experts to instal it but make detailed inspection that it meets your needs and have regular detailed training for judges and staff especially when they are new to the job. And check it every time you use it—both before and after use. While problems can sometimes be fixed on the spot with live CCTV evidence, because they are noticed at the time, videotaping for later use requires more care. It is usually too late to go back. You do need to have good equipment properly installed and know how to use it and this costs money to achieve. It has taken a lot of time, effort and money to get this done but without it frustration and system failures follow.

Children are Different

The witnesses are equally critical however. Adults are used to all this technology but not to going to court—for children it is far worse and for abused children more so. The problems for them go on and on and usually their parents and friends can't really solve them. They may indeed add to them.

With children far more than with adults it is necessary to (a) keep the child away from the abuser and his supporters; and (b) make sure he or she knows what is going on and what is going to happen. This requires both physical separation from the abuser and his supporters and impartial help in coping with the unknown and fearsome world of courts and all that involves.

The separation issue involves provision of appropriate physical facilities not just in the courtroom itself, but in the court precincts and at the remote witness place. Fortunately, both pre-recording and the use of a remote CCTV link make the issue of separation much less significant.[15] In Perth, a new purpose-built court building was designed to enforce separation. Children's evidence is given from the Children's Witness Service facilities. Other courts built in recent decades in major centres also take the issue into account.

Separation of child complainants and other victims and vulnerable witnesses, especially in remote areas where communities are small and often far from protective help, is still a special problem—not in the court evidence aspect but outside that, in the street or court precincts.

[15] By the way, the result of pre-recording is that 'clearing the gallery' to protect the complainant is not an issue in running the trial and rarely is necessary for any reason.

Child Witness Service

I now turn to the issue of impartial help. The Law Reform Commission of Western Australia recommended that:

> The Attorney General, in consultation with others should establish a programme for the preparation of children under 16 who have to give evidence in court proceedings.
>
> Under the programme persons with appropriate training and experience in child communication and court processes should be appointed to prepare child witnesses for the giving of evidence, and to be available to assist them whenever appropriate before, during and immediately after the trial process.
>
> Written publications and videos should be produced and should be readily available to child witnesses and other interested persons.

This was done and the Child Witness Service has been a tremendous success. With a small staff it does all these things. Two things are vital—proper funding, proper facilities being part of that, and in my view the Service being independent of prosecution and the court. To my knowledge, no one has ever criticised its work. Children are referred to it by police, prosecutors and others. It is housed adjacent to but separate from the court in child-friendly rooms and with CCTV links to courts. It familiarises children with the courtroom, reassures them that a verdict of not guilty is not one that they have lied, that they won't see or meet the accused or his supporters and prepares children for their evidence by explaining processes, roles, showing them how it works, keeping them and their supportive family advised of dates, times and places and so on.[16] The Child Witness Service operates independently of the larger Victim Support Service with a coordinator who is a social worker with child specialisation, and a small staff of other social workers and, in remote areas, volunteers. It is funded by government and has developed specialised facilities and techniques.

The child is always accompanied during his or her evidence by a support person of his or her choosing, usually using a Child Witness Service officer and a court officer. The court officer deals with oaths or affirmations, exhibits, the electronic equipment etc. Neither at any time of course coaches or discusses the evidence with the child or at all.

The facility for giving evidence should, if possible, be close enough to the actual courtroom for the child to be quickly supplied with any exhibit, photograph etc, on which they are to be questioned. Hopefully the court officer will already have been given proposed exhibits.

[16] One other thing—the Child Witness Service can and does act as an advocacy group for funding legislative and other changes, and a wider Reference Group it established helps support it.

So you must have the court equipment, the support facilities and the child witnesses properly looked after. These requirements apply both to live CCTV evidence and to pre-recordings.

Leadership

My strong view is that for the system to work for children you also need good legislation, good judges and a supportive bureaucracy. To achieve these things, a lot depends on planning and maintaining good structures. Difficulties have occurred in Western Australia and elsewhere when these matters are not vigorously cared for. Mistakes have been made in different places in a number of ways: lack of an appropriate legislative base, over-rigid legislation, under-resourcing, lack of consultation between relevant bureaucracies and between bureaucracies and the judiciary.

The implementation of such systems is a matter for the bureaucracies responsible for funding, installing and maintaining physical resources. Their use in court systems is a matter for the judiciary and court staff and for those providing relevant services to children. Inevitably consultation is needed. Multi-disciplinary arrangements are needed both initially and over time.

In my view it is important that within the judiciary persons with an interest in the area of the taking of children's evidence be identified and enrolled to take leadership of the implementation and continued monitoring of these matters.

Issues

The process of pre-recording though is thought by some to add to the court's workload. A judge and courtroom are allotted for the special hearing to pre-record the child's evidence, a hearing that generally is listed for half a day. In some cases longer may be needed but often less. Then, at trial, when the video pre-recording is played as the child's evidence, a judge and his or her staff, as well as the prosecutor and defence counsel, sit in court for the duration of the playing of the pre-recorded evidence. Pre-recording thus increases judicial hearing time.

That increase of judicial time also directly increases the time of defence counsel. Defence counsel must fully prepare the defence case. The special hearing to pre-record the child's evidence is the only opportunity for the defence to cross-examine the child. Then, some months or even years later, defence counsel must again prepare the matter for the trial before judge and jury. There are undoubtedly further costs for the defence when the child's evidence is pre-recorded prior to trial.

There are social and legal benefits as I have said. The argument is the balance between improving the evidence and reducing the stress for children on one hand, and judicial and court administrative issues on the other.

Inter-State Assessments

An academic inquiry comparing the position in Western Australia with that in Queensland and New South Wales in 2002 by Eastwood and Patton commented:[17]

> All children in Western Australia (except one child who chose not to) gave evidence via CCTV—70 per cent gave the evidence at trial and 30 per cent fully pre-recorded their evidence months prior to trial.[18] Therefore, complainants gave evidence only once. In Western Australia, the use of CCTV for an 'affected child' under the age of 16 years at the time of complaint is mandatory where it is available, unless the child chooses to give evidence in court ... In practice, CCTV facilities in Western Australia are of a very high standard and widely used.
>
> The findings in Western Australia contrasted with the uncertainty and trauma suffered by children in eastern jurisdictions who faced the possibility or the reality they would give evidence in court in the presence of the accused.
>
> The reasons why courts are reluctant to allow children the use of CCTV were presented by some legal participants in eastern jurisdictions with comments that use of CCTV erodes the rights of the accused, the child would not take giving evidence seriously, conviction rates would fall, or that the child is needed in court living out the trauma to get a result. There is also evidence where CCTV provisions are discretionary, that prosecutors may discourage the child from using CCTV in the belief that a conviction is more likely.
>
> In contrast, prosecutors, defence lawyers and judges in Western Australia commented on the effectiveness of the legislation and the mandatory use of CCTV. Prosecutors reported it facilitated the child's evidence because the child exhibits better concentration, is more attentive and less traumatised by the experience. Defence counsel in Western Australia noted it has not affected the rights of the accused, understood it was designed to prevent further damage to the child and believed its use does not affect conviction rates.
>
> ...
>
> Children in other jurisdictions would benefit from similar legislation which protects them from facing the accused in the courtroom.

More recently a number of other enquiries have recommended adoption of the system. As indicated elsewhere in this volume some other jurisdictions have done so.

[17] The report is conveniently summarised in Christine Eastwood and Wendy Patton, *The Experiences of Child Complainants of Sexual Abuse in the Criminal Justice System*, AIC Trends and Issues Paper No 250, May 2003 available at www.aic.gov.au.

[18] These percentages have varied over time depending on available facilities, on legislative changes and on court delay times.

A recent author comments as follows:[19]

> Adopting the approach taken in Western Australia is likely to benefit … in terms of reducing delays, particularly when adjournments are granted on the day of trial due to changes in legal representation, legal arguments and issues surrounding the admissibility of portions of the child's tape. … Enabling the child complainant to give evidence uninterrupted by delay would inevitably mean that the memory of the child would be fresher and therefore more accurate. Additionally, the child can have the process over and done with early on so that the child can move on with his or her life. For example, the child complainant may need to seek counselling, which may have been postponed in order to avoid tainting his or her evidence. Another advantage is that, where a re-trial is required after a hung jury, aborted trial or successful appeal, the child's evidence may be presented in the form of the same videotape.
>
> It has been argued that there may be tactical disadvantages caused to the accused … By cross-examining the child complainant well before trial, the defence is forced to reveal its case prior to trial, and may allow the prosecution to gather further evidence to meet any arguments put forward by the defence. However, the accused already has an obligation to provide prior notice of certain lines of defence arguments, such as the requirement to give notice of an alibi defence. Furthermore, in circumstances where the court considers it would be in the interests of the administration of justice, the court may order further disclosure by the defence …
>
> It is submitted that the Western Australian approach should be adopted. Scepticism has been expressed as to whether it would be effective, since taking the child complainant's evidence in isolation from other evidence in the case may ultimately require the child to be recalled at trial so that additional material or evidence can be put. However, it has been shown to be rare for a child in Western Australia to be recalled to give further evidence at trial.

She then adds referring to the 2002 inquiry by Eastwood and Patton:

> A study which interviewed child complainants from Queensland, New South Wales and Western Australia revealed that when asked whether the child complainant would report sexual abuse again if it were repeated, only 44% in Queensland and 33% in New South Wales indicated they would, compared to 64% in Western Australia. The higher response from child complainants in Western Australia may be an indicator of the more accommodating provisions that exist in that State.

[19] J Zhou, 'Challenges in Prosecuting Child Sexual Assault in New South Wales' (2010) 34 *Criminal Law Journal* 306.

Appendix I

On Western Australian reforms in the area of tendency, similar fact, propensity and coincidence, the report of the National Child Sexual Assault Reform Committee, chaired by Annie Cossins and published by the University of New South Wales, *Alternative Models for Prosecuting Child Sex Offences in Australia: Report of the National Child Sexual Assault Reform Committee* (2010) commented:

> 3.2.81 At common law, unless evidence of each complainant is cross-admissible in relation to the counts concerning the other complainants, separate child sexual assault trials will be ordered (*De Jesus* (1986) 68 ALR 1; *R v Hoch* (1988) 165 CLR 292). However, the cross-admissibility of the evidence of two or more complainants is dependent on, not only the evidence revealing 'striking similarities' or an underlying unity, system or pattern, but also passing the *Pfennig* test—that there is no rational view of the evidence consistent with the innocence of the accused. At common law, if there is a reasonable possibility of concoction, then there is a rational view of the evidence that is consistent with the accused's innocence. As such, the evidence of two or more complainants will not be cross-admissible.
>
> 3.2.82 The Western Australian reforms in the form of ss 133 and 31A have changed the common law in several respects in relation to the conduct of sexual assault cases which involve two or more complainants.
>
> (i) concoction has been removed from the admissibility equation and is now a matter for the jury when determining the weight to be given to the evidence of each complainant;
>
> (ii) the common law 'striking similarities' test is no longer the test for determining the probative value of the evidence and has been replaced with a significant probative value test under s 31A(2)(a);
>
> (iii) the *Pfennig* 'no rational view of the evidence' test has been abrogated and replaced with a less stringent balancing test under s 31A(2)(b);
>
> (iv) a joint trial can still be held even if propensity evidence is not cross-admissible; and
>
> (v) it is envisaged that the prejudice arising from the admission of propensity evidence can be cured by a warning.

Appendix II

Evidence Act 1906 (Western Australia), sections 106I and 106K

106I. Visual recording of child's evidence, application for directions

(1) Where a Schedule 7 (i.e. the provision limiting classes of matters to be pre-recorded) proceeding has been commenced in a court, the prosecutor may apply to a judge of that court for an order directing—
  [(a) deleted]
  (b) that the whole of the affected child's evidence (including cross-examination and re-examination) be—
    (i) taken at a special hearing and recorded on a visual recording; and
    (ii) presented to the court in the form of that visual recording,

  and that the affected child not be present at the proceeding.

(2) The accused is to be served with a copy of, and is entitled to be heard on, an application under subsection (1).

106J. Deleted.

106K. Child's evidence in full, special hearing to take and record

(1) A judge who hears an application under section 106I(1)(b) may make such order as the judge thinks fit which is to include—
  (a) directions, with or without conditions, as to the conduct of the special hearing, including directions as to—
    (i) whether the affected child is to be in the courtroom, or in a separate room, when the child's evidence is being taken; and
    (ii) the persons who may be present in the same room as the affected child when the child's evidence is being taken;
  (b) subject to section 106HB(3) (i.e. admissibility of 'ABE' interviews), directions, with or without conditions, as to the persons, or classes of persons, who are authorised to have possession of the visual recording of the evidence,

and, without limiting section 106M (i.e. provisions as to altering prerecording without approval) but subject to section 106HB(3), may include directions and conditions as to the giving up of possession and as to the playing, copying or erasure of the recording.

(2) An order under subsection (1) may be varied or revoked by the judge who made the order or a judge who has jurisdiction co-extensive with that judge.

(3) At a special hearing ordered under subsection (1)—
  (a) the accused—
    (i) is not to be in the same room as the affected child when the child's evidence is being taken; but
    (ii) is to be capable of observing the proceedings by means of a closed circuit television system and is at all times to have the means of communicating with his or her counsel;

(b) no person other than a person authorised by the judge under subsection (1) is to be present in the same room as the affected child when the child's evidence is being taken;
(c) subject to the control of the presiding judge, the affected child is to give his or her evidence and be cross-examined and re-examined; and
(d) except as provided by this section, the usual rules of evidence apply.

(4) If an order is made under subsection (1), nothing in this section or section 106I prevents a visually recorded interview from being presented under section 106HB (see above) as the whole or a part of the affected child's evidence in chief at the special hearing, and in that event the judge may give directions as to the manner in which the visually recorded interview is to be —
(a) presented at the special hearing; and
(b) recorded on, incorporated with or referred to in the visual recording of the evidence taken at the special hearing.

(5) Where circumstances so require, more than one special hearing may be held under this section for the purpose of taking the evidence of the affected child, and section 106I and this section are to be read with all changes necessary to give effect to any such requirement.

Appendix III

GUIDELINES FOR CROSS-EXAMINATION OF CHILDREN AND PERSONS SUFFERING A MENTAL DISABILITY

1. Preamble

   These guidelines are meant to provide assistance to counsel as to the appropriate approach to take when cross-examining in criminal proceedings child witnesses and witnesses suffering from mental disabilities. The guidelines are not meant to be rules of the District Court and are not meant to limit or restrict the ability of counsel to represent the interests of the client (subject to s 26 of the *Evidence Act*, other rules of evidence and rules of professional conduct).

2. Guidelines

   2.1 Counsel should address the witness by the name the witness prefers. For a young child this will usually be the child's first name. (Counsel calling the witness should generally inform the Court and opposing counsel of the name the witness prefers before the witness is called.)

   2.2 Questions should be short and simple.

   2.3 A witness should be given an adequate opportunity to consider the question, formulate a response and then give an answer. This will generally be longer than is required for the average adult witness. Quick fire questions are to be avoided.

   2.4 As a general rule a witness' answer should not be interrupted except where it is necessary to ensure the witness responds to the question or to prevent the witness giving inadmissible evidence. It is to be taken into account that such witnesses may require greater leeway in formulating an oral response to a question.

   2.5 The tone of the questions should not be intimidating, annoying, insulting or sarcastic. Likewise the volume of counsel's voice should not be intimidating.

   2.6 Terminology used in questions should be age or mental capacity appropriate.

   2.7 Legalese is to be avoided (for example, 'I put it to you', 'my learned friend', 'his Honour').

   2.8 A young child should not be accused of 'lying' except where the defence case is that the child is deliberately telling lies. Rather, counsel should suggest the 'witness' version is 'not correct', or is 'wrong' or the child should be asked whether an alternative version has occurred. The purpose of this guideline is to emphasise that counsel should normally avoid an unnecessary allegation that a witness is 'lying' which may cause distress to the witness.

   2.9 The witness should not be subject to unduly repetitive questioning.

2.10 Counsel should not mix topics or switch between topics. Events should be dealt with in a logical and/or chronological sequence.

2.11 In cases where the witness clearly is incapable of understanding inconsistencies and the inconsistencies only go to the issue of reliability, counsel should give consideration to limiting or abandoning cross-examination on otherwise proven inconsistencies. In such cases counsel should seek a ruling from the trial judge as to whether proven inconsistencies can be relied upon in the closing address without comment that the inconsistencies were not the subject of cross-examination.

Appendix IV

OTHER MATERIALS

There have been a plethora of inquiries, reports, seminars, academic articles and the like published in Australia over the last 20 years into matters relevant to this paper. Among the vastness may be noted, in addition to those cited in this chapter, for example:

Australasian Institute of Judicial Administration *Bench Book for Children Giving Evidence in Australian Courts* (2010) available at www.aija.org.au/Child Witness Bch Bk / Child%20Witness%20BB%20Update%202010.pdf

N Friedman and M Jones 'Children Giving Evidence of Sexual Offences in Criminal Proceedings: Special Measures in Australian States and Territories' (2005) 14 *Journal of Judicial Administration* 157 at 161.

Law Reform Commission, Queensland, *The Receipt of Evidence by Queensland Courts: The Evidence of Children* (QLRC R55 Part 2A, December 2000), available at www.qlrc.qld.gov.au/Publications.htm.

Law Reform Commission, Victoria, *Sexual Offences: Law and Procedure. Final Report* (2004) available at www.lawreform.vic.gov.au.

K Sleight, 'Managing Trials for Sexual Offices—A Western Australian Perspective', (Paper delivered at AIJA Criminal Justice in Australia and New Zealand—Issues and Challenges for Judicial Administration Conference, Sydney, September 2011) available at www.aija.org.au/conferences-and-seminars/past-aija-programs.

5

Cross-Examining the Child Complainant: Rights, Innovations and Unfounded Fears in the Australian Context

ANNIE COSSINS

Introduction

Over the last 20 years, Australian jurisdictions have engaged in wide-ranging reforms in relation to sexual assault trials. We have found that reforms, such as changes to competency requirements, special investigative teams for interviewing children and the introduction of screens and closed-circuit television (CCTV) have significantly increased the number of child sexual assault cases going to trial in Australia.[1]

Twenty years ago, it was highly controversial to even consider that a child could give evidence outside the courtroom because it was thought this would prohibit a jury from assessing the credibility of a child 'in the flesh'. Prosecutors warned that juries would never convict in such circumstances.

The first Australian jurisdiction to introduce legislation to enable the use of CCTV during a child's evidence-in-chief and cross-examination in criminal trials was Western Australia in 1991. It was another six years before New South Wales introduced similar legislation and then several more years before all other Australian States and Territories adopted these reforms, although there are differences in terms of the breadth and scope of the legislation.[2] Nowadays, the fact that a child gives evidence via CCTV is an everyday, unremarkable occurrence.

Many lawyers and judges in the Eastern States of Australia were then alarmed to learn of another outlandish idea from Western Australia that involved pre-recording

[1] J Cashmore, 'The Prosecution of Child Sexual Assault: A Survey of NSW DPP Solicitors' (1995) 28 *Australian and New Zealand Journal of Criminology* 32; P Gallagher and J Hickey, *Child Sexual Assault: An Analysis of Matters Determined in the District Court of New South Wales during 1994* (Sydney, Judicial Commission of New South Wales, 1997).

[2] For a comparison of the legislation, see A Cossins, *Alternative Models for Prosecuting Child Sex Offences in Australia* (Sydney, National Child Sexual Assault Reform Committee, UNSW, 2010).

a child's evidence-in-chief and cross-examination soon after the child's first report to police and some months before trial. In the Eastern States, some wondered whether the good people in the West had taken leave of their senses.

In fact, out of all reforms, the pre-recording of a child's cross-examination has been the most controversial reform to protect vulnerable witnesses because it appears to infringe the accused's right to a fair trial. Yet from the child's and prosecution's point of view, it is the most reliable method for enabling children to give their best evidence, that is, at a time when their report to police is fresh in their memories.

Other innovations have evolved in particular Australian jurisdictions according to the politics of the day and problems arising in particular cases. For example, New South Wales was the first jurisdiction in Australia to allow the pre-recorded police (investigative) interview of a child to be admitted as the child's evidence-in-chief after a Royal Commission inquiry into the policing of child sex offences.[3] However, this form of pre-recording has only been adopted in three other Australian jurisdictions.[4] This particular innovation ensures that a child is not required to appear to give essentially the same evidence a second time and allows the jury to see and hear the child close to the time and the age at which the child reported to police. Another innovation in New South Wales arose out of a controversial gang-rape appeal in which the accused had one of his convictions quashed and a retrial ordered. Because the complainant refused to participate in the retrial, legislation was introduced to ensure that the evidence of all sexual assault complainants is recorded for subsequent use at retrials.[5]

Victoria introduced the first specialist case management for sex offences in Australia in the form of a specialist sex offences list (SOL) in its Magistrates' and County Courts. The purpose of the SOL is to track all cases relating to a charge for a sex offence in order to reduce delay, to assign vulnerable witness facilities to cases and to 'provide a greater level of consistency in the handling of these cases', 'in recognition of the unique features of such cases including the difficulties faced by complainants'.[6] In the County Court of Victoria, this list ensures that sexual assault cases are listed for trial within three months of committal, although extensions can be granted.[7]

Despite these wide-ranging reforms in Australian jurisdictions, there is still a long way to go since the conviction rate at trial is very low for child sex offences.

[3] Royal Commission into the New South Wales Police Service, *Final Report—Volumes IV and V: The Paedophile Inquiry* (Sydney, The Government of the State of New South Wales, 1997).

[4] Criminal Procedure Act 1986 (NSW), ss 306R, 306U; Crimes Act 1914 (Cth), s 15YM; Criminal Procedure Act 2009 (Vic), s 367; Evidence Act 1906 (WA), s 106H(2c). The Commonwealth and WA legislation only applies to children, whereas the Victorian and NSW legislation applies to children and cognitively impaired witnesses.

[5] See Division 3 (Special provisions relating to retrials of sexual offence proceedings), Criminal Procedure Act 1986 (NSW).

[6] This information is taken from the website of the Victorian Magistrates' Court www.magistratescourt.vic.gov.au/wps/wcm/connect/Magistrates+Court/Home/Specialist+Jurisdictions/Sexual+Assault/MAGISTRATES+-+Sexual+Offences+List, accessed 21 September 2009.

[7] Practice Note PNCR 2-2008 of the County Court of Victoria.

For example, for the years 2004–06, it was an average of 26.2 per cent in the higher courts and 14.9 per cent in the local courts of New South Wales. In 2004, 62 per cent of defendants were acquitted of all child sex offence counts compared with an acquittal rate of 44 per cent for *all* offences in the higher courts of New South Wales. There was also a high drop-out rate after a child's first report to police with child sex offences withdrawn before trial at a rate of 32.9 per cent compared with 23.5 per cent of assault charges.[8]

The combination of low conviction rates, high attrition rates and low guilty plea rates, led Fitzgerald to conclude that 'the number of proven charges [of sexual and indecent assault was] less than 16 percent of the number of incidents' reported to police for the 10-year period 1995 to 2004 which represented a 'very stable' 10-year trend.[9]

The reasons for low conviction rates are many and varied, although the conduct of child sexual assault proceedings is very likely to be largely responsible for court outcomes.[10] One key aspect of these proceedings is the style and nature of the cross-examination of children, the topic to be addressed in the remainder of this chapter.

Adopting the Western Australia Reforms in other Jurisdictions

Six jurisdictions in Australia now permit the pre-recording of the whole of a child complainant's evidence, that is, Victoria, Queensland, South Australia, the Australian Capital Territory and the Northern Territory, in addition to Western Australia.[11] New South Wales only permits the pre-recording of the child's evidence-in-chief so that the child must be available for cross-examination when the trial is conducted.[12]

For example, in Victoria, the pre-recording (known as the VATE process)[13] takes place during a pre-trial hearing where, in the absence of a jury, the child is examined in chief in the presence of a judge and the accused's defence counsel. The child's cross-examination is then recorded along with any re-examination.

[8] These data are taken from J Fitzgerald, 'The Attrition of Sexual Offences From the New South Wales Criminal Justice System', *Crime and Justice Bulletin* No 92 (Sydney, NSW Bureau of Crime Statistics and Research, 2006). Unfortunately, there are no more recent data on conviction rates in Australia. In 2004, only 45% of defendants in the NSW higher courts pleaded guilty compared with 65.1% of defendants charged with assault and a guilty plea rate of 70.7% for all offences combined.

[9] Ibid, 2.

[10] See further Cossins (n 2) and Spencer, ch 1.

[11] Criminal Procedure Act 2009 (Vic), ss 369–370; Evidence Act 1977 (Qld), s 21AK; Evidence Act 1906 (WA), s 106I; Evidence Act 1929 (SA), s 13; Evidence (Miscellaneous Provisions) Act 1991 (ACT), s 40S; Evidence Act 1939 (NT), ss 21A–21B.

[12] Criminal Procedure Act 1986 (NSW), s 306U.

[13] VATE process stands for video or audio taping of evidence.

The accused is not permitted to be in the courtroom while the child's evidence is pre-recorded but may observe the child using CCTV facilities and must at all times be able to communicate with his/her defence counsel. The VATE pre-recording is then admissible as evidence in a subsequent trial as if the recording was the live testimony of the child. It may also be used in any subsequent retrial.

In some jurisdictions, the pre-recording procedure has been extended to cognitively impaired complainants in sexual assault trials. The Queensland legislation, for example, covers 'special witnesses' who are defined as those suffering from a mental, intellectual or physical impairment who would be disadvantaged as a witness, those suffering severe emotional trauma and those who would be so intimidated as to be disadvantaged as witnesses.[14]

Advantages and Disadvantages of these Procedures

In a review of pre-trial procedures in sexual assault trials, the Australian Law Reform Commission (ALRC) recently identified the benefits of pre-recording a child's evidence as follows:[15]

— improvements in the quality and reliability of evidence;
— facilitating pre-trial decisions by the prosecution and the defence;
— helping with the scheduling and conduct of the trial; and
— minimising systemic abuse of child witnesses.

Overall, pre-recording allows both parties to gauge the strength of the prosecution's case well before trial, which assists the prosecution in deciding whether or not to proceed to trial and the defence in deciding whether or not to plead guilty.[16] Other benefits include the fact that the child is then able to 'move on' with her or his life without the anxiety of having to give evidence at the upcoming trial and to engage in therapy without fear of her or his evidence being contaminated.[17]

As a result of the ALRC's review of pre-recording procedures in Australia, it recommended that both child and adult complainants of sexual assault should be

[14] Evidence Act 1977 (Qld), s 21A(1). The South Australian legislation goes even further by allowing the evidence of a vulnerable witness to be pre-recorded if s/he has been subject to threats of violence or retribution or has reasonable grounds to fear violence or retribution in connection with the proceedings (Evidence Act 1929 (SA), s 4).

[15] Australian Law Reform Commission and New South Wales Law Reform Commission, *Family Violence: Improving Legal Frameworks (Consultation Paper)* (Sydney, Australian Law Reform Commission, 2010) 800–01.

[16] Australian Institute of Judicial Administration Committee, 'Children Giving Evidence', *Bench Book for Children Giving Evidence in Australian Courts* (Melbourne, AIJA, 2009) 116.

[17] J Cashmore, 'Innovative Procedures for Child Witnesses' in HL Westcott, GM Davies and R Bull (eds), *Children's Testimony: A Handbook of Psychological Research and Forensic Practice* (Chichester, Wiley, 2002) 213.

able to give the whole of their evidence by way of a pre-recording.[18] At the same time, defence counsel object to this particular reform on the grounds that it is unfair for them to cross-examine the prosecution's chief witness before the trial has begun[19] and that further issues for cross-examination are likely to come up during the trial.

In fact, most jurisdictions have provided for this possibility. For example, under s 376(1) of the Victorian Criminal Procedure Act 2009, a child complainant (whose cross-examination has already been pre-recorded) may be subject to further cross-examination at trial if the court gives leave. There is a presumption against further cross-examination unless the court is satisfied one of the following matters exist:

(i) the accused is seeking leave because of becoming aware of a matter of which the accused could not reasonably have been aware at the time of the recording; or

(ii) if the complainant were giving direct testimony in the proceeding, the complainant could be recalled, in the interests of justice, to give further evidence; or

(iii) it is otherwise in the interests of justice to permit the complainant to be cross-examined or re-examined.

Other drawbacks that have been identified in the Australian context include the quality of the pre-recording which may make it hard to hear and see the child. However, in most modern courtrooms in New South Wales and Western Australia, for example, state-of-the-art technology using large screens and good quality audio facilities have overcome this problem. If a child's pre-recorded investigative interview is to be used as their evidence-in-chief in court, it may be affected by untrained or poorly trained interviewers.[20]

While a video-recording of a child's evidence is said to lack 'the immediacy and persuasiveness' of a child's live testimony,[21] empirical evidence shows that jurors are not adversely affected by this form of evidence. In fact, although such reforms were designed to address the vulnerability of child witnesses and to remove the traditional barriers that had been thought to prevent the successful prosecution of child sex offences, such reforms do not appear to have any effect on the likelihood of conviction.

[18] Australian Law Reform Commission and New South Wales Law Reform Commission, *Family Violence—A National Legal Response (Final Report)* (Sydney, Australian Law Reform Commission, 2010) 1233.

[19] Australian Law Reform Commission and New South Wales Law Reform Commission (n 15) 800.

[20] Ibid, 801; PC Snow and MB Powell, 'Getting the Story in Forensic Interviews with Child Witnesses: Applying a Story Grammar Framework' (Report to the Criminology Research Council Grant: CRC 04/04-05) (Canberra, Australian Institute of Criminology, 2007); MB Powell, K Roberts and B Guadagno, 'Particularisation of Child Abuse Offences: Common Problems When Questioning Child Witnesses' (2007) 19 *Current Issues in Criminal Justice*, 64–74.

[21] Australian Law Reform Commission and New South Wales Law Reform Commission (n 15) 801.

For example, in 2004 a comprehensive British study found there was no evidence that conviction rates were affected by the availability of special measures for vulnerable witnesses.[22] Two very recent Australian studies have confirmed these views. Taylor and Joudo conducted a mock jury study to investigate the impact of pre-recorded evidence or evidence given via CCTV on jury perceptions in sexual assault trials. They found that the mode of presentation of evidence had no impact on jurors' perceptions of the defendant, the complainant or the defendant's guilt.[23]

Similar findings were reported by Cashmore and Trimboli who found that a majority of jurors from 22 child sexual assault trials did not have a negative reaction to viewing a child's pre-recorded interview (as evidence-in-chief), or to a child giving evidence via CCTV. Out of 241 jurors, 84 per cent stated that 'the pre-recorded tape of the child's evidence-in-chief helped either "a lot" ... or "quite a bit" ... in understanding the child's evidence'.[24]

With regard to the police interview being used as evidence-in-chief, jurors appreciated seeing the child give a first-hand account in their own words close to the time when the report was first made. In addition, 90.3 per cent of 277 jurors in 25 trials considered the use of CCTV as 'quite fair' or 'very fair' to the complainant, whilst 88 per cent held the same views in relation to the defendant.[25]

There was also a high level of understanding by jurors about the reasons for using CCTV such as the need to reduce the stress on the child, provide a safe environment for the child, the child's age, the nature of the alleged offence, or the relationship between defendant and complainant. While this study did not study the use of pre-recorded cross-examination, there is no reason to expect jurors would react differently to that aspect of a child's evidence.

I understand that in England objections to the use of pre-recorded evidence remain because of the perceived infringement of the accused's right to cross-examine witnesses and that this right is enshrined under Article 6 of the European Convention on Human Rights. This leads to another question: how absolute is the right of an accused person to cross-examine the witnesses against him or her?

The Right to Cross-examine: An Absolute Right?

In Australia, we have a federal system of government as does the USA. Unlike the situation when the American colonies declared their independence from Britain, a charter of rights was not enshrined in the Australian constitution when Australia

[22] B Hamlyn, A Phelps, J Turtle and G Sattar, *Are Special Measures Working? Evidence from Surveys of Vulnerable and Intimidated Witnesses (Home Office Research Study 283)* (London, Home Office, 2004).

[23] N Taylor and J Joudo, *The Impact of Pre-Recorded Video and Closed Circuit Television Testimony by Adult Sexual Assault Complainants on Jury Decision-Making: An Experimental Study* (Canberra, Australian Institute of Criminology, 2005).

[24] J Cashmore and L Trimboli, 'Child Sexual Assault Trials: A Survey of Juror Perceptions' (2006) *Crime and Justice Bulletin* No 102 (Sydney, NSW Bureau of Crime Statistics and Research, 2006) 5.

[25] Ibid, 6.

gained independence from Britain in 1901. Nor has our Federal Parliament since enacted a Bill or Charter of Rights as has occurred in England and Canada.[26] Two jurisdictions in Australia have enacted human rights legislation but this legislation only operates within the jurisdictional limits of the State of Victoria and the Australian Capital Territory.[27] This means most citizens and non-citizens in Australia are forced to rely on the common law and the limited provisions of the Bill of Rights enacted in 1688 to protect their civil and human rights, including the right to cross-examine witnesses against them.

Most people would agree that the right to cross-examination is based on the widely accepted belief that cross-examination is 'the primary evidentiary safeguard of the adversary trial process'[28] and that the defendant's *inability* to effectively test the prosecution's case will infringe the fair trial principle.[29] Yet commentators are rarely able to articulate how that right would be affected if cross-examination were more tightly regulated.[30]

The Australian High Court has held that the rights of an accused under the fair trial principle are not absolute and are subject to 'the interests of the Crown acting on behalf of the community'.[31] Indeed, the concept of fairness is not fixed and immutable and 'may vary with changing social standards and circumstances',[32] which means that it is inextricably 'bound up with prevailing social values'.[33] The concept of fairness can take into account the interests of the victim,[34] including the desirable goal of encouraging victims to report sexual offences to the police, as well as minimising the re-traumatisation experienced by sexual assault complainants during the trial process.

In recent times, both Australian Parliaments and government bodies have begun to accept that the right to cross-examination by the defendant is not an absolute

[26] Human Rights Act 1998; Canadian Bill of Rights (SC 1960, c 44).

[27] Under s 22(2)(g) of the Human Rights Act 2004 (ACT) a person has a guarantee 'to examine prosecution witnesses, or have them examined, and to obtain the attendance and examination of witnesses on his or her behalf under the same conditions as prosecution witnesses'. Presumably, pre-recording would not infringe this guarantee. Under s 25(2)(g) of the Charter of Human Rights and Responsibilities Act 2006 (Vic), a person is entitled to the minimum guarantee 'to examine, or have examined, witnesses against him or her, unless otherwise provided by law'. This wording indicates that the right to cross-examine is not absolute and can be limited.

[28] L Ellison, 'The Protection of Vulnerable Witnesses in Court: an Anglo-Dutch Comparison' (1999) 3 *International Journal of Evidence and Proof* 29, 35.

[29] *S v The Queen* (1989) 168 CLR 266; *Dietrich v R* (1992) 177 CLR 292; *R v McHardie and Danielson* [1983] 2 NSWLR 733; *R v McLennan* [1999] 2 Qd R 297; *R v Khan* [2003] NSWSC 849; *Stack v State of Western Australia* [2004] WASCA 300.

[30] C Eastwood and W Patton, *The Experiences of Child Complainants of Sexual Abuse in the Criminal Justice System* (Brisbane, Queensland University of Technology, 2002) 127; NSW Legislative Council, Standing Committee on Law and Justice *Report on Child Sexual Assault Prosecutions* (Parliamentary Paper No 208) (Report 22) (Sydney, NSW Parliament, 2002) 69.

[31] *Dietrich v R* (1992) 177 CLR 292 at 335, per Deane J; quoting *Barton v R* (1980) 147 CLR 75 at 101, per Gibbs ACJ and Mason J.

[32] *Dietrich v R* (1992) 177 CLR 292 at 328, per Deane J.

[33] Ibid at 364, per Gaudron J.

[34] Ibid at 357, per Toohey J.

right.[35] For example, reforms in Australia that now prevent an unrepresented defendant from personally cross-examining a sexual assault complainant show:

(i) that the legitimate expectations of an accused under the fair trial principle are to be balanced against the needs of sexual assault complainants and the benefits to the community at large; and
(ii) the unfettered right to cross-examine prosecution witnesses is not necessarily absolute and can be subject to controls where necessary.[36]

This means there is a precedent for making reforms to the cross-examination process.

Should we go Further? Other Problems with Cross-examination

In a recent article, I examined whether reforms to cross-examination in child sexual assault trials should go much further by, for example, restricting defence counsel's ability to put questions to the child or by abolishing particular styles of cross-examination.[37]

In order to consider such radical reforms, it is necessary to examine the extent to which cross-examination is used as an oppressive tool for intimidating and confusing children, rather than a forensic tool for exposing a dishonest witness. In particular, is cross-examination more properly described as a procedure for manufacturing false evidence?

There has been a considerable amount of research on the use of the 'strange language' of the courtroom and its impact on children.[38] Because many of the objections to cross-examination are made without any empirical basis, it is important to engage with the research literature to better inform the criminal justice reform agenda.

[35] In such a situation, the complainant can only be cross-examined by a person appointed by the court who will ask the complainant questions requested by the accused. See, for example, Criminal Procedure Act 1986 (NSW), s 294A.

[36] See, further, *R v TA* (2003) 57 NSWLR 444 at 446, per Spigelman CJ. In the UK, ss 34–39 of the Youth Justice and Criminal Evidence Act 1999 prohibit an unrepresented accused from cross-examining a child witness.

[37] A Cossins, 'Cross-Examination in Child Sexual Assault Trials: Evidentiary Safeguard or an Opportunity to Confuse? (2009) 33 *Melbourne University Law Review* 68.

[38] M Brennan and R Brennan, *Strange Language: Child Victim Witnesses under Cross-examination* (Wagga Wagga, CSU Literacy Studies Network, 1998); M Brennan, 'Cross Examinations of Child Witnesses' (1994) VII *International Journal of the Semiotics of Law* 51; M Brennan, 'The Discourse of Denial: Cross-Examining Child Victim Witnesses' (1995) 23 *Journal of Pragmatics* 71; R Zajac and H Hayne, 'I Don't Think That's What *Really* Happened: The Effect of Cross-Examination on the Accuracy of Children's Reports' (2003) 9 *Journal of Experimental Psychology* 187; R Zajac, J Gross and H Hayne, 'Asked and Answered: Questioning Children in the Courtroom' (2003) 10 *Psychiatry, Psychology and Law* 199.

It probably goes without saying that jurors' verdicts are influenced by the consistency of children's evidence and jurors' perceptions of their credibility, although a recent Australian jury study has verified this empirically.[39] It is no surprise, therefore, that both of these features are the subject of persistent attack during cross-examination. In fact, this Australian study showed that juror perceptions of children's consistency and credibility affected their verdicts.

There is, however, a distinct mismatch between what lawyers and jurors believe children's inconsistency indicates (unreliability and lack of veracity) and the research literature. In other words, 'the emphasis on consistency may be misplaced' since inconsistencies in 'children's accounts of sexual abuse do not indicate that their claims are false'.[40]

Two studies have specifically analysed the phenomenon of inconsistent evidence given by children in response to cross-examination-style questions. The first by Zajac, Gross and Hayne analysed 2,935 cross-examination questions from 18 trial transcripts. They found that children's responses to defence questions showed 'high rates of misunderstanding *and* compliance with leading and closed questions, and a low rate of clarification seeking'.[41] In fact, 76 per cent of children made changes to one or more aspects of their evidence in chief as a result of cross-examination. Ninety-five per cent of these changes were made in response to either leading questions, credibility-challenging questions or both.[42]

The authors then conducted a second study to determine whether children's changes to their evidence during cross-examination constituted a change *towards* the truth or *away* from the truth. To answer this, Zajac and colleagues examined the effect of cross-examination on 46 children's reports of a contrived event in which the children actually participated.[43]

All children were interviewed six weeks after the event using open-ended questions as well as more specific questions about two actual things that had happened (photo taken, siren on police car) and questions about two things that did not happen (trying on handcuffs, seeing a lady report a stolen bike). Eight months[44] after this direct examination, they were interviewed by a different interviewer using cross-examination-style questions and language in order to try to persuade the children to change their accounts of what happened, or to admit that their answers might have been wrong.

Zajac and colleagues reported that 85 per cent of children 'changed at least one of their original responses during cross-examination and one-third … changed

[39] Cashmore and Trimboli (n 24).

[40] Ibid, 14.

[41] Zajac, Gross and Hayne (n 38) 206.

[42] Ibid, 204.

[43] The event involved a tour of a New Zealand police station during which the children had their thumbprint recorded and 'mug shot' taken. They were also shown a jail cell and a police car with the lights and siren turned on.

[44] The eight month period is the average delay in New Zealand between when a child first reports and the matter goes to trial.

all of their original responses'.[45] These findings were highly consistent with their previous study of court transcripts in which 76 per cent of children were found to have made one or more changes to their evidence during cross-examination, as discussed above.

The next question to be addressed by the researchers was whether the changes made by 85 per cent of the children were changes that corrected earlier mistakes, or did the children make changes to answers that were originally correct? Zajac and colleagues reported that 'children were just as likely to change a correct answer under cross-examination … as they were to change an answer that had initially been incorrect'.[46] As well, a small group of children who had been given misinformation prior to being questioned were, unexpectedly, found *not* to be more susceptible to probing cross-examination. This means that children who had given accurate answers during evidence-in-chief were somehow influenced or persuaded during cross-examination to change their previous accurate accounts of what had happened at the police station.

This may have been due to either a weakened memory of the event and greater susceptibility to suggestion (since cross-examination occurred 9.5 months after the visit to the police station) and/or because of 'compliance with suggestions' that the children knew to be incorrect.[47] Zajac and colleagues concluded that 'cross-examination not only proved to be unsuccessful in discrediting inaccurate children (i.e., [the] misled children [who had been] questioned about false events), it also decreased the accuracy of children who were initially correct'.[48]

Confirming what a number of inquiries have suggested, this study shows that cross-examination, which is ostensibly designed to flush out the dishonest witness, was incapable of achieving that task with five- and six-year old children. Rather it achieved what has long been thought to be its main aim in child sexual assault trials—producing inconsistencies or retractions by a majority of the children who participated in the study.

In other words, cross-examination was not able to discriminate between true and false testimony and produced inaccuracies in children who had previously given accurate accounts. The question is whether these inaccuracies are produced within the actual courtroom. Since the cross-examination questions used in the study were based on the questioning styles used by defence counsel in child sexual assault trials, and because children are cross-examined under much more intimidating conditions than those used in Zajac and colleagues' study in a public forum by people unknown to them and for considerably longer periods of time, it is highly likely that cross-examination will produce similar inaccuracies during child sexual assault trials.

45 Zajac and Hayne (n 38) 190.
46 Ibid, 191.
47 Ibid, 192.
48 Ibid, 191.

Other Alternatives to Cross-examination

The current debate in Australia is not about whether to pre-record a child's evidence-in-chief and cross-examination, but what can be done to control oppressive and misleading styles of cross-examination. It is impossible to know how many trials result in acquittals as a result of cross-examination producing inaccurate testimony but in the interests of justice, such styles of questioning ought to be prohibited.

However, my previous review of Australian inquiries into children's evidence over a 14-year period[49] has shown that we have four key problems to face in relation to the cross-examination of children:

(i) mental abuse, intimidation and humiliation by defence lawyers are relatively common occurrences in child sexual assault trials in Australia;
(ii) defence counsel deliberately use complex and leading questions to produce inaccuracies and inconsistencies in children's testimony;
(iii) mock jurors' pre-existing beliefs about sexual assault influenced their decisions *more than* the facts of the case and the manner in which the evidence was given; and
(iv) these beliefs are likely to be reinforced by cross-examination that taps into common myths and stereotypes.

The question is whether it is in the public interest for jurors to make decisions based on what amounts to manufactured inaccuracies, particularly since other evidence strongly suggests that cross-examination which confirms pre-existing beliefs on the part of jurors will influence jury decision-making.[50] If a fair trial necessarily involves *preventing* the contamination of a child's evidence then there is a need to consider the ways in which the cross-examination process can be reformed.

It may have been hoped that the introduction of measures allowing children to pre-record their evidence or give live evidence from another location via CCTV (with support persons present) would protect them 'from the full rigour of adversarial-style proceedings'.[51] Despite these innovations, a recent evaluation in New South Wales found that the style and patterns of cross-examination have remained unchanged, judges are reluctant to intervene to prevent improper cross-examination,[52] and there is no evidence to show that children's susceptibility to suggestive styles of cross-examination is reduced by vulnerable witness protections.

[49] See Cossins (n 2).

[50] Taylor and Joudo (n 23); GS Goodman and A Melinder, 'Child Witness Research and Forensic Interviews of Young Children: A Review' (2007) 12 *Legal and Criminological Psychology* 1.

[51] Ellison (n 28) 34.

[52] J Cashmore and L Trimboli, *An Evaluation of the NSW Child Sexual Assault Specialist Jurisdiction* (Sydney, NSW Bureau of Crime Statistics and Research, 2005); Cashmore and Trimboli (n 24).

However, '[t]he difficult issue in relation to child witnesses is to what extent the normal methods of cross-examination to attack a witness's credit should be restricted to give proper recognition of the child's particular vulnerability'.[53] Evidence shows that judges are reluctant to intervene in relation to cross-examination because of 'concern about jeopardising a fair trial ... and/or concern regarding the approach to be taken' by courts of appeal.[54] In fact, empirical evidence from a study of child sexual assault trials shows that judges are not more likely to intervene to protect *vulnerable* witnesses from improper cross-examination.[55]

Recommendations for reform in this area have tended to focus on educating judges with the expectation they will become more interventionist and that professional conduct rules should specifically proscribe intimidating and harassing questioning of child witnesses.[56] Such approaches are, however, unlikely to affect the way that child sexual assault trials are conducted since every jurisdiction in Australia already has legislation which allows a trial judge to disallow certain types of questions put to a witness in a criminal trial while barristers' professional associations have adopted similar rules.

Trial judges now have a positive duty to control improper questions in some jurisdictions,[57] irrespective of whether or not the other party has raised an objection. However, anecdotal evidence from barristers and students observing trials suggests this reform in New South Wales, at least, has had very little impact. This is likely to be due to the fact that there is still a large degree of discretion for judges to decide whether or not questions are improper.

Yet '[i]f it is accepted that misleading, confusing, intimidating, harassing, offensive, oppressive, humiliating and insulting questions negatively affect the

[53] K Sleight, 'Commentary on the Video "A Case for Balance"—the Issue of Judicial Control of Cross-Examination' (paper presented at the Biennial District and County Court Judges Conference, Fremantle, Western Australia, 27 June–1 July 2007) 3.

[54] Australian Law Reform Commission, NSW Law Reform Commission and Victorian Law Reform Commission, *Uniform Evidence Law Report (ALRC Report 102; NSWLRC Report 112; VLRC Final Report)* (Sydney: Australian Law Reform Commission, 2005) 152; quoting Judge Ellis; Cashmore and Trimboli's analysis of 17 child sexual assault trials in the NSW Pilot Program confirmed this anecdotal evidence. They found that judicial intervention to protect children during cross-examination was unusual, with only 20.6% of judicial interventions in the study being made to control cross-examination: Cashmore and Trimboli (n 52).

[55] Cashmore and Trimboli (n 52).

[56] Australian Law Reform Commission and Human Rights and Equal Opportunity Commission, *Seen and Heard: Priority for Children in the Legal Process* (Sydney, Australian Law Reform Commission, 1997).

[57] See s 41 of the NSW, Victorian, Tasmanian and ACT Evidence Acts (known as the Uniform Evidence Acts or UEA). Section 41 defines an improper question as: misleading, confusing, intimidating, harassing, offensive, oppressive, humiliating or insulting. In Australian common law jurisdictions, the regulation of improper questions varies from jurisdiction to jurisdiction, although most do not place a duty on the trial judge to disallow improper questions. For example, s 26 of the Evidence Act 1906 (WA), s 21 of the Evidence Act 1977 (Qld) and s 16 of the Evidence Act (NT) state that a court *may* disallow improper questions. In South Australia, judicial regulation is limited to scandalous and insulting questions (Evidence Act 1929 (SA), s 25). Like the UEA, some common law jurisdictions stipulate the matters that the court may take into account in disallowing improper questions, such as age or mental disability (see, for example, Evidence Act 1977 (Qld), s 21(2)).

reliability of evidence and bring the criminal justice process into disrepute',[58] reform of the cross-examination process ought to be guided by the public interest in ensuring that verdicts are based on the most accurate evidence. This would mean discarding the discretion that allows judges to decide whether or not an improper question should be disallowed. If, as the research literature indicates, admissible evidence can become inconsistent, skewed or inaccurate because of the *method* used to elicit that evidence during cross-examination then the legitimate public interest in the goals of justice in relation to child sexual assault are undermined.

Recommendations for the Way Forward

The findings from various reports, studies and inquiries into the way children are treated within the criminal justice system lead to the inevitable conclusion that cross-examination is inappropriately used to exploit children's age and developmental vulnerability and may impede children's psychological recovery.

The research literature also tells us that the techniques of cross-examination are an important defence method for changing the accuracy of children's evidence, constructing children as unreliable and, thus, influencing a jury's decision as to the guilt or innocence of the accused, with empirical evidence showing that jurors' perceptions of consistency and credibility affect their verdicts.

In order to produce real change to the cross-examination process, reforms will need to go further than allowing a child to give evidence via CCTV or pre-recording their evidence, or imposing a judicial duty to disallow improper questions.

Education of judges is also unlikely to provide a comprehensive solution to the problems of protecting children from the rigours of cross-examination since there are no consequences for judges if they do not intervene to protect vulnerable witnesses. Because there is some evidence to show that judges do not change their approach to protecting children during cross-examination, even with educational packages, other protections for vulnerable witnesses during cross-examination are required.[59] As well, lawyers and judges who are untrained in child development will not necessarily recognise that a child is stressed or confused or is answering questions they do not understand.

Since it is not the goal of a cross-examiner to ask age-appropriate questions (nor are they likely to possess the skills to do so), this requirement ought to be imposed upon them. All together, I have come up with a package of five recommendations which are based on the recognition that the legitimate expectations of an accused under the fair trial principle must be balanced against the needs of

[58] T Henning, 'Control of Cross-Examination—A Snowflake's Chance in Hell?' (2006) 30 *Criminal Law Journal* 133, 136.

[59] Cashmore and Trimboli (n 52).

complainants and the expectations of the community at large. This recognises the fact that, in Australia at least, the right to cross-examine prosecution witnesses is not an unfettered right and can be subject to controls where necessary in the public interest.

To some these reforms will appear to be radical. Arguably, they are required to meet the equally radical phenomenon that the type of cross-examination questions permitted in child sexual assault trials are the same type that studies have shown produce inaccurate evidence by children, and the type that police and other professionals are *discouraged* from using for fear of contaminating a child's evidence.[60]

These five recommendations are set out below.[61] The first has been drafted to prohibit suggestive questions or statements that are designed to persuade children to agree with the propositions or suggestions put to them. In other words, what is not permitted during the investigative interview of children (in order to ensure that the children's evidence is not contaminated) ought not to be permitted during cross-examination.

The second recommendation amounts to a prohibition on asking children the same questions or making the same statements more than once because of the risk that the children's answers will be affected by suggestion or the desire to please authority figures, rather than the children's memory and experience.

The third recommendation is designed to prohibit questions or statements made by the defence that directly accuse children of lying or being a liar, given the damaging effects of such allegations on children's mental health. Such questions can be re-phrased (for example, 'Are you sure you're telling the truth?') without directly accusing the child of lying.

Recommendation 1: Suggestive questions during the cross-examination of child witnesses in sexual assault trials

(1) This section applies to prescribed sexual offence proceedings.
(2) During cross-examination, the court must disallow a question put to a witness under the age of 18 years, or inform the witness that it need not be answered, if the question suggests a particular answer to which the witness is asked to agree.

Recommendation 2: Repetitive questions during the cross-examination of child witnesses in sexual assault trials

(1) This section applies to prescribed sexual offence proceedings.
(2) During cross-examination, the court must disallow a question put to a witness under the age of 18 years, or inform the witness that it need not be answered, if the question is repetitive.
(3) For the purposes of sub-section (2), a question is repetitive where the content of the question is largely the same as that of a previous question asked of the same witness.

[60] Snow and Powell (n 20).
[61] They were first published in Cossins (n 37).

Recommendation 3: Questions about lying during the cross-examination of child witnesses in sexual assault trials

(1) This section applies to prescribed sexual offence proceedings.
(2) During cross-examination, the court must disallow a question or statement put to a witness under the age of 18 years, or inform the witness that it need not be answered, if the question directly suggests that the witness is a liar, or is lying, or has lied.
(3) For the purposes of sub-section (2), examples of questions and statements that are prohibited include but are not limited to:
 (a) You're lying, aren't you?
 (b) You're a liar, aren't you?
 (c) It's all lies.
 (d) What you've said is a pack of lies.

These three recommendations are aimed at ensuring that inaccuracies are not produced by the typical questions used by defence counsel during cross-examination. This would enhance the fairness of the trial from the perspectives of the complainant, the defendant and the community since it would reduce the extent to which juries base their verdicts on inaccurate testimony.

The fourth recommendation places restrictions on the use of prior inconsistent statements by the defence. This would mean that, before the defence can cross-examine a child on a prior inconsistent statement, the judge must be satisfied that the statement *is* a prior statement about a matter central to the facts in issue, that it is in fact inconsistent and does not relate solely to a trivial or irrelevant matter. This would prevent a child from being cross-examined on a prior inconsistent statement which is only relevant to the child's credibility. This is recommended on the grounds that there is no evidence that inconsistencies in children's accounts are the result of lying and are more likely to be the result of cognitive development or the style of questioning.[62]

Recommendation 4: Questions about a prior inconsistent statement during the cross-examination of child witnesses in child sexual assault trials

(1) This section applies to prescribed sexual offence proceedings.
(2) During cross-examination, the court must disallow a question put to a witness under the age of 18 years, or inform the witness that it need not be answered, if the question is about a prior inconsistent statement made by the witness, unless the court is satisfied that the prior statement:
 (a) is in fact inconsistent with the witness's evidence given in court;
 (b) is a prior statement about a matter relevant to a fact in issue in the trial; and
 (c) does not relate solely to a trivial or irrelevant matter.

[62] H Dent, 'The Effects of Age and Intelligence on Eyewitnessing Ability' in H Dent and R Flin (eds), *Children as Witnesses* (Chichester, John Wiley & Sons, 1992); L Geddie, S Fradin and J Beer, 'Child Characteristics Which Impact Accuracy of Recall and Suggestibility in Preschoolers: Is Age the Best Predictor?' (2000) 24 *Child Abuse & Neglect* 223; S Ghetti, GS Goodman, ML Eisen, J Qin and SL Davis, 'Consistency in Children's Reports of Sexual and Physical Abuse' (2002) 26 *Child Abuse & Neglect* 977.

All of the above four recommendations are likely to decrease the length of cross-examination, and hence the trial, by reducing the number of questions put to a child, preventing the use of repetitive questions and reducing confusion in the child witness. The restriction of questions that directly accuse a child of lying may also result in less stress and trauma to the child and enhance their ability to give their most accurate evidence.

Nonetheless, these recommendations would need to be accompanied by improved training of prosecutors and judges about the differences between suggestive and non-suggestive questions to ensure that they are able to object to, and disallow, such questions. However, these recommendations, on their own, are unlikely to be sufficient to prevent the manufacture of inaccurate evidence.

That is why I have proposed a fifth recommendation. This involves the use of court-appointed intermediaries (such as social workers, psychologists or other relevant professionals) trained in child cognition, language and development to assess defence questions during the cross-examination of a child complainant. The role of this intermediary would be to advise the trial judge on whether or not each cross-examination question is age-inappropriate, suggestive in content, misleading, confusing, oppressive, intimidating, humiliating, repetitive, or unable to be understood by a child of the particular complainant's age.[63] In addition, the intermediary would be able to advise the court about how to rephrase a particular question so that the child can understand it. This recommendation would also ensure that recommendations one to four can be put into practice. In particular, recommendation five is justified on the grounds that:

> [i]n order to maximise the ability of children to give accurate evidence, it is essential that they are asked questions appropriate to their cognitive level. This is not fundamentally different from ensuring that witnesses who cannot communicate in English are questioned via an interpreter, in a language they can understand.[64]

Recommendation 5: Court-appointed intermediaries in child sexual assault trials

(1) This section applies to prescribed sexual offence proceedings.
(2) A question must not be put to a witness under the age of 18 years during cross-examination *unless* the question has been assessed by a court-appointed intermediary, trained in the linguistic skills and cognitive development of children, and the intermediary has stated their opinion to the court as required by this section.
(3) The intermediary must state their opinion to the court as to whether or not the question is:

[63] There is provision for the use of an intermediary under s 29 of the Youth Justice and Criminal Evidence Act 1999 (UK) which gives a court the power to order the examination of certain types of vulnerable witnesses using an intermediary during the witness's live or pre-recorded evidence-in-chief, cross-examination and/or re-examination. The intermediaries in use in England, however, have a more limited role than is envisaged under Recommendation 5. See, further, ch 1 by JR Spencer for a discussion of the UK intermediaries.

[64] Victorian Law Reform Commission, *Sexual Offences: Final Report* (Melbourne, Victorian Law Reform Commission, 2004) 312.

   (a) able to be understood by a person of the witness's particular age and cognitive development; and
   (b) an improper question.
(4) For the purposes of sub-section (3)(b), a question is improper if it:
   (a) is misleading or confusing; or
   (b) is annoying, harassing, intimidating, offensive, oppressive, humiliating or repetitive; or
   (c) is put to the witness in a manner or tone that is belittling, insulting or otherwise inappropriate; or
   (d) has no basis other than a stereotype (for example, a stereotype based on the witness's sex, race, culture, ethnicity, age or mental, intellectual or physical disability).
(5) Where the intermediary concludes that a question put to a witness during cross-examination is not able to be understood by the witness or is an improper question, the intermediary must advise the court about whether or not the question can be re-phrased and, if so, how it can be re-phrased. If the court accepts the opinion of the intermediary, it must disallow the question unless the question can be re-phrased.

This recommendation is akin to appointing an interpreter to ensure that cross-examination questions are not only able to be understood by a particular child according to their cognitive development, but also that cross-examination questions do not breach provisions which are designed to prevent improper questions. There is both anecdotal and empirical evidence[65] that children do not seek clarification when they misunderstand a question hence the need for someone in the courtroom to monitor cross-examination questions to prevent children from giving answers to questions that are beyond their cognitive development.

Conclusion

Pre-recording of evidence is beneficial in a number of ways, including the fact that it ensures that children's evidence is given when they make their first report, thus enhancing the accuracy of their evidence, particularly in jurisdictions which have long delays between charge and trial.

However, pre-recording does not tackle the endemic problems that exist in relation to the actual purpose and function of cross-examination in a child sexual assault—rather than being a method for uncovering untruthful child witnesses, empirical evidence shows that it is a process that manufactures inaccurate evidence.

[65] NSW Legislative Council, Standing Committee on Law and Justice (n 30) 64–65; Zajac, Gross and Hayne (n 38).

The package of reforms proposed in this chapter would enhance the fairness of the trial from the perspective of the complainant, the defendant and the community since they would reduce the extent to which juries base their verdict on inaccurate testimony. Some will argue that the above reforms will impede the rights of the accused to fair trials. But what is the nature of those rights? Whilst there is a common law right to cross-examine witnesses, previous reforms to cross-examination in Australia show that this right is not absolute and can be subject to controls in the interests of justice. There is certainly no case law that states that the right to cross-examine extends to attempts to produce or manufacture inaccurate evidence. If cross-examination is considered the best method for testing the accuracy of a witness's evidence, then the present method used in child sexual assault trials is clearly not appropriate to that task. Because judges are acknowledged to play a legitimate role in 'protecting complainants from unnecessary, inappropriate and irrelevant questioning',[66] these reforms, informed as they are by the research literature, merely limit the right to cross-examine in ways that will actually improve the quality of the evidence given by children in child sexual assault trials.

In conclusion, this chapter has documented the evidence which justifies the need for the package of reforms set out above. Arguably, such a package is required to achieve *real* cultural change in the courtroom. If lawyers themselves would not allow their own children to be complainants within the adversarial system[67] then communities and governments owe it to *other people's* children to change that system.

[66] *R v TA* (2003) 57 NSWLR 444 at 446, per Spigelman CJ.

[67] Eastwood and Patton (n 30); NSW Legislative Council, Standing Committee on Law and Justice (n 30).

6

An Idea Whose Time has Come: The Reform of Criminal Procedure for Child Witnesses in New Zealand[1]

EMILY HENDERSON

Around 750 children appear in the New Zealand criminal courts as complainants or witnesses every year.[2] Although their situation has improved markedly since the early 1980s, it is still far from satisfactory. We have ongoing problems with delays before trial, with cross-examination and with access to the available special measures. However, proposals have been made recently for significant new measures, including pre-recording the entirety of children's evidence and a new intermediary system based loosely on continental European models.[3]

New Zealand is a parliamentary democracy of approximately 4 million people in an area roughly equivalent to that of the United Kingdom. Its criminal justice system is derived from the British model and remains very similar: witnesses must appear at trial to give their evidence and be cross-examined; the jury trial has been retained for offences punishable by two years' or more imprisonment;[4] and New Zealand's evidence and criminal laws are also still very similar to their British parents, although both have been codified.[5]

The basic process is that police investigate complaints and interview witnesses. Children should be interviewed in specialist facilities by trained forensic interviewers and their interviews digitally recorded (the equivalent of 'ABE' (Achieving Best Evidence) interviews). The police then lay charges in court. The police prosecute many cases themselves using in-house lawyers, or Police Prosecutors, but if the matter is serious (or 'indictable') it passes to the district Crown Solicitor.[6]

1 My thanks to Thomas Biss, Professor Fred Seymour and Dr Kirsten Hanna for reading drafts of this chapter. However, the views expressed in this chapter (and all remaining errors) are, of course, my own.

2 S Power *Alternative Court Processes for Child Witnesses* Press Release 5 October 2011, media release, beehive.govt.nz.

3 Ibid.

4 Previously 3 months' imprisonment: extended to two years by the Criminal Procedure (Reform and Modernisation) Bill passed 4 October 2011.

5 Crimes Act 1961; Evidence Act 2006.

6 My thanks to Michael Smith, Crown Solicitor, Northland for clarifying this information.

Once the Crown Solicitor receives a file from the police, he or she decides whether to continue with the prosecution, decides what charges will be proceeded with, instructs the police on any further investigations and deals with all pre-trial and trial matters. At trial the Crown will usually apply for child witnesses to use their forensic interview videos as their evidence-in-chief and to give the remainder of their evidence via live link or screens. They may also have a support person in the courtroom. Cases involving child witnesses should be given priority fixtures.

This chapter describes the development of New Zealand's criminal procedure and evidence law relating to child witnesses, the current situation, and the government's intended reforms.

The History

Up until the early 1990s, the position of most child witnesses in New Zealand was, as in most of the common law world, extremely bleak. However, from the late 1970s and early 1980s onwards a wave of concern about the failure of criminal justice processes to both meet the needs of, and gather adequate evidence from, child witnesses swept across most of the common law world. Many commentators began to discuss reforming criminal evidence law and procedure to remove barriers to children's effective participation in trials. They also began to consider a range of alternatives to conventional testimony, including recording the child's evidence-in-chief, recording the child's entire testimony, the use of live links, and the use of intermediaries to assist in questioning children.

The New Zealand government also began to consider reforming the criminal process for child witnesses. In 1984 and 1985, the legislature enacted major changes to the law of evidence and procedure relating to rape complainants; these gave child complainants of sexual crime their first real protections. The requirement that the evidence of complainants in sexual offence trials be corroborated was abolished.[7] Further, rape complainants were excused from appearing at oral committal proceedings,[8] and judges were given discretion to clear the public galleries when they testified.[9] Alleged child victims could also have support persons in court.[10]

In late 1985 the government established the 'Advisory Committee on the Investigation, Detection and Prosecution of Offences Against Children', an interdisciplinary[11] inter-departmental committee, to 'recommend any necessary changes to protect children from needless trauma' during criminal investigations.[12]

[7] Section 23AB Evidence Act 1908, inserted by s 3 Evidence Amendment Act (no 2) 1985.

[8] Section 185C Summary Proceedings Act.

[9] Section 138 Criminal Justice Act 1985.

[10] Section 375A(2)(h) & (3)(b) Crimes Act 1961 inserted by s.5 Crimes Amendment Act (No 3) 1985.

[11] Including doctors, psychiatrists, lawyers and judges.

[12] Letter 9.12.1985 Minister of Police to Ministers of Justice, Education and Health.

This became known as the 'Geddis Committee' after its chair, Dr David Geddis, a pediatrician who was also chair of the National Advisory Committee on the Prevention of Child Abuse established in 1981. After consulting widely with 230 organisations and individuals, and having had some 400 people participate in discussions nationwide,[13] the Committee reported in 1988.

Meanwhile, the Justice Ministry also began considering legislative reform.[14] In September 1987 the Minister of Justice, Geoffrey Palmer, declared to Parliament the government's intention to amend the existing legislation to 'allow the evidence of victims of sexual violence cases to be presented to the court through means of video camera, monitors, and screens'.[15]

The Geddis Committee's Report included similar recommendations but its scope was much wider. The Report began by debunking a range of common myths and misconceptions about children's reliability generally and about sexual abuse complaints specifically.[16] It then highlighted problems with the status quo, including the intimidating courtroom environment[17] and the inappropriateness of cross-examination.[18]

The Report recommended, inter alia, reform of the investigative process to include joint police/social welfare investigations utilising skilled interviewers.[19] It also suggested that children be prepared for trial by visiting the court and meeting the judge.[20] The Report recommended that children not appear at oral committal proceedings and that cases involving child witnesses be given priority when scheduling cases.[21]

Turning to the trial itself, the Report recommended removing the competency test,[22] giving expert witnesses a greater role, and relaxing restrictions on hearsay. It recommended that when children testified they be screened from the defendant,[23] that counsel and judges remove their wigs and gowns[24] and that the court be

[13] D Geddis Private or Public Nightmare: Report of the Advisory Committee on the Investigation, Detection and Prosecution of Offences Against Children New Zealand, 1988, 8–9.

[14] Justice Dept Minute Lewin to Hoffman 13.9.1988; Letter Secretary of Justice to Minister of Justice 14.10.1988, attaching Cook A and Whitney L *Child Sexual Abuse Cases Heard in the Criminal Court: Proposals for Reform* unpublished, Ministry of Justice 1988.

[15] 29/9/87 Capital Letter.

[16] Geddis (n 13) 17–19.

[17] Ibid, 23.

[18] Ibid, 20–21.

[19] Ibid, 11–15, 20.

[20] Ibid, 23.

[21] Ibid, 22.

[22] Ibid, 16.

[23] The first successful application was in May 1988 in *R v Rihari* T4/88 Whangarei High Court per Hillyer J, following *R v K* T8/88 Wellington DC 16.2.1988. The Crown were also successful in *R v Vloet (No 2)* T34/88 13.6.1988 and *R v Accused T19/88* Wellington High Court 22.7.1988. There was controversy regarding the threshold for admitting a screen: see *R v O'Brien* T53/88 June 1988; *R v Henderson (No 1) T12/88* 20 July 1988. In December *Rihari* was approved by the Court of Appeal.

[24] Geddis (n 13). In 1996 wigs were dispensed with in all courts (Practice Direction 25.3.1996).

closed.[25] The Report also endorsed some use of live link, pre-recorded evidence and intermediaries.[26]

The Committee recognised that, by the mid 1980s, some New Zealand practitioners were already videotaping children's disclosure interviews for legal (rather than therapeutic) purposes,[27] including criminal investigations.[28] It also noted that several of its suggested reforms (including screens; removing wigs and gowns; closing the court; preventing publication of the complainant's identity; and preparatory visits to the court) had already been allowed under the court's inherent jurisdiction. These practices had been instigated, independently of the government, by small groups of police, clinicians, doctors and prosecutors who began working together in child abuse investigations in the early 1980s.[29]

The Evidence Amendment Act 1989

At the end of 1989, Parliament passed the Evidence Amendment Act 1989, which introduced a series of alternative methods of testifying in sexual cases for complainants aged under 17.[30] Such children could have their forensic interview played to the court instead of having to give evidence-in-chief; they could also give their evidence-in-chief and/or any cross- and re-examination via live link, from behind a screen or even from:

> behind a wall or partition, constructed in such a manner and of such materials as to enable those in the courtroom to see the complainant while preventing the complainant from seeing them, the evidence of the complainant being given through an appropriate audio link,[31]

always provided the jury, judge and counsel (but not the defendant) could see the witness. They could also have their entire testimony (including cross- and re-examination) pre-recorded outside the courthouse with counsel and judge in attendance.[32] Under section 23E(4) the judge could also direct that:

[25] Ibid, 23.

[26] Ibid, 25–26.

[27] J R Spencer and R Flin *The Evidence of Children: The Law and the Psychology* London, Blackstone Press 1993, review procedure internationally, 166–72.

[28] Geddis (n 13) 25. By mid 1988 there were already several agencies nationally with dedicated video suites for recording children's evidence: eg the Hastings Memorial Hospital Children's Development Unit (for the Family Court only), the first Evidential Video Unit in South Auckland, and the New Plymouth White House, all established in 1987 as joint police/DSW initiatives and, in May 1988, the Miriam Centre, an NGO in Whangarei. The last three were largely created as bases for the interdisciplinary police investigative teams established in the early 1980s.

[29] By late 1986 the new process was well enough established to enable the first national guidelines, the *Guidelines on the Investigation and Management of Child Sexual Abuse* to be written.

[30] Section 23C(b) Evidence Act 1908.

[31] Section 23F Evidence Act 1908. This is clearly a version of the Libai 'child courtroom': see D Libai (1969) 'The Protection of the Child Victim of a Sexual Offence in the Criminal Justice System' (1969) 15 *Wayne Law Review* 977–1032.

[32] Section 23E(a)–(e) Evidence Amendment Act 1989.

> any questions to be put to the complainant shall be given through an appropriate audio link to a person, approved by the Judge, placed next to the complainant, who shall repeat the question to the complainant.[33]

The Act also allowed for expert evidence regarding the extent to which the child's behaviour was consistent with having been sexually abused and restricted the defendant's right to personally cross-examine children or mentally impaired persons.[34] The Act abolished the judicial practice of requiring corroboration of children's evidence and of routinely warning juries to treat children's evidence with suspicion.[35]

This was remarkably radical legislation, exceeding even the recommendations of the UK Pigot Report released in 1989, and enacted several years in advance of similar legislation in comparable commonwealth jurisdictions such as South Africa, Canada, Australia and the UK. Unfortunately, within a very short period, some of these reform initiatives were abandoned.

After the Act

The standard procedure for child witnesses in New Zealand's criminal courts quickly became the use of the forensic interview video as evidence-in-chief, with the child appearing at trial to be cross-examined using live link or screens. The Act's other alternatives were overlooked.

The author uncovered only three instances where intermediaries were used after the Act,[36] only one of which (where an evidential interviewer was asked by the judge to put a very few questions to a child on behalf of the prosecutor) resulted in evidence which was put to the jury.[37] In the first of the other two cases, an application to use an intermediary succeeded but proceedings were withdrawn before trial.[38] In the second instance, the judge, prosecutor and defence counsel convened to examine the child at the offices of the social worker who acted as intermediary. The judge stopped proceedings when the child could not enunciate the meaning of 'truth'.[39] There is also one instance of an unsuccessful application

33 Section 23E(4) Evidence Amendment Act 1989.

34 Section 23F Evidence Act 1908.

35 Section 23H(b) of the Evidence Act 1908 inserted by s 3 Evidence Amendment Act 1989. The provision was later repeated in s 125(1) Evidence Act 2006. For the previous practice see *R v Parker* [1968] NZLR 325.

36 In 1987 the Hastings Hospital Child Development Unit began video-recording children's disclosures for the Family Court and allowed counsel present behind one-way glass to put questions via the interviewer. Newspaper article dated 11.8.1987 from unknown newspaper in collection of Ministry of Justice Archives. There is one other instance involving an unreported criminal case in 1974 which was overturned on appeal (personal communication from the psychologist who acted as intermediary).

37 Personal communication with the intermediary.

38 The Working Party on Child Witnesses *Child Witnesses in the Court Process: A Review of Practice and Recommendations for Change* Wellington, Ministry of Justice 1996 briefly mentions this, 157.

39 Personal communication with intermediary.

for pre-recording.[40] The option of an audio-linked walled space within the courtroom[41] seems never to have been attempted.[42]

Why Were Options Ignored?

The reasons for the failure of the intermediary, walled space and pre-recording options, even though they had been very much part of the ministerial vision, are not clear. However, it has been stressed internationally that governmental investment in infrastructure, training and organisation is necessary for reforms to succeed.[43] The New Zealand government did not make any such investments beyond some bare-bones regulations. Practitioners were left to sort things out for themselves.

Unfortunately, the practitioners had no experience with, and little awareness of the possibilities of, full pre-recording or the use of intermediaries. On the other hand, several practitioner groups had established expertise in, and even practice guidelines for, forensic interviewing[44] and some even piloted live link in anticipation of the Act.[45] Videos, screens and live link had already been accepted by the courts under their inherent jurisdiction, so it is not surprising that practitioners continued to focus on developing and consolidating these options.

Further, the early 1990s were years of intense activity for practitioners involved in child abuse investigations. The courts grappled with the new Act and with video interviews in particular, ultimately taking a generally supportive approach

[40] Working Party on Child Witnesses (1996) briefly mentions one successful pre-trial application to pre-record the evidence of an autistic child, 157.

[41] Section 23F Evidence Act 1908.

[42] New Zealand is not alone in having ignored useful legislative reforms: Queensland practitioners largely ignored 1991 legislation permitting pre-recording until the legislature made it mandatory and Western Australian practitioners still ignore their 2003 provision for intermediaries for children. England and Wales have not brought their 1999 provision for pre-recording into force either.

[43] See, eg, K Sleight *Managing Trials for Sexual Offences—A Western Australian Perspective* AIJA Conference 7–9 September 2011, Sydney; H Jackson ch 4; Australian Federal Police & Prosecutions *Responding to Sexual Assault: The Challenge of Change* Canberra, A.C.T.: Australian Federal Police, Australian Capital Territory Office of the Director of Public Prosecutions 2005, 131, 148; C Eastwood and W Patton *The Experiences of Child Complainants of Sexual Abuse In the Criminal Justice System* 2002; J Cashmore and L Trimboli *An Evaluation of the NSW Child Sexual Assault Specialist Jurisdiction Pilot* 2005, http://203.3.186.80/lawlink/bocsar/ll_bocsar.nsf/vwFiles/L18.pdf/$file/L18.pdf (last accessed 17 February 2012).

[44] In 1988, aware the Bill would allow forensic interview videos into court and determined to prevent a lengthy teething period, a group of Auckland practitioners developed forensic interviewing guidelines which were used in the first forensic interview video admitted under the new Act (but before the regulations governing videos came into force): *R v Accused* CA32/91 [1992] 1 NZLR 257 (CA). The eventual regulations in fact did not deal with interview methodology. The 1988 guidelines were not superseded and, as updated in 1996 and 2007, apply today.

[45] In July 1989, before the Act passed, Lower Hutt police piloted live link in the Wellington High Court (under its inherent jurisdiction). Chief Justice Sir Thomas Eichelbaum was 'cautiously enthusiastic,' about the results (*The Evening Post* 18.7.1989, 5).

to the new practices and the pre-existing forensic interview video guidelines.[46] Further, the Chief Justice and the Chief District Court Judge, recognising the problems delay caused children, in 1992 ordered that trials involving child witnesses be given priority when scheduling.

Investigative interviewers were also busy, first with the establishment of an annual national training programme in 1990 and then in the early 1990s with the national establishment of new Evidential Interview Units, the need to develop a professional organisation, and the need to monitor standards amongst the increasing numbers of new practitioners.[47]

A further but quite different factor may have affected practitioners' willingness to experiment with the less familiar options. The early 1990s also saw widespread public controversy about child abuse investigations and interviewers, particularly as the result of various well-publicised scandals both outside[48] and inside New Zealand[49] where it was alleged that poor and aggressive interviewing had contaminated children's disclosures.[50] The 1993 Ellis trial brought public suspicion of child abuse investigators to its highest pitch.

Crèche worker Peter Ellis was convicted of 16 sexual offences against pre-schoolers in his care following a large-scale investigation that included the forensic interviewing of over 100 children and split the local community in Christchurch and a trial marked by lengthy and aggressive cross-examination of the interviewers. Ellis, together with a vocal group of supporters, continues to maintain his innocence, and has appealed several times, based largely on criticisms of the interviewing. However, the courts (and several prominent international experts) have always rejected the appeals and exonerated the interviewers' methodology and technique.[51] Nonetheless, the Ellis case still raises hackles nationally and

[46] See case law review by M-E Pipe and M Henaghan 'Accommodating Children's Testimony: Legal Reform in New Zealand' in B Bottoms and G Goodman (eds) *International Perspectives on Child Abuse and Children's Testimony: Psychological Research and Law* Newbury Park, CA, Sage Publications 1996, 151–54.

[47] K Wilson 'Forensic Interviewing in New Zealand' in M-E Pipe, M Lamb, Y Orbach and A Cederborg (eds) *Child Sexual Abuse: Disclosure, Delay, and Denial* New York, Routledge 2007 describes the ongoing annual peer tape review conferences for statutory interviewers and the review of data from all video unit interviews annually, which began in the early 1990s.

[48] Eg the UK Orkney and Cleveland Inquiries.

[49] Eg the Ward 24 inquiry in Christchurch unearthed significant poor practice contrary to the accepted best practice standards of the time: C Brett 'Hospital Staff in Breach of Guidelines' *The Christchurch Star* 7 June 1989; 'Doors Opened On Ward 24' *The Christchurch Star* 7 June 1989; R McLeod 'The Spence Case: A Private and Public Nightmare' *North and South* July 1989; L Hood *City Possessed: The Christchurch Civic Creche Case* Longacre, Dunedin 2001, 153, 162–63.

[50] The Orkney and Cleveland Inquiries and also the series of 1986 Family Court decisions in England and Wales criticising interviewing practices at Great Ormond Street Hospital. The NZ Minster of Police's comments in Hansard 27.4.1989, 2.5.1989 and 16.2.1989 regarding child protection teams in 1989 serve as a good example of the extent of concerns.

[51] See *R v Ellis (Nos 1–4)* [1993] 3 NZLR 329; *R v Ellis* (1994) 12 CRNZ 172; *Ellis v R* [1998] 3 NZLR 555; *R v Ellis* [2000] 1 NZLR 513. The tapes were also passed by UK authority Professor Graeme Davies and Canadian expert Dr Louise Sas; cf Hood *City Possessed* (n 49).

provokes anxiety amongst current forensic interviewers. In such a context it is hardly surprising that practitioners' enthusiasm for innovation diminished.

In the mid 1990s, various evaluations of the criminal justice system's treatment of child witnesses were undertaken. While forensic interviewing standards were not criticised, otherwise the evaluations revealed an uncoordinated and flawed system.[52] Delays had worsened. Despite the judicial direction to give priority to cases involving child witnesses, by 1996 they took nearly eight months to process—about a month longer than other cases.[53]

There were also serious concerns about lawyers' developmentally inappropriate questioning, especially in cross-examination, and about judicial reluctance to intervene.[54] Defence counsel still promoted as viable defence theories the Geddis Report had criticised as spurious or exaggerated (such as that the child had imagined the abuse).[55]

Further, since the Evidence Amendment Act only applied to children alleging that they had been abused sexually, other children were still in an invidious position, although the courts extended some protections to these witnesses using their inherent jurisdiction. Even for children protected by the Act, applications for videotaped evidence-in-chief and live link were usually made only for under-12s, while older children were generally only offered screens.[56] Thus, child abuse trials continued to be 'confusing, frustrating, and ultimately disempowering for many participants'.[57]

Reengaging with Reform

In 1996 both the Law Commission and the Working Party of the Courts Consultative Committee[58] released proposals for further action, the Working Party focusing on infrastructure, while the Commission focused on evidence law. The Working Party recommended, inter alia, practical measures for fast-tracking cases involving child witnesses and the development of a national court

[52] B Lash *Time Taken to Process Sexual Offence Cases Through the Courts* Wellington, Ministry of Justice 1995; E Davies and F Seymour 'Questioning Child Complainants of Sexual Abuse: Analysis of Criminal Court Transcripts in New Zealand' (1998) 5(1) *Psychiatry, Psychology and Law*; E Davies, E Henderson and F Seymour 'In the Interests of Justice? The Cross-examination of Child Complainants of Sexual Abuse in Criminal Proceedings' (1997) 4(2) *Psychiatry, Psychology and Law* 217–29; E Henderson 'Psychological Research and Lawyers' Perceptions of Child Witnesses in Sexual Abuse Trials' in D Carson and R Bull (eds) *Handbook of Psychology in Legal Contexts* (2nd edn) Chichester, Wiley 2003.

[53] Lash (n 52) 4, 13; Davies and Seymour (n 52) 16.

[54] Davies and Seymour (n 52); Davies, Henderson and Seymour (n 52); Henderson (n 52); later transcript analyses by R Zajac, J Gross and H Haynes 'Asked and Answered: Questioning Children in the Courtroom' (2003) 10 *Psychiatry, Psychology and Law* 199 made similar findings.

[55] Davies, Henderson and Seymour (n 52); Henderson (n 52).

[56] Davies and Seymour (n 52).

[57] F Seymour *A Reasoned Response to Child Sexual Abuse* unpublished presentation to Department of Psychology, University of Auckland, 12 August 2009.

[58] Working Party (n 38).

preparation programme for children. The Law Commission's 1996 discussion paper[59] recommended that the competency test for children be abolished and that everyone, including children, be deemed eligible to testify.[60] It also recommended extending the special measures to all witnesses,[61] introducing support persons for all complainants, and expanding the intermediary provision to allow intermediaries to rephrase answers as well as questions.[62] It also suggested that expert witnesses might be appointed to 'advise the court and counsel on the most appropriate way to question' witnesses with 'comprehension difficulties'.[63] Finally, it recommended re-introducing pre-recording.[64]

In its final proposals in 1999, the Law Commission stood by most of its original recommendations, including pre-recording.[65] The Commission also proposed enlarging judges' powers to control examination questions,[66] and extending restrictions on defendants personally cross-examining witnesses[67] to 'all complainants and child witnesses in sexual cases, and ... domestic violence cases' with a discretion to include any witness.[68] However, although the Commission recommended allowing a wide range of 'communication assistance',[69] it withdrew its support for intermediaries, despite backing from the great majority of responses to its 1996 paper.[70] Although the government adopted the Working Party's

[59] New Zealand Law Commission *The Evidence of Children And Other Vulnerable Witnesses: A Discussion Paper [PR26]*. Wellington, New Zealand Law Commission 1996 ('NZLC 1996').

[60] New Zealand Law Commission *Evidence: Reform of the Law* Report 55 vol 1 1999 retrieved from http://www.lawcom.govt.nz/sites/default/files/publications/1999/08/Publication_56_163_R55%20Vol%201.pdf (last accessed 17 February 2012).0Vol%201.pdf ('NZLC 1991(1)', para 329; New Zealand Law Commission *Evidence: Evidence Code and Commentary* Report 55 vol 2 www.lawcom.govt.nz/UploadFiles/Publications/Publication_64_227_R55%20Vol%202.pdf ('NZLC 1999(2)'), para C294. Many comparable jurisdictions had either already removed or were discussing removal of the test: eg by 1984 20 US states had abolished special competence requirements for children and included it in R 601 Federal Rules of Evidence (Whitcomb 5) and the UK abolished the test in the 1991 Criminal Justice Act 1988, s 33A.

[61] In sections 105(1)(a)(iii) and 106(1) of the Law Commission's draft Code (n 61).

[62] NZLC (1999)(1) (n 60) paras 167–76.

[63] Ibid, para 176. Later, UK intermediaries combined these roles.

[64] NZLC (1996) (n 59), paras 144–58. It is not clear from the report that the Law Commission appreciated that provision for full pre-recording had in fact already been enacted.

[65] NZLC (1999)(1) (n 60) paras 459–60; NZLC 1999(2) (n 60) paras 103–06.

[66] Section 14(a) Evidence Act 1908 disallowed 'scandalous or indecent questions'. The Commission recommended a discretion to exclude 'any question that the judge considers intimidating, improper, unfair, misleading, needlessly repetitive, or expressed in language that is too complicated for the witness to understand', taking account of a broad range of factors including the witness's 'age or maturity ... any ... disability ... the linguistic ... background of the witness' and the nature of the case, NZLC 1999 vol 2 (n 60), s 85, and see also paras C320–22.

[67] Section 23F Evidence Act 1908.

[68] NZLC (1999)(2) (n 60) para C341; s 95.

[69] Ibid, para C310; s 81.

[70] The Commission cited research suggesting that interpreters for severely disabled adult witnesses were inaccurate and influenced by their own preconceptions, raising concerns that courts could not monitor the accuracy of intermediaries' translations for such witnesses. However, severely disabled adults were likely to be much less common users of intermediaries than young children and the use of intermediaries was never mandatory. The same problem must arise with ordinary translation but it has never been suggested that we exclude witnesses who cannot speak English.

recommendation of a national courts education programme for children,[71] other reform would wait until the government achieved its long-term goal of a comprehensive evidence code[72] in the Evidence Act 2006.

The Evidence Act 2006: An Overview

The Evidence Act 2006 ['the Act'] codified New Zealand's evidence law, replacing all pre-existing legislation and incorporating many of the Law Commission's 1999 recommendations. This section describes the Act's provisions together with the findings of a recent study into actual practice. The study, *Child Witnesses in New Zealand Criminal Courts: A Review of Practice and Implications for Policy*, was conducted by the Auckland University of Technology's Dr Kirsten Hanna, a linguist, and Dr Emma Davies, a psychologist, together with other researchers, and funded by the New Zealand Law Foundation with contributions from the Ministry of Social Development, Ministry of Justice and the New Zealand Police.

The study considered two groups of criminal cases involving child witnesses under 17 years old over the period 2008–09. The first group ('the trial group') included 69 trials involving 71 children.[73] The second group consisted of pre-trial applications on behalf of 134 children for directions authorising the use of special measures for upcoming criminal trials ('the modes group').[74] Additionally, Hanna also undertook a detailed analysis of transcripts of 18 children's forensic interviews and courtroom examinations.[75] Accordingly, we have reasonably clear information about current practice in New Zealand, despite a notable lack of statistical information in this area collected by the government.

The Evidence Act 2006 makes every person eligible to testify and removes the special test of competence for children.[76] Witnesses aged 12 and over must take an oath or give an affirmation but children under 12 can give evidence which in principle has equal weight provided the judge tells them of the importance of telling the truth and not lying and the child promises to tell the truth.[77] Alternatively, the child may still testify and their testimony has the weight of sworn evidence if

[71] A pilot programme was favourably reviewed in 2003 and rolled out nationally in 2004.

[72] See eg NZ Law Commission 'Striking the Balance NZLC PP51', Wellington, 2002; 'Seeking Solutions: Options for Change to the New Zealand Court System PP52', Wellington, 2002; 'Delivering Justice for All NZLC R85', Wellington, 2004.

[73] K Hanna, E Davies, E Henderson, C Crothers and C Rotherham *Child Witnesses in New Zealand Criminal Courts: A Review of Practice and Implications for Policy* NZ Law Foundation, Auckland 2010, 20–21.

[74] K Hanna, C Crothers and C Rotherham 'Children's Access to Alternative Modes of Evidence' in ibid, 93, 96.

[75] K Hanna 'Questioning Children' in Hanna et al (n 73) 58–60.

[76] Section 71 Evidence Act 2006.

[77] Section 77(2) and (3) Evidence Act 2006.

the judge directs that it be so.[78] The Act reiterates the provision from the 1989 Act that, except in special circumstances, the judge must not warn the jury to regard children's evidence with special caution.[79]

The 2006 Act also extended eligibility for the special measures. Any witness who meets the criterion may depart from the 'ordinary way' of giving evidence and instead testify in an 'alternative way'.[80] If any alternative is directed, the judge must warn the jury that it is prescribed by statute and that no inference adverse to the accused is to be drawn from its use.[81] The alternatives are described broadly and inclusively: provided that 'the defendant is able to see and hear the witness'[82] the witness may testify:

> (i) while in the courtroom but unable to see the defendant or some other specified person; or
> (ii) from an appropriate place outside the courtroom …; or
> (iii) by a video record made before the hearing of the proceeding.[83]

Moreover:

> any appropriate practical and technical means may be used to enable the Judge, the jury (if any), and any lawyers to see and hear the witness giving evidence, in accordance with any regulations.[84]

The Act also incorporated the Law Commission's recommendation that interpreters[85] be able to provide a wide range of 'communication assistance'. The Act allows interpreters to provide

> any … assistance that enables or facilitates communication with a person who:
>
> (a) does not have sufficient proficiency in the English language to:
> (i) understand court proceedings conducted in English; or
> (ii) give evidence in English; or
> (b) has a communication disability.[86]

The Act omits overt mention of the earlier 1989 Act's options for an audio-linked walled enclosure within the courtroom, full pre-recording and intermediaries.[87] This makes New Zealand both the earliest Commonwealth country to allow such measures and the only country to remove them, although, with some

[78] Section 77(4) Evidence Act 2006.
[79] Section 125 Evidence Act 2006.
[80] Section 103(1) Evidence Act 2006.
[81] Section 123 Evidence Act 2006.
[82] Section 103(1)(c) Evidence Act 2006. Even this, however, comes with a (thus far untested) loophole: 'except where the Judge directs otherwise'.
[83] Section 105(1)(a) Evidence Act 2006.
[84] Section 105(1)(b) Evidence Act 2006.
[85] Section 80 Evidence Act 2006.
[86] Section 4 Evidence Act 2006.
[87] Although its broad provision for 'communication assistance' may permit assistance similar to that of an intermediary. Section 80 Evidence Act 2006.

imagination, the broad description of the special measures and 'communication assistance' might be interpreted as still allowing these measures.[88]

Hanna et al found little evidence of imagination in the use of special measures in 2008–09. The status quo of the 1990s prevailed and the only special measures used or applied for were the forensic interview as evidence-in-chief, screens and live link. The most common combination was the forensic interview and live link at trial for cross-examination. Forty-five per cent of children in the trial sample, including all children under 13 and 31 per cent of those over 13, testified in this way while 21 per cent used videos and screens (although Hanna et al also found that approximately a third had not had a forensic interview and so could not apply to use a video[89]). Eighteen per cent used a screen only, while 1 per cent used only live link. Fourteen per cent of the children (all aged 15 or older) testified in the ordinary way.[90]

The Act also states that complainants are 'entitled' to, and other witnesses may apply for, a support person.[91] There is no restriction on who may be appointed. However, Hanna et al found that 30 per cent of children had no supporter. Further, although most supporters were family members, counsellors or social workers, 20 per cent were court personnel.[92] This is unfortunate because support persons are intended to help witnesses derive strength from the proximity of someone with whom they have a close relationship.[93]

Under the Act, no one is automatically eligible to use a special measure but anyone, including a defendant, may apply. Prosecutors, however, must apply for directions as to how child complainants testify, even if they do not seek special measures.[94]

There is a different threshold for applications for child complainants as opposed to other witnesses. In either case, the judge 'must' consider 'the need to ensure' the 'fairness of the proceeding', that there is a 'fair trial' [95] and the catch-all 'any other factor that is relevant to the just determination of the proceeding.'[96] The judge must also consider the child's preference as to mode of testifying[97] and the need to 'minimise' the child's 'stress' and to 'promote their recovery'.[98] Where the witness

[88] Imagination was applied in 2010 to full pre-recording: see below.

[89] 34% of the trial group and 27% of modes group: Hanna, Crothers and Rotherham (n 74) 98–99.

[90] K Hanna 'The Police and Court Processes' in Hanna et al (n 73), 17, 38–40. Similarly, most applications (43%) were for the forensic interview and live link. 22% applied for forensic interview video and screens, 34% for screens only and 1% for live link only: Hanna, Crothers and Rotherham (n 74), 99. Overall, screens were more popular than live link, with 44% of applications seeking live link compared to 56% seeking screens: Hanna, Crothers and Rotherham (n 74) 101.

[91] Section 79(1) and (2) Evidence Act 2006.

[92] Hanna et al (n 73) 7.

[93] Hanna 'Police and Court Processes' in ibid, 48.

[94] Section 107(1) Evidence Act 2006.

[95] Section 107(4)(a)(i) and (ii).

[96] Section 107(4)(c) Evidence Act 2006.

[97] Section 107(4)(b) Evidence Act 2006.

[98] Section 107(4)(b)(i) & (ii) Evidence Act 2006.

is a child complainant, those are the only considerations that apply. However, for other witnesses the court 'may' also consider an inclusive and discretionary list of other factors. The judge 'may' consider:

(a) the age or maturity of the witness;
(b) the physical, intellectual, psychological, or psychiatric impairment of the witness;
(c) the trauma suffered by the witness;
(d) the witness's fear of intimidation;
(e) the linguistic or cultural background or religious beliefs of the witness;
(f) the nature of the proceeding;
(g) the nature of the evidence that the witness is expected to give;
(h) the relationship of the witness to any party to the proceeding;
(i) the absence or likely absence of the witness from New Zealand;
(j) any other ground likely to promote the purpose of the Act.

However, although it is mandatory that the courts consider witnesses' views, Hanna et al found that 60 per cent of children in the trial sample were not consulted:[99] only 16 per cent of the younger children but 51 per cent of the older children.[100] This is unfortunate in light of research strongly suggesting that child witnesses are less stressed if they are consulted.[101]

Hanna et al found that the defence opposed 24 per cent of the special measure applications. When applications are opposed, not only is there a hearing but the prosecution are almost always directed to brief an expert witness (usually a private clinical psychologist). However, Hanna et al found that the defence ultimately consented to nearly half of the applications they initially opposed (of the rest, eight were granted and three rejected, but there were no data for the remaining six).[102] This indicates a significant expenditure of time and resources for no real purpose.

Although police investigations were completed reasonably quickly,[103] there were significant delays between the accusers' first court appearances and the trials. The mean delay was 15.68 months,[104] nearly twice that in the 1990s when delays were last surveyed.[105] When the children finally reached court, Hanna et al found

[99] Hanna 'Police and Court Processes' in Hanna et al (n 73) 36.

[100] Ibid, 36–37. Of the 29 consulted, 8 preferred to testify in the ordinary way. Eleven of the 12 who had been forensically interviewed preferred to use their videos as their evidence-in-chief (and all were allowed to do so) and then use live link or a screen. Of the 16 remaining children, 8 preferred live link or a screen and 8 preferred the ordinary method. 79% of the children were allowed their preferred mode: ibid, 37.

[101] NZLC 1999(1) & (2) (n 50); Cashmore and Trimboli (n 35).

[102] Hanna et al (n 73) 9–10, Hanna, Crothers and Rotherham (n 74) 101. In only 9 of the contested cases did Hanna et al find clear information about the grounds for opposition: Hanna, Crothers and Rotherham (n 74), 102–06.

[103] Half of the police investigations in the trial sample completed within 1.6 months and a mean delay of 3.35 months: Hanna 'Police and Court Processes' in Hanna et al (n 73) 24.

[104] Ibid.

[105] Lash (n 52).

that, despite a direction to prosecutors to call children as early as possible,[106] they spent an average of nearly three hours waiting to testify. Sixty four per cent only began testifying at midday or later and, although 58 per cent completed their evidence on their first day at court, 42 per cent had to return.[107] Those children waited on average four-and-a-half hours before being sent away.[108] The average time children spent testifying was three hours (ranging between 16 minutes and 11 hours).[109]

Moreover, Hanna's analysis of the courtroom transcripts showed that lawyers often still use developmentally inappropriate language when examining children, particularly when cross-examining.[110] Cross-examination questions were overwhelmingly closed, leading and inappropriately complex.[111] Further, in addition to high rates of inappropriate vocabulary and grammar, the cross-examination transcripts still show frequent use of questioning tactics long identified as problematic for children. Moreover, lawyers' questioning styles and techniques did not vary depending on the age of the child.[112]

Whilst the type of inappropriate language used had changed slightly since Davies and Seymour surveyed cross-examination transcripts in 1996, inappropriate language was roughly as common as it had been.

Whilst under cross-examination a significant percentage (of what was still quite a small sample) of children exhibited signs of distress: 35 per cent of the younger children and 25 per cent of the older children wept. Conversely while some had wept in examination-in-chief the numbers were far lower. Only 10 per cent of the younger and 18 per cent of the older children wept at that stage of proceedings.[113]

The 2006 Act also includes a strong restatement of the judge's common law power to disallow unfair, misleading or needlessly repetitive questions, including questions outside the witness's comprehension. This might be expected to prompt judges to take greater control of inappropriate questioning.

Hanna et al found that the frequency of judicial interventions had increased since the mid 1990s. In 1996, Davies and Seymour found that judges intervened only six times (and not out of concern for the intelligibility of the questions) in 26 criminal trials involving child complainants and witnesses.[114] In the 16 transcripts Hanna analysed, judges intervened 38 times in 10 of the 16 trials, often to point

[106] National Guidelines for Agencies Working with Child Witnesses NZ Government, 20 June 2011, 12.

[107] Hanna 'Police and Court Processes' in Hanna et al (n 73) 49. 35% had to come to court on 2 days and 6% had to come back on a third day. One returned to court on 4 days, on 2 of which he testified.

[108] Ibid, 49.

[109] Ibid, 50.

[110] Hanna 'Questioning Children' in Hanna et al (n 73).

[111] Ibid; E Davies, E Henderson and K Hanna 'Facilitating Children to Give Best Evidence: Are There Better Ways to Challenge Children's Testimony?' (2010) 34 *Crim L J* 347, 351–52.

[112] Davies et al (n 111) 65.

[113] Hanna 'Police and Court Processes' in Hanna et al (n 73) 51–52.

[114] Davies and Seymour (n 52); Hanna 'Questioning Children' (n 73) 88.

out comprehension issues.[115] However, these interventions were still far too infrequent to control the full extent of problematic questioning. This finding does not suggest that statutory encouragement of judicial intervention is an effective cure for inappropriate cross-examination.

In summary, there are still significant problems with the situation of child witnesses in the New Zealand criminal court. Access to protective measures is patchy, delay has worsened considerably, and the language of cross-examination in particular remains a serious issue.

Recommendations

In their conclusion, Hanna et al set out a series of recommendations which included both proposals to improve use of the existing legislation and also two far-reaching procedural reforms, based upon a review of current practices internationally.[116]

The first of these was that New Zealand deal with delay by adopting Western Australia's highly successful practice of pre-recording children's entire evidence well in advance of trial. The second was that New Zealand consider introducing some type of intermediary system to alleviate problems with conventional cross-examination. Several jurisdictions in the common law accusatorial tradition already use intermediaries to either relay or to monitor lawyers' questions and children's answers.[117] However, Hanna et al saw flaws in these models because none of them are able to deal with inappropriate questioning completely. Accordingly, they suggested going beyond these models to one based on continental European systems such as Norway's, where specialist examiners (such as psychologists or trained police interviewers) question children under the supervision of judges, prosecutors, and defence counsel. Hanna et al suggested that defence counsel would have the power to compel the specialist examiners to explore issues but that the examiners would conduct the questioning according to standards of best practice in forensic interviewing rather than those of conventional cross-examination.[118]

The Future

These proposals have generated considerable interest in New Zealand. The current Minister of Justice, Simon Power, was already engaged in reforming criminal

[115] Hanna 'Questioning Children' (n 73).

[116] E Henderson 'Innovative Practices in Other Jurisdictions' in Hanna et al (n 73) ch 5.

[117] Eg England, South Africa and the US. See Hanna et al (n 73) ch 5 and Henderson, ch 3.

[118] E Davies, K Hanna and E Henderson 'Implications for Future Legislation and Practice' in Hanna et al (n 73) 173–78.

procedure generally[119] and was investigating further reform to protect adult complainants of sexual offences.[120] Power responded strongly to the new information about the plight of child witnesses, declaring that '[i]mproving the experience of children in the criminal justice system is my first priority', and deploring that 'the adversarial process, and in particular cross-examination, can actually undermine the quality of evidence given by vulnerable children'. At his instigation, the Ministry began exploring further reforms and in particular began to explore models from continental Europe, including Austria and Germany.[121]

Almost simultaneously, in late 2010, the Crown Solicitor for Auckland, relying upon the breadth of the 2006 Act's provision for video-recording, began applying to fully pre-record all children's evidence.[122] In December Judge Wade in the District Court delivered a comprehensive and well-researched judgment allowing one such application.[123] By May 2011, 13 children's evidence had been pre-recorded, using a new Ministry of Justice protocol,[124] and many more applications were filed across the country.

That many practitioners supported significant reform became clear when in early 2011 the Ministry of Justice released an issues paper about child witnesses. The paper floated various reform options, including pre-recording and intermediaries[125] and a presumption in favour of special measures.[126] Unsurprisingly, the Children's Commissioner and the New Zealand Psychological Society were 'strongly in favour' of these proposals.[127] Less predictably, the New Zealand Law Society was also 'strongly in favour of increasing the use of alternative ways', commenting that pre-recording 'should be the usual, but not the mandatory, method of proceeding' and also supporting the exploration of an intermediary system.[128] It seemed that, as in the late 1980s, governmental and professional intent were converging.

Meanwhile, further work in mid 2011, by members of the same team that produced the AUT study of child witnesses discussed above, refined their earlier vision as to

[119] The Summary Proceedings Amendment Act (No 2) 2008 reformed the committal process while the Criminal Disclosure Act 2008 created a new timetabled disclosure regime. The Criminal Procedure Act 2011, now being phased into operation, further reforms pre-trial procedure, introducing, inter alia, a formal case management process and increasing the use of technology in courts www.legislation.govt.nz/act/public/2011/0081/61.0/DLM3359962.html (last accessed 17 February 2012).

[120] Eg see Taskforce on Sexual Violence.

[121] S Power Speech to University of Canterbury Workshop, 19 April 2011; see also S Power, Speech to Working with Sexual Violence Symposium 6 May 2011.

[122] Sections 103, 105 and 107 of the Evidence Act 2006.

[123] *R v Sadlier* unreported, Auckland District Court, CRI-2010-044-4165, 7 December 2010 per Wade J.

[124] Based upon that in Western Australia as described by Jackson, ch 4.

[125] Ministry of Justice Alternative Pretrial and Trial Processes for Child Witnesses in New Zealand's Criminal Justice System ('Issues Paper') 27–28.

[126] Ibid, 16.

[127] F Seymour, S Blackwell and J McDougall Submission on Behalf of the NZ Psychological Society 21 February 2011; Children's Commissioner Submission to Ministry of Justice 21 February 2011.

[128] NZ Law Society Submission to Ministry of Justice on behalf of the NZ Law Society 21 February 2011.

how a more radical intermediary system might work.[129] A series of mock trials were held using approximations of the English,[130] the South African[131] and Norwegian[132] intermediary systems to examine a 'child' (played by a forensic interviewer). Senior barristers acted as prosecutor and defence. An experienced forensic interviewer and a speech and language therapist took turns as the intermediary. The trials were observed by members of the judiciary, the Bar and other interested professionals.

The English and South African systems were perceived as insufficient to prevent poor cross-examination but the Norwegian system raised concerns that defence counsel had insufficient control over the questioning to satisfy the accused's right to challenge the evidence. Discussion amongst the participants and observers introduced the idea of another possible model, the 'topic' model whereby the specialist questions the child via live link from the courtroom in two discrete parts corresponding to evidence-in-chief and cross-examination, under the direction of, first, the prosecutor and then the defence counsel. The questioning proceeds 'topic by topic' with counsel able to direct the examiner as to the next area for questioning.

However, in August 2011 the Court of Appeal released its decision on two of the Auckland pre-recording applications.[133] Whilst accepting that the Evidence Act permits pre-recording, the Court of Appeal limited its use to extreme situations, such as where the witness is dying. The decision is based upon a very reductive interpretation of the benefits of pre-recording and a very suspicious reading of its potential dangers. The decision largely overlooked the extensive empirical evidence and international literature which might have allayed its fears. Thus, in marked contrast to its history of facilitating child witness law reform, the Court effectively halted pre-recording under the existing legislation.[134]

However, in early October 2011 the government announced that it intends to introduce significant new reforms for child witnesses aimed at decreasing stress and increasing the reliability and accuracy of their evidence.[135] The government aims to reduce delays to under six months by introducing:

> a legislative presumption that all children under the age of 12 give their evidence by video record or CCTV [aka live-link]. This will increase efficiency in the court process by removing the requirement that prosecutors make an application to the court … [and] a legislative presumption in favour of pre-recording a child's entire evidence (under the age of 12) including cross-examination and re-examination at a pre-trial hearing conducted in an age appropriate setting. This presumption would apply unless

[129] K Hanna, E Davies, E Henderson and L Hand *Questioning Child Witnesses: Exploring the Benefits and Risks of Intermediary Models* Institute of Public Policy, AUT University, Auckland, September 2011, funded by the New Zealand Law Foundation and the J R Mackenzie Trust.

[130] See Plotnikoff and Woolfson, ch 2.

[131] See Henderson, ch 3.

[132] See Myklebust, ch 8.

[133] *R v M* (CA335/2011); *R v E* (CA339/2011) unreported decision of the NZ Court of Appeal 30 June 2011, per Glazebrook, Chambers and Arnold JJ.

[134] Sleight (n 43); see also E Henderson 'Case and Comment: *R v M, R v E*' (2011) 35 *Crim L J* Oct 2011 300.

[135] Cabinet Domestic Police Committee *Minute of Decision* DOM Min (11) 10/1; Power (2011) n 1.

> there was good justification why a child should not give evidence in this way … [and] a requirement to hold pre-recording evidence hearings within a specified timeframe. This has the potential to reduce the waiting time for children giving evidence to less than six months.[136]

The government also intends '[c]larify[ing] legislation which guides the way in which pre-recording operates in the courts … [so that] a child witness could be recalled for further questioning only when absolutely necessary'.[137] Further, the government proposes to improve the questioning of children by introducing 'specialist intermediaries trained in the cognitive development and language comprehension of children, to improve the questioning of child complainants (under the age of 18) in court'.[138] However, more recently still there are suggestions that the projected reforms are stalling for want of cash.[139]

The model of intermediary system is still under discussion. The Minister of Justice's references to Norwegian, Austrian and German examples suggest that the model will be more radical than those currently used in comparable jurisdictions in the English-speaking legal world.

Conclusion

> 'Nothing is more powerful than an idea whose time is come.'[140]

New Zealand is a small country but one with a great openness to innovation. Whilst its small size enables it to effect change quickly, those changes sometimes lack the momentum the weight of a larger country might give them.

In 1989 New Zealand was the first Commonwealth country to introduce a comprehensive package of special measures for child witnesses. However, it was not able to carry through on all of the options the legislation made available. It is now again on the cusp of potentially revolutionary reforms with the potential to markedly improve both child witnesses' experience of the criminal trial and also the accuracy and reliability of the evidence they give.

New Zealand has great hopes for the future. However, it is also to be hoped that, whatever legislation the government eventually presents, it will make an adequate investment in the necessary infrastructure in order to realise the full potential of these very important ideas—whose time, one hopes, has come.

[136] Power (n 2).
[137] Power (n 1).
[138] Ibid.
[139] D Cheng 'Child Witness Reforms Stalled By Lack of Funding' *New Zealand Herald* 2 Feb 2012.
[140] Victor Hugo *Histoire d'un Crime* 1877.

7

Child Witnesses in Austria

VERENA MURSCHETZ

Introduction

The title of my chapter is, in line with the title of the conference, child witnesses. I have to stress, though, that the specific pre-trial procedures in place in Austria only apply to child victims and not to child witnesses who are not suspected victims of the offence under investigation. Therefore, I focus on the specific procedures that apply to child victims and briefly explain how other child witnesses are questioned. Before describing these specific procedures, I first review the prosecution system and the trial structure in Austria because it differs in many respects from the British, Australian and New Zealand models. To facilitate understanding, I have translated the relevant provisions of the Code of Criminal Procedure and provide these in the Appendix at the end of the chapter.

Prosecution System and Court Structure

Inquisitorial Model

The prosecution system in Austria does not include such characteristics of adversarial trials as cross-examination and is considered inquisitorial though to differentiate the modern procedure from its medieval forbear Austrian lawyers prefer to give it the label 'akkusatorisch'.[1]

Pre-trial Phase

Until 2008, the Austrian pre-trial model involved investigative judges actively leading the investigation and gathering the relevant evidence (through the police).

[1] EE Fabrizy, *Die österreichische Strafprozessordnung*, 11th edn (Vienna, Manz Verlag, 2011) 37–38; V Murschetz, 'The U.S.-American Jury System—An Insight from a Civil Lawyer's Perspective' in G Grabher and A Gamper (eds), *Legal Narratives: European Perspectives on U.S. Law in Cultural Context* (Vienna, Springer Verlag, 2009) 158, 165.

In practice, though, it was mostly the police who conducted the investigation without much interference from the judge. The Criminal Code Reform Act, which entered into force in January 2008, completely restructured the pre-trial phase by putting the public prosecutor in charge of the proceedings and giving the judge the role of independent arbiter deciding on requests by the police or prosecutors to employ coercive measures.[2]

The Role of the Prosecutor

The person officially in charge in the pre-trial phase today is the public prosecutor, who is, since 2008, formally considered an organ of the judiciary by the Constitution (Art 90a B-VG). But it should be stressed that public prosecutors are hierarchically structured and are bound by the instructions of the office of the senior public prosecutor and ultimately of the Minister of Justice. The latter is entitled to give directions to the prosecution office not only regarding policy but also regarding prosecution decisions in individual cases.[3] Public prosecutors are (theoretically) regarded as neutral and objective, and are trusted to weigh up the case for both sides. They are expected to take into account not only inculpatory but also exculpatory evidence.[4] Because prosecutors are officially in charge they should control and oversee the proceedings, ordering investigative measures or carrying them out directly, although this rarely happens in practice.

The Role of the Police—the Relationship between Police and Prosecution Services

In practice, the police conduct the majority of investigations independently of the prosecutors, presenting them with completed files only at the conclusion of the investigation. Contact with the prosecutors tends to happen before that if the police wish to exercise coercive powers that require formal prosecutorial orders and judicial warrants. In these cases, the prosecutors have to formally order these measures and are responsible for seeking judicial warrants or detention orders.[5]

Once investigations by the police are completed, the files are handed to the prosecutors who then decide whether or not to prosecute.[6] The defence have a right to access the file and can request further lines of investigation or the questioning of additional witnesses. Prosecutors or police are obliged to act on such requests, carrying them out or denying them, with the defence having the right to appeal denials to the court.[7]

[2] Code of Criminal Procedure Reform Act *Bundesgestzblatt I* 2004/19; K Schwaighofer, *Die neue Strafprozessordnung* (Vienna, Wiener Universitätsverlag, 2008) 17–32; FA Koenig and C Pilnacek, 'Das neue Strafverfahren—Überblick und Begriffe' (2008) *Österreichische Juristen-Zeitung* 10–17, 56–63.

[3] Fabrizy (n 1) 37–38, 59–60. However, it is rare for the Minister to do so; if he or she does, the instruction must be in written form and accompanied by reasons.

[4] Ibid, 36.

[5] M Vogl, '§ 99 'top' in H Fuchs and E Ratz (eds), *Wiener Kommentar zur Strafprozessordnung* (Vienna, Manz Verlag, 2008) 22.

[6] Fabrizy (n 1) 242–43.

[7] C Bertel and A Venier, *Strafprozessrecht*, 5th edn (Vienna, Manz Verlag, 2011) 37–42.

Decisions about whether or not to prosecute are primarily governed by the 'principle of legality'. In general, police and prosecution have to investigate all offences that come to their attention and prosecutors have to continue proceedings if there is sufficient evidence.[8] Only very limited reasons not to prosecute, such us the use of diversion, exist, and these are not elaborated in this chapter.[9]

The Role of the Judge

In the pre-trial phase, judges are limited to decisions relating to the use of coercive investigative measures such as search and surveillance, to pre-trial detention, and to the contradictory interrogation of child victims, as explained in detail below.[10]

The Importance of the Pre-trial Investigative Stage

The pre-trial phase is a crucial and important part of the Austrian criminal procedure. During this phase, all relevant evidence is gathered and collected in the case dossier. If the prosecutors decide to bring charges, they file those in court, together with the supporting case dossier containing all the evidence considered important, including all the relevant witness statements, exhibits etc. All information relevant not just to the determination of guilt but also to sentencing (eg the defendant's prior convictions and other background information) is included. Because there are no separate conviction and sentencing stages, judges are required to consider both together, using all relevant evidence.

Witness statements are generally prepared by the police who conduct pre-trial questioning, writing the witnesses' statements for signature. Hardly any specific rules of evidence apply. So long as information is relevant, it may be presented in the dossier. The defence has a general right to access the case dossier in the pre-trial phase and may request that further statements be added and that additional matters be investigated. If the request is declined, an appeal is possible.[11] The right to access is limited only when ongoing investigations would be endangered by access. Once dossiers reach the court, judges control the case. It is their job to decide if the evidence is sufficient for the matter to go to trial, which they usually do. The judges then set trial dates and summon the relevant witnesses (taken from the dossier).[12]

To complete the picture it should also be mentioned that guilty pleas cannot be offered, and that plea bargains are not possible in the pre-trial and trial phases.

8 Fabrizy (n 1) 37–38, 516.

9 See for instance §§ 191, 192, 194 Code of Criminal Procedure.

10 Bertel and Venier (n 7) 64–65; Fabrizy (n 1) 252–53.

11 Fabrizy (n 1) 124–28, 216–17.

12 Again the importance of the dossier has to be mentioned. It stems from the fact that it is used by the trial judge to prepare for the trial and during the trial as well. Even though all the evidence, meaning all the statements and information, should be orally presented at the trial as well, the judge will always keep in mind what the witnesses and the accused have stated to the police in the investigative phase. Bertel and Venier (n 7) 19.

The prosecution is required to proceed with cases if none of the reasons for non-prosecution (such as for diversion[13]) apply. The general principle governing the Austrian Criminal Procedure is what could be translated as the principle of 'material truth-finding'. The proceedings are supposed to discover the 'material' truth not just the formal truth as presented by the parties. Therefore confessions do not end the proceedings but require the courts to be convinced by independent evidence presented at trial that the statements are true.

The Trial Stage

Court Types

There are three types of first instance courts:

- — One professional judge sitting alone in either the District or the Regional Court will decide on minor cases, generally cases with possible sentences of up to one year or up to five years' imprisonment, respectively.[14]
- — One professional judge and two lay judges hear cases together in Regional Courts when the alleged offences could require possible sentences of more than 5 years' imprisonment.[15]
- — A jury of eight lay judges and three professional judges hear cases involving the most serious offences such as murder, aggravated robbery, and treason in the Regional Court. The jury of eight lay judges independently decides on guilt or acquittal without giving reasons.[16] The sentence is then determined together with the three professional judges. Only a very limited number of cases fall under the jurisdiction of such juries.[17]

The Trial

Role of the Judge

Judges are in charge of trial proceedings. They play active and dominant roles, deciding which evidence to hear and questioning the witnesses.

Principles of 'Orality' and 'Immediacy'

Even though case dossiers containing all evidence are available to trial judges, the main trial is supposed to operate on the basis of the principles of 'orality' and 'immediacy'. All evidence has to be presented orally in court and the immediate or first-hand evidence, rather than written statements, need to be presented at trial.

[13] § 192 Code of Criminal Procedure.

[14] § 31 Absatz 4 Code of Criminal Procedure.

[15] § 31 Absatz 3 Code of Criminal Procedure.

[16] A description of the specifics of the Austrian jury trial can be found in Murschetz (n 1) 165–71.

[17] § 31 Absatz 2 Code of Criminal Procedure. S Seiler, *Strafprozessrecht*, 11th edn (Vienna, Wiener Universitätsverlag, 2010) 42–45.

In principle, therefore, fact-finders should be persuaded of the guilt of the accused on the basis of oral evidence presented in court, not on the basis of the statements contained in the pre-trial dossier.[18] In some exceptional circumstances, however, written statements may substitute for direct evidence. The exceptions relevant to this chapter are:

— if the witness has died, cannot be found, is very sick or too old, is out of the country for a long period, or is for other significant reasons not available to the trial court;[19]
— if the witness rightfully refuses to testify at trial and the statements were made during the 'contradictory interrogation' procedure, which is the specific procedure used for child victims, explained in detail later;[20]
— if the witnesses refuses to testify at trial, without having the right to do so.[21]

Case Dossier

Notwithstanding the limitations on the use of written statements instead of oral testimony, the material contained in the case dossiers is used by judges not just in preparation for trial, but to conduct trials, carry out the questioning and to be able to give a reasoned verdict. Without the dossiers, judges would be dependent on the evidence presented by the parties at trial, which is not foreseen in the Austrian system.

To appreciate the importance of the statements collected at the pre-trial stage, one has to imagine witnesses or defendants not remembering some of the details at trial, changing their minds or not saying much. Under these circumstances, judges may confront the witnesses or defendants with their pre-trial testimony and eventually might also place more weight on what was said at the pre-trial stage. This can happen because the statements were made closer in time to the events in question without opportunity for reflection or interference by counsel.

One problem with this approach is that there is no real equality of arms at the pre-trial stage and the rights of the accused are not adequately protected. For example, when witness statements are obtained and recorded by the police, generally neither the accused nor defence counsel have a right to be present or to ask questions. Furthermore, police can prohibit counsel from being present when the accused are interrogated and even when they are allowed to be present, the Code prohibits lawyers from actively participating in any way.[22]

[18] K Kirchbacher, '§ 252' in H Fuchs and E Ratz (eds), *Wiener Kommentar zur Strafprozessordnung* (Vienna, Manz Verlag, 2009) 5; Bertel and Venier (n 7) 18–20; Fabrizy (n 1) 48–50.
[19] § 252 Absatz 1 Ziffer 1 Code of Criminal Procedure.
[20] § 252 Absatz 1 Ziffer 2a Code of Criminal Procedure.
[21] § 252 Absatz 1 Ziffer 3 Code of Criminal Procedure.
[22] The inadequacy of this rule is commented on in Murschetz 'Das Recht auf Verteidigerbeistand während der (ersten) Einvernahme § 164 Abs 2 StPO—geglückte Regelung oder unzulänglicher Kompromiss?' (2010) *Österreichische Juristen-Zeitung* 650–56.

Presentation of Evidence

The ways in which evidence is presented in the Austrian system differ vastly from the adversarial prosecution model and affect the way the testimony of child witnesses is introduced.[23] Because judges play dominant and active roles, they decide which evidence to hear and they do the questioning. Only secondarily can prosecuting and defence lawyers question witnesses as well. Questioning by the defence is probably less confrontational and more neutral than in adversarial systems, because aggressive questioning might suggest that the judges' questioning was inadequate. Because judges conduct the questioning, no formal distinction between prosecution and defence witnesses exists.

The Austrian system does not contain what Spencer has called 'the adversarial package'. In particular, there is no distinction between examination-in-chief and cross-examination. Evidence is instead presented in the form of a narrative, with witnesses allowed to recount events without significant interruption by the judges or the parties. As Spencer pointed out in the introductory chapter, the witness 'is questioned by a person operating from a neutral standpoint, whose aim is to get the witness to tell the truth'. Questioning is not conducted by a party 'whose agenda is to persuade the court that their account is incomplete, or that they are lying or mistaken'.

Hardly any evidentiary rules are applied. Specifically, there is no need for corroboration and a hearsay rule does not exist. The rules that do exist apply to evidence given by all witnesses and do not deal with irrelevancy or prejudice.[24] Rather, the principle of 'free assessment of evidence' applies, meaning that judges are only guided by scientific knowledge and the principles of logic and common sense.[25] Judges are trusted to weigh the evidence correctly, making the required distinctions between hearsay and immediate evidence, or between trustworthy and unreliable evidence etc.

Accused persons have the right to remain silent. They are always asked to testify first; if they then wish to exercise the right to remain silent, they must refuse to answer questions asked of them. Defence counsel do not decide whether or not to call the accused as witnesses; in practice, they tend to testify to avoid giving the impression that they are guilty by refusing to speak. When the accused do give evidence, they are not required to tell the truth but they cannot untruthfully implicate others in the offence.[26]

The Role of Victims

Victims in General

Victims have specific rights both before and during trial, including the rights to be kept informed about case progression, to be given access to case dossiers, and

[23] Regarding the differences between an adversarial model and the Austrian system see Murschetz, (n 1) 158, 165.

[24] Bertel and Venier (n 7) 129.

[25] Seiler (n 17) 36; also Bertel and Venier (n 7) 20.

[26] Fabrizy (n 1) 558–59.

the right to pose questions for witnesses at trial. They also have the right to appeal against prosecution decisions not to lay charges[27] and the right to be present at the 'contradictory interrogation'.[28]

Victims of Sexual Offences or Offences Involving Threats or Violence

In addition to these rights, victims of sexual offences or offences involving threats or violence also have access to free legal representation[29] and 'psycho-social' support both before and during the trial, regardless of their financial capacity.[30] The psycho-social support is intended to prepare victims to withstand the proceedings with all their attendant burdens.[31]

Child Witnesses (Under the Age of 14)

The Code of Criminal Procedure does not specify an age limit for witnesses. Case law and literature suggest that from the age of five years children are generally considered to be qualified as witnesses, whereas between three and four years of age they have to be specifically qualified.[32] Child witnesses under the age of 14 also have the right to have support persons present during questioning.[33] They can be family members, but are mostly people working for victim-protection organisations.

[27] There exists no general right of private prosecution. Only a small number of specified offences must be brought by way of a private prosecution. Other than that, if the prosecutor decides not to press charges, the victim is entitled to an appeal (to the single judge of the lower court) against this decision. Appeals are brought frequently, but are overruled in most cases. If the court does decide to act on the appeal, it can direct the prosecutor to carry out further investigations or to review the case, but it cannot instruct the prosecutor to lay charges. In case of a diversion proceeding the victim is not entitled to appeal against a prosecution decision to divert. In practice though, the victim will have been consulted about it in advance. Seiler (n 17) 26, 182–83, E McDonald and Y Tinsley, *From "Real Rape" to Real justice* (Wellington, VUP 2011) 464.

[28] § 66 Code of Criminal Procedure, see Bertel and Venier (n 7) 48.

[29] This representation is funded by the state at the rate of € 78 per hour.

[30] If the victim has suffered loss or damage as a result of the offence, he or she is entitled to take part in the proceedings as a 'civil participant' in order to make a (civil) compensation claim. For that matter he or she is entitled to have legal representation at the trial. The legal counsel may then participate in the proceedings and set out the basis for the reparation claim. He or she may ask for further evidence to be heard for the purposes of proving the claim and may also ask the witnesses questions. In case of a 'civil participant' the court is then obliged to make a finding as to the claim as part of the overall verdict, by sustaining or overruling it or by not deciding on it and directing the participant to seek for compensation in civil proceedings. If the prosecutor decides to drop the charge, after he or she has filed it with the court, the victim can take over the prosecution as a 'subsidiary prosecutor' (§ 72 Code of Criminal Procedure) McDonald and Tinsley (n 27) 464, 465.

[31] Bertel and Venier (n 7) 49.

[32] HJ Bart, 'Kinder als Zeugen im Strafverfahren—insbesondere als Opfer sexuellen Mißbrauchs' (1998) *Österreichische Juristen-Zeitung* 818, 819.

[33] § 160 Absatz 3 Code of Criminal Procedure.

Testimony of Child Victims

Child Victims

Child victims are victims who have not completed their 14th year of age at the time of the questioning.

Contradictory Interrogation Procedure

Development and General Definition

Previously, the evidence of child victims was commonly introduced at trial in the form of statements made during police questioning at the pre-trial stage, without the parties being present. Even though, as mentioned earlier, witnesses are (in accordance with the principles of 'orality' and 'immediacy') generally required to testify orally at trial, this is not compulsory when witnesses are 'unavailable' for significant reasons. Child victims, especially of sexual offences, were frequently considered 'unavailable' because experts usually considered the repeated questioning involved too traumatic and likely to cause further psychological harm to the child victims.[34] This arrangement was of course considered problematic with respect to the defendants' rights to a fair trial as set forth in Art 6 ECHR (European Convention on Human Rights). Therefore a procedure, termed 'contradictory interrogation', was introduced in 1993. It was designed on the one hand to mitigate the trauma and stress suffered by child witnesses giving evidence at trial and on the other hand to guarantee specifically the defendants' right to confront witnesses.

Under this procedure, victims under the age of 14 provide their evidence at a 'contradictory' pre-trial hearing. It is called contradictory because the parties—prosecution, defendant and (other) victims—have a right to be present and to use their right to witness-confrontation, and are therefore able to contradict or confront the witness. Having participated in this contradictory interrogation procedure, children have the right to refuse any further testimony. Instead of appearing again, the children's statements are recorded and played at trial.[35]

[34] K Schwaighofer, 'Anmerkungen zu einigen Zeugen- und Opferschutzbestimmungen der StPO und ihre Umsetzung durch die Rechtsprechung' in R Moos (ed), *Festschrift für Udo Jesionek zum 65. Geburtstag* (Vienna and Graz, Neuer Wissenschaftlicher Verlag, 2002) 501–04; Bart (n 32) 818, 819.

[35] K Kirchbacher, '§ 165 StPO' in H Fuchs and E Ratz (eds), *Wiener Kommentar zur Strafprozessordnung* (Vienna, Manz Verlag, 2009) 53–54; Schwaighofer, ibid, 499–500.

Requirements

Timing

The contradictory interrogation usually happens during the pre-trial stage and in addition to questioning of victims by the police (and sometimes by the prosecutor), rather than instead of such questioning. A pilot project in Vienna is currently evaluating this requirement for double questioning by exploring whether contradictory interrogation, ideally within a month of the initial report to the police, could substitute for police questioning. The pilot project also requires the participation of two rather than the single expert witness provided for at present.[36]

Parties Involved

In the existing procedure, the contradictory interrogation is conducted privately, before a 'pre-trial judge', with the prosecutor, defence and victims having the right to be present. The questioning is conducted, on behalf of both sides, either by the judge or an expert, subject to the pre-trial judge's decision, depending on the vulnerability of the child. During questioning of the child, support persons are always present.[37]

Procedure

Examination in Separate Child-Friendly Rooms

If the child is under the age of 14 and the offence is of a sexual nature, the child has to be interviewed in a separate room, without the parties present. This applies automatically. If the child is a victim of any other type of crime, the use of two rooms is mandatory if requested by the victim or the prosecutor. Separate rooms are used to guarantee that children do not have to come in contact with the accused. The rooms are in the court house and are considered child friendly, decorated with little chairs, toys etc. They are usually equipped with microphones and two video cameras showing the child victim from the front and the side. The parties can view and hear the questioning live on two TV screens in a separate courtroom, but there is no live connection to the parties in the interview room.[38]

Examination by Judge

If a judge is asking the questions, he or she will be in the same room as the victims and support persons. Once the judge has finished questioning, he or she goes to the other room and ask the parties what additional questions they have. The judge then returns to the room in which the children are located and puts those additional questions. If one of the parties objects to any of the proposed

[36] See below.

[37] Kirchbacher (n 35) 56; H Hinterhofer, *Zeugenschutz und Zeugnisverweigerungsrecht im österreichischen Strafprozess* (Vienna, Wiener Universitätsverlag, 2004) 118.

[38] Kirchbacher (n 35) 54–55; K Bruckmüller and IC Friedrich, 'Getrennte Räume in Gerichtsgebäuden zum Schutz von Opfern einer Straftat' (2008) *Richterzeitung* 93.

questions, the judge determines whether the questions are appropriate. Judges can also refuse to ask questions suggested by the parties on their own initiative, if they consider them unnecessary, inappropriate or irrelevant. The judges' pre-trial refusals to pose questions cannot be challenged per se. The defence can only mention at trial that they wanted to ask such questions and then appeal any resulting convictions.[39] Because there is no live connection, the parties cannot interrupt, intervene or object to the questioning. This can only be done when the judges return to the rooms where the parties are situated.[40]

The judges conducting contradictory interrogations are not the judges conducting the main trials, but are pre-trial judges. In the Austrian system, pre-trial judges are never allowed to hear cases at trial, because they are considered biased. This accusatorial model thus constitutionally requires the investigation process and the trial process to be separated.[41]

Examination by Expert

Alternatively, experts can carry out the questioning. In such cases, the experts sit with the children, who also have support persons. The judges, prosecutors and defence lawyers again are not connected to the hearing but can follow it on a TV screen. The preferred practice is for judges to communicate their questions to the experts and for the judges and parties to offer further questions—if necessary—during brief intermissions.[42]

Who conducts these interviews varies from place to place. Within the jurisdiction of the Innsbruck Regional Court, almost all contradictory interrogations are carried out by judges, whereas in Vienna the questioning is almost always conducted by experts rather than judges. The contradictory hearings are transcribed and may also be recorded at the judges' discretion. Today video-recording is the standard procedure.

Consequences

If child victims have given evidence in contradictory hearings, they have the right to refuse any further testimony before or at trial. Before the contradictory questioning starts, therefore, children are informed of their rights and duties, including the right to refuse any further appearances. Children are asked at this stage if they prefer not to testify again, and if so, will not be summoned or contacted again. The right to refuse further examination therefore exists once children have been subjected to contradictory interrogation, no matter how much time has passed between then and trial. In case of very long delays it might be sensible to

[39] Defence can ask for a 'Zwischenerkenntnis' (an intermediate decision) and appeal on grounds of § 281 Absatz 1 Ziffer 4 Code of Criminal Procedure.

[40] Kirchbacher (n 35) 58; McDonald and Tinsley (n 27) 465–67.

[41] Bertel and Venier (n 7) 64–65; Seiler (n 17) 59, 120.

[42] M Eder-Rieder and C Frank, 'Rechtsbelehrung durch den psychiatrischen-psychologischen Sachverständigen gegenüber den zu befragenden bzw zu untersuchenden Zeugen und Beschuldigten im Strafprozess' (2001) *Richterzeitung* 186, 188.

ask victims again whether they wanted to exercise their rights, but this is not done regularly.[43] Children must decide whether to exercise their right to refuse further testimony themselves. It is not up their legal guardians.[44]

Of course, victims could waive their rights and choose to give evidence again, but this only happens in cases of adult victims of sexual offences. When it does occur, the same procedure as in the pre-trial stage is used: the victims are questioned by trial judges in a room separated from the parties and give evidence via video. Such re-examinations hardly ever happen.

If contradictory interrogations have been carried out, the transcripts are read and the recordings are presented at trial. Case law has established that not only these records but also all other written statements given before the contradictory procedure may be presented at trial instead of 'live' testimony.[45]

Problems/Issues

The contradictory interrogation proceedings allow prosecutors and defendants to participate, but do not require their presence. The Code permits the procedure to be used even in the absence of the prosecutor or the defendant. If, for instance, defendants have been summoned properly and do not appear, the contradictory interrogations go ahead—something which happens now and then.[46]

Furthermore, defence counsel are allowed to be present, but do not have to be there, so there is no mandatory representation. This is especially problematic when the main trial requires mandatory representation, as do most sexual offences. In these cases, the questioning during the main trial has to be carried out in the presence of counsel, whereas questioning during the pre-trial contradictory hearing, which substitutes for questioning at the main trial, may take place without legal assistance. Because these proceedings do not involve mandatory representation, defendants have no right to free legal representation.[47] In an obiter dictum at the end of last year, however, the Supreme Court indicated that this rule might not stand much longer.[48]

Difficulties may also arise because the parties are in different rooms when the victims are being questioned. Because there is no two-way communication,

[43] Hinterhofer (n 37) 332.

[44] Ibid, 330. Some require the consent of the child for exercising the right to refuse further testimony, but the consent of the legal guardian if the child wants to waive his right: ibid, 331.

[45] Kirchbacher (n 18) 23; Fabrizy (n 1) 408, 573. As long both parties knew or could have known of their content.

[46] A Birklbauer, 'Anforderungen an eine kontradiktorische Zeugenvernehmung außerhalb der Hauptverhandlung' (2002) *Anwaltsblatt* 512, 514.

[47] K Schwaighofer, 'Zur Verwertbarkeit kontradiktorischer Zeugenaussagen' (2006) *Österreichische Juristen-Zeitung* 235, 237.

[48] E Ratz, '§ 281 Abs 1 Z 2 und 3 StPO' in H Fuchs and E Ratz (eds), *Wiener Kommentar zur Strafprozessordnung* (Vienna, Manz Verlag, 2011) 25–26.

At least the right to free legal representation under the rule of § 61 Abs 2 Z 3 StPO might apply, which grants assistance of counsel paid for by the state in cases dealing with difficult issues of facts or issues of law, EvBl 2010/63.

it is impossible for the parties to object to the ways some questions are posed or to ask for clarification. Instead, the parties have to wait until the break to ask for additional questions. Initially, communication between the judge and counsel was permitted by way of wireless microphone, but this practice stopped because it was found that the communication could be overheard using walkie talkies.

Another very problematic issue is that further questioning is not possible when further matters come to light after the pre-trial hearing which the parties, especially the defence, would like to question the child about. Sometimes during further investigation or during the main trial new evidence or new facts do indeed come to light and are relevant to the case. Case law has established that, by giving evidence in the contradictory interrogation, child victims have the full and unlimited right to refuse to give any further testimony and cannot be coerced to appear again. However, the Supreme Court has indicated that defence requests for further questioning might be valid in exceptional cases where decisive new facts come to light, provided the defence can demonstrate that the witness might be willing to testify again.[49] In any event, child victims cannot be coerced to testify. Victims must voluntarily agree to appear again, and this hardly ever happens.

Testimony of Child Witnesses who are not Victims

As mentioned before, contradictory interrogation is mandatory for child victims.[50] In such cases the following rules apply. If the child is under 14 years of age and the offence is a sexual offence contradictory interrogation in two rooms is mandatory. When children are victims of any other offences, contradictory interrogation in two rooms is mandatory if the children request it. The same applies to adult victims of sexual offences who then gain the right to refuse any further testimony or questioning (especially any re-appearance at trial).

Contradictory interrogations are possible for child witnesses who are not victims as well, either upon the victim's or the prosecutor's request, at the judge's discretion. The procedure is always allowed if there is any danger that the questioning of the witness will not be possible during trial for factual or legal reasons.[51] Importantly, however, child witnesses who are not victims do not have the right to

[49] Ratz (n 48) 25–26; Bart (n 32) 818, 822.

[50] § 165 Absatz 3 Code of Criminal Procedure.

[51] Ultimately it is a matter for the judge to determine whether the contradictory interrogation procedure ought to be used in such cases, and he or she will usually be guided by what the victim wants.

refuse any further testimony once they have been subjected to the contradictory questioning. They are summoned to appear again at trial.[52]

Testimony of Adult Victims of Sexual Offences

Adult victims of sexual offences have to be questioned via contradictory interrogation in the pre-trial phase if they request it and they have the right to refuse any further testimony once the interrogation has taken place. Other witnesses can request the procedure, but do not gain the right to refuse further appearances.

Conclusion

I hope this chapter has clearly demonstrated the way child victims give evidence in Austrian criminal proceedings. The model presented is a workable solution in a prosecution system following inquisitorial principles, especially because such systems do not call for (live) cross-examination of witnesses. As such the 'contradictory interrogation model' limits the negative effects on children and also grants (some) defence rights to the accused. It is not flawless, though, especially with regard to the lack of mandatory legal representation for defendants when victims/witnesses are questioned and the fact that new evidence cannot be sufficiently contested. Compared to the previous rules, however, the model appears to be a major improvement.

[52] Bart (n 32) 818, 822.

Appendix

Relevant Provisions in the Code of Criminal Procedure (Strafprozessordnung, or StPO)[53]

Section 156 (1): The obligation to testify does not apply to the following:

1. Persons who would have to testify in proceedings against a relative …;
2. Persons who might have been injured by the act alleged against the accused who are under the age of fourteen at the time of their examination, or who might have been injured in their sexual sphere by the accused, provided that the parties to the proceedings have had the opportunity to participate in a previous contradictory examination (section 165, 247).

Section 165: **(1)** Where the examination of the accused or of a witness at trial could become impossible for factual or for legal reasons, a contradictory examination, together with audio or visual recording, may be held.

(2) The court must conduct the contradictory examination at the request of the public prosecutor, in which case sections 249 and 250 shall apply. The court must grant the public prosecutor, the accused, the victim, … and their representatives the opportunity to participate in the examination and to ask questions.

(3) At the request of the public prosecutor or where the court so rules ex officio, during the examination of a witness, in the interests of that witness (and in particular on account of his youth or his emotional or physical condition), or in any case where this is necessary to establish the truth, the opportunity to participate shall be restricted so that the participants in the proceedings (paragraph 2) and their representatives can exercise their right to ask questions through an audio-visual transmission without being present at the examination. In such a case an expert may be given the task of conducting the examination, in particular where the witness is under the age of fourteen. In any case precautions shall be taken to ensure so far as possible that the witness does not have to come in contact with the accused or any other party to the proceedings.

(4) A witness who is under the age of fourteen and who might have been injured in his sexual sphere by the accused must be examined by the court in the way described in paragraph 3. All other witnesses mentioned in section 156 (1) numbers 1 and 2 must be examined this way if they themselves or the public prosecutor so requests.

Section 252 (1): Transcripts of the depositions of the co-accused and witnesses, transcripts of other evidence, official memoranda and other official documents containing statements of witnesses or of the co-accused, experts' testimony as well as audio and visual recordings of the examination of the co-accused or witnesses may be read out or shown in the following cases only. In all other cases they shall be considered null and void:

[53] Author's translation.

1. when the witness has since died; when his whereabouts is unknown or when his appearance can not be arranged on account of old age, illness, weakness or a distant place of residence or other significant reason;
2. when the witness in the main trial contradicts his prior testimony;
2a. when the witness lawfully refuses to give further testimony and the parties were given the opportunity to participate in a judicial examination (section 165 …);
3. when the witness refuses further testimony without having the right to do so; and finally
4. when the prosecutor and accused agree to it.

Aussagebefreiung

§ 156. *(1) Von der Pflicht zur Aussage sind befreit:*

1. *Personen, die im Verfahren gegen einen Angehörigen (§ 72 StGB) aussagen sollen, wobei die durch eine Ehe oder eingetragene Partnerschaft begründete Eigenschaft einer Person als Angehöriger für die Beurteilung der Berechtigung zur Aussageverweigerung aufrecht bleibt, auch wenn die Ehe oder eingetragene Partnerschaft nicht mehr besteht;*
2. *Personen, die durch die dem Beschuldigten zur Last gelegte Straftat verletzt worden sein könnten und zur Zeit ihrer Vernehmung das vierzehnte Lebensjahr noch nicht vollendet haben oder in ihrer Geschlechtssphäre verletzt worden sein könnten, wenn die Parteien Gelegenheit hatten, sich an einer vorausgegangenen kontradiktorischen Einvernahme zu beteiligen (§§ 165, 247).*

Kontradiktorische Vernehmung des Beschuldigten oder eines Zeugen

§ 165. *(1) Eine kontradiktorische Vernehmung sowie die Ton- oder Bildaufnahme einer solchen Vernehmung des Beschuldigten oder eines Zeugen ist zulässig, wenn zu besorgen ist, dass die Vernehmung in einer Hauptverhandlung aus tatsächlichen oder rechtlichen Gründen nicht möglich sein werde.*

(2) Die kontradiktorische Vernehmung hat das Gericht auf Antrag der Staatsanwaltschaft in sinngemäßer Anwendung der Bestimmungen der §§ 249 und 250 durchzuführen (§ 104). Das Gericht hat der Staatsanwaltschaft, dem Beschuldigten, dem Opfer, dem Privatbeteiligten und deren Vertretern Gelegenheit zu geben, sich an der Vernehmung zu beteiligen und Fragen zu stellen.

(3) Bei der Vernehmung eines Zeugen ist in seinem Interesse, besonders mit Rücksicht auf sein geringes Alter oder seinen seelischen oder gesundheitlichen Zustand, oder im Interesse der Wahrheitsfindung auf Antrag der Staatsanwaltschaft oder von Amts wegen die Gelegenheit zur Beteiligung derart zu beschränken, dass die Beteiligten des Verfahrens (Abs. 2) und ihre Vertreter die Vernehmung unter Verwendung technischer Einrichtungen zur Wort- und Bildübertragung mitverfolgen und ihr Fragerecht ausüben können, ohne bei der Befragung anwesend zu sein. Insbesondere wenn der Zeuge das vierzehnte Lebensjahr noch nicht vollendet hat, kann in diesem Fall ein Sachverständiger mit der Befragung beauftragt werden. In jedem Fall ist dafür Sorge zu tragen, dass eine Begegnung des Zeugen mit dem Beschuldigten und anderen Verfahrensbeteiligten möglichst unterbleibt.

(4) *Einen Zeugen, der das vierzehnte Lebensjahr noch nicht vollendet hat und durch die dem Beschuldigten zur Last gelegte Straftat in seiner Geschlechtssphäre verletzt worden sein könnte, hat das Gericht in jedem Fall auf die in Abs. 3 beschriebene Art und Weise zu vernehmen, die übrigen im § 156 Abs. 1 Z 1 und 2 erwähnten Zeugen dann, wenn sie oder die Staatsanwaltschaft dies beantragen.*

§ 252. (1) *Protokolle über die Vernehmung von Mitbeschuldigten und Zeugen, Protokolle über die Aufnahme von Beweisen, Amtsvermerke und andere amtliche Schriftstücke, in denen Aussagen von Zeugen oder Mitbeschuldigten festgehalten worden sind, Gutachten von Sachverständigen sowie Ton- und Bildaufnahmen über die Vernehmung von Mitbeschuldigten oder Zeugen dürfen bei sonstiger Nichtigkeit nur in den folgenden Fällen verlesen oder vorgeführt werden.*

1. *wenn die Vernommenen in der Zwischenzeit gestorben sind; wenn ihr Aufenthalt unbekannt oder ihr persönliches Erscheinen wegen ihres Alters, wegen Krankheit oder Gebrechlichkeit oder wegen entfernten Aufenthaltes oder aus anderen erheblichen Gründen füglich nicht bewerkstelligt werden konnte;*
2. *wenn die in der Hauptverhandlung Vernommenen in wesentlichen Punkten von ihren früher abgelegten Aussagen abweichen;*

2a. *wenn Zeugen die Aussage berechtigt verweigern (§§ 156, 157 und 158) und die Staatsanwaltschaft und der Angeklagte Gelegenheit hatten, sich an einer gerichtlichen Vernehmung zu beteiligen (§§ 165, 247);*

3. *wenn Zeugen, ohne dazu berechtigt zu sein, oder wenn Mitangeklagte die Aussage verweigern; endlich;*
4. *wenn über die Vorlesung Ankläger und Angeklagter einverstanden sind.*

8

The Position in Norway

TROND MYKLEBUST

Introduction

Since 1913, Norway has pioneered effective forensic interviewing of children. The legal process in Norway differs from that in many other countries to the extent that alleged child victims do not appear as live witnesses in court. Instead the video is 'evidence-in-chief' replacing the children's need to testify in open court. Instead children can put the incidents behind them and, if necessary, receive help from the child welfare service. In this chapter I explain how Norway seems to have found a way to ensure that child witnesses provide valuable information, early, and are then freed from the legal processes, without compromising the rights of accused perpetrators.

Demographic Data

With a land mass of 323,787 km^2 and 4.9 million inhabitants, Norway has the second lowest population density in Europe, with 15 inhabitants per km^2. A rough climate, poor soil and difficult terrain mean that a large part of the country is unsuitable for settlements or agriculture, and almost 80 per cent of the population live in urban settlements. According to Statistics Norway,[1] (depicted in Figure 1) 1,114,400 (23 per cent) of the 4.9 million inhabitants in January 2011 were under 18 years of age. Of these, approximately 368,000 were between 0 and 5 years, 425,000 between 6 and 12 years, 193,000 between 13 and 15 years, and 128,000 between 16 and 18 years, with 79 per cent of the children living in urban settlements. In 2010 about 13,800 children entered the country as immigrants, while 4,800 migrated from Norway. The majority (9,500) of the immigrant children came from Poland[2] while the majority of immigrant parents are from Pakistan, Somalia and Iraq. In total, immigrants and people born in Norway to immigrant parents constitute 600,900 persons or 12.2 per cent of Norway's total population.[3]

1 www.ssb.no/.

2 www.ssb.no/emner/02/barn_og_unge/2011/bef/.

3 www.ssb.no/innvandring_en/.

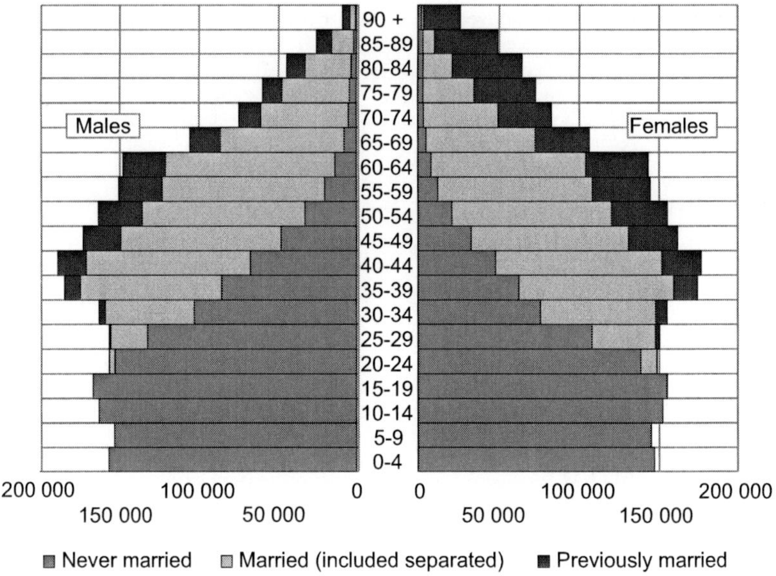

Figure 1. Population by age, gender and marital status 1 January 2011[1]
Source: www.ssb.no

Police Education and Training

All police officers in Norway complete a three-year bachelor's degree at the Norwegian Police University College (NPUC) before beginning patrol work or embarking on further specialised training also available at NPUC. Approximately 40 per cent of the undergraduate students at NPUC have credits from other universities or university colleges before they start studying at NPUC, and the average applicant is 22.5 years old.[4] The first and third years of undergraduate study mainly involve theoretical courses on campus, while in their second year the students are assigned to one of the 27 police districts in Norway for practical training under the guidance of personal mentors and supervisors. The NPUC students are not employed or salaried by the police. Like other bachelor's students they are entitled to financial grants and loans from Lånekassen[5] (the Norwegian state educational loan fund). In 2010 and 2011, 720 students were accepted each year with 37 and 39 per cent respectively being female. Of the approximately

[4] Statistics from the NPUC database presented at the Norwegian Police University College Board meeting 4.10.2011.

[5] www.lanekassen.no/.

8,000[6] serving officers in Norway 22 per cent are female and the government is committed to raising this percentage.[7]

The Number of Investigative Interviews of Children

Although the numbers of reported offences, including the numbers of reported cases of child sexual abuse (CSA) are recorded, there is no official public register of the number of investigative interviews of children conducted every year. However, the author has been collecting the exact numbers of interviews from each of the police districts from the start of videotaped interviewing in 1994. As illustrated in Figure 2, the number increased tenfold from 1994 to 2010 with 207 and 2,073 interviews respectively.

These statistics suggest that the police take children more seriously today, although one should also bear in mind that there has been a general increase in the number of criminal cases in the same period, and that an increasing number of these interviews are not related to sexual abuse. Nevertheless, several senior investigators argue[8] that the communication and cooperation between the

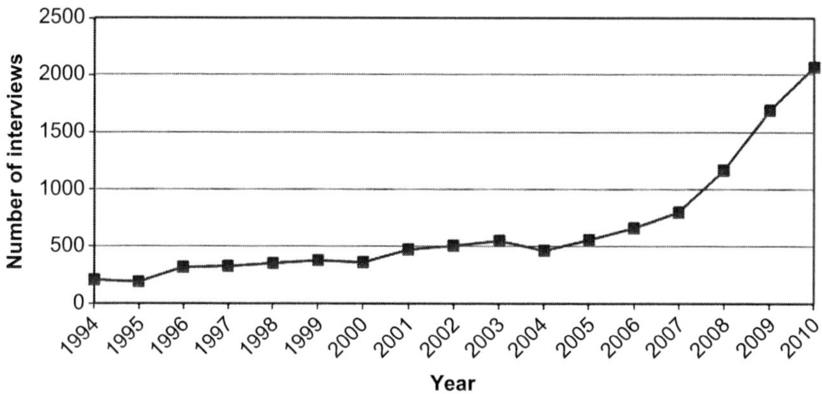

Figure 2. The number of investigative interviews of children 1994–2010

[6] Reported by the Norwegian Police Directorate, August 2011. Personal conversation: Kvernen, 26t September 2011.

[7] Politidirektoratet *Politiet mot 2020 Bemannings og kompetansebehov i politiet Rapport mai 2008* [The Norwegian police towards 2020. Manning and competence requirements. Report May 2008] (Oslo, Politidirektoratet, 2008).

[8] T Myklebust 'Politiavhør som metode' [Investigative interviews as a method] in T Myklebust and G Thomassen (eds) *Arbeidsmetoder og metodearbeid i politiet* [Working methods within the police] (Oslo, PHS Forskning, 2010) 45–97.

child welfare service, the social services and themselves have changed positively, resulting in children being interviewed earlier and more often.

The Norwegian Criminal Justice System

As already indicated in the first chapter of this book, in the international literature,[9] in official web pages[10] and in publications by the Norwegian Ministry of Justice and Police,[11] Norway's relatively informal criminal legal system is quite distinct from most strongly inquisitorial systems although the trial process in particular contains significant inquisitorial elements.

Trials are led by professional judges. As stated in the *domstolloven*[12] [Act relating to the courts of justice], the ordinary courts are of three types: *tingrett* [District Courts], *lagmannsrett* [Courts of Appeal] and *Høyesterett* [Supreme Court]. The courts hear both civil and criminal cases. The courts do not take up cases of their own accord. Criminal cases are brought before the courts by the prosecution authority[13] within the police (*politiadvokatene*), the public prosecutors (*statsadvokatene*) or the Director of Public Prosecutions (*Riksadvokatemebetet*). All cases before the courts are presided over by a professional judge. As regulated in Chapter 3 in *domstolloven*, the professional judges are always law graduates and civil servants appointed by the King-in-Council. *Inntillingsrådet for dommere* [Judicial Appointments Board for Judges] is an independent body and makes recommendations for judicial appointments. A judge must be a Norwegian citizen, achieve the highest standard both personally and professionally,[14] and can only be dismissed by court judgment. In the courts of first instance there are several deputy judges. They are legally qualified and appointed to a court for a limited period, in order to give law graduates practical experience of the courts. These assistant judges preside over proceedings in court and decide cases just like other judges, with certain restrictions. All judges are independent in their adjudication and all penal cases are to be dealt with pursuant to the provisions of

[9] K Hanna, E Davies, E Henderson, C Crothers and C Rotherham, *Child Witnesses in the New Zealand Criminal Courts: A Review of Practice and Implications for Policy* (Auckland, Institute of Public Policy, 2010).

[10] www.domstol.no/en/.

[11] Royal Ministry of Justice and the Police and Royal Norwegian Ministry of Foreign Affairs *Administration of Justice in Norway. A Brief presentation* 3rd edn (Oslo, Royal Ministry of Justice and the Police and Royal Norwegian Ministry of Foreign Affairs, 1998).

[12] Lov om domstolene [Act relating to the courts of justice] (1915-08-13).

[13] Lov om rettergangsmåten i straffesaker (Straffeprosessloven) 22.mai 1981 nr 25 [The Criminal Procedure Act of 22 May 1981 No 25] Chapter 6.

[14] Lov om domstolene [Act relating to the courts of justice] Chapter 3 Section 55 (for more information see www.domstol.no/en/).

the *Straffeprosessloven*[15] [Criminal Procedure Act].[16] Chapter 22 sets out how the main hearing should be conducted. The following sections describe the examination procedure:

> **Section 289:** The hearing of the actual matter to which the indictment relates begins with the reading aloud of the indictment. The president of the court shall then ask the person indicted whether he pleads guilty and shall urge him to follow the proceedings carefully. The prosecutor then addresses the court to explain the substance of the indictment and to mention briefly the evidence that will be produced. On application defence counsel may be allowed to make short comments in connection with what the prosecutor has said.
>
> **Section 290:** Any reproduction in the court record or a police report of any statement that the person indicted has previously made in the case may only be read aloud if his statements are contradictory or relate to points on which he refuses to speak or declares that he does not remember, or if he does not attend the hearing. The same applies to any written statement that he has previously made in relation to the case.
>
> **Section 291:** Evidence shall first be produced by the prosecutor and then by defence counsel unless they agree on another sequence. The party producing the evidence may, if necessary, briefly explain the significance of the matters that he or she is seeking to prove.
>
> **Section 294:** The court shall in its official capacity ensure that the case is fully clarified. For this purpose it may decide to obtain new evidence and to adjourn the hearing.
>
> **Section 296:** Witnesses who can give evidence that is deemed to be of significance in the case should be examined orally during the main hearing if special circumstances do not prevent this. At such examination any reproduction in the court record or a police report of any statement that the witness has previously made in the case may only be read aloud if the witness's statements are contradictory or relate to points on which he refuses to speak or declares that he does not remember. The same applies to any written statement that the witness has previously made in relation to the case.
>
> **Section 298:** In a case relating to a sexual felony or misdemeanor, the reading aloud, video-recording or audio recording of a statement made by a witness less than 16 years of age before court or pursuant to the provisions of section 239 shall take the place of a personal examination unless the court for special reasons finds that the witness should give evidence at the main hearing. The same procedure may be followed if the witness is mentally retarded or similarly handicapped. The same procedure may also be followed

[15] Lov om rettergangsmåten i straffesaker (Straffeprosessloven) 22.mai 1981 nr 25 [The Criminal Procedure Act of 22 May 1981 No 25].

[16] At present there is no official English translation of the Straffeprosessloven (see note 15) in Norway. For the present chapter the author has translated the sections referred to. This translation is largely based on the unofficial translation of the Criminal Procedure Act (with amendments of 30 June 2006 NO. 53) by Walford et al (2006) (www.ub.uio.no/ujur/ulovdata/lov-19810522-025-eng.pdf). The present translation is of the Criminal Procedure Act updated 24 June 2011 NO. 32. Finding exact English equivalents for the Norwegian legal terms and concepts involved was not an easy task. In some cases the translation is no more than an approximation since there are no equivalents. The author of this chapter would like to thank Michael Lamb, John Spencer, Gavin Oxburgh and Morten Holmboe for their advice and adjustments in my translations.

in cases relating to other criminal matters when it is in the interests of the witness to do so.

Section 302: Written evidence shall be read aloud by the person producing the evidence unless the court decides otherwise.

Section 303: After the examination of each individual witness and after the reading aloud of each piece of written evidence the person indicted should be given an opportunity to speak.

Section 304: When the production of evidence is completed, first the prosecutor and then defence counsel may address the court. Each of them is entitled to speak twice. When the defence counsel has finished, the person indicted shall be asked whether he has any further comment to make. If the person indicted does not understand Norwegian, or if he is deaf, at least the proposals made by the prosecutor and defense counsel must be brought to the knowledge of the person indicted.

Section 305: In deciding what is deemed to be proved only the evidence produced at the main hearing shall be taken into consideration.

Appeals against judgments of the District Court or the Court of Appeal are regulated in Chapter 23 of the Criminal Procedure Act.[17] In short, a higher court cannot, of its own accord, instruct a lower court how it should handle individual cases. If one party takes a decision further, the higher court can decide that the lower court must hear the case again. As stated in section 306:

Error in the assessment of evidence in relation to the issue of guilt cannot be grounds for appeal to the Supreme Court. As regards a judgment of the Court of Appeal in a case that involves a trial by jury, no appeal to the detriment of the person charged may be brought against the application of law with regard to the issue of guilt unless the ground of appeal is that the recorded explanation by the president of the court of the applicable legal principles was wrong.

Lay judges are selected by municipal councils for four years at a time.[18] In the District Courts the lay judges sit on the bench, in the Court of Appeal either on the bench or in the jury box. There are no lay judges in the Supreme Court.

Compared to other countries, the cooperation between the police and the prosecution service in Norway is also somewhat distinctive. In England and Wales, the police direct the entire investigation and consult the Crown Prosecution Service for legal advice on whether the case is ready for court purposes. In Norway, the police conduct the initial investigation and work together with prosecutors throughout the investigation.

In other Nordic countries such as Sweden, a preliminary pre-investigation is undertaken by the police, following which the prosecution office decides whether a full investigation is warranted. The full investigation is then led by the police

[17] Straffeprosessloven (n 15).
[18] Lov om domstolene (1915-08-13) Chapter 4.

and transferred to the prosecution office to consider whether there is sufficient evidence for prosecution.

In comparison with some more overtly inquisitorial systems, Norway has, like adversarial systems, a strong preference for oral evidence and examination. There is no tradition of aggressive, adversarial cross-examination in Norway and the judge-led direct examinations by the prosecution and defence are relatively informal in terms of evidence rules and procedure.

Complainants or victims do not become parties to proceedings in Norwegian criminal cases and have the same status as other witnesses. However, since 1981[19] alleged victims of sexual assault and some violent offences are entitled to state-funded counsel and separate legal representation. Such legal representatives have several roles as regulated in Chapter 9 of the Criminal Procedure Act.

> **Section 107c:** Counsel for the aggrieved person shall protect the latter's interests in connection with the investigation and the main hearing of the case. Counsel shall also give the aggrieved person such additional assistance and support as is natural and reasonable. Counsel shall be notified and shall be entitled to be present at the examination of the aggrieved person by the police and the court during investigation. Counsel is also entitled to be present at the main hearing of the case. When the hearing of the evidence is concluded, the court may decide that counsel shall withdraw. At the examination of the aggrieved person, counsel is entitled to put further questions. Counsel is entitled to object to questions that are not relevant to the case or that are put in an improper manner. During the examination in court the aggrieved person shall be allowed to comment on procedural issues that concern the said person. Counsel shall further be allowed to comment on civil legal claims pertaining to the aggrieved person even when the claim is presented by the prosecuting authority.

In CSA cases this involves supporting the children and their guardians through the pre-trial stages, accompanying the children to police interviews, notifying them about case progression, contacting appropriate support agencies, representing the children's interests at trial, and claiming economic compensation[20] for young victims from the defendants.

Historical Development

Norway's first Criminal Procedure Act of 1887 made no special provisions for investigative interviews of children. To the extent that children were questioned or asked to testify at all, they were treated the same way as adults. In the mid 1920s, Norway experienced a massive and heated discussion about sexual offences, which were believed by many to be increasingly frequent and more severe than

[19] A Robberstad *Bistandsadvokaten Ofrenes stilling i straffesaker* [State-funded counsel and the aggrieved person's position in criminal cases] (Oslo, Universitetsforlaget, 2003).

[20] See straffeprosessloven § 107a.

before.[21] It was claimed that children who had been sexually abused were further humiliated when dealt with by the legal authorities. At the time, children had to give repeated statements, first to the police in one or several interviews, then as part of the preliminary judicial inquiry (which was a required intermediate stage when dealing with serious crimes), during the adjudication at the main hearing and even at appeal. In the process, children were confronted by several members of the court, prosecutors, defence lawyers and the accused, all asking questions about events that may have taken place long before, and which the children had already described repeatedly.

In celebration of its 50th anniversary, the Norwegian Women's National Council published a book in 1957 containing reports from the Council's meetings and an outline of its history. Regarding the Council's national congress in Kristiansand in July 1913, the book reports:

> During the Council's '5 minutes session', Porsgrund Women's Council put forward a motion to attempt to amend the law concerning investigative interviews of children who have fallen victim to sexual felonies. The motion was subsequently included in the N.K.N's working plan. Numerous lectures and visits to the Minister of Justice followed. Although there was full agreement, it was difficult to bring about this highly called for amendment, which eventually came in 1926. (Norwegian Women's National Council, 1957, p 181)[22]

The Council's initiative brought about an amendment in the legislation, which came into effect in 1926. To the author's knowledge, this made Norway the first country in Europe to statutorily outline how investigative interviews in CSA cases should be conducted. According to the new legislation, children were to give accounts to judges outside the courtroom, and preferably they were interviewed by judges only. Moreover, the upper age limit was set at 16 years, which coincided with the age of consent at the time. The legislative amendments were not motivated solely by child welfare considerations. It was also noted that statements given immediately after abuse occurred were more detailed than statements given during hearings taking place long after the sexual offences had been committed.

Because the investigative interview had to be conducted outside court, it was assumed that neither the accused nor the defence counsel was entitled to be present during the interviews. Consequently, children were interviewed by judges in chambers or in closed courtrooms. The judges asked questions and recorded the answers themselves or else dictated the children's responses for later transcription. Most often, summaries rather than verbatim accounts were recorded. Using these summaries, the judges independently assessed the children's reliability. These

[21] NOU 1992: 16 *Sterkere vern og økt støtte for kriminalitetsofre* [Norwegian Official Report (NOU) 1992: 16. Stronger protection and increased support to victims of crime] (Ministry of Justice and the Police) (Oslo, Justisdepartementet, 1992).

[22] Norske Kvinners Nasjonalråd *Norske Kvinners Nasjonalråd 1904–1954* [Norwegian Women's National Council 1904–1954] (Flisa boktrykkeri, NKN, 1957).

reliability assessments were normally recorded as the judges' conclusions, but the reasoning was not recorded.

The 1926 Act was supported by both public prosecutors and senior judges of the Court of Appeal. In a detailed comment on the new Act, however, the Director General of Public Prosecutions expressed his doubts, including reservations about risks to the rights of accused offenders. According to the Official Norwegian Report, or green paper, the rationale for the 1926 law reform was rather limited. The reform was motivated by a number of well-publicised trials in which children had been subjected to thorough and emotionally distressing interrogation. It is no exaggeration, therefore, to say that the reform was more emotionally than rationally justified.

Except for a few modifications, the heart of this legislation was sustained in the new Criminal Proceedings Act of 1981[23] which came into effect in 1986. Changes to the original 1926 scheme included the following:

- The upper age limit for investigative interviews under judicial supervision was lowered from 16 to 14 years.
- It was stated that repeated interviews of children should, if possible, be avoided.
- Well-qualified persons were required to assist and conduct the interviews.
- The interviews were to be audio-taped whenever possible.

However, in the Act of 1981 exceptions could be made if children were distracted during the interviews. At the time, many courts either lacked recording devices, or were equipped with devices of such poor quality that it was difficult to transcribe what was said during the interviews. Then came the Bjugn case in 1992.

The *Bjugn* case

In brief, seven adults in the small community of Bjugn in north-west Norway were arrested in 1992 on suspicion of sexually abusing and raping children in a kindergarten. The incidents reported by the children included ritualised abuse. During the subsequent investigation, the police conducted more than 550 interviews of 220 witnesses and conducted 61 judicial hearings with 40 children. Parents, psychological experts and the authorities were convinced that a paedophile circle was operating in the community.

Charges against six of the seven suspects were later dropped and after a trial lasting two-and-a-half months, the remaining defendant was acquitted in 1994.

[23] Lov om rettergangsmåten i straffesaker (Straffeprosessloven) 22.mai 1981 nr 25 [The Criminal Procedure Act of 22 May 1981 No 25]. See in particular second paragraph in section 234 and section 239.

Thirty-three children received compensation from the state, suggesting that CSA had taken place, and there is continued controversy about whether the main suspect was correctly identified. The complaints about this case, such as criticisms of the interviewers' competence, style of questioning and the length of delays between the alleged abuse and the interviews, resemble those made in other highly publicised cases such as the *McMartin* and *Wee Care* (Kelly Michaels) cases in the USA, and the *Roum* case in Denmark.[24]

Following an evaluation of the Bjugn case by the General Director of Public Prosecution in Norway,[25] the following recommendations were made:

- Specialised police interviewers instead of psychologists or social workers should interview children.
- Police interviewers should be given additional advanced training.
- New regulations specifying how these interviews should be conducted were introduced

The new regulations and guidelines[26] stated that investigative interviews of children should only be conducted by qualified interviewers who had been specially trained. Assuming that specially trained police officers would elicit more information from children than officers without such training, substantial resources and effort have been invested in increasing the competence of the police officers conducting these interviews. At NPUC, the interview training is based on scientifically and research-based techniques.[27] The child interviewers are the most qualified interviewers in Norway and have dedicated most of their professional careers to investigative interviews of children.

[24] H Kringstad *Bjugnformelen* [The Bjugnformula] (Oslo, Tiden Norsk Forlag, 1997); T Myklebust and RA Bjørklund 'The effect of long-term training on police officers' use of open and closed questions in field investigative interviews of children (FIIC)' *Journal of Investigative Psychology and Offender Profiling* 165, 181.

[25] Riksadvokaten *Riksadvokatens gjennomgang av den såkalte Bjugn-saken* [The Director of Public Prosecutions, An evaluation of the Bjugn case] (Oslo, Riksadvokaten, 1994).

[26] Justisdepartementet [Ministry of Justice and the Police] *Rundskriv G-70/98 om forskrift 2 oktober 1998 nr 925 om dommeravhør og observasjon og om endringer i straffeprosessloven, straffeloven og påtaleinstruksen* [Regulations concerning out-of-court judicial examination and observation and concerning legislative amendments to the Criminal Proceedings Act, the Criminal Code, and the Prosecution Instructions] (Oslo, Det Kongelige Justis- og politidepartement, 1998).

[27] T Myklebust *Analysis of field investigative interviews of children conducted by specially trained police investigators* (published PhD thesis) (Oslo, UniPub-University of Oslo, 2009); Politihøgskolen *Studieplan for videreutdanning: Kommunikasjon mellom avhører og barn i dommeravhør* [The Norwegian Police University College, Specialisation in communication between children and interviewers in investigative interviews of children] (Oslo, Politihøgskolen, 2009); KT Gamst and Å Langballe (2004) *Barn som vitner—En empirisk og teoretisk studie av kommunikasjon mellom avhører og barn i dommeravhør. Utvikling av en avhørmetodisk tilnærming* [Children as witnesses—An empirical and theoretical study of the communication between the interviewer and the child in investigative interviews of children. Development of a methodological approach] (published PhD thesis) (Oslo, UniPub-University of Oslo, 2004); KT Gamst *Profesjonelle barnesamtaler. Å ta barn på alvor* [Professional conversations with children. Taking children seriously] (Oslo, Universitetsforlaget, 2011).

How the Interviews are Conducted

When sexual abuse or violent offences against children are alleged, 'investigative interviews under judicial supervision' are conducted. In 2008 the upper age limit was increased from 14 to 16 years, though children between 14 and 16 years are entitled to give their statements in person, if they prefer.[28] The examination of children outside the trial is regulated by the Criminal Procedure Act section 239 subsection 1 and 2, which reads as follows:

> In the case of an examination of a witness who is under 16 years of age or a witness who is mentally retarded or similarly handicapped in cases of sexual felonies or misdemeanors, the judge shall take the statement separately from a sitting of the court when he finds this desirable in the interests of the witness or for other reasons. The judge shall in such cases as a general rule summon a well-qualified person to assist with the examination or to carry out the examination subject to the judge's control. When it is possible and due consideration for the witness or the purpose of the statement does not otherwise indicate, the examination shall be recorded on a video cassette and if necessary on a separate audio recorder. On the same conditions the defence counsel of the person charged shall as a general rule be given an opportunity to attend the examination. The same procedure may also be used in cases concerning other criminal matters when the interests of the child so indicate.

In practice, the police are typically contacted by the child's guardian or the child welfare service with information about the suspected abuse. The receiving police officer contacts the local police prosecutor who assigns the case to one of the investigators in charge who then notifies the local court that an interview is required. The court allocates a judge to supervise while the interviewer prepares an interview plan, which is then presented to the judge before the interview is scheduled. The child's examination should take place as early as possible and by regulation no later than 14 days after the report to the police. If no defendant has been named, a lawyer will be present to represent his or her interests but in these cases a second interview will later be necessary for the defendant to challenge the specific accusations.

The interview is conducted by highly trained police officers in specially designed video interview suites, whilst the judge, prosecution, defence lawyers and state-funded counsel to the complainant observe the interview in an adjoining monitor room via video link. The interview process and the presence of observers in the monitor room are normally explained to children in developmentally appropriate terms.

The interviewer first conducts an interview in accordance with his/her professional skills and when he/she considers it complete, the interviewer takes a break

[28] The Ministry of Justice regulations of 28 June 1985 concerning Prosecution Instructions, Section 8–12. Revised 4 April 2008; No 321. Entered into force on 1 July 2008.

to consult counsel and the judge, leaving the camera running. The judge gives both parties the opportunity to suggest topics or identify contradictions that they want investigated. The interviewer then returns to the interview room to address these issues and then consults the observers again. This process continues until the judge and counsel are satisfied. The child then leaves the interview room, meets his/her guardian and the interview is finished. The interview is transcribed, and this transcript accompanies the video and other case documents to the police prosecutor, who decides what steps to take next. The child can be re-interviewed, in which case the same process will be followed, but re-interviewing is very rare. After the investigation is finished the case is sent to the State Public Prosecutor for indictment or withdrawal of charges.

The decision of the prosecuting authority may be appealed by way of complaint to the immediately superior prosecuting authority. Decisions not to prosecute, to waive prosecution, to issue optional penalty writs or bills of indictment, or to defer the execution of sentences can be appealed to the prosecuting authorities[29] by

— the person adversely affected by the decision;
— other persons with a legal interest in the complaint, such as the alleged victim or his/her guardian if the victim is under 18 years of age;
— an administrative body—provided the decision concerns its area of administrative responsibility.

The right to appeal by way of complaint cannot be exercised by any person who is entitled to bring the decisions before the court. Nor can a person who has been charged appeal by complaining against a decision that institutes prosecution before a court. No complaint can be brought against the administrative decisions of the Director of Public Prosecutions.

As in the other Nordic countries—Norway, Sweden, Finland, Denmark, and Iceland—the video of the child's interview is accepted in court as the evidence-in-chief, thus negating the need for the child to attend court, provide evidence or be cross-examined. In other words, the child's involvement in the judicial process almost always comes to an end after the interview, even if the case is appealed.

As emphasised in Hanna et al's review of interview practice, the Norwegian process manages to circumvent some of the problems experienced elsewhere. Children's evidence is obtained early and the risks of inappropriate cross-examination are avoided by using specially trained interviewers and restricting counsel's involvement. Further, interviewing the children in special suites away from the police station and courtroom keeps the number of people involved to a minimum. Children are also given state-funded legal representatives: '[the] Norwegian process manages to avoid at least some of the objections raised by adversarial advocates to inquisitorial processes, especially the unfairness of preventing

[29] Section 59a Criminal Procedure Act.

the defence from challenging the evidence fully. Norway retains the essential two-party nature of the adversarial proceeding.'[30]

Discussions Regarding the Norwegian System

There are several arguments and discussions in Norway regarding the ways in which the investigation, investigative interviews and court procedures involving children are conducted, with some suggesting a conflict between the principles of The European Convention on Human Rights (ECHR) and the UN Convention on the Rights of the Child (UNCRC).

Since World War II there has been a strong focus on human rights exemplified by the 'Helsinki declarations'. This focus on human rights has implications for police work in relation to suspects, witnesses and victims. The ECHR, ratified by the European Council on 4 November 1950, states in Article 6 that all suspects have the right to a fair trial:

> In the determination of his civil rights and obligations or of any criminal charge against him, everyone is entitled to a fair and public hearing within a reasonable time by an independent and impartial tribunal established by law. Judgment shall be pronounced publicly but the press and public may be excluded from all or part of the trial in the interests of morals, public order or national security in a democratic society, where the interests of juveniles or the protection of the private life of the parties so require, or to the extent strictly necessary in the opinion of the court in special circumstances where publicity would prejudice the interests of justice (Article 6.1).

With respect to interviews of children, Article 6.3 paragraph d is also relevant:

> Everyone charged with a criminal offence has the following minimum rights: ... to examine or have examined witnesses against him and to obtain the attendance and examination of witnesses on his behalf under the same conditions as witnesses against him.

Norway was the second country to ratify the ECHR (15 January 1952) and the Convention entered into force in Norway on 3 September 1953. The subsequent Protocols to the Convention were also ratified shortly after they were opened for ratification.[31] The Convention is incorporated into the Norwegian legislation.

The 1989 UNCRC gave special rights to children, however. The main purpose of this Convention was to ensure the best interests of the child in all regards. Of special interest to the present chapter is Article 34:

[30] Hanna et al (n 9) 163–64.

[31] M Matningsdal 'The Influence of the European Convention for the Protection of Human Rights and Fundamental Freedoms on Norwegian Criminal Procedure' (2007) *Scandinavian Studies of Law* 399, 418.

> Sexual exploitation—The child has the right to protection from all forms of sexual exploitation and sexual abuse. For these purposes the state shall take all appropriate national and international measures (Article 34).

Although this Convention is more than twenty years old, I have found very little scientific work evaluating the effect of the Convention on investigative interviews of children.[32] In contemporary Norway, there is discussion among lawyers, practitioners, politicians and NGOs about practical difficulties of ensuring that suspects are fairly tried while the best interests of children are protected.

The Norwegian Supreme Court has stated[33] that defendants should have the opportunity to examine witnesses and evidence and to respond to accusations through their defence counsel, also known as the principle of contradiction or *audi alteram partem*. This is in accordance with the Criminal Procedure Act (CPA) section 239, subsection 1 and 2 (see above). The implications of the ECHR for the protection of human rights and fundamental freedoms under Norwegian criminal procedure were reviewed by Supreme Court judge Matningsdal in 2007.[34] He concluded that the Norwegian case law regarding child witnesses 'today is clearly in accordance with the case law of the European Court' (p 408).

The relationship between the provision of the CPA and ECHR have been addressed in several cases, including Rt-1990-319.[35] In this CSA case[36] the accused had not been present or represented by defence counsel when the child was examined, and was sentenced to eight months' imprisonment. After an assessment of the circumstances, in which the Supreme Court considered the problems that arise when children are believed to have been sexually victimised, it was concluded that the procedure did not violate the ECHR.

In case Rt-1994-748[37] defence counsel had not attended the first investigative interview of the child, which was presented at trial, but the request for a new examination/interview was refused. The Supreme Court set aside the conviction on the grounds that the child's statement constituted the primary evidence in the case. In Rt-1999-586, the Supreme Court held that 'if the statement is to be used as evidence at the trial—and when the statement is an important piece of evidence in the case—the rule must be that the person charged shall have had the

[32] S Maffei *The European Right to Confrontation in Criminal Proceedings. Absent, Anonymous and Vulnerable Witnesses* (Groningen: European Law Publishing, 2006); KH Søvig *Barnets rettigheter på barnets premisser: utfordringer i møtet mellom FNs barnekonvensjon og norsk rett* (vol. nr 115) [Children's rights based on their immaturity: challenges between the UN Convention on the Right of the Child and the Norwegian justice] (Bergen, Det juridiske fakultet, 2009).

[33] Rt 1999-586. See n 35.

[34] Matningsdal (n 31).

[35] *Norsk Retstidende*, ie the journal in which the judgments and decisions of the Supreme Court and the Appeals Selection Committee of the Supreme Court are published. Reference format is Retstidende-Year-Page (eg Rt-1990-319).

[36] Referred to by Matningsdal (n 31).

[37] Ibid, 407.

opportunity to examine the witness through his defence counsel, if necessary at a new examination'. Since children's statements are considered to be the evidence-in-chief in most CSA cases, Matningsdal concluded that the Supreme Court will not accept the use of interviews conducted by a judge at a separate sitting of the court if the defendant has not had the opportunity to submit questions to the witness through his defence counsel[38] However, if the defence counsel has not been present at the first examination, the statement can be used if defence counsel were present at a second interview and examination.

In the 2010 case of *A S v Finland*,[39] an applicant charged with sexual abuse of a child contended that his defence rights had not been respected in the criminal proceedings against him in that the courts had made use of a video-taped interview with the alleged victim although he had not been afforded an opportunity to put questions to the child. The European Court of Human Rights stated in paragraph 56:

> In acknowledging the need to strike a balance between the right of the defendant and those of the alleged child victim, the Court finds that the following minimum guarantees must be in place: the suspected person shall be informed of the hearing of the child, he or she shall be given an opportunity to observe that hearing, either as it is being conducted or later from an audiovisual recording, and to have questions put to the child, either directly or indirectly, in the course of the first hearing or on a later occasion.

In its overall conclusion, the Court found that the child's video-recorded account constituted the only direct evidence leading to the applicant's conviction. It also found that the lack of opportunity to put questions to the child involved such limitations on the applicant's defence rights that he could not be considered to have received a fair trial. Furthermore the Court found that the applicant did not waive his right to contest the child's account by putting questions to the boy. It thus followed that there had been a violation of Article 6 §1 and Article 6 §3(d).

The Norwegian system contrasts with practices in England and Wales with respect to the adversarial cross-examination (see Spencer, chapters one and eight). There seems to be a consensus[40] in Norway in favour of investigative interviews conducted under

[38] Ibid, 418; ch 17 in M Matningsdal, *Siktedes rett til å eksaminere vitner. Opplesning av politiforklaringer, anonyme vitner og dommeravhør av barn* [The defendant's right to examination of witnesses] (Bergen, Fagbokforlaget, 2007).

[39] *A S v Finland* App no 40156/07 ECtHR, 28 September 2010.

[40] J Andenæs and T G Myhrer *Norsk straffeprosess* [The Norwegian Criminal Procedure Act] (Oslo, Universitetsforlaget, 2009); HK Bjerke and E Keiserud *Straffeprosessloven. Lov av 22. mai 1981 nr.25 om rettergangsmåten i straffesaker med senere endringer. Bind II (3.utg.)* [The Criminal Procedure Act. Volume 2, 3rd edn] (Oslo, Universitets-forlaget, 2001); R Hennum 'Dommeravhør og menneskerettigheter: konvensjonspraksis om særlig sårbare vitner' [Investigative interviews of children in Norway and the ECHR] in OK Fauchald, H Jakhelln and A Syse (eds) *Dog fred er ej det bedste: Festskrift til Carl August Fleischer på hans 70-års dag 26.august 2006* (Oslo, Universitetsforlaget, 2006) 247, 261; Matningsdal (n 31) 418; M Matningsdal, *Siktedes rett til å eksaminere vitner* (n 38) ch 17); A Robberstad *Bistandsadvokaten. Ofrenes stilling*

judicial supervision, with opportunities to challenge the witness by suggesting questions for interviewers to pose. I am not aware of any studies comparing the cross-examination of children in Norway as opposed to England and Wales, but my review of selected examinations in England, Wales and Australia leads me to ask: Which of the questions asked in the cross-examination could not have been raised during the investigation or at an earlier stage of the process? My answer is: None. And I think the questions would have been better contextualised, phrased better and asked more age-appropriately if they had been asked by the interviewer during the video-recorded investigative interview, rather than during cross-examination by defence counsel.

Child Advocacy Centres

The first Child Advocacy Center was established in the US in 1985. The chief goals were to ensure that children are not further victimised by the intervention systems designed to protect them (more child-friendly criminal investigations with fewer interviews in less intimidating settings) and to create a place where the different authorities involved could come together to investigate allegations of child sexual abuse while treating the victims. Initially another goal was to increase successful criminal prosecution of child sexual abuse, but Connell[41] has argued that investigative functions may undermine therapeutic effectiveness. The therapist who is focused on gathering evidence to assist in the prosecution of the case has stepped out of the role of therapist and instead is conducting a series of investigative interviews, possibly without the objectivity or neutrality necessary to protect the interest of justice. There is a wide agreement in the forensic area that the roles of forensic evaluations and clinical treatment should be distinct roles to be fulfilled by different people, and for this reason, the therapist's participation as a member of the investigative team may be inappropriate and professionally ill advised. The police officer needs to gain valid information about the alleged offence, while the mental health worker focuses on the child's psychological well-being. The following table shows some of the dimensions along which forensic and clinical work differ.

i straffesaker [The state-funded counsel and the aggrieved persons position in criminal cases] (Oslo, Universitetsforlaget, 2003).

[41] M Connell 'The Extended Forensic Evaluation' in K Kuehnle and M Connell (eds) *The Evaluation of Child Sexual Abuse Allegations. A Comprehensive Guide to Assessment and Testimony* (New Jersey, Wiley, 2009) 451, 487.

Table 1. Differences between forensic and clinical work*

Dimension	Forensic	Clinical
Client	Court	Child
Context	Legal	Therapeutic
Stance	Neutral	Supportive
Type of data	Just the facts	Subjective experience
Structure	More structure	Less structure
Data-gathering method	Non-leading	Some leading
Fantasy	Only the real	Some pretend
Documentation	Extensive: video	Less extensive: notes
Collateral contacts	Extensive	Some contacts
Length of involvement	1–3 sessions	Several/many
Product	Long report	Short report

*Adapted from KC Faller 'Forensic and Clinical Interviewer Roles in Child Sexual Abuse' in KC Faller (ed) *Interviewing Children About Sexual Abuse. Controversies and Best Practice* (Oxford, Oxford University Press, 2007); KC Faller and M Everson *Forensic and Clinical Issues With Children Who May Have Been Sexually Abused: Potential Conflict Between the Child's Best Interest and the Legal System*, unpublished manuscript (University of Michigan, School of Social Work, 2003).

Internationally, the opening of Child Advocacy Centres has challenged the understanding of the roles of the practitioners involved. Interviewing police officers need to understand the different perspectives of police officers and health care workers, for example. According to Conell[42] and her colleagues, health care personnel working with children are concerned with the children's unique understanding and not with the objective reality that is of concern to the police.

Child Advocacy Centres in the Nordic Countries

In 1998, Iceland was the first of the Nordic countries to introduce a Child Advocacy Centre, along the US model;[43] it was followed by Sweden in 2006, and Finland (Åland) and Norway in 2007. There are nationally differences, with the Swedish model being less stringent than the Norwegian, for example. In their

[42] Kuehnle and Connell, ibid, and Connell's chapter therein, 451, 487.

[43] SL Jackson 'A USA National Survey of Program Services Provided by Child Advocacy Centers' (2004) *Child Abuse & Neglect* 411, 421.

evaluation of the Swedish model, Åstrøm and Rejmer[44] reported significant regional differences with respect to such factors as the target clientele, the professionals represented, the interview strategies and the recording procedures. Similar differences are evident across the Nordic countries. In Iceland, interviews are conducted by psychologists or criminologists, in Sweden and Norway by the police, and in Finland by both police officers and psychologists.

Statens Barnehus *in Norway*

The desire to protect the best interests of children and provide them with appropriate treatment and support has been on the Norwegian political agenda for several years. Based on the US Child Advocacy Center model, and in order to improve the investigative interviews and coordinate both the forensic interviews and clinical treatment and support, the Norwegian government implemented the first *Statens Barnehus* (SBH) [Child Advocacy Centre] in 2007. By 2011 there were seven[45] SBH, with the eighth[46] to be opened in 2012. At the SBH the forensic interview, medical examination and therapeutic consultations all take place under the same roof. There is a specially designed interview room that allows the interview to be recorded directly to DVD, with video links to a conference room at the SBH. The conference room serves as a courtroom, with all legal representatives present, as described earlier in this chapter.

In practice, the police or child welfare service contact the centre when abuse is alleged. The SBH then calls a meeting with the police and the child welfare service. The meeting takes place at the SBH with one of the staff members appointed as the child's contact person. The reported case is then discussed and case-relevant information given by the child welfare service to the police. After the meeting the police consider how to proceed before calling another meeting to explain their decisions. The forensic interview is then planned in detail as described earlier, with contact between the prosecution and the judge leading the interview. At the SBH some judges also allow representatives of the child welfare service to monitor investigative interviews. This has led to a debate among professionals because there are no regulations concerning their role. Some judges allow them to be present while others exclude them from the monitoring room. The procedure[47] for the forensic interview was described earlier in this chapter.

[44] K Åstrøm and A Rejmer *Det blir nog batter för barnen. Slurapport i utvärderingen av nationell försöksverksomhet med barnahus 2006–2007* [Presumably it will be better for the children. Evaluation of the National project of Child Advocacy Centres in Sweden 2006–2007] Research Report 2008:7 (Lund, Lund University, 2008).

[45] Bergen 2007; Hamar 2007; Kristiansand 2008; Trondheim 2009; Tromsø 2009; Oslo 2009; Stavanger 2010.

[46] The next *Statens Barnehus* will be opened in Ålesund in 2012. This according to the National Budget for 2011, presented to the *Storting* (Norwegian Parliament) as Report no 1 (2010–2011) on 5 October 2010. The National Budget presents the government's programme for the implementation of economic policy and projections for the Norwegian economy.

[47] Justisdepartementet [Ministry of Justice and the Police] Rundskriv G-70/98 om forskrift 2 oktober 1998 nr 925 om dommeravhør og observasjon og om endringer i straffeprosessloven,

After the forensic interview of the child, a medical doctor can (if necessary and if he or she is present) consult and physically examine the child. A representative of the SBH then evaluates the child and starts the therapeutic treatment/discussions. The child's contact at the SBH follows up to make sure that the child is treated appropriately. The therapeutic treatment will, if necessary, be provided locally by the health service and the child welfare service in the municipality where the child lives. The SBH have no responsibilities for the child after that.

Many of the practitioners argue that the introduction of the SBHs improved the conditions in which children are interviewed, and provided a context in which the necessary steps can be taken to ensure that the investigative teams are well instructed and receive feedback on the quality of their interviews so that they perform work of the highest quality.

Ongoing Challenges

After evaluating the Bjugn case, the Director of Public Prosecution in Norway drew attention to the effect of temporal factors on children's accounts, focusing on everything that might affect children's memories after offences have taken place. Children's memories are so easily affected by such things as conversation with other children, parents, siblings and other persons that most police officers instruct parents not to talk with the children about the case before the forensic interview has taken place. Health care workers, on the other hand, stress the importance of encouraging children to give their perspectives on the events that have taken place in order to prevent traumatic stress disorders. Health care workers also believe that children slowly come to understand better what has taken place whereas police officers are expected to conduct as few interviews as possible—typically only one—with children.

Unfortunately, this desire to limit interviewers to a single interview is not well grounded. Several researchers[48] have claimed that repeated interviews including misleading questions create distress by generating painful memories and increase the likelihood that children respond erroneously. The potentially distressing effect of repeated interviewing has not been studied, and the effects on children's

straffeloven og påtaleinstruksen [Regulations concerning out-of-court judicial examination and observation and concerning legislative amendments to the Criminal Proceedings Act, the Criminal Code, and the Prosecution Instructions] (Oslo, Det Kongelige Justis- og politidepartement, 1998).

[48] S Garven, JM Wood, RS Malpass and JS Shaw 'More than Suggestion: The Effect of Interviewing Techniques From the McMartin Preschool Case' (1998) *Journal of Applied Psychology* 347, 359; JA Quas and H Lench (2007) 'Arousal at Encoding, Arousal at Retrieval, Interviewer Support, and Children's Memory for a Mild Stressor' (2007) *Applied Cognitive Psychology*, 21, 289–305; VF Reyna, RE Holliday and T Marche (2002) 'Explaining the Development of False Memories' *Developmental Review* 436, 489; J Qin, JA Quas, AD Redlich and GS Goodman 'Children's Eyewitness Testimony: Memory Development in the Legal Context' in E Cowan (ed) *The Development of Memory in Childhood* (Hove, Psychology Press, 1997).

accuracy have been studied in the experimental laboratory but not in the field. La Rooy, Lamb and Pipe[49] reported that many researchers failed to distinguish between the effects of repeated interviewing, the effects of suggestive contamination, and the effects of normal forgetting over time. Indeed, their review of thirty studies concluded that, under some conditions, repeated interviews of children could be beneficial; how and when children are interviewed is more important than how many times they are interviewed. The possibility of suggestive contamination[50] is the major justification for limiting interviewers to one interview and further research is needed on the impact of the interviewer's identity and training, the length of delays before and between the interviews, the age of the child and the suggestiveness of the interviews.

It is hoped that use of the SBHs addresses internationally recognised problems with the quality of investigative interviewing. In 1987 Fisher, Geiselman and Raymond[51] were the first to report that interviewing police officers frequently interrupted interviewees and asked inappropriate questions. Other analyses[52] of investigative interviews with witnesses and suspects around the world similarly found that interviewers typically asked many *closed*, *direct*, *leading* and *suggestive* questions, while seldom asking *open* questions. Similar problems have been observed in interviews of children and adults by interviewers from varied professional backgrounds in Australia, England and Wales, Estonia, Israel, Norway, Sweden, Finland and the USA.[53] The problem in all these countries is a

[49] D La Rooy, ME Lamb and ME Pipe 'Repeated Interviewing: A Critical Evaluation of the Risks and Potential Benefits' in K Keuhnle and M Connel (eds) (n 41) 327, 361.

[50] ME Lamb, I Hershkowitz, Y Orbach and PW Esplin *Tell Me What Happened. Structured Investigative Interviews of Child Victims and Witnesses* (Chichester, John Wiley & Sons, 2008); ME Lamb, D La Rooy, LC Malloy and C Katz *Children's Testimony: A Handbook of Psychological Research and Forensic Practice* (2nd ed) (Chichester, John Wiley & Sons, 2011).

[51] RP Fisher, RE Geiselman and DS Raymond 'Critical Analysis of Police Interview Techniques' (1987) *Journal of Police Science and Administration* 177, 185.

[52] G Oxburgh, T Myklebust and T Grant 'The Question of Question Types in Police Interviews: A Review of the Literature from a Psychological and Linguistic Perspective' (2010) *International Journal of Speech, Language and the Law* 45, 66.

[53] AC Cederborg, Y Orbach KJ Sternberg and ME Lamb 'Investigative Interviews of Child witnesses in Sweden' (2000) *Child Abuse & Neglect* 1355, 1361; C Clarke and R Milne *National Evaluation of the PEACE Investigative Interviewing Course. Police Research Award Scheme.* Report No: PRAS/149 (London, National Crime Faculty, 2001); K Kask 'Dynamics in Using Different Question Types in Estonian Police Interviews of Children' (2011) *Applied Cognitive Psychology.* Published online in Wiley Online Library (www.wileyonlinelibrary.com) DOI: 10.1002/acp.1831; K Kask *Trying to Improve Child and Young Adult Witnesses' Performance* PhD thesis University of Leicester, 2008; J Korkman, P Santtila and NK Sandnabba 'Dynamics of Verbal Interaction Between Interviewer and Child in Interviews with Alleged Victims of Child Sexual Abuse' (2006) *Scandinavian Journal of Psychology* 109, 119; J Korkman, P Santtila, M Westeråker and NK Sandnabba 'Interviewing Techniques and Follow-up Questions in Child Sexual Abuse Interviews' (2008) *European Journal of Developmental Psychology* 108, 128; ME Lamb, I Hershkowitz, KJ Sternberg, PW Esplin, M Hovav, T Manor and L Yudilevitch 'Effects of Investigative Utterance Types on Israeli Children's Responses' (1996) *International Journal of Behavioral Development* 627, 637; Myklebust (n 27); Myklebust and Bjørklund (n 24); Oxburgh, Myklebust and Grant (n 52); MB Powell and CH Hughes-Scholes 'Evaluation of the Questions Used to Elicit Evidence about Abuse from Child Witnesses: Australian Study' (2009) *Psychiatry, Psychology and Law* 369, 378; KE Sternberg, ME Lamb, I Hershkowitz, P Esplin, A Redlich and N Sunshine 'The Relationship Between Investigative Utterance Types and the Informativeness of Child Witnesses'

gap between knowledge and practice, with interviewers not implementing best practices even if they know them and think they are complying. Accordingly, it was hoped that the Norwegian SBH might foster co-operation among the professionals involved, thereby improving the quality of interviewing. Several researchers[54] have indicated that team-based cooperation generates better communication and practice than individual focus. Evaluation of the SBH has just begun in Norway and a report is expected in April 2012. A parallel examination of the procedures relating to the interviews of children is also being conducted.

Regulations of 2 October 1998

Norwegian legislation does not specify how forensic interviews should be conducted. Section 12 of the Norwegian Regulations[55] essentially provides a checklist of what the interviewer should inform and admonish the child to do. On the other hand, this section does not indicate how this should be done, other than stating that the interview must be adapted to the age and mental development of the witness:

> **Section 12 How to conduct the interview**
>
> Prior to the interview, the witness shall as a general rule receive information about who is going to attend the interview and where they will be located. As a general rule, the witness shall also be told that the interview will be videotaped or recorded on tape.
>
> The person who conducts the interview must admonish the witness to tell the whole truth, cf. section 128 of the Criminal Proceedings Act. The admonition must be adapted to the age and mental development of the witness.
>
> The interview must be adapted to the age and mental development of the witness, and to the circumstances in general …

Comments on the Regulations are similarly vague:

> The Ministry does not find it expedient to outline rules about the contents of interview methods/interviews in the Regulations. Leading questions are only one of the interview methods which are problematic. Similar objections can be made to, among others, the

(1996) *Journal of Applied Developmental Psychology* 439, 451; C Thoresen, K Lønnum, A Melinder, U Stridbeck and S Magnussen 'Theory and Practice in Interviewing Young Children: A Study of Norwegian Police Interviews 1985–2002' (2006) *Psychology, Crime & Law* 629, 640.

[54] Eg JA Cannon-Bowers, E Salas, and S Converse 'Shared Mental Models in Expert Team Decision Making' in NJ Castellan (ed) *Individual and Group Decision Making* (Hillsdale New Jersey, Lawrence Erlbaum Associates, 1993); CD Hardin and ET Higgins 'Shared reality: How social verification makes the subjective objective' in RM Sorrentino and ET Higgins (eds) *Handbook of motivation and cognition: Foundations of social behavior* (New York, Guilford Press, 1996).

[55] Regulations of 2 October 1998 no 925 concerning investigative interviews and observation, and concerning legislative amendments to the Criminal Proceedings Act, the Criminal Code, and the Prosecution Instructions. Translated for this chapter from Norwegian to English by the author.

> use of hypothetical questions. The objective of the investigative interview is to clarify the facts, and it is not possible for the Ministry to recommend one specific interview method. The main point is that the interview is conducted within the legal frameworks which apply for the interview in question, and that the interviewer is properly informed about these legal frameworks. The interview method applied must be adapted to the age, personality and maturity of the child, and to the nature of the case and the interview situation. It is important that the interviewer's conversation with the child is characterised by neutrality with regard to whether or not the alleged abuse has taken place. Furthermore, it is important that it is the child's version which comes to light, and not, for example, the abuser's version, or that of the parents or the interviewer ... In case the interviewer is called to appear as a witness in court, he or she must be ready to explain how the interview was carried out. (Comments on Regulations of 2 October 1998 no 925 Section 12, pp 30–31).

These comments specify that interviewers are required to know the legal framework and must also clarify and conduct the interview according to 'the age, personality and maturity of the child, and according to the nature of the case and the interview situation' and 'as witness in court, he or she must be ready to explain how the interview was carried out'. That is to say, concrete demands are made of interviewers as regards both the objective of the interview and their knowledge of why and how the interview was undertaken.

Proposition no 33 of the Norwegian *Odelsting* (1993–94)[56] explains that the well-qualified person instructed to conduct the interview:

> should have special knowledge of children's manner of speaking and behaviour, and be familiar with the judicial system's requirements as concern interviews. In addition, the interviewer should possess the ability to inspire confidence and establish the rapport necessary to make the child talk. Deciding which persons are best qualified will therefore not only be a matter of educational background, but also depend on the persons' other educational qualifications, experiences, and personal qualities.

The latter requirement has consequences for the Norwegian Police University College's recruitment strategies and priorities, as well as for the training of interviewers.

Regulations do not specify where the interview suites should be located or how they should be equipped, except that they should provide a 'child-friendly environment'. In some cases, children must travel long distances to get to the 'child friendly' interview suites. Obviously care has to be taken not to exhaust children before the interviews are conducted.

The upcoming examination of the 1998 Regulations[57] should make clear both the objectives of the interview and the empirical knowledge of how the interviews should be conducted, addressing such issues as the number of investigative

[56] Proposition no 33 (1993–94) of the *Odelsting* concerning the act of amendments to the Criminal Proceedings Act (to strengthen the position of victims of crime). The system of the *Odelsting* and *Lagting* was abolished as of 1 October 2009. Until this time, three-quarters of the members of the *Storting* were members of the *Odelsting*. The *Odelsting* considered all Bills before sending its decision to the *Lagting*.

[57] Regulations of 2 October 1998 (n 55).

interviews and the identity of those monitoring the interviews. Increased forensic psychological understanding of investigative interviews may ensure greater security under the law, so that guilty people get punished, whereas innocent people are acquitted. To achieve this, the regulations need to be empirically updated and all the practitioners in the process must become familiar with, and know the limitations of, the methods and procedures in use. Researchers, decision-makers and practitioners need education and must, through mutual cooperation, contribute to further development of this field to strengthen the legal protection of the persons involved.

The Way Ahead

In my PhD thesis,[58] I analysed 100 investigative interviews of children by the special trained interviewers in Norway. Consistent with the results of research elsewhere, my findings raised challenging questions for the police officers, their leaders, training facilitators, institutions such as the Norwegian Police University College, and academics and researchers: the interviewers and officers knew how interviews should be conducted and were aware of the strengths and weaknesses of different strategies, but did not implement this knowledge when conducting interviews. As a result, I am convinced that future training should be group focused, involving the same groups and in the same environments where day-to-day work takes place, with emphasis on planning and evaluation of each of the officers' contributions, using empirically tested procedures and protocols. Similar knowledge needs to be implemented in the courts.

Summary

Since 1913, Norway has pioneered effective forensic interviewing. The tenfold increase in the number of interviews conducted over the last 16 years shows that we do take children's testimony seriously. The legal process in Norway, and in the other Nordic countries, differs from that in many other countries to the extent that alleged child victims do not serve as live witnesses in the court. Instead the video is 'evidence-in-chief' replacing the children's need to testify in open court. Children can put the incidents behind them and, if necessary, receive help from the child welfare service. According to the Norwegian Supreme Court, the case law and procedure is clearly in accordance with the case law of the European Court. However, the low population density makes travel distances longer, for both children and police. To ensure the best interests of the child and provide them with

[58] Myklebust (n 27).

appropriate treatment and support, the Norwegian government has opened seven *Statens Barnehus* (Child Advocacy Centres). The procedure (Regulations) is being examined and the models (*Statens Barnehus* versus the interviews conducted in special interviews suites at the police stations, in courts or at the child welfare service) are being evaluated. Both nationally and internationally interviewers, teaching institutions, research environments, legislative authorities and the court of law are all responsible for improving the quality of investigative interviewing. This work will be pursued in the spirit of the Norwegian Women's National Council who in 1913 took the first steps to improve interviews of children. 'Everybody agreed; yet still it was difficult to bring about the necessary changes!'[59]

[59] Norske Kvinners Nasjonalråd (n 22) 181.

9

Conclusions

JR SPENCER[1]

In this concluding chapter a series of related questions will be addressed, the perspective being that of English law. To help the reader follow the thread of the argument, here at the outset is a list of those questions:

(i) Does section 28 of the Youth Justice and Criminal Evidence Act 1999, which provides for pre-trial cross-examination, contain a scheme that can be made to work?
(ii) If section 28 proves workable, will it solve all the problems that arise from the cross-examination of children?
(iii) Is it possible to alter or 'tame' the process of cross-examination so that, when it takes place, it is more attuned to the capacities of children?
(iv) Alternatively, would it be feasible to dispense with cross-examination altogether, at least in certain cases?
(v) What other means, apart from adversarial cross-examination, exist to enable the credibility of child witnesses to be tested?

(i) Is Section 28 Workable?

The text of this section has already appeared as an appendix to chapter one, but for the convenience of readers here it is again:

28.— Video recorded cross-examination or re-examination.

(1) Where a special measures direction provides for a video recording to be admitted under section 27 as evidence in chief of the witness, the direction may also provide—
  (a) for any cross-examination of the witness, and any re-examination, to be recorded by means of a video recording; and
  (b) for such a recording to be admitted, so far as it relates to any such cross-examination or re-examination, as evidence of the witness under cross-examination or on re-examination, as the case may be.

[1] I am grateful to Joyce Plotnikoff and Danya Glaser for their helpful comments on this chapter. The remaining errors are my own.

(2) Such a recording must be made in the presence of such persons as Criminal Procedure Rules or the direction may provide and in the absence of the accused, but in circumstances in which—
  (a) the judge or justices (or both) and legal representatives acting in the proceedings are able to see and hear the examination of the witness and to communicate with the persons in whose presence the recording is being made, and
  (b) the accused is able to see and hear any such examination and to communicate with any legal representative acting for him.

(3) Where two or more legal representatives are acting for a party to the proceedings, subsection (2)(a) and (b) are to be regarded as satisfied in relation to those representatives if at all material times they are satisfied in relation to at least one of them.

(4) Where a special measures direction provides for a recording to be admitted under this section, the court may nevertheless subsequently direct that it is not to be so admitted if any requirement of subsection (2) or Criminal Procedure Rules or the direction has not been complied with to the satisfaction of the court.

(5) Where in pursuance of subsection (1) a recording has been made of any examination of the witness, the witness may not be subsequently cross-examined or re-examined in respect of any evidence given by the witness in the proceedings (whether in any recording admissible under section 27 or this section or otherwise than in such a recording) unless the court gives a further special measures direction making such provision as is mentioned in subsection (1)(a) and (b) in relation to any subsequent cross-examination, and re-examination, of the witness.

(6) The court may only give such a further direction if it appears to the court—
  (a) that the proposed cross-examination is sought by a party to the proceedings as a result of that party having become aware, since the time when the original recording was made in pursuance of subsection (1), of a matter which that party could not with reasonable diligence have ascertained by then, or
  (b) that for any other reason it is in the interests of justice to give the further direction.

(7) Nothing in this section shall be read as applying in relation to any cross-examination of the witness by the accused in person (in a case where the accused is to be able to conduct any such cross-examination).

When the section was first enacted in 1999, changes to the rules of criminal procedure and evidence fell within the purview of the Home Office, whose officials seem to have taken the firm view that it was not workable. Hence it was not brought into force, even on an experimental basis.[2] Some years later there was a redistribution of responsibilities when the Ministry of Justice was created and these matters were transferred to the new department. Shortly after that, in 2008, the Ministry of Justice set up an internal working group consisting of a judge, representatives of the police, the Crown Prosecution Service and officials from various government departments to consider whether section 28 might be workable. This reached the conclusion that, properly managed, it could be made to work, and that it would be of significant help in cases involving vulnerable

[2] See Laura Hoyano, 'Coroners and Justice Act 2009: (3) Special Measures Directions Take Two: Entrenching Unequal Access to Justice?' [2010] *Crim LR* 345, 348–49.

witnesses, particularly children. In so concluding, it distanced itself from some of the fears that had been expressed in a consultative document emanating from the government several years before.[3] Though not published to the world at large, in September 2011 the conclusions of this working party were circulated and discussed at a large seminar organised by the Ministry of Justice, attended by invited representatives of all the different professional groups involved in the workings of the criminal justice system. The discussion at this seminar was constructive and it seems that the main obstacle to the implementation of section 28 is now concern about the cost, particularly if new technical equipment for the courts should be required. As this book goes to press, discussions on this topic are still taking place within the Civil Service. Ultimately, the decision to implement section 28 is one for the Minister of Justice, who must bring the provision into force by issuing a Commencement Order. Whether the Minister will do so, and if so when, is likely to depend on the outcome of these discussions.

(ii) If Section 28 is Workable, Will it Solve all the Problems that Arise from the Cross-examination of Children?

The answer to this question, I believe, is that it will ameliorate some of the current problems, but not solve all of them. This is for two reasons: first, though the pre-trial cross-examination under section 28 will take place earlier than a live cross-examination conducted at the eventual trial, in many cases there will still be a substantial delay between the cross-examination and the ABE interview[4] (and, of course, an even longer one between cross-examination and the matters that gave rise to the proceedings); and secondly, it seems to be envisaged that the pre-trial cross-examination, when it happens, will be conducted in the same way as a cross-examination taking place at trial—a method which gives rise to many problems.

First Problem—Delay

Section 28, it should be noted, does not create the legal basis for a new investigative measure, to be managed by the police as an add-on to the procedure for the

[3] Office of Criminal Justice Reform, *Improving the Criminal Trial Process for Young Witnesses: A Consultation Paper* (June 2007). When reviewing it, Laura Hoyano described this document as 'notably thin on evidence and analysis': 'The Child Witness Review: Much Ado About Too Little' [2007] *Crim LR* 849, 852.

[4] ABE stands for 'Achieving Best Evidence'. ABE interviews are those conducted with a view to criminal proceedings under guidance contained in an official document called *Achieving Best Evidence in Criminal Proceedings; Guidance on Interviewing Victims and Witnesses, and Guidance on Using Special Measures*. See ch 1 above, at n 31.

ABE interview. Instead it provides for pre-trial cross-examination to be ordered as a 'special measure' by a judge of the court before which the defendant will eventually be tried, as part of the package of 'special measures' designed to facilitate vulnerable witnesses giving evidence created by part II chapter I of the Youth Justice and Criminal Evidence Act 1999. It follows that a section 28 pre-trial cross-examination could not take place until a prosecution has been instituted and an application has been made to a judge who is competent to make the order. In the light of this, how great, in reality, is the time-lag likely to be between the ABE interview and the pre-trial cross-examination?

In a case that is destined to be heard in the Crown Court, as the majority of cases grave enough to justify the use of the procedure will be, the following steps will be necessary before the pre-trial cross-examination takes place: (i) the prosecution must be formally instituted; (ii) the case must be considered by the magistrates' court, which is the point of entry for all criminal cases, including those that the Crown Court will eventually deal with; (iii) the file must be transferred from the magistrates' court to the Crown Court; (iv) the prosecutor must make a formal application to the Crown Court for the section 28 'special measure' to be ordered; (v) a judge of the Crown Court must decide whether to grant it or not, and if it is granted, must set a date for the pre-trial cross-examination to be carried out.

Where the case is simple, and the defendant willing to co-operate, these different stages could be made to follow each other quickly, so that the resulting interval could be relatively short. In these circumstances the sequence leading to an expedited pre-trial cross-examination would be as follows. The police, having already discussed the matter with the CPS, would 'charge' (ie formally accuse) the defendant immediately after the ABE interview. A copy of the charge would be sent at once to the magistrates' court, where its arrival would have the legal effect of starting the prosecution. The defendant's 'first appearance' in the magistrates' court would then follow almost immediately. If the police were holding the defendant in police custody after charge his 'first appearance' in the magistrates' court would be on that day or the next;[5] and if the police had released him, having bailed him to appear at the next sitting of the court, his first appearance would again follow quickly. From the magistrates' court the case would then move on to the Crown Court by one or other of two expedited routes. If the offence charged was 'indictable only', ie a grave crime such as rape, which only the Crown Court is competent to try, the case would be 'sent for trial' by the magistrates at once and without any consideration of the evidence.[6] In such a case the file would arrive in the Crown Court almost immediately after the defendant's 'first appearance'. If the defendant was charged with an offence triable 'either-way', ie a less serious offence, such as sexual assault, which the magistrates themselves could try, a proper hearing before the magistrates would normally be necessary in order to decide the court in which it should be tried; but where child witnesses are involved the CPS

[5] Or the next but one if a Sunday or Bank Holiday intervenes: PACE 1984 s 46.

[6] Crime and Disorder Act 1998 s 51.

can override the normal process by issuing what is called a 'notice of transfer',[7] which could also move the case into the Crown Court immediately after 'first appearance'. The CPS having made its application for pre-trial cross-examination at the same time as the case was sent or transferred for trial, a Crown Court judge would then deal with the application quickly. The defendant, thinking that an early pre-trial cross-examination would serve his interests—as it is at least conceivable he might—would then join the prosecution in requesting an early date. And assuming a properly equipped courtroom and a judge were available, a pre-trial cross-examination could take place within perhaps two or three weeks of the ABE interview.

In reality, however, the delay is likely to be greater than this, even in a simple case. First, as everybody with practical experience of the criminal justice system knows, complications can arise even in apparently straightforward cases. As a barrister once put it, 'Getting a trial up and running can be like trying to get two pandas to mate: not only does everything have to be in alignment but you also need to be extravagantly lucky.'[8]

Secondly, even in a simple case the defence may be unwilling to cooperate in fixing an early date for the pre-trial cross-examination. Defendants, and guilty ones in particular, often see advantages in spinning the proceedings out. They may reason, for example, that the longer the time the child is waiting to be cross-examined the greater the chance of a retraction. And for such a defendant, section 28 and the detailed arrangements envisaged for its practical application make it possible to extend the minimum period between the ABE interview and the pre-trial cross-examination by at least a month.

This is because the detailed scheme proposed[9] for the operation of section 28 envisages that the pre-trial cross-examination will normally take place after two things have happened: (i) the prosecution has 'complied with its duty of disclosure' by informing the defence of any material not previously disclosed which 'might reasonably be considered capable of undermining the case for the prosecution … or of assisting the case for the accused'[10] and (ii) the defence have filed the 'defence statement' in which, as English law stands, they inform the court and the prosecutor of the grounds on which they propose to fight the case, and also of the witnesses—if any—whom they intend to call. To file a defence statement, the law[11] currently allows the defendant 28 days from when the prosecution carries out its 'duty of disclosure', the step (i) previously mentioned. This means that, even where the prosecution carries out its duty of disclosure as soon as a prosecution is begun, a dilatory defendant can slow things down by insisting on his full four weeks for the filing of the defence statement.

[7] Criminal Justice Act 1993 s 53.

[8] Alex McBride, *Defending the Guilty*, Viking, London, 2010, 232.

[9] By the Working Party—see above.

[10] Criminal Procedure and Investigations Act 1996 s 3(1).

[11] The Criminal Procedure and Investigations Act 1996 (Defence Disclosure Time Limits) Regulations 2011 (SI 2011 No 209).

For this timetable for pre-trial cross-examination there are two good reasons, at any rate in principle. First, the judge who will be presiding at the pre-trial cross-examination needs to know the broad lines of the defence in order to control the cross-examination. Secondly, after receiving the defence statement the prosecution is required to take another look at the material that has been collected in the course of the investigation to see whether, in the light of the defence statement, there is some further matter which the defence in fairness ought to be informed about, and which the prosecution did not initially disclose because it did not perceive it to be potentially helpful to the defence. Further material of this sort might well be something the defence would wish to ask the child about in cross-examination. So in principle it is right that the cross-examination of the child should not take place until such material, if it exists, will have reached the hands of the defence. But if necessary, as it probably is, this timetable for pre-trial cross-examination has an obvious disadvantage. It means that even in the simplest cases, the delay between the ABE interview and the pre-trial cross-examination is likely to be at least six or eight weeks if the defendant drags his heels—as against the two or three weeks which might be achieved where the defence is willing to cooperate. This problem, however, needs to be placed in perspective. Even if delayed to this extent, the pre-trial cross-examination would still take place considerably earlier than it would if, as now, it was held at trial.

Where the case is complicated, the period between the ABE interview and the section 28 pre-trial cross-examination will almost invariably be longer. The typical complication will be the existence of a body of material which arguably bears upon the credibility of the witness, and which the defence—quite understandably—wants to look at before planning the cross-examination. This material could be records relating to the child or her family held by the local authority social services department; hospital records; records held by schools or children's homes; or the records of investigations by other police forces into earlier allegations that the child has previously made. In the first place, the prosecution, if the material has reached its hands, will have to consider it and decide whether it is material it should disclose to the defence under its general 'duty of disclosure'. This is likely to take time, and so delay the prosecution in taking the first of the two stages, described above, which must normally be completed before the section 28 pre-trial cross-examination will take place. And secondly, and more seriously, material of this sort may be in the hands of third parties who are unwilling to hand it over. In this case, either the prosecution or the defence will have to apply to the court for an order requiring the third party to disclose it. If the third party resists the application, a court hearing will be necessary to resolve the matter—which will inevitably take yet more time. A variant on this theme is where the material is already in the hands of the prosecutor, but the prosecutor believes that the public interest requires that it should go no further. Here too an application to the court will be required, for the issue to be decided by a judge. Where this happens, the delay between the ABE interview and the cross-examination could extend to four or five months, rather than the six or eight weeks mentioned at the end of the previous paragraph. If the going gets really difficult, it might be even longer still.

Part of the problem here is that the law on what is called 'third-party disclosure' in England and Wales is currently obscure. In France, the *juge d'instruction* who is responsible for the pre-trial phase of a prosecution of a grave offence has, by statute, the express power to take any legal step which 'he considers useful towards the discovery of the truth';[12] but in English law the position is not so simple. A comprehensive account of the current law on third-party disclosure, so far as it is possible to give one, would run to many pages.[13] As so much legal uncertainty exists as to what confidential material a third party can be made to hand over, whether to the prosecution or to the defence, there is plenty of room for legal argument when this situation arises; and legal argument takes time, as well as money. In practical terms, the police and the CPS could sometimes minimise the possible delay between the ABE interview and the pre-trial cross-examination by planning ahead, and negotiating with third parties in advance. But in this type of case, the current state of the law means that a considerable delay between the ABE interview and the cross-examination will often be inevitable.

If there will often be a substantial delay between the ABE interview and the pre-trial cross-examination made possible by section 28, this does not, of course, mean that section 28 is useless. First, for various reasons, a cross-examination conducted ahead of trial can be managed in a way that is less stressful for the child than a cross-examination conducted at the trial itself. One obvious improvement is likely to be that the child is not kept waiting outside the courtroom for a day and half, as with the four-year-old girl in the *Barker* case.[14] Secondly, even if there is a substantial delay, it is likely to be shorter than it would have been if the child was to be cross-examined at the trial. And thirdly, if the police, the CPS and the courts are prepared to cooperate, there should also be many cases in which the delay is relatively short.

But the possibility of substantial delays in certain types of case, in particular where 'third party disclosure' is an issue, does suggest that there ought in principle to be a mechanism for an 'expedited cross-examination' at which, at a much earlier stage, the defence would be able to put questions to the child about the basic facts that are alleged—with the possibility of a further cross-examination to explore issues of credibility, should the disclosure process, when completed, eventually reveal any, and should the court, on being informed of them, decide that it is appropriate for the child to be questioned about them. Such an 'expedited cross-examination' could not be arranged within the framework of section 28 because, as we have already seen, section 28 can only operate after criminal proceedings have

[12] *Code de procédure pénale*, article 81, paragraph 1.

[13] For a detailed analysis, see Laura Hoyano and Caroline Keenan, *Child Abuse—Law and Policy Across Boundaries*, Oxford, Oxford University Press, 2010, 553–68.

[14] See ch 1, p 9 above and pp 200–01 below. Also J R Spencer and Rhona Flin, *The Evidence of Children, the Law and the Psychology*, 2nd edn (London, Blackstone Press, 1993), 270–76.

been instituted. So as the law stands, it could only be done informally, by the police offering it as an 'optional extra' to the defence, should they wish to avail themselves of the possibility. And if so done, it would presumably not displace the right to insist on a 'proper' cross-examination later, either pre-trial under section 28, or at trial.[15]

Second Problem—the Method of Adversarial Cross-examination

Secondly, replacing cross-examination at trial with cross-examination conducted ahead of trial is of limited value to child witnesses, and to the process of accurate fact-finding, if what is permitted to take place pre-trial will always be the same sort of adversarial cross-examination, conducted in the same sort of way that cross-examinations of child witnesses are usually conducted when they take place at trial.

To repeat what has been said in earlier chapters of this book, and in many other places too, it is beyond question that the traditional adversarial cross-examination, when applied to child witnesses who are either young or vulnerable, is unsatisfactory. This is for two reasons. First, the traditional adversarial cross-examination is not a reliable method of either testing the truthfulness of what the child has previously said, or of obtaining from them further information that is accurate, and hence it does not help the court to reach a decision in accordance with the truth. Secondly, for children it is potentially abusive.

Taking the first point first, the problem is that the traditional adversarial cross-examination involves, or indeed actually centres upon, the asking of leading questions: that is, questions that suggest the answer the questioner desires. Suggestive questions have a tendency to produce answers that are inaccurate because they conform to the suggestion, rather than to the truth. It is for this reason that police officers, psychiatrists and social workers are strongly discouraged from asking them in investigative interviews. It is also the reason why even lawyers are banned from asking them when examining in-chief the witnesses appearing for the side they are representing. The more suggestible the witness, the stronger the likelihood of their accepting the suggestion the question contains; and children, particularly young children, are in general more suggestible than adults. Similarly, the greater the gulf in age and status between the questioner and person questioned, the harder the person questioned will find it to resist the pressure to give the questioner the answer he has made clear he wants to hear, whether true or false; and the gulf in age and status between barristers and children, especially young ones,

[15] Though the fact that the defence had the chance to put questions would presumably improve the chances of the child's statement then being admitted as hearsay evidence, should the Crown seek its admission on that basis: see section (iv) of this chapter, below.

is obviously much greater than that between barristers and experienced police officers or barristers and hardened criminals.[16]

All this is common sense and hardly needs scientific evidence to prove it. But such evidence does indeed exist. As we saw earlier in this book, studies where children are exposed to the sort of suggestive questioning allowed in cross-examination have indeed been carried out, and they clearly demonstrate that common sense is right: when applied to young children, the traditional sort of cross-examination risks producing evidence that is inaccurate.[17] It is also borne out by those who have practical experience of children and of the courts. Thus a child psychiatrist who has extensive experience of the courts once wrote:

> As an experienced expert witness, I can confirm that there is not the slightest chance of a traumatised sexually abused child surviving cross-examination by a barrister. That is not to be unduly critical of lawyers but simply to state plain common sense.[18]

And similarly, an Australian magistrate once stated that cross-examining children is '… like shooting rats in a barrel … it's easy to confuse them and make out they're telling lies'.[19]

That the traditional, adversarial, 'Old Bailey-style'[20] cross-examination is not a reliable method of testing the evidence of children is increasingly accepted by the senior judiciary, at any rate in England and Wales.

In *Re W (Children) (Family Proceedings: Evidence)*[21] the Supreme Court had to consider when, if ever, children should be required to give live evidence, and undergo cross-examination, in care proceedings—civil proceedings in which the state applies to remove a child from a family where it is at risk of harm. In a judgment in which the other four Justices agreed, Baroness Hale said this:

> [25] The court is unlikely to be helped by generalised accusations of lying, or by a fishing expedition in which the child is taken slowly through the story yet again in the hope that something will turn up, or by a cross-examination which is designed to intimidate the child and pave the way for accusations of inconsistency in a future criminal trial. On the other hand, focussed questions which put forward a different explanation for certain events may help the court to do justice between the parties.

A civil court, she went on to say, must 'factor in what steps can be taken to improve the quality of the child's evidence and at the same time decrease the risk of harm to the child', and in doing so it should not

[16] A further point is that suggestibility increases as time passes between the events and the questioning—as it will necessarily have done where, as usual, a substantial period elapses between the ABE interview and the cross-examination.

[17] Plotnikoff and Woolfson, ch 2; Cossins, ch 5.

[18] Eileen Vizard, letter *The Independent*, 30 October 1987.

[19] Quoted by Mark and Roslin E Brennan in *Strange Language—Child Victims Under Cross Examination*, Wagga Wagga, 1988, 3.

[20] For the benefit of foreign readers, the Old Bailey, properly called the Central Criminal Court, is the Crown Court in central London, where many of the most sensational criminal trials take place.

[21] *Re W (Children) (Family Proceedings: Evidence)* [2010] UKSC 12, [2010] 1 WLR 701.

> [27] assume that an 'Old Bailey style' cross-examination is the best way of testing that evidence. It may be the best way of casting doubt upon it in the eyes of the jury but that is another matter.

Similarly, in *W and M*[22] the Criminal Division of the Court of Appeal upheld the defendants' convictions for attempted rape despite the fact that the alleged victim, a little girl of eight, had changed her initial account significantly under cross-examination at the Old Bailey. The Court of Appeal held that the convictions—evidently based on the account the girl had given in her ABE interview—were nevertheless to be considered safe notwithstanding her change of tune under cross-examination. In so holding, the Court of Appeal said:

> [30] There is undoubtedly a danger of a child witness wishing simply to please. There is undoubtedly a danger of a child witness seeing that to assent to what is put may bring the questioning process to speedier conclusion than to disagree.

And the court also went on to say:

> [31] ... Most of the questions which produced the answers which were chiefly relied on [by the defence], unlike many others, constituted the putting of direct suggestions with an indication of the answer: 'This happened, didn't it?' The consequence of that is, as the judge remarked, that it can be very difficult to tell whether the child is truly changing her account or simply taking the line of least resistance.

To the problem of suggestion there is added the further and equally troubling problem of cross-examiners using age-inappropriate language. In chapter two we saw how at least half of the young witnesses in Plotnikoff and Woolfson's study recognised that in court they had been asked questions that they failed to understand—and yet over half of them had muddled through without asking for clarification, despite being told that they could do so. Again to state the obvious, if a witness (of whatever age) has not understood the question, the answer it provokes will not help the court to elucidate the truth. A fortiori, nothing should be read into the witness's failure to respond to a statement in the form of an assertion ('... and then X happened ...') which the witness has not understood was intended as a question at all.[23]

Turning to the second point, the traditional 'Old Bailey-style' cross-examination is potentially abusive for child witnesses because it inflicts on them an experience that is often stressful and unpleasant. Again, this is something that common sense suggests. And once again, there is research evidence that amply shows that common sense is right. The New Zealand study by Hanna and others quoted by Henderson in chapter six of this book reported that during cross-examination 35 per cent of the young children and 25 per cent of the older children were reduced to tears;[24] and in chapter two, Plotnikoff and Woolfson describe the unfavourable reactions to the experience of the child witnesses they interviewed

22 *W and M* [2010] EWCA Crim 1926.
23 Plotnikoff and Woolfson, ch 2.
24 See ch 6, at 126.

in the course of the study. It is hard to disagree with the opinion a predominantly civil judge once expressed to this author in the course of conversation: 'However much we try to set the child at ease and make the court child-friendly, for children adversarial cross-examination is a form of secondary abuse.'[25]

The most stressful aspect of a cross-examination is likely to be when the cross-examiner accuses the witness of telling lies; an element a cross-examination is almost certain to contain where the case is basically the child's word against the defendant's and the defendant takes the only line available to him—namely that the child has made the accusation up. This is a tricky issue, because if the essence of the defence case is that the child is telling lies, questioning has to be allowed which at least suggests the child is lying, even though the suggestion will be hurtful—and particularly hurtful if the child is in fact telling the truth. The child may indeed be lying, and if he is, questions of this sort will probably be necessary to expose this. An object lesson to this effect was the trial in 2002 of the first group of youths accused of murdering the ten-year-old boy, Damilola Taylor. The key prosecution witness was a girl, aged 12 at the time of the killing and 14 at the time of trial, who claimed to have seen the defendants committing the murder. At trial her evidence was discredited, to the point where the judge directed the jury to disregard it, in a cross-examination which some people at the time criticised as brutal. But there is no doubt that she was lying—as was shown when, at another trial four years later, forensic evidence led to the conviction of a different group of youths for the offence.[26] But if a child has to be confronted with the possibility that he or she has lied, there are ways and ways of doing it. This will be discussed in the next section of this chapter, which examines the question whether adversarial cross-examination can be adapted to make it a suitable means of testing the evidence of children. That is to say, a procedure that is less stressful to them and more likely to produce accurate information, rather than information that is inaccurate.

(iii) Is it Possible to 'Tame' Adversarial Cross-examination?

The initial hurdle to taming cross-examination is the one already identified by Plotnikoff and Woolfson in chapter 2, Henderson in chapter 3 and Cossins in chapter 5: namely that adversarial cross-examination is widely perceived by the

[25] Though that said, research suggests that children whose evidence is believed can find the experience of giving evidence empowering: J Quas, G Goodman, S Ghetti, K Alexander, R Edelstein, A Redlich, I Cordon and DPH Jones, *Childhood Sexual Assault Victims: Long-term Outcomes After Testifying in Criminal Court.* (2005) Monographs of the Society for Research in Child Development, 70, serial no 280, vii–145.

[26] *Preddy and others*, Central Criminal Court, September 2006; BBC News, 20 September 2006.

legal profession as serving purposes which have little if anything to with ensuring that the evidence of witnesses conforms to what Continental lawyers call 'material truth'. In the eyes of many, it exists to serve two other, potentially very different, purposes. First, it is seen as a vehicle for counsel to put before the fact-finder—in grave cases, a jury—his client's version of events. As a New Zealand barrister once candidly explained to a researcher: 'In a trial I have three speeches: my opening, my cross-examination, and my closing.'[27] And secondly, it is seen as a vehicle for discrediting the witness: for making his or her testimony appear, in the eyes of the fact-finder, less worthy of belief than otherwise it might be. As a precondition to any meaningful discussion of 'taming' cross-examination, it must be accepted that the first of these additional purposes is improper, and the second proper only to the extent that the cross-examination makes the witness seem less credible for good reasons rather than for bad ones.

There is no reason for counsel to use his cross-examination of a witness as a vehicle to put his client's case before the court because counsel has other opportunities for this in the form of an opening and a closing speech.[28] In the light of this, it seems odd—at least to observers not brought up within the legal system—that anyone should ever imagine that this is a proper purpose for a cross-examination at all, let alone one that justifies imposing an unpleasant experience on any witness, let alone a witness who is a child. The practice of allowing defence counsel, in particular, to make use of cross-examination in this way may have its roots in legal history. At one time, those accused of felony were required to defend themselves in person. Then when they were first allowed the assistance of counsel, counsel were only permitted to argue points of law on their behalf, and to examine and cross-examine witnesses; they were not permitted to address the court on behalf of their client, the accused being required to do any speech-making for himself—assuming he was sufficiently articulate to do so.[29] At this point in legal history, the only way that defence counsel could put their clients' case before the court was by exploiting their cross-examination of the prosecution witnesses for this purpose; and that is what they did, with the connivance of the judges. The need for this 'bending of the rules' expired in 1836, when those accused of felony were allowed counsel for all purposes, including the making of a closing speech.[30] But it looks as if the practice of bending cross-examination to this end, once established, was permitted to continue, even though there was no longer any need for it.

Moving to the second point, cross-examiners should not be permitted to discredit witnesses by tactics that make them and their evidence seem less credible

[27] Emily Henderson, 'Persuading and Controlling: The Theory of Cross-examination in Relation to Children', in H Westcott, G Davies and R Bull (eds), *Children's Testimony: A Handbook of Psychological Research and Forensic Practice* (Chichester, Wiley 2002) 279, 282.

[28] Or in summary trials, where the advocates for each side usually make one speech only, the opening speech in the case of the prosecutor, and the closing speech in the case of the defence advocate.

[29] See generally John H Langbein, *The Origins of Adversary Criminal Trial*, Oxford, Oxford University Press, 2003, and especially from 171 onwards.

[30] Trial for Felony Act 1836, 6 & 7 Will. IV c114.

than they really are because the overall aim of criminal proceedings, in an adversarial system as well as in an inquisitorial one, is the conviction of the guilty and the acquittal of the innocent.[31] Rules of criminal procedure and evidence should therefore serve that end, rather than the opposite. Thus, to state the obvious again, prosecutors should not be permitted to use techniques that tend to produce the conviction of the innocent, and defenders should not be permitted to use techniques that tend to produce the acquittal of the guilty.

Indeed, behind most of the rules of criminal procedure and evidence this guiding principle can be discerned. It is for this reason, obviously, that neither prosecutors nor defenders are permitted to bribe or threaten their opponents' witnesses to make them stay away from court or change their evidence when they get there; anyone who did so would commit the crime of conspiracy to pervert the course of justice. Similarly, neither prosecutors nor defenders are permitted to incite their witnesses to lie; to do so would be to commit subornation of perjury, another criminal offence. A little less obviously, an advocate is not permitted to call a witness in support of his case whose evidence he knows full well is false (as against one whose evidence he suspects might be so). Thus the Code of Conduct of the Bar provides that a barrister 'must not deceive or knowingly or recklessly mislead the Court';[32] and more particularly, if defending a client who has confessed to him his guilt, counsel must not 'suggest that some other person has committed the offence charged, or call any evidence which the barrister must know is false having regard to the confession'.[33] To break these rules amounts to professional misconduct and could in some circumstances also constitute a criminal offence.[34] And similarly, prosecutors are not permitted to make inflammatory closing speeches, aimed at the hearts of the jurors rather than their heads, in the hope of persuading them to convict despite the flimsy nature of the evidence.[35] It follows, surely, that advocates when cross-examining witnesses should not be permitted to use techniques that discredit them unfairly—that is, make their evidence appear

[31] In the past, hard-bitten practitioners at the criminal Bar have tended to dispute this, claiming that 'the adversarial system' has nothing to do with the discovery of the truth. But this position is impossible to maintain in the light of the 'overriding objective', the official statement of aims and objectives, which since 2005 has been the opening statement in §1.1 of the Criminal Procedure Rules: '(1) The overriding objective of this new code is that criminal cases be dealt with justly. (2) Dealing with a criminal case justly includes (a) acquitting the innocent and convicting the guilty …'. Nor is it possible to square this position with judgments from the higher courts invoking the 'overriding objective' to condemn adversarial tactics tending to produce the opposite result—such as unveiling, on the day of the trial, an 'ambush defence' which, though implausible, the prosecution cannot then and there rebut; eg *R (DPP) v Chorley Justices* [2006] EWHC 1795.

[32] Code of Conduct of the Bar of England and Wales, §302.

[33] Ibid, Written Standards for the Conduct of Professional Work, §12.4.

[34] The common law offence of perverting the course of justice consists of 'any act or course of conduct tending or intended to interfere with the course of public justice': *Archbold, Criminal Pleading, Evidence and Practice* (2012) §28.2.

[35] See *Puddick* (1865) 4 Foster and Finlason 497, 176 ER 662, where Crompton J rebuked prosecution counsel in a rape case for urging the jury to convict by telling them 'that to acquit the prisoner of rape would be to commit the girl of perjury'. Cf Bar Code, Written Standards (n 33) §10.1: 'Prosecuting counsel should not attempt to obtain a conviction by all means at his command.'

weaker than it is, assuming the matter is rationally approached. This is because, if witnesses on one or other side are made to look like fools or liars when they have told the truth, this will reduce the likelihood of a truthful verdict. A fortiori, advocates should not be permitted to use techniques which, by confusing the witnesses, tend to make them deliver evidence that is factually inaccurate.

What amounts to discrediting a witness 'unfairly' is, of course, to some extent a matter of debate. The rules on this are not immutable, and have changed from time to time as opinion has developed. At one time, the law regarded it as acceptable to attempt to discredit the complainant in a rape case by cross-examining her at length about her sex life if it had previously been other than completely chaste; a scandalous state of affairs which Parliament redressed by legislation putting limits on this sort of questioning.[36] At one time, too, the law regarded it as permissible to attack the credibility of an opponent's witnesses by confronting them with almost any piece of discreditable behaviour in their past; another unsatisfactory state of affairs which led, in 2003, to the enactment of a law forbidding the questioning of witness about matters of bad character except with judicial leave, to be granted only where the behaviour in question is bad enough to cast real doubt upon their credibility[37]—a change in the letter of the law which is widely said to have produced a noticeable change in the way that witnesses are treated in the courts.[38] And in setting the limits where child witnesses are concerned, it should be borne in mind that it is particularly easy to discredit children.

Against that background, I believe that for children adversarial cross-examination could in principle be 'tamed' by making the following changes to what at present often happens. First, contrary to what too often happens now, the questions should be put in language that the witness can understand. This point is so obvious that there is no need to elaborate it further. Secondly, as well as being expressed in language children can understand, questions in cross-examination should be put in an order that avoids confusing them. At present it is widely regarded as acceptable for cross-examiners to put questions out of logical sequence and to jump around from topic to topic—a practice sometimes justified as a way of uncovering the fact that the witness has memorised his testimony and is reciting it by rote;[39] though in reality, questioning that jumps from topic to topic without the clues routinely given in normal conversation to indicate a change of subject seems as likely to confuse a truthful witness as to trip up a lying one.[40] A further problem related to the order of questions is the mixing up of questions designed to test the witness's sincerity with questions designed to elicit

[36] The current legislation is s 41 of the Youth Justice and Criminal Evidence Act 1999.

[37] Criminal Justice Act 2003 s100.

[38] Hoyano and Keenan (n 13) 759: 'the asymmetry which the common law had constructed, allowing open season on ordinary witnesses whilst shielding the defendant from such attacks (subject to forfeiture) has been reversed'.

[39] Louise Ellison, 'The Mosaic Art?: Cross-examination and the Vulnerable Witness' (2001) 21 *Legal Studies* 353, 360–61.

[40] See Brennan (n 19) 64–65.

further information. Questions of the first sort, which usually imply that the witness is untruthful, are likely to upset the witness. In the case of a young witness the effect will often be to reduce the child to tears, a state in which he or she will find it difficult to think clearly and to produce accurate answers to questions of the second sort, those intended to elicit further information. Questions of these two types should be kept apart and asked in separate phases.[41]

Thirdly, as Cossins suggests in chapter five, there should be a ban on asking the child the same question (or confronting the child with the same statement) more than once. This is because of the risk that the child, overawed by being questioned by someone who appears to be an authority figure, will think the original answer was unacceptable and give a different answer in a desire to please.

Fourthly, 'leading questions'—that is, suggestive questions—should be strictly limited. In particular there should, when dealing with little children, be a ban on 'tag questions': questions put in the form of an assertion, with 'isn't it?' or 'didn't he?' tagged onto the end of them. As Plotnikoff and Woolfson explain in chapter two, children often misunderstand tag questions and end up saying 'yes' when they mean 'no', and 'no' where they mean 'yes'. Even where this does not happen, strongly suggestive questions can press a child (and particularly a young one) into outwardly agreeing with the suggestion, though they inwardly do not. And strongly suggestive questions can sometimes plant a false idea in the mind of a witness, causing them to assent to a suggestion, in the incorrect belief—temporary or permanent—that it is true. The most insidious and harmful are said to be those which presume a false premise—'Did it hurt when he stuck it in you?' when the witness has said nothing about penetration.

Fifthly, limits should be placed on questions that directly or indirectly amount to accusations that the witness is a liar. Child witnesses are not infrequently asked the general question 'Do you ever tell lies?', or to put it more gently, 'Do you ever tell fibs?' A cross-examiner would not be permitted to put such a question to an adult witness unless he or she had some objective basis for believing that the witness was a bigger liar than the rest of the population, and similarly, such a question should not be put to a child except where this is so. Inevitably, almost everybody tells 'white lies' occasionally, particularly on social occasions. Few people would be candid enough to copy Groucho Marx and say 'I've had a perfectly wonderful evening, but this wasn't it.' And an honest adult's answer to the question 'Do you ever tell lies?' should be 'No more frequently than you do.' But this level of sophistication is not to be expected of a child who, even if he or she is truthful about important matters, is likely to find the question very awkward and embarrassing. A child witness will usually be driven to answering such a question with a 'Yes' or 'No'; the first of which will discredit him or her unfairly, and the second of which will almost certainly be a lie.

[41] A point I have tried to explain at greater length elsewhere: Spencer and Flin (n 14) 273–74.

A more difficult issue is how far, if at all, a child witness should be confronted with a specific accusation of having told a lie, where the essence of the defence case is that the child's evidence is untrue. Assuming that the child is old enough to be submitted to a cross-examination at all—a topic which is to be discussed later—then in fairness to the defendant this must usually be done. But as previously mentioned, there are many ways of doing it.

In its crudest and most heavy-handed form, the 'Old Bailey' way of doing this would be to take the witness step by step through his evidence-in-chief again, at the end of each step interjecting, in the form of a question, something that is in truth a comment: 'That's not true, is it? You made that up too, didn't you?' If a child witness has to be confronted with the accusation that his or her evidence is false, this can and should be done shortly and simply and without going through a pantomime of this sort. The point was made by the Court of Appeal in *Barker*:[42]

> [42] … When the issue is whether the child is lying or mistaken in claiming that the defendant behaved indecently towards him or her, it should not be over-problematic for the advocate to formulate short, simple questions which put the essential elements of the defendant's case to the witness, and fully to ventilate before the jury the areas of evidence which bear on the child's credibility. Aspects of evidence which undermine or are believed to undermine the child's credibility must, of course, be revealed to the jury, but it is not necessarily appropriate for them to form the subject matter of detailed cross-examination of the child and the advocate may have to forego much of the kind of contemporary cross-examination which consists of no more than comment on matters which will be before the jury in any event from different sources. Notwithstanding some of the difficulties, when all is said and done, the witness whose cross-examination is in contemplation is a child, sometimes very young, and it should not take very lengthy cross-examination to demonstrate, when it is the case, that the child may indeed be fabricating, or fantasising, or imagining, or reciting a well rehearsed untruthful script, learned by rote, or simply just suggestible, or contaminated by or in collusion with others to make false allegations, or making assertions in language which is beyond his or her level of comprehension, and therefore likely to be derived from another source. Comment on the evidence, including comment on evidence which may bear adversely on the credibility of the child, should be addressed after the child has finished giving evidence.[43]

Finally, and related to the last point, the cross-examination should not be exploited as an occasion for making comments. Unlike some of the other practices mentioned in the previous paragraphs, which are in principle permitted, interspersing cross-examination with comments is in principle forbidden.[44] In practice,

[42] *Barker* [2010] EWCA Crim 4; the facts of the case are described in chs 1 & 9, and at 200–01 below.

[43] Though with due respect to the Court of Appeal, child psychologists and child psychiatrists are likely to say that discovering whether a child is telling the truth or not by questioning can sometimes be a harder job than these words suggest—particularly if a false belief has become implanted in the child's mind, so that he or she is then repeating it in sincerity.

[44] *Archbold* 2012 §8-217. The rule dates back at least as far as *Hardy's case* (1794) 25 St Tr 199, 754, where Eyre CJ rebuked defence counsel as follows: 'Mr Gibbs, I am sorry to interrupt you, but your questions ought not to be accompanied with those sort of comments: they are the proper subject of

however, it is widely permitted. In truth some limited degree of comment has to be permitted, because one of the permitted purposes of cross-examination is to confront the witness with the allegation that he or she is lying or mistaken where (as often) this is the theory the cross-examiner is seeking to put forward, and it is difficult to confront a witness in this way without saying, at least by implication, 'I don't believe you'. However, apart from the inevitable implied comment of this sort, cross-examiners should adhere to the instructions given in the leading manual for practitioners, which is 'cross-examination must not be used for making comments, which should be confined to speeches'.[45]

Is it realistic to think that adversarial cross-examination might be tamed so as to make it suitable for witnesses who are young, or otherwise vulnerable? To do so would involve something of a revolution in the practices and attitudes of the criminal Bar, which at first sight might seem difficult to achieve. However, at the time this chapter goes to press[46] the senior judiciary are doing their best to make this revolution happen.[47] In January 2012 the Judicial College[48]— the body, funded by the government but managed by the judges, that is responsible for training judges—published official guidance for judges confronted with cases where witnesses are children.[49] This advises judges, at the start of such a case, to lay down 'ground rules' as to the way in which the examination of child witnesses is to be conducted. As the matters to be considered, it lists the following:

Directions to both advocates at 'ground rules' discussions

— Adapt questions to child's developmental stage, enabling *this* child's 'best evidence'
— Ask short, simple questions (one idea at a time)
— Follow a logical sequence
— Speak slowly, pause and allow child enough time to process questions (for younger children, almost twice as much)
— Allow full opportunity to answer
— Avoid question types which may produce unreliable answers. 'Tag' questions (e.g. 'He didn't touch you, did he?') are particularly complex. Put more directly e.g. 'Did Jim touch you?' (and if the answer is 'yes') 'How did Jim touch you?' (Use name not pronoun)
— Avoid allegations of misconduct without reasonable grounds. Being accused of lying, particularly if repeated, may cause a child to give inaccurate answers or to agree simply to bring questioning to an end

observation when the defence is made. The business of cross-examination is to ask all sorts of acts, to probe a witness as closely as you can; but it is not the object of a cross-examination to introduce the sort of periphrasis as you have just done.' (Note that this was said in the course of a trial for treason where, unlike in trials for felony, defence counsel were permitted to address the jury.)

45 *Archbold*, ibid.

46 In March 2012.

47 For a comment expressing caution, see Adrian Keane, 'Towards a Principled Approach to the Cross-examination of Vulnerable Witnesses [2012] *Crim LR* (in press).

48 Formerly known as the Judicial Studies Board.

49 *Judicial College Bench Checklist*, http://www.judiciary.gov.uk/publications-and-reports/guidance/2012/jc-bench-checklist-young-wit-cases (accessed February 25 2012).

— Do not ask children to give their address aloud unless for a specific reason
— Do not ask children to demonstrate intimate touching on their body. Use a body diagram
— How child is to be questioned about matters arising from third party disclosure
— How defence case is to be put. For younger children, inform jury of evidence believed to undermine credibility, but do not necessarily address in detailed cross-examination (see *R v Barker* [2010] EWCA Crim 4)

This guidance builds on the observations of the Court of Appeal in *Barker*, which were quoted and reinforced in two other important cases decided during the later part of 2011: *Wills*,[50] and *E*.[51] Both of these cases involved defendants who sought to appeal against their convictions on the ground that, by laying down 'ground rules' of this sort, the trial judge had unfairly hampered their counsel in doing their proper job —and in both cases their appeals were resoundingly rejected. In the first, the Court referred, with approval, to a report published in March 2011 by the Advocacy Training Council,[52] which recommended the course of action that the judge had taken here. In the second, the Court specifically rejected the defendant's complaint that his counsel had not been allowed to 'put his case' to a prosecution witness, a little girl of five, whom the defendant was accused of gravely injuring by punching her in the stomach, and who the defendant said had hurt herself by falling out of bed.

> [28] … The real complaint here, in our view, is that the defence was deprived of the opportunity to confront C in what we might venture to call 'the traditional way'. It is common, in the trial of an adult, to hear, once the nursery slopes of cross-examination have been skied, the assertion: 'You were never punched, hit, kicked as you have was suggested, were you?' It was precisely that the judge was anxious to avoid and, in our view, rightly. It would have risked confusion in the mind of the witness whose evidence was bound to take centre stage, and it is difficult to see how it could have been helpful. Putting the same thing a different way, we struggle to understand how the defendant's right to a fair trial was in any way compromised simply because Mr Whitehead was not allowed to ask: 'S did not punch you in the tummy, did he?' …

In rejecting the defence submission, the Court of Appeal referred to the 'overriding objective' set out in the Criminal Procedure Rules, which imposes on the judge a duty to manage a trial so as to produce a just result.[53]

All this is a good start. But what happened in the trial of Stephen Barker in May 2009 suggests that there is still a long way to go before these lessons are fully internalised by the Bar. This was a high-profile case, tried in the spotlight of publicity in the most famous criminal court in the land. Yet the cross-examination of the

[50] [2011] EWCA Crim 1938, [2012] 1 Cr App R 2.

[51] [2011] EWCA Crim 3028. The judgment in this case was delivered by Lady Justice Rafferty, who when still a barrister had been a member of the Pigot Committee.

[52] Advocacy Training Counsel of the Bar of England and Wales, *Raising the Bar: The Handling of Vulnerable Witnesses, Victims and Defendants in Court* (2011). Information about what this body is and what it does can be found on its website at www.advocacytrainingcouncil.org

[53] See note 31 above.

four-year-old girl was a textbook example of the way that it should not be done. Having put the child through the 'Do you ever tell fibs?' routine, defence counsel proceeded to ask a series of leading questions, many of them 'tag questions', and some of them convoluted ones, with double negatives and several different questions rolled into one, of which the following is an example: 'So you don't tell fibs and Curly Kate asked you—in the tape—whether Stephen ever touched you and you said he didn't. Stephen never touched you with his willy, did he? Did he?'[54] The advocate responsible for this was not a novice, but an experienced QC who, incidentally, writes articles in the legal press about the cross-examination of children.[55] And in the face of this the judge, who was also experienced, did not intervene.

Furthermore, even if suitable rules are laid down, there is still the practical problem of enforcement. What is a judge to do where an advocate, though well aware of the points made in the previous paragraphs, decides that it is in his client's interests to ignore them? Most counsel consider it both bad practice and bad tactics to bully a child witness, but there are some like the barrister whom Esther Rantzen encountered at a public meeting, who told her: 'I don't care what sort of monster my client is, my job is to break the child—and I'll do whatever is necessary to achieve this.'[56] Faced with counsel who persists in asking inappropriate questions there are limits to what even the most conscientious judge can do. As the judge whose words are quoted in chapter two explained, 'You can only interrupt or send the jury out so many times. If I interrupt four out of seven questions, I can't do it again … Their role is to get the client off and they will.' One of the cardinal sins of a judge, as denounced by the Court of Appeal on many occasions, is 'entering the arena': intervention in the case on a scale that gives the impression that the judge has taken sides. For most judges, the need to avoid falling into this trap makes it difficult to exercise to the full the powers of control that the law in theory gives them.

To ensure cross-examination is 'fit for purpose' as far as child witnesses are concerned, it seems that two further measures would be necessary in addition to training. First, to avoid problems of misunderstanding, adequately trained intermediaries should be used as appropriate to the needs of the witness. All children are eligible under the legislative provision: guidance suggests that where any child seems unlikely to be able to recognise a problematic question or tell the questioner that he or she has not understood, then assessment by an intermediary should be considered.[57] And secondly, it would be necessary to couple training with a system of official accreditation and evaluation for those who are permitted to take cases

[54] Two further examples are given in ch 2 above, and more are to be found in the report of the Court of Appeal decision, [2010] EWCA Crim 4, which can be found at www.bailii.org/ew/cases/EWCA/Crim/2010/.

[55] Bernard Richmond QC, 'Cross-examining Young Witnesses' (2011) 175 *Criminal Law and Justice Weekly* 69–70.

[56] Personal communication from Esther Ranzen.

[57] For a list of the matters to be considered, see box 2.1 on p 23 of *Achieving Best Evidence* (n 4).

where child witnesses are involved—not only for counsel, but probably for judges too.

Where children are very immature, or have serious communication problems, or are highly vulnerable, there is surely no sensible alternative to the use of an intermediary in the full sense of the word: not the intermediary as used in the courts today, who merely intervenes when counsel's questions are beyond the child's comprehension, or the 'intermediary as a megaphone'[58] who merely 'translates' the questions into a form the child can understand, but the intermediary who is given a list of issues that the other side wishes to explore, and is then allowed to ask the questions in his or her own way. This was, of course, one of the options that the Pigot Committee proposed, albeit only by a majority:[59]

> … The majority propose that the judge's discretion, which we have already permitted, should extend where necessary to allowing the relaying of questions from counsel through a paediatrician, child psychiatrist, social worker or person who has the child's confidence. In these circumstances nobody except for the trusted party would be visible to the child, although everyone with an interest would be able to communicate, indirectly, through the interlocutor.
>
> We recognise that this would be a substantial change and we realise that there will be unease at the prospect of interposing a third party between advocate and witness. Clearly some of the advocate's forensic skills, timing, intonation and the rest, would be lost, and it is, of course, possible that a child might be confused by being subjected to testing questioning from someone regarded as a friend. Nevertheless we do not find these objections conclusive. Where it is absolutely impossible for counsel to communicate successfully with a child there is, in our view, no great difference of principle between someone who can do so and the employment of an interpreter where a witness cannot speak English. Neither technique is entirely satisfactory but both can prevent the loss of crucial evidence without which the court cannot do justice.

The one dissentient from this proposal was the member of the committee who was a barrister, Anne Rafferty, who thought the problems could be solved by 'allowing greater opportunities for counsel to establish a rapport with the child'. She thought the intermediary would 'hinder rather than assist counsel in conducting the case'—a respectable objection. But among the reasons other barristers have given are that the system would 'remove the theatre of confrontation' and that it would 'reduce defence lawyers' ability to use their communicative superiority over children to avoid bringing out the truth'.[60] To anyone who is not a lawyer, these look like reasons to support the proposal rather than to oppose it.

[58] Henderson, ch 3, p 65.

[59] Report, reprinted as ch 10 below, §§2.32 and 2.33.

[60] E Davies, K Hanna, E Henderson and L Hand, *Questioning Child Witnesses—Exploring the Benefits and Risks of Intermediary Models*, Institute of Public Policy, AUT University (New Zealand), 29.

(iv) Is it Possible to Dispense with Cross-examination?

In the previous sections of this chapter, and indeed in the previous chapters of this book, we have seen that the cross-examination of children—and especially of very young children—is a major problem, and one to which the solutions are not easy. That prompts the question, could we simply do without it?—at least in certain cases. As discussed below, this raises once again the question of what the purpose of cross-examination is—testing the evidence with the explicit intention of getting at the truth, or discrediting the witness.

However, the immediate objection to this is a formal one. The European Convention on Human Rights, an international instrument by which the United Kingdom is bound,[61] appears to guarantee it, at any rate for defendants. So far as relevant, Article 6 of this Convention provides that

1. In the determination of his civil rights and obligations or of any criminal charge against him, everyone is entitled to a fair and public hearing within a reasonable time by an independent and impartial tribunal established by law…
2. Everyone charged with a criminal offence shall be presumed innocent until proved guilty according to law.
3. *Everyone charged with a criminal offence has the following minimum rights*:

   …

   d *to examine or have examined witnesses against him* and to obtain the attendance and examination of witnesses on his behalf under the same conditions as witnesses against him. (emphasis added)

A similar provision is also to be found in the United Nations Covenant on Civil and Political Rights, another instrument by which, as a matter of international law, the United Kingdom is also bound.[62] It was partly in response to the requirements of these Conventions that Austria and Norway, where at one time the evidence of children would usually be put before the court without the chance for the defence to ask their questions, adopted the systems that were described in chapters seven and eight above.

It should be noted, however, that the right that is guaranteed by these Conventions is not the right to cross-examine witnesses adversarially, but the right 'to examine witnesses or to have them examined'. From the case law from the European Court of Human Rights at Strasbourg it is clear that the right is sufficiently protected in a system where the defence is permitted to propose questions that are then asked on its behalf by other people—as in Austria and Norway. In *SN v Sweden*[63] a defendant was convicted of a sexual offence against a child on

[61] And incidentally drafted with the principles of the common law in mind: see ch 1, n 49.

[62] Article 14(3)(e).

[63] *SN v Sweden* (2002) 39 EHRR 13.

the basis of tape-recorded police interviews with the child complainant, before one of which the suspect's lawyer had agreed with the police office which aspects of the case he wished to be explored. In dismissing the defendant's application the Strasbourg Court said:

> Having regard to the special features of criminal proceedings concerning sexual offences ... [Article 6(3)(d)] cannot be interpreted as requiring in all cases that the questions be put directly by the accused or his or her defence counsel, through cross-examination or other means.

Furthermore, according to the case law of the Strasbourg Court, the defendant's right to a 'fair trial' under Article 6 of the Convention is not infringed just because the conviction was based on evidence some part of which came from a source to which the defence was unable to put its questions, or to have its questions put; the defendant's right is only liable to be infringed if the unquestioned source was the 'sole or decisive' evidence on which the conviction is based. And according to the latest case-law from the Strasbourg Court, even a conviction where such evidence is the 'sole or decisive' element will not invariably infringe the defendant's right to a fair trial. In *Al-Khawaja and Tahery v UK* the Grand Chamber held that it is permissible for a court to convict in such circumstances, even where the central core of the prosecution case consists of hearsay evidence, provided (i) there is a serious reason why the original maker of the statement cannot be produced for questioning by the defence and (ii) sufficient safeguards are provided to compensate the defence for the resulting disadvantage. In so ruling, the Grand Chamber also held that, intelligently applied, sufficient safeguards were provided by the hearsay provisions of the CJA 2003.[64]

So could the hearsay provisions of the CJA 2003 be used to enable the cross-examination of child witnesses—or at any rate, very young or highly vulnerable child witnesses—to be dispensed with? In certain circumstances they could. As we saw in chapter one, these provisions were used in the case of *J (S)*,[65] in which a man was accused of sexually penetrating a little girl aged two-and-a-half, to put before the court the statements she had made to various people indicating that the defendant was the person who had done it. Could they be used more widely, to put before the court the out-of-court statements of child witnesses where a cross-examination would be stressful for the child and, in reality, serve no useful purpose?

They could certainly be so used where both prosecution and defence are prepared to agree to this, because section 114(1)(c) of the CJA 2003 explicitly provides that hearsay evidence is admissible where 'all parties to the proceedings agree to it being admissible'. In practice, this provision is likely to be used in cases where neither side

[64] Applications Nos 26766/05 and 22228/06; judgment given on 15 December 2011. In so holding, the Grand Chamber accepted the arguments put forward by the UK Courts in *Horncastle* [2009] UKSC 124, [2010] 2 AC 373. For an evaluation, see Spencer, 'Hearsay Evidence at Strasbourg: a Further Skirmish, or the Final Round? [2012] *Archbold Review*, Issue 1, 5-8.

[65] *J (S)* [2009] EWCA Crim 1869; see page 6 above.

disputes the truth of what the witness said—as where, for example, a child describes an attack but cannot identify the attacker, and the defence admit the attack took place but deny the defendant committed it. In practice, too, it is occasionally used where the defence do dispute what the witness said, but agree with the prosecution that a cross-examination would serve no useful purpose. An example is the recent case of *Watts*,[66] a case where the defendant was accused of sexual offences against a group of disabled adults with severe communication problems. They had been video-interviewed, with patience and persistence, by an intermediary, and the tapes of the resulting interviews were put before the court. At trial, the defence elected not to attempt to cross-examine the witnesses and concentrated its efforts 'on the areas of evidence which advanced the defendant's case that the allegations against him were false'. The resulting conviction was upheld by the Court of Appeal.

If the 'other side' (in reality, usually the defence) are not prepared to agree as they did in *Watts*, then the situation is more difficult. If the witness is 'unavailable' for any of the list of reasons set out in section 116 of the Act then the hearsay statement could be used. These reasons are death, unfitness to testify through bodily or mental condition, absence abroad,[67] disappearance,[68] and fear;[69] the list does not include 'the experience of testifying orally would be needlessly stressful for the witness and serve no useful purpose'. In principle, the evidence of an absent witness could be admitted for this reason under the 'inclusionary discretion' given to the court by section 114(1)(d) of the Act. But the case law on this provision generally discourages its use to admit hearsay statements of absent witnesses whom it is physically possible to produce to give live evidence at trial but who are reluctant to testify, or when the parties wishing to make use of their statements are reluctant to call them.[70] For hearsay statements of absent children to become generally admissible on the ground that cross-examination would be stressful and serve no useful purpose would require either a change of attitude by the courts towards the use of the 'inclusionary discretion' by the courts, or an amendment to the statutory provisions by Parliament.

Would this be, in principle, a desirable development? In my view, and that of many professionals involved in child abuse cases who are not lawyers, it would.

[66] *Watts* [2010] EWCA Crim 1824; [2011] *Crim LR* 68.

[67] To be precise 'that the relevant person is outside the United Kingdom and it is not reasonably practicable to secure his attendance': s 116(1)(c).

[68] '... that the relevant person cannot be found although such steps as it is reasonably practicable to take to find him have been taken': s 116(1)(d).

[69] '... that through fear the relevant person does not give (or does not continue to give) oral evidence in the proceedings, either at all or in connection with the subject matter of the statement, and the court gives leave for the statement to be given in evidence': s 116(1)(e). By section 116(3), '... "fear" is to be widely construed and (for example) includes fear of the death or injury of another person or financial loss'.

[70] The case-law is voluminous and not altogether consistent. Decisions discouraging the use of s 114(1)(d) in these circumstances include *O'Hare* [2006] EWCA Crim 2512; *Finch* [2007] EWCA Crim 36, [2007] 1 WLR 1645; *McEwan v DPP* [2007] EWHC 740 (Admin), 171 JP 308; *Ibrahim* [2010] EWCA Crim 1176; *Eed* [2010] EWCA Crim 1213; and *Z* [2009] EWCA Crim 20, [2009] 1 CrAppR 34 (500). Cases condoning its use include *Seton* [2010] EWCA Crim 450 and *Burton* [2011] EWCA Crim 1990.

It is simply wrong, surely, to impose on children—or even adult witnesses—an experience that is stressful if it will not really serve the ends of justice. And there are cases, surely, where this is so. Where the child is very young, like the little girl in *Barker*,[71] it is difficult to see what a cross-examination conducted a significant time after the ABE interview is likely to achieve, other than stress for the child—even if it is conducted out of court and ahead of trial under section 28 of the Youth Justice and Criminal Evidence Act 1999, and without the 'Old Bailey' features that were criticised above. A very little child, surely, will have already given by that stage all the useful information that he or she has to give. A cross-examination at this later stage might, of course, give the defence the chance to discredit the child by confusing him or her or pushing him or her into an insincere retraction. But as argued above, that should not be accepted as a proper function of cross-examination.

The views expressed in the previous paragraph are obviously heretical, at any rate from the perspective of those—apart from the police—whose sphere of action is the criminal justice system. And with that in mind, it should be stressed that they are expressed subject to three qualifications. First, we are talking here about children who, like the little girl in the *Barker* case, are very young,[72] or older ones who have severe learning disabilities or who for other reasons are highly vulnerable—for example, because they have been severely traumatised. Secondly, even in these cases it would be preferable, surely, if the defence (as it will in practice nearly always be) were given the opportunity, where this is practicable,[73] to have its most important issues explored with the child at the time of the ABE interview. This would obviously be helpful to the defendant, at any rate if he is innocent, and it would also be helpful to the prosecution, because the tribunal of fact is bound to give more weight to statements of absent witnesses to whom the defence have had some minimal chance to put their questions than it would to statements made by those to whom the defence have been unable to put any questions whatsoever. Thirdly, I believe that, particularly in this type of case, we need to consider other possible methods for testing and evaluating the evidence of children, as a substitute for—or in some cases, to supplement—cross-examination.

(v) Other Possible Methods of Testing the Evidence of Children

When an allegation by a child is relevant to civil proceedings the court will adopt a completely different method of assessing its truthfulness or otherwise from what

[71] [2010] EWCA Crim 4; see 186 above and 200–01 below.

[72] It is difficult to state a precise age limit, but if one were to be fixed by statute I think it should be those under six.

[73] In Norway, as we saw in ch 7, where an interview takes place at this stage and the defendant has not yet been identified, a lawyer is nominated to look after the interests of the defence.

is done in the criminal courts. In the first place, in civil proceedings the child will not usually be subjected to cross-examination. Indeed, until the important Supreme Court decision in *Re W*[74] there was actually a presumption against calling children as live witnesses in civil proceedings, created on the basis that the experience of giving oral evidence and undergoing adversarial cross-examination was almost certain to be harmful to them. In *Re W* the Supreme Court, overturning previous case law, said that the civil courts should not operate on the basis of any such presumption: instead, the decision as to whether a child should be called as a witness should be made, on a case-by-case basis, without any preconceptions. The decision, said the Supreme Court, requires examining and weighing up a number of factors.

In broad terms the Justices said that 'the court will have to weigh up two considerations: the advantages that that will bring to the determination of the truth and the damage it may do to the welfare of this or any other child'. As regards the first consideration, specific factors to consider will include the importance or otherwise of the child's evidence in relation to the issues the court has to decide, what other evidence there is, and the quality of the ABE interview, if there is one. In the context of the second consideration, the court mentioned the following as relevant:

> [26] The age and maturity of the child, along with the length of time since the events in question ... the support which the child has from family or other sources, or lack of it, the child's own wishes and feelings about giving evidence, and the views of the child's guardian and, where appropriate, those with parental responsibility. We endorse the view that an unwilling child should rarely, if ever, be obliged to give evidence. The risk of further delay to the proceedings is also a factor: there is the general principle that delay in determining any question about a child's upbringing is likely to prejudice his welfare ...There may also be specific risks of harm to this particular child. Where there are parallel criminal proceedings, the likelihood of the child having to give evidence twice may increase the risk of harm. The parent may be seeking to put his child through this ordeal in order to strengthen his hand in the criminal proceedings rather than to enable the family court to get at the truth. On the other hand, as the family court has to give less weight to the evidence of a child because she has not been called, then that may be damaging too. However, the court is entitled to have regard to the general evidence of the harm which giving evidence may do to children, as well as to any features which are particular to this child and this case. That risk of harm is an ever-present feature to which, on the present evidence, the court must give great weight...

The decision in *Re W* has resulted in 'an increase of applications for permission for children to be cross-examined'.[75] As to how many of these applications succeed, no official data is available; but the author's conversations with practitioners suggests that most of them do not, and in the end the position is little changed.

[74] In *Re W (Children) (Family Proceedings: Evidence)* [2010] UKSC 12, [2010] 1 WLR 701.

[75] J Mitchell, 'Children Giving Evidence: The Practical Implications of *Re W*' *Family Law*, August 2011, vol 41, 817–26, 817.

Part of the reason for this difference of practice is that civil and criminal proceedings are to some extent pursuing different objectives. When dealing with matters affecting children the civil courts regard the welfare of the child as centrally important.[76] In criminal proceedings, in contrast to civil proceedings, the central aims are the conviction of the guilty and the acquittal of the innocent, and it is generally believed—quite rightly—that the legal system must do everything it can to avoid the wrongful conviction of the innocent. From this it inevitably follows that child witnesses must give their evidence orally, and submit to cross-examination, to the extent that it is necessary to achieve these aims, and in particular the second one. But it does not follow that in criminal proceedings we must therefore simply forget the welfare of the child, and assume that cross-examination is invariably essential. The position, surely, is that cross-examination of child witnesses has to be accepted where the practice is more likely to lead the court towards a truthful outcome; but equally, it does not have to be accepted where it does not. In particular, there is no reason why a traditional cross-examination should be required in circumstances where, for reasons discussed in the previous sections of this chapter, it is unlikely to have this effect.

A second difference in the way the evidence of children is tested in the civil courts is that, when considering whether a child has told the truth, the civil courts stress the importance of examining the child's statement in context. As one judge put it:

> A judge in difficult cases such as this has to have regard to the relevance of each piece of evidence to other evidence and to exercise an overview of the totality of the evidence in order to come to the conclusion whether the case put forward by the party making the allegation has been made out to the appropriate standard of proof.[77]

This 'holistic approach' is possible in a civil case because both rules of evidence and the method of trial are radically different from those in operation in criminal proceedings. In a civil case there is no hearsay rule and 'evidence' is anything that is logically relevant to the issues that the court is called upon to decide. In consequence, in a civil case '[T]here is often a mass of documentary evidence, much of it hearsay, from which a picture can be built up or inferences drawn.'[78] This evidence will be put together in a file, which together with the oral evidence will form the basis of the arguments at the hearing, and in a difficult case the judge will take the file, together with the notes of evidence, and study them with care before producing a reasoned judgment. In a criminal case, things are very different. The rules of evidence tend to suppress anything that is technically 'hearsay' in

[76] Indeed the tone is set by s 1(1) of the Children Act 1989, which provides that: 'When a court determines any question with respect to (a) the upbringing of a child, or (b) the administration of a child's property or the application of any income arising from it, the child's welfare shall be the court's paramount consideration.'

[77] Stephen Wildblood QC, sitting as a High Court Judge, in *ID v B (Flawed Sexual Abuse Enquiry)* [2006] EWHC 2987 (Fam), [2007] 1 FLR 1245, at [27].

[78] Baroness Hale in *Re W* [2010] UKSC 12, at [10].

favour of the evidence of those witnesses who depose before it orally. The tribunal of fact—whether a jury or a bench of magistrates—will not have a file. And the result will be that, in a case involving a child witness, everything is likely to centre upon the child's oral evidence: typically in the form of an ABE interview, and the subsequent cross-examination. The result is that the fact-finders, in practice, have to decide the case on the basis of a 'snapshot' picture of what the child witness has said at one particular point. To those who, like child psychiatrists, have to make decisions in their work as to whether what a child has said is true, this 'snapshot' method of fact-finding is counter-intuitive. Professionals who find themselves in this position believe that the proper way to make such a decision is to look carefully at the way the suspicions first arose and the way in which the child's account developed afterwards. They look at exactly what the child said on the first occasion that it spoke of the matter, the circumstances under which the account was given, the influences (if any) that had been or might have been brought to bear, and the way the account has subsequently evolved;[79] the same method, in other words, that a competent judge in a civil case would adopt.[80]

A third big difference in the way the evidence of children is evaluated in civil proceedings is that judges in civil cases are more willing than they are in criminal cases to allow experts—psychiatrists and psychologists—to give the court their opinion as to whether a child who claims to have been abused is telling the truth or not.[81] In *Re MN and R (Minors) (Sexual Abuse: Expert Evidence)*[82] the Civil Division of the Court of Appeal, after some hesitation in earlier cases, ruled that it was permissible in civil proceedings for experts of this sort to give this type of evidence; though in so holding, the Court of Appeal was careful to stress that the credibility of the child was ultimately a question for the judge, and the judge was free to disregard the expert evidence if he or she was not convinced by it.

The criminal courts, by contrast, generally refuse to allow psychiatrists or psychologists to give their opinions on the credibility of witnesses. The principle on which the criminal courts operate is that the question whether a 'normal' witness is telling the truth or not is something which ordinary people—whether jurors or magistrates—are able to decide for themselves and without the need for expert help; and this is true whether the witness is young or old. If one side attempts to call an expert to bolster the credibility of their witness this is condemned as 'oath-helping',[83] a practice which is strictly forbidden. Thus in *Robinson* the Court of Appeal quashed a man's conviction for sexual offences against a 15-year-old girl,

[79] For a classic example of this technique being applied in a forensic context by a psychological expert in Sweden, see 'Was Lars Sexually Assaulted? A Study in the Reliability of Witnesses and of Experts', (1958) 56 *Journal of Abnormal and Social Psychology* 385.

[80] For a practical example, see the Court of Appeal judgment in *Re B (Allegation of Sexual Abuse: Child's Evidence)* [2006] EWCA Civ 773, [2006] 2 FLR 1071.

[81] See generally Hoyano and Keenan (n 13) 887 ff.

[82] *Re MN and R (Minors) (Sexual Abuse: Expert Evidence)* [1996] 4 All ER 239, [1996] 2 FLR 195.

[83] Historically, oath-helping, alias 'wager of law', was the ancient practice under which a litigant was sometimes entitled to prove his case by taking a formal oath that it was just, accompanied by a group of 'oath-helpers' who swore together with him. The underlying theory was that if a person's friends and

because at trial the Crown had been permitted to call an educational psychologist to give opinion evidence in support of the girl's credibility.[84]

By and large, the same approach is taken to attempts to call psychologists or psychiatrists to undermine the credibility of the witnesses for the other side. In *R v D and others*,[85] the Criminal Division of the Court of Appeal accepted that it is in order for the defence to call a psychiatrist and a psychologist to criticise the way child witnesses have been interviewed—but out of order for them to express their views on whether the children were credible, holding that the trial judge in the case in hand had been right to forbid this. Similarly, in *G v DPP*[86] the Divisional Court upheld the refusal of a Crown Court (on appeal from a magistrates' court) to admit as defence evidence a report from a psychologist applying a graphic technique called 'THEMA' (Thematic Emergence of Anomaly), intended to cast doubt on the veracity of child witnesses. In so holding, the Divisional Court quoted with evident approval the words of the Crown Court when refusing to admit the evidence:

> ... In this case we are dealing with perfectly normal children and we feel that we do not require help from Dr. Shepherd in dealing with these matters. When dealing with young children it is better for the court to determine these by listening to the children and forming our own views. None of us has derived any assistance from reading this report, not to say that the observations are bad, some are good, some indifferent and some bad. The good points we could have seen for ourselves without his assistance. This is a report that has cost a lot of money at public expense...

At first sight, it looks distinctly odd that the criminal courts routinely turn their backs on this sort of evidence when the civil courts are prepared to admit it. One would have thought that if expert help was seen as potentially helpful to a civil court confronted with the question of whether a child has told the truth, a criminal court would find it potentially helpful too.

All in all, it is difficult to avoid the conclusion that the methods used by civil courts to evaluate the truth or otherwise of the evidence of little children are much more rational than the methods—or to be accurate, the one and only method, namely cross-examination—relied on by the criminal courts. If this is right, it follows that the criminal courts would improve the accuracy of their fact-finding if they were to adopt some or all of the methods used in civil proceedings. If this were done, it would obviously make the criminal process more successful in convicting the guilty. And no less obviously, it would also make it more

neighbours were prepared to risk eternal damnation on his behalf, this was a sure guarantee that he was honest. After many years of desuetude it was formally abolished by the Civil Procedure Act 1833.

[84] *Robinson* (1994) 98 Cr App R 370; the decision is questionable, because the child was far from 'normal'. According to the Court of Appeal, she was 'illiterate, mentally defective and had the mental capacity of a seven or eight-year old' and 'was mentally within the bottom 1 per cent of 15-year-olds'.

[85] *R v D and* others, unreported, 3 November 1995. The case is described in detail by Hoyano and Keenan (n 13) 893–94.

[86] *G v DPP* [1998] QB 919, [1998] 2 WLR 609.

efficient at protecting the innocent who are falsely accused. This point was made, by implication, by a defence solicitor in an online 'blog' in which the writer criticises the *Barker* case, arguing that the resulting law and practice exposes innocent people to the risk of wrongful conviction. Whilst this document contains much with which the editors of this book would disagree, among the good points that it makes are these:

> Research shows that in assessing reliability, what is of particular importance is not simply techniques used to generate the evidence, but the context of the case as it develops, and the characteristics of the child.
>
> One point can be agreed. It was futile to attempt to cross-examine the child [in the *Barker* case] about what had really happened—even though it led to the denial rejected by the jury.[87]

Unfortunately, transplanting the techniques of the civil courts into criminal courts is not as simple as it sounds, because they do not fit easily with several 'classic' features of the English criminal trial. The first of these classic features is a fact-finder in a contested criminal trial that is almost invariably a group of lay people: in a grave case, a jury of 12 persons, selected at random from the electoral roll. The second classic feature is the fact that, unlike in a civil case, the fact-finders in criminal proceedings come to the case 'cold'. Whereas the judge in a civil case will have a file to study in advance, and to refer to afterwards when reaching a decision, a jury (or indeed a bench of lay magistrates in a summary trial) will know nothing of the case apart from what is put before them at the trial, almost all of it in the form of oral evidence; and it will be on the basis of the impressions left by the oral evidence, and nothing else, that the fact-finder is then expected to make an immediate decision. In consequence, in criminal proceedings it is difficult to avoid taking the 'snapshot approach' to the evidence of children.

The fact-finder being a panel of lay people also helps to explain why, in criminal proceedings, the judges are reluctant to admit expert evidence about the credibility of witnesses. Though the traditional explanation is that judges believe jurors to be exceptionally gifted at telling truthful witnesses from liars, the real reason, one suspects, is the opposite: that judges are afraid that jurors, unlike judges, will be too easily bamboozled by expert evidence the quality of which is poor. As Hoyano and Keenan put it, 'The absence of the seasoned judicial mind as the trier of fact is probably the primary reason why the criminal courts have been very reluctant to countenance expert evidence commenting on a witness's reliability ....'[88] This reluctance is encouraged by another classic feature of the English criminal trial, which is that expert knowledge is placed before the court through expert witnesses who are chosen by the parties—who will obviously tend to select the experts whose evidence fits the case they wish to put before the court, rather than the experts who are most competent, whom the court would presumably prefer

[87] www.chrissaltrese.co.uk/commentary.html.
[88] Hoyano and Keenan (n 13) 892.

to hear from if it had the choice. In consequence, judges rightly feel that if such evidence were permitted in criminal proceedings it would probably generate more heat than light. In civil proceedings involving children, by contrast, the court will often hear from experts commissioned by the Child and Family Court Advisory Service (CAFCASS), whose stance, unlike that of experts called by the parties, is more likely to be neutral.[89]

The fact that the techniques used by the civil courts for evaluating the credibility of children fit ill with jury trial obviously reduces the chances of adopting them in criminal proceedings. For many people jury trial appears to be totemic: a topic on which emotions run so high that any rational discussion of its merits is impossible. And this fact, regrettably, renders equally difficult the rational discussion of any procedural reform that might impinge upon it. In my view, however, those who believe that the criminal courts could usefully borrow some of the fact-finding techniques of the civil courts should not on this account give up, and should be prepared if necessary to argue the case for changes in the structure of the courts before which accusations of child abuse are tried. As long ago as 1949 a joint committee of the British Medical Association and The Magistrates' Association discussed the composition of the courts for trying child abuse cases in a report entitled *The Criminal Law and Sexual Offenders.*[90] Having set out a long list of the practical difficulties that result from the use of juries in these cases, it said:[91]

> If the law could permit these cases to be tried at assizes or quarter sessions[92] by the presiding judge, recorder or chairman, assisted by two magistrates of experience in the work of a juvenile court,[93] the difficulties of the present system would be overcome. Some such method is, the Committee thinks, the only practicable way in which the undesirable strain on child victims, which the present methods involve, can be avoided.

Heretical as this long-forgotten suggestion might appear to some, it surely merits serious consideration. What is at stake is not only the 'undesirable strain on child victims' but also the need for accurate fact-finding: something which is required in order to secure the acquittal of the innocent as well as the conviction of the guilty.

This last excursus has taken us away from the central topic of this book, which is children and cross-examination. It is to this topic that we should finally return.

Concluding Remarks

This book of essays resulted from a conference. The conference in turn was a direct result of the *Barker* case, to which references have been made in this chapter

[89] See Spencer and Flin (n 14) ch 9.
[90] Published as a pamphlet by the British Medical Association.
[91] At §30.
[92] The courts which the Crown Court replaced in 1971.
[93] Nowadays called the 'Youth Court'.

and elsewhere. After the trial and the dismissal of the defendant's appeal the police officers in the case contacted the editors of this book, whom they knew to be interested in the problems of children's evidence, to express their concern about the treatment that the legal system had imposed upon the key witness at the trial. To remind readers of what they have already heard, this witness was a child who was alleged to be the victim of an anal rape. At the age of four-and-a-half, she was brought to the Old Bailey to undergo a live cross-examination about matters she had described at an ABE[94] interview a whole year earlier. To produce her at the court for this it was necessary for her carers to get her up at 6 am. When she arrived, the court was not ready for her and, after waiting for the whole day, she was then sent home unheard. After another early start and another morning waiting at the court, she was then cross-examined in the afternoon, by which time she was very tired. And when it eventually took place, the cross-examination, if judged as a procedure meant to test the evidence of children to determine whether it is reliable, was inept and served no useful purpose.

The police officers were surely right to find this shocking. There is no necessity for little children to come to court to undergo a cross-examination live at trial because provision for pre-recording exists in section 28 of the Youth Justice and Criminal Evidence Act 1999, if only the government could be persuaded to bring it into force. From the experience of other countries, some of which has been described in the earlier chapters of this book, we know that systems of this sort can indeed be made to work. And if there is a will, then surely a way can be found to conciliate the defendant's right to question his accusers with the capacities of little children, and the need to protect them from needless stress and harm.

[94] 'ABE interviews' are explained at n 4 above.

HOME OFFICE

Report of

The Advisory Group on Video Evidence

REPORT OF THE ADVISORY GROUP ON VIDEO-RECORDED EVIDENCE

MEMBERS OF THE ADVISORY GROUP ON VIDEO-RECORDED EVIDENCE

His Honour Judge Thomas Pigot, QC, Chairman, Common Serjeant of London

Mr Anthony Kilkerr, Detective Chief Superintendent, Metropolitan Police

Mr Roy Parker, Assistant Director of Social Services, Metropolitan District of Sunderland

Miss Anne Rafferty, Barrister

Professor Jennifer Temkin, University of Buckingham

Mr Kirk Coulson-Gilmer, Secretary

To the Right Honourable Douglas Hurd CBE, MP, Home Secretary

On 20 June 1988 the establishment of an advisory group to consider the use of video recordings as a means of taking the evidence of children and other vulnerable witnesses at criminal trials was announced in the House of Commons. In your letter of invitation the following terms of reference were set out:

> "to look in greater depth than has so far been possible at the idea that video recordings of interviews with child victims (and possibly other victims of crime) should be readily admissible as evidence in criminal trials".

2. Your letter also explained the context in which the advisory group would work and the particular concerns which it would address:

> "The background, as you are probably aware, is that, during the passage of the Criminal Justice Bill, there has been a growing body of support for a change in the law, so that video recordings of interviews with victims could be readily used as evidence in trials for child abuse. In some parts of the country the police and social services are running joint schemes under which child victims are interviewed soon after the alleged assault, and the interview is video-recorded. The idea is that these recordings should be admissible and be capable of forming the child's evidence-in-chief. Its supporters argue that they will enable a fresher account to be before the court, and reduce the distress which the criminal process causes for the child.
>
> "Immediately attractive as this idea is, we have had some doubts about whether it would actually have the effect of making things easier for the child victim, and can see grounds for fearing that it might make matters worse. If the accused contested his guilt, the child would not be spared having to give evidence again at the time of the trial, since we could not contemplate removing the right of the accused to have such a crucial witness cross-examined at his trial. There could also be problems over editing the tape, which may well contain material which would be inadmissible for other reasons, and it is not altogether clear what effect the prospect of use in court would have on the extent to which the original interviews served their main purpose of aiding the police and the caring agencies.
>
> "These doubts have led us to conclude that the time is not yet ripe for a change in the law. But our minds are by no means closed to the idea that such a change might be made at some time in the future. We find it difficult to assess how much weight to give to the doubts which I have mentioned, and would like to mount a more detailed study of the practical implications. Hence the idea of an advisory group.

> "Although it is in the context of child abuse that the idea has gained ground, it clearly has wider implications, and an argument—although probably a less compelling one—could be mounted for allowing the evidence-in-chief of other vulnerable groups to be given in this way, subject to cross-examination. I should certainly not wish to exclude this wider dimension from the remit of the advisory group and would welcome its being given some attention also."

3. With the exception of one recommendation, (paras 2.32–2.34), from which Miss Rafferty dissents, our report is unanimous.

4. Those to whom acknowledgements are due are mentioned in an annex to the report. It would be wrong to single out any of the many individuals and organisations from which we received so much assistance for special mention here, but we do owe a particular debt of gratitude to the Scottish Law Commission and Sheriff Gordon Nicholson QC. The Commission has carried out a detailed and comprehensive study of questions relating to children and other vulnerable witnesses in the Scottish criminal courts. It issued a discussion document before our initial meeting and will shortly publish its own proposals. We found some of the ideas which the Commission canvassed extremely helpful in developing our recommendations and we benefited greatly from our discussions with the responsible Commissioner, Sheriff Nicholson.

5. We should like to offer our special thanks to Mr Kenneth Ashken of the Crown Prosecution Service and Mr Richard Weatherill of the Criminal Policy Department, Home Office who attended our meetings as observers and gave us much useful advice and assistance. We also wish to pay tribute to Mr Kirk Coulson-Gilmer, our Secretary, who was responsible for much of the organisation of our work and for producing successive drafts of our report. Despite all the help and advice which we have received the conclusions and recommendations which follow are our sole responsibility.

CONTENTS

CHAPTER 1

BACKGROUND AND METHODS OF WORKING

Introduction

1.1 This chapter describes the circumstances which led to the Government's decision to set up an advisory group on video-recorded evidence and explains how the group understood and approached its task. Because perceptions about the prevalence of child abuse and the questionable effectiveness of existing legal rules and procedures in dealing with it were important factors which helped to promote public, professional and parliamentary interest in the use of video-recordings in criminal proceedings, we devote part of the chapter to a necessarily attenuated account of the statistical and research background to that problem. We then look briefly at the ways in which other jurisdictions have modified procedures to accommodate child witnesses. After this we review the parliamentary debates which preceded the inception of an advisory group. Finally we consider how the group set about taking evidence and drawing its conclusions.

Research and statistics

1.2 During the mid-1980s a variety of surveys of the general public and of health service professionals, some of which were well-publicised, suggested that many more sexual offences were being committed, and had previously been committed, against children than was hitherto generally recognised. This possibility received much consideration following events in Cleveland. At the same time a number of notorious and extremely disturbing cases, such as those of Jasmine Beckford and Kimberley Carlisle, drew attention to the problem of the physical abuse of children. As a result we think there is now a widespread impression that the incidence and severity of all types of child abuse have increased markedly in recent years.

1.3 The only continuous large-scale survey of the problem is the NSPCC's child protection register research which contains annual estimates of incidence based upon the analysis of child protection registers in areas containing some 9% of the child population in England and Wales. A report of this research, Child Abuse Trends in England and Wales 1983–1987, was published in July 1989. This indicates that in those years the known cases of sexual abuse of children increased from 0.08 to 0.65 per thousand, or eight-fold, and that the physical injury rate rose by one third, while the number of children registered with serious or fatal injuries doubled. In 1988 the Department of Health conducted its first national survey of child protection registers. The findings are broadly in line with those of the NSPCC, although they indicate a lower overall incidence of abuse. Its survey shows that nearly 25,000 children were on Child Protection Registers because of various types of abuse at 31 March 1988 and that a further 14,400 had been registered because of 'grave concern'.

1.4 Child abuse is sometimes said to exemplify the classic iceberg description of disease. The number of cases which surface will depend upon the vigilance and awareness of parents, police, professionals, teachers and carers and the willingness of victims to disclose their experiences. It can be argued that trends of the sort recorded by the NSPCC are caused by a heightened general consciousness of the problem of abuse and a lessening reticence by children and adults alike in speaking about it, and that they do not constitute empirical evidence of a real underlying increase in scale.

1.5 There is, we think, a risk that acceptance of this argument might lead to an unconscious complacency about the problem in general and, in particular, about the need to reform the law so that the criminal courts can more easily take evidence from children. We wholly accept that the true extent of child abuse is, and will necessarily remain, unknown. However, increases of the proportions mentioned in the number of cases reported may well reflect a considerable increase in the actual incidence of offences committed.

1.6 The NSPCC research also contains some disturbing findings about the effectiveness of the criminal justice system in dealing with abuse once it comes to light. Prosecutions were planned in only 9% of the physical abuse cases and 28% of the sexual abuse cases which the Society considered in the whole period 1983–1987. In its evidence to us the Society was inclined to ascribe this to an unwillingness by the children to give evidence and an unwillingness by parents to put their children through a traumatic court experience.

1.7 There are no centrally collected national statistics about the total number of offences committed against children, except where the age of the victim is a component of the offence and a prosecution results. Offences such as unlawful sexual intercourse with a girl under 16 and indecency with children are included, but rape and assault are not. The number of such prosecutions, mainly but not exclusively for sexual offences, increased from 3,229 in 1983 to 3,723 in 1987: a rise of only 17% during a period when the NSPCC's evidence suggests an increase of much more substantial proportions in the number of such offences coming to the attention of the authorities. In itself this is tenuous evidence upon which to conclude that existing criminal procedures are less effective than necessary where the victim is a child. As we shall see, however, police officers, social workers and other specialists who deal with these cases have few doubts about the truth of such a proposition. Their evidence seemed to suggest that the recorded growth in the number of offences committed against children has not been matched by a corresponding increase in prosecutions because a high proportion of the crimes now coming to light are committed against the very young who are unable to testify in the criminal courts.

1.8 It appears to us to be highly desirable that more detailed national statistics about the victims of crime and the reasons for discontinuing or failing to proceed with potential prosecutions should be collected on an agreed basis and made available to policy-makers. In this context the questions which we wished to put—'how many offences cannot be prosecuted because the principal witness or victim is a young child?' and 'how often do prosecutions fail because child witnesses cannot cope with court procedures?'—simply could not be answered except in a limited, imprecise or anecdotal way.

Other Jurisdictions

1.9 In considering the potential use of video technology and other techniques and changes to improve the position of child witnesses we were naturally eager to take due account of developments in other jurisdictions, especially those similar to our own. An excellent occasion to supplement the published material on this subject was provided by the international conference on children's evidence in legal proceedings held at Selwyn College, Cambridge in June 1989. We are indebted to the organisers, Mr John Spencer of Cambridge University, Sheriff Gordon Nicholson QC, Dr Rhona Flin of Robert Gordon's Institute of Technology, Aberdeen and Professor Ray Bull of Glasgow College, as well as to the other speakers and participants, for this opportunity. We do not think it would be useful here to explain in detail how other countries approach the question of children's evidence and so we confine our remarks to what we have identified as matters of general principle.

1.10 We consider the issue of the competence of child witnesses at more length later. What emerged from our review of other systems was, however, that in almost every western jurisdiction which we considered other than England and Wales provisions are in force or are proposed which would enable the criminal courts to hear what relevant evidence very small children are able to give in criminal proceedings. Few jurisdictions other than our own, or those derived from it, completely exclude the testimony of a witness as valueless purely by reason of his or her age. The age and understanding of a child are, of course, highly relevant to the weight which is placed upon the evidence, but effective age limits for witnesses have become increasingly rare.

1.11 Different approaches to reform have been taken in other common law jurisdictions. In South Australia a child can testify on the same terms as an adult if he or she can respond rationally to questions, give intelligible evidence and promises to tell the truth. Even if this is not possible a very small child's evidence is to be considered in the light of his or her cognitive development if there is some other confirmation of the account which the child gives. In some states in the USA a child's evidence given during a video-recorded interview is simply to be treated in the same way as other testimony given at a 'live' hearing by adults. The point is that even jurisdictions constrained by the scepticism of the common law tradition towards the value of young children's evidence are devising techniques which enable it to be heard. Whether this relates to changed perceptions about the truthfulness of children, or to growing international concern about the extent of the problem of child abuse, we are not qualified to say.

1.12 A second aspect of international practice which struck us forcibly was the prevalence of the use of pre-trial, out-of-court ways of taking children's evidence. These are used not only in inquisitorial systems, where for example in France the 'juge d'instruction' has an investigatory role, but also where there is an essentially adversarial structure, for instance in Norway, Denmark and Sweden. The techniques employed range from the Israeli method, which enables a 'child examiner' to appear in court on behalf of a victim of child sexual abuse, to special provisions which allow out-of-court statements by child witnesses, especially when video-recorded in a prescribed way, to be shown to the court in Canada and many parts of the USA, Europe and, now, some Australian jurisdictions.

1.13 At this stage we think it worth emphasising that, in other parts of the world where the quality of justice is not inferior to our own, listening to what very small children have to say and providing suitable means for children to describe their experiences outside the public arena of the courtroom is not regarded as unusual, unreasonable, or a threat to the principle that the prosecution must discharge the burden of proof.

Parliamentary proceedings

1.14 During the passage of the Criminal Justice Act 1988, which was to contain provisions allowing witnesses to give evidence from outside the courtroom by live television link (section 32) and abolishing special requirements relating to the corroboration or confirmation of children's evidence (section 34), proposals were advanced which would also have made video-recorded interviews with child witnesses conducted by police officers and social workers admissible as evidence in criminal proceedings. The principal debate on this question took place on 20 June 1988 in the House of Commons when Sir Eldon Griffiths moved the second reading of a new clause which would have permitted video-recorded interviews with the alleged victims of sexual offences under the age of 14 to be put in evidence. This amendment would also have provided for the cross-examination of such witnesses, using the live television link system, to take place through an intermediary: a social worker, child psychiatrist or probation officer. The clause enjoyed substantial all-party support.

1.15 The proposal had been developed from the increasingly widespread practice of carrying out a single, formal interview with child victims of alleged sexual abuse at which the police, social workers and, where appropriate, other professionals can each ask or have asked questions relevant to the concerns of their particular agencies. This eliminates duplication of effort and reduces the stress upon children which is likely to result from repeated interviews. Joint interviews are now often video-recorded. The sponsors of the clause saw the admissibility of such material in court, coupled with the employment of a child specialist to question the young witness, as an important step towards improving the position of child witnesses and enabling the courts to hear their evidence more often.

1.16 In the course of the debate it became clear that Members of Parliament held differing opinions about both the principle and the practicalities of such a change. This was also the position during similar debates in Standing Committee and in the House of Lords. The Minister with responsibility for the Bill, Mr John Patten, identified the main areas of controversy in replying to the debate. There was disagreement about whether admitting a pre-recorded interview with a child would increase or diminish the stress experienced by that child during courtroom cross-examination. There were arguments for and against the use of a specialist interlocutor to replace the defendant's chosen counsel in questioning a child witness. Moreover it was not clear how far existing techniques used by the police and social services to interview children, which have therapeutic and investigative aims, could be successfully employed for evidential purposes.

1.17 Mr Patten expressed the Government's view that these problems required further careful and detailed consideration. He then announced the establishment and composition of the advisory group, making it clear that the group would not confine its inquiries to the evidence of children, but would also consider how video technology might assist with the evidence of other vulnerable witnesses such as rape victims and the disabled.

The advisory group

1.18 The group met on twenty five separate occasions. We viewed video-recorded interviews with child victims of alleged sexual offences conducted by clinicians at Great Ormond street Hospital for Sick Children, by joint police and social services teams at Bexley and West Yorkshire and by NSPCC workers in Coventry. We considered written and oral evidence submitted to us by members of the judiciary and legal professions, the police, social workers, paediatricians, psychiatrists, academics and a range of voluntary and professional organisations concerned with the welfare and protection of children (Annex A). We studied a substantial amount of published material relating to children's evidence and interviews with abuse victims. Before finalising our conclusions and recommendations we received advice about the central legal and practical questions from specialists and policy-makers.

1.19 As our enquiries progressed we became increasingly clear about two issues. First, the framework of co-operation between the police and social services and the personal and technical skills and resources necessary to conduct and video-record interviews with child witnesses are widely available and are capable of rapid development to meet forensic requirements if, as a matter of policy, this is thought to be desirable. Second, it is not sensibly possible to divorce consideration of video-recorded evidence by children from consideration of the criteria which govern the eligibility of children to testify at all, and of the special rules which limit the reliance which can be placed upon the evidence of the complainant where the offence charged is of a sexual nature. For this reason chapter 5 of the report is devoted to legal issues other than those most directly related to video recordings as evidence.

1.20 In chapter 6 we consider procedural issues in relation to the prosecution system. It seems to us that one of the most substantial difficulties faced by children, other vulnerable witnesses, and, indeed, most witnesses, is the extraordinary and, in our view, quite unacceptable delay which they must often endure before cases come to court. We explain how we believe serious cases involving children in particular might be expedited and we look at the implications of this for the magistrates' courts.

Conclusion

1.21 We are grateful to all of those who assisted us. It is not possible in a report of this nature to explain the detailed views of individual witnesses. Nevertheless we think it is important to stress that where our recommendations do not reflect the evidence of some of the specialist medical, paediatric and psychiatric witnesses which we considered we do not wish to question the scientific validity of their views, but only to record our reservations about the applicability of these in the context of a criminal trial. Similarly, some of the specialist legal witnesses suggested that we might address issues which bear upon children and other vulnerable witnesses but which, like the rules which govern the admissibility of evidence about an accused's propensities or previous convictions, have much wider implications. We have chosen not to do so, but this is not because we consider that the present position is necessarily satisfactory, only that we think the issues are beyond our terms of reference, however interpreted.

1.22 In this report we are concerned with aspects of the law which, in a democracy, cannot safely be left to politicians and lawyers alone. Members of the general public have a deep, significant and legitimate interest in these questions. We have attributed considerable weight to the views expressed to us by representatives of many organisations dedicated to the welfare of children. Their opinions are based upon wide experience and should not be lightly dismissed or stigmatised as anecdotal.

CHAPTER 2

ADMISSIBILITY

Introduction

2.1 This chapter focuses on the central issue of whether video-recorded evidence by child witnesses of the sort already described should become admissible in criminal proceedings. In particular we examine the present law and the main arguments for reform and reservations which have been expressed about change. We include some necessarily brief consideration of the views of those who gave or sent evidence to us and we set out our principal conclusions and recommendations.

The existing law

(i) The rule against hearsay

2.2 Video-recorded interviews and most other out-of-court statements are not normally admissible in criminal proceedings because they contravene the rule against hearsay. The rule, which does not appear in any statute and has never been definitively formulated judicially, is described in this way in *Archbold*, the leading authority on criminal pleading, evidence and practice; "Former statements by any person … may not be given in evidence if the purpose is to tender them as evidence of the truth of the matters contained in them, unless they were made by the defendant and constitute admissions of fact relevant to those proceedings".[1] This means that if a child makes an allegation in a recorded interview the recording cannot be given as evidence at trial whether or not the child attends to testify in person.

(ii) Hearsay exceptions

2.3 There are numerous common law and statutory exceptions to the hearsay rule. Hearsay statements are admissible if they are deemed to be sufficiently close and relevant to the material facts of an offence: for instance, spontaneous exclamations by victims or bystanders may be repeated as evidence in some cases. Statements made by deceased persons in certain circumstances are received in spite of the rule. Previous statements in which a witness contradicted his evidence may also be given in court, but such material is not usually regarded as a hearsay exception because technically it is only evidence of the witness's credibility and

---

[1] Forty third edition, 1988, vol 1 page 1084.

not of the truth of the facts which it contains. Two statutory exceptions are of special relevance here.

2.4 The Children and Young Persons Act 1933 contains provisions in sections 42 and 43 which enable a child's sworn deposition to be put in evidence at trials for certain violent and sexual offences if attendance in court would involve serious danger to the child's life or health. The deposition must be made before a magistrate, the accused or his legal representative must have an opportunity to cross-examine the child and both the Crown Court and the magistrates' court must be satisfied of the child's condition on qualified medical evidence. These stringent provisions are rarely, if ever, used.

2.5 The Police and Criminal Evidence Act 1984 and the Criminal Justice Act 1988 have both made substantial in-roads into the hearsay rule as it applies to documentary evidence. Section 23 of the 1988 Act provides that a statement made by a person in a document (which is defined to include tapes and video-recordings) shall be admissible if direct oral evidence by that person would be admissible where various conditions are met. These are that the person is dead, mentally or physically unfit to attend the trial, abroad in circumstances in which it would not be reasonably practical to secure his attendance, or if he is missing and all reasonable steps have been taken to find him without success. Statements made to the police and others charged with the investigation of crime are also admissible if the person does not give oral evidence through fear or because he is being kept out of the way. The provisions are subject to the general judicial discretion to exclude admissible evidence because admitting it would be unfair: 'more prejudicial than probative', and to a statutory duty to exclude such evidence if the court is of the opinion that inclusion would be contrary to the interests of justice.

2.6 It is notable that when the 1988 Act was introduced the Government sought to extend the readier admissibility of documentary evidence without imposing a pre-condition that the witness should be unavailable to attend in person. It was simply proposed that where the maker of a statement gave oral evidence as well this should not be treated as strengthening or confirming his documentary evidence where the two coincided. A narrower provision passed into law largely because of fears expressed in Parliament about the erosion of the oral tradition of the English trial. If the Government's original proposals, which were based on recommendations made by the Roskill Committee on fraud trials, had been enacted it would also now be possible for video-recorded interviews to be admitted whether or not a child gave evidence in person, provided that the court was satisfied that this was in the interests of justice.

2.7 We are not disposed to attempt to assess in any detail how far the 1988 Act will operate to allow video-recorded interviews to be put in evidence. It seems to us that this will largely depend upon how the courts approach the question of the mental fitness of witnesses to attend and the concept of non-attendance through fear. But we are satisfied that the provisions are unlikely to affect the admissibility of evidence by the generality of children and other vulnerable witnesses.

2.8 In a number of jurisdictions similar to our own previous statements by witnesses who testify at a trial can be given in evidence. The inherent defects of hearsay may be argued to be cured by the presence in court of both the maker of the statement and the person to whom it was made, where they can be examined about the circumstances. It seems to us that the terms of our appointment postulate the continued existence of the hearsay rule in its present form and the focus of our deliberations has therefore been upon whether and how a special exception relating to video recorded evidence might be made. Nevertheless we should point out that a more general change relating to prior statements by witnesses would have the effect of allowing video recordings and much other material now excluded to be put in evidence. This raises wider questions about the law of evidence than those particular to children and other vulnerable witnesses, but we think that if such a change were introduced it would have a marked effect in these cases. Here we simply say that we are not convinced as a matter of principle that a court which has heard a nervous, hesitant and perhaps confused account from an alleged victim should necessarily be prevented from drawing conclusions about its truthfulness from consideration of the way in which the offence was first described in the words of the person it was reported to.

The arguments for admissibility

2.9 Almost all of those who submitted evidence to us believed that the existing law is far too restrictive and that some general provision ought now to be made for video-recorded evidence to be admissible, especially in child abuse cases. Their arguments have two main aspects. One may be said to centre on the child's welfare and the other upon the integrity of the evidence. These are related, but for convenience we consider them separately.

(i) The child's welfare

2.10 All of the submissions which we received that addressed the matter indicated that most children are disturbed to a greater or lesser extent by giving evidence in court. The confrontation with the accused, the stress and embarrassment of speaking in public especially about sexual matters, the urgent demands of cross-examination, the overweening nature of courtroom formalities and the sense of insecurity and uncertainty induced by delays make this a harmful, oppressive and often traumatic experience. Moreover, because children are less clearly able to understand the reason for the demands which are placed upon them and have fewer developed intellectual and emotional resources than adults to help them cope with these, the effects are generally agreed to be peculiarly injurious and very often long-lasting.

2.11 The admissibility of video-recorded interviews would relieve some of these pressures. The child would know that an account of his or her experiences had already been shown to the court before it became necessary to testify and the time spent giving evidence would accordingly be briefer and less stressful than at present. Indeed the availability and admissibility of video recordings is said by some to have led to a significant increase in guilty pleas in the United States and might therefore be thought likely to remove the necessity for many children to give formal evidence at all. The information which we received about this was not conclusive, however, and we are inclined to think that much would depend upon the details of any enabling provision and the way in which the courts apply it in practice.

2.12 We are satisfied that a majority of children are adversely affected by giving evidence at trials for serious offences under existing circumstances. We attach particular importance to the psychiatric opinion we received which suggests that not only do abused children who testify in court exhibit more signs of disturbed behaviour than those who do not, but that the effects of a court appearance are most severe and prolonged in those who have suffered the worst abuse and those without family support. We received evidence on this point from paediatricians, psychiatrists, social workers and a range of organisations and individuals with professional and voluntary responsibility for child care and the care of victims. This led us not only to endorse the case already explained for relieving the stress upon child witnesses, but also to wonder whether the nature and extent of the problem is fully comprehended by the legal profession and the wider public. We cannot emphasise strongly enough that those children who are clearly upset or who break down in the witness box simply manifest openly the effects of a much more generally harmful experience.

2.13 We acknowledge that in important respects the possibility of giving evidence by live television link from outside the courtroom in trials for violent and sexual offences which was made available to children under the age of 14 by section 32 of the Criminal Justice Act 1988 has improved matters. Direct confrontation with the accused can be avoided and the pressures of speaking in public about embarrassing matters reduced. It is too early to make a thorough assessment of this innovation, which is being carefully monitored and evaluated. Nevertheless the difficulties created by the court context, particularly in relation to cross-examination and the delays and formalities all, to a large extent, persist. It is even possible that in some cases the new system itself could make children feel more isolated and insecure. It may place a greater burden upon the child witness, who must cope with intrusive technology and a sense of remoteness from contemporaneous proceedings, than other solutions which we have considered.

2.14 The evidence which we received and our own knowledge and experience all suggest to us that quite radical changes are now required if the courts are to treat children in a humane and acceptable way. Regardless of the evidential considerations we see the advent of video technology as an opportunity for achieving this. Our own detailed proposals are set out later. At present, however, we think it important to identify two principles which seem to us to follow from the most rudimentary appreciation of the child's welfare. First, the proceedings or part of the proceedings in which a child witness is involved should be disposed of as rapidly as is consonant with the interests of justice. Second, children should give evidence in surroundings and circumstances which do not intimidate or overawe them and there should be the smallest possible number of people present.

(ii) The evidence

2.15 Because of the problems already mentioned it is widely agreed that parents and guardians are often unwilling for children to give evidence and that when children do testify these difficulties sometimes inhibit the giving of a full account and, on occasion, prevent the courts from receiving coherent evidence at all. Clearly this leads to some unjustifiable acquittals. We also received evidence from police officers and social workers that many hundreds of cases cannot be pursued successfully each year because children seem unlikely to make effective or legally competent witnesses under present circumstances. As a result some child victims are left with feelings of anger, resentment, frustration and even guilt which many experts believe could be to some extent dispelled by legal procedures which enabled them to speak fully and freely. Other consequences are that because offenders are not dealt with by the courts they are free to reoffend and that where abuse has occurred within the family it can be the victim rather than the perpetrator who is removed. These are sometimes described as instances of secondary victimisation. We think this situation must be contrary to the public interest and that it distinguishes many cases which involve child witnesses quite sharply from most other criminal cases. In these it may sometimes simply be difficult to obtain a conviction under existing, largely effective, rules and procedures. Where child witnesses are concerned the existing process is quite fundamentally flawed.

2.16 Evidence which we received from practitioners, psychiatrists, social workers and the police suggested that if an interview takes place shortly after the child's first allegation or disclosure it will usually provide the freshest account least tainted by subsequent discussions and questioning.

2.17 It is also established beyond dispute that children generally recall past events most accurately when subject to the least stress. This is a finding which relates to children's memories in general and does not just apply to those children who find it impossible to cope under particular circumstances. It seems to us that this means the formality and solemnity of the courtroom context which are often thought to promote truthfulness by witnesses may actually have a deleterious effect on the fullness and accuracy of children's testimony.

2.18 The group finds these arguments highly persuasive. We are convinced that admitting video recordings of fairly conducted interviews with child witnesses made as early as possible in informal surroundings will give the courts access to an important and often crucial source of evidence. We also think that the quality of evidence which children give on cross-examination will improve where this takes place in informal surroundings as soon as can practicably be arranged. Regardless of the child's welfare we think such changes can only be in the interests of justice.

Objections and procedural questions

2.19 None of those who made submissions to the group disputed the existence of the difficulties which we have identified in existing systems for taking and testing children's evidence. But a few questioned whether a procedural solution could be devised which lessened the stress experienced by children, enabled children's evidence to be properly tested and at the same time preserved the essential structure of the trial.

2.20 The most widely-held reservation to which our attention was drawn was that the admissibility of video-recorded interviews would not relieve the pressure upon child witnesses since cross-examination would be necessary in any case and that the stress experienced by children might actually increase because opposing counsel would take the child through the whole recorded account in great detail exposing the minutest discrepancies.

2.21 To us this argument is controvertible. As we have seen previous out-of-court statements are already admissible if they contradict the account which a witness gives in court. Indeed the prosecution should inform the defence if such material exists. We find the explanation that this only constitutes evidence of a witness's credibility and not of the facts to be rather a subtle distinction. What it means in child abuse cases now is that where a previous statement exists it may be adduced by the defence to undermine an opposing witness but not by the prosecution. We know that this has already occurred in practice with video recordings on at least one occasion. It follows that the potential difficulty feared by those who think admitting video-recorded interviews would worsen the position of child witnesses is already substantially present without commensurate benefits for the child or the court.

2.22 Of course we agree that cross-examination is essential. Indeed in appointing the group the Home Secretary made it clear that a proposal which did not allow for this would be unacceptable. We are, however, convinced that it is both possible and desirable to use video technology to alter the context in which this takes place so that it becomes a less oppressive experience for the child and a more informative exercise for the court than at present.

2.23 A further reservation expressed to us was that a procedure which allowed for the admissibility of video recordings was simply contrary to the practice of the courts developed over many years and that all other possibilities should be explored first. We have already seen that many exceptions to the hearsay rule are already permitted according to circumstances, but the essential point, it seems to us, is that the practices and procedures of the courts were developed many years before the technology which now allows us to treat child witnesses more considerately. Lord Normand's words are sometimes cited as an explanation for the practice of excluding out-of-court statements: "the truthfulness and the accuracy of the person whose words are spoken to another witness cannot be tested by cross-examination and the light which his demeanour would throw on his testimony is lost".[2] It seems to us that video recording can be employed in ways which meet these objections at every point as well as the needs of the child and the court.

2.24 A final concern about video-recorded interviews, expressed to us by lawyers, was that where a child does not tell the truth in the first place a procedure which allowed the recording to be given as evidence-in-chief is likely to influence the child to adhere to a false account. Where the child gives evidence for the prosecution it is thought that this might lead to unsafe convictions. We understand however that, contrary to the traditional view, recent research shows that untruthful child witnesses are comparatively uncommon and that, like their adult counterparts, they act out of identifiable motives. It is the business of counsel to probe this on cross-examination. We would be seriously concerned about this matter if it were proposed entirely to excuse the child from cross-examination. As it is we believe that giving the court access to a recording of the original allegation as well as access to the child will make it more rather than less difficult for falsehoods to be consistently sustained.

Our proposals

2.25 We have concluded that a video-recorded interview in which a child witness gives information relevant to the commission of an offence should, in principle, be admissible at a trial on indictment. Committal proceedings and matters relating to summary trials are discussed in chapter 6. At this point we simply make clear that if the prosecution proposes to rely upon such a recording the defence should have access to it as soon as possible. Once such a case comes within the jurisdiction of the Crown Court we then propose that the prosecution should be able as of right to apply for the child witness to be examined and cross-examined at an out-of-court hearing which would be itself video-recorded and later shown to the trial jury. In deciding whether to apply for a child to give evidence in this way the prosecution would always be guided by the child's own wishes. Where a child was manifestly unsuited to undergo cross-examination in open court by reason of age or temperament, however, the prosecution should be able to override an expressed preference to do so and apply for an out-of-court hearing.

---

[2] *Teper v R* [1952] 1 A.C. 480.

2.26 We have concluded that children who come within the ambit of our proposals, which are described below in greater detail, ought never to be required to appear in public as witnesses in the Crown Court, whether in open court or protected by screens or closed circuit television, unless they wish to do so. This principle, we believe, is not only absolutely necessary for their welfare, but is also essential in overcoming the reluctance of children and their parents to assist the authorities. It would create a certainty which, we suggest, would enable many more prosecutions to be pursued successfully and therefore enhance the protection afforded to the very young by the courts.

2.27 Preliminary hearings would always take place under the supervision of the trial judge and they would be governed by the existing rules of evidence. Where such a hearing was to be held, and a video-recorded interview was also to be put in evidence, it would be necessary first for the judge to rule upon the admissibility of the recording at a pre-trial application before the witness was questioned because the recording would substantially replace examination-in-chief.

2.28 This pre-trial application would take place in chambers or another suitable place. Advocates and the accused would be present but the child witness would not. In deciding whether a recording should be admitted in whole or part the judge would hear arguments from both sides, take account of the Code of Practice which we discuss in chapter 4, and if necessary exercise his common law discretion to exclude evidence which was likely to be unfair in its effect—'more prejudicial than probative'. We consider that in those rare cases in which a judge decides to exclude an interview entirely he should be required to give reasons for doing so in order that those responsible for the conduct of such interviews can take proper account of these in future.

2.29 At the subsequent preliminary hearing the judge would provide for the examination and cross-examination of the child witness in informal surroundings and these proceedings would be video-recorded and shown at the trial. The arrangements, we think, should be within the judge's discretion, but we propose that wigs and gowns should always be removed and that he should control cross-examination with special care. It will usually be appropriate to hold the hearing in a room in the court building which is suitably equipped. With smaller children it may sometimes be desirable to use a purpose-built interview suite at a hospital or similar place. In such cases it will be important for the courts to liaise with the police and social services about the availability of accommodation and facilities. The only prescription we would make here is that the proceedings should be as informal as possible, nobody should be present in the same room as the child apart from the judge, advocates and a parent, guardian or supporter for the child, and that where evidence is given for the prosecution the defendant or defendants should be able to view the proceedings through a two-way mirror or closed-circuit television and instruct those representing them, through an audio link.

2.30 The leading case of *Smellie* (1919),[3] indicates that there is no right of confrontation in English law and we believe that defendants should be specifically prohibited by statute from examining child witnesses in person or through a sound or video-link. The limitation which this places upon the defence is, in our view, far less significant than the damage which can be inflicted upon the child and the interests of justice if, in certain circumstances, such an exercise is allowed to take place.

2.31 We envisage that the video-recorded interview, or as much of it as is to be admitted, will be shown to the child at the preliminary hearing and that he or she will be asked to confirm the account which it gives and to expand upon any aspects which the prosecution wishes to explore. After this cross-examination will take place. Where no video recording is put in evidence we assume that evidence-in-chief and cross-examination will take place in the usual sequence. In some cases new issues or evidence may later arise during the course of the subsequent public trial which make it necessary to recall the child. We recommend that this should be carried out under the same conditions as the first examination.

2.32 A majority of the group has concluded, particularly in view of the recommendations which we will make subsequently about the competence of child witnesses, that the trial judge should be able to make special arrangements for the examination of very young or very disturbed children at the preliminary hearing if he thinks this is appropriate. The majority propose that the judge's discretion, which we have already permitted, should extend where necessary to allowing the relaying of questions from counsel through a paediatrician, child psychiatrist, social worker or person who enjoys the child's confidence. In these circumstances nobody except for the trusted party would be visible to the child, although everyone with an interest would be able to communicate, indirectly, through the interlocutor.

2.33 We recognise that this would be a substantial change and we realise that there will be unease at the prospect of interposing a third party between advocate and witness. Clearly some of the advocate's forensic skills, timing, intonation and the rest, would be lost, and it is, of course possible that a child might be confused by being subjected to testing questioning from someone regarded as a friend. Nevertheless we do not find these objections conclusive. Where it is absolutely impossible for counsel to communicate successfully with a child there is, in our view, no great difference of principle between the use of someone who can do so and the employment of an interpreter where a witness cannot speak English.

---

[3] 14 Cr. App. R. 128.

Neither technique is entirely satisfactory but both can prevent the loss of crucial evidence without which the court cannot do justice.

2.34 Miss Rafferty dissents from the arguments explained in the two preceding paragraphs. In her opinion the intervention of a specialist interlocutor would hinder rather than assist counsel in conducting the case. She believes that the difficulty which has been explained should be overcome by allowing greater opportunities for counsel to establish a rapport with a child witness before the hearing takes place.

2.35 At the trial itself we think that the video-recorded interview, where available and approved by the judge, should be shown at the point at which the child would now give evidence-in-chief and that the video recording of the preliminary hearing should be shown at the place where cross-examination would normally follow. The press should be able to view this material at trial.

2.36 It remains to consider what age limit should apply to the special measures which we have proposed. In the United States individual states have applied limits as various as 10 and 17 years of age to similar measures. A number of those who gave evidence to us indicated their belief that all children under 16 should benefit from any change in the law. Inevitably this is a difficult and perhaps impossible judgment to make but in our opinion the general age limit should coincide with the legally accepted point at which a child becomes a young person, and the measures should apply in respect of violent offences to all witnesses under 14. Where sexual offences are concerned we believe there are obvious different and special considerations and we think the measures should be available to witnesses under 17. We consider the position of older vulnerable witnesses in relation to our proposals in chapter 3.

2.37 It seems to us that the new procedures should apply at trials on indictment for violent and sexual offences and offences of child cruelty and neglect. Section 32 of the Criminal Justice Act 1988, which introduced live television links, provides a precedent and a detailed definition of these. In addition we think that video-recorded interviews should be admissible at trials for comparable offences in the juvenile courts. We reject the proposition that alleged victims alone should benefit from the special procedures. Although some American states have adopted this approach it is clear to us that child witnesses of some of the very worst violent and sexual offences are as badly affected by the experience as some victims. Moreover, children are all too often witnesses of sexual offences against other children.

2.38 We are convinced that the difficulties which exist in bringing those who commit offences against children to justice and the damage which courts often inflict upon many children both constitute grave and hitherto intractable social problems. We think that the development of video technology gives us an opportunity to find fair and humane solutions to these. Our proposals are radical but, we believe, entirely practical. They are an attempt to harness technological progress to the interests of the child and of justice in a way which preserves the traditional fairness, if not the traditional forms, of the English trial.

2.39 In the next three chapters we explain how our proposals might apply to older vulnerable witnesses, the circumstances under which we believe the initial video-recorded interview should be made and why we think other major changes to the law of evidence are necessary.

CHAPTER 3

OTHER VULNERABLE WITNESSES

Introduction

3.1 The group was also asked to consider the possible application of video technology as a means of taking the evidence of adult witnesses who might be especially vulnerable to the worst effects of testifying in open court. In this chapter we explore the concept of vulnerability in that context and explain how we think the proposals which we have already put forward in relation to children might eventually be extended to other classes of witness.

Some general considerations

3.2 In principle there is no obvious reason why measures designed to reduce the stress experienced by witnesses and so ensure that the court receives clearer and fuller testimony should be permanently restricted to children. It would, for example, be difficult to justify allowing a sixteen year old to give evidence at a preliminary hearing while insisting that a slightly older badly-traumatised rape victim, a mentally handicapped person or a very frail and elderly witness should always undergo cross-examination in open court, however great the distress this caused.

3.3 Nevertheless children may be identified according to age. Unless the benefits of video technology are to be available to all witnesses, which is neither possible nor desirable, vulnerable adults who are to be eligible to benefit from it must be defined with some certainty. Plainly this presents difficulties. For example, not all elderly people will find it hard to give evidence in open court, although some younger adults might suffer an unreasonable degree of stress when doing so.

Vulnerability

3.4 For these reasons it seems to us that it will be necessary to create a test of eligibility, or vulnerability, that addresses all the relevant factors, which the party wishing to adduce evidence using the special techniques must satisfy in respect of its witness before this is permitted.

3.5 In our view evidence given in these new ways should eventually be admissible at trials on indictment for sexual and violent offences and at comparable trials in the juvenile court if the court is satisfied that an adult witness would be likely to suffer 'an unusual and unreasonable degree of mental stress' if required to give evidence in open court. The court would have regard to the age, physical and mental condition of the witness, the nature and seriousness of the offence charged and of the evidence which the witness was to give. It would take account of information from those responsible for the physical or mental health or welfare of the witness which was advanced in support of the application and would hear objections from the opposing party before reaching its decision. There should, we think, be a rebuttable presumption that all alleged victims of serious sexual offences are vulnerable witnesses. The general evidence on this point seems to us to be overwhelming.

3.6 We think that rules of this sort would be sufficiently flexible to enable traumatised, elderly and handicapped witnesses who cannot always testify or be examined satisfactorily under existing circumstances to give a fuller account and, at the same time, restrictive enough to ensure that video technology was not used in inappropriate cases. We do not believe that experienced judges would find it unduly difficult to make the necessary distinctions.

3.7 Once an application made by a witness to give evidence in a special way because of his or her vulnerability has been granted, we suggest that the trial judge should have a substantial degree of discretion to decide which of the new techniques we have described should be employed. For example if a video-recorded interview with a rape victim has been made admitting this may sometimes be sufficient to relieve the stress which she is likely to suffer through giving 'live' evidence in open court. On the other hand with an elderly or mentally-handicapped witness an out-of-court preliminary hearing may sometimes be essential.

Available techniques

(i) Video-recorded interviews

3.8 At present in most cases a video-recorded interview with the adult vulnerable witness will not have been made when he or she is first interviewed by the police and will not, therefore, be available to the court. We do not, however, think that any enabling provision should exclude the possibility of such an interview being put in as evidence-in-chief in the way we have proposed in relation to child witnesses. There are some cases—and we would particularly cite those involving badly traumatised victims of sexual offences or mentally-handicapped witnesses—where this would be sensible, humane, advantageous to the court and fair, provided that some provision was also made for cross-examination. This may, of course, pose some difficulties for the police, who will have to assess in each case whether a recording is likely to be worthwhile. We think, however, that it should be possible to identify some categories of witness, for example rape victims, where video recording should usually take place.

(ii) Preliminary hearings

3.9 If our main proposals are accepted and extended to adult vulnerable witnesses one technique employed to take their evidence will be the video-recorded preliminary hearing. We anticipate that this would be conducted in much the same way as similar hearings involving child witnesses: on an informal basis, with the accused person excluded but able to view the proceedings and communicate with his legal representatives. We would suggest that an accused should not be able to cross-examine a vulnerable witness in person. As with child witnesses we believe that in these exceptional cases it is necessary to restrict an accused's right to represent himself in the interests of justice.

3.10 We think the important points about such preliminary hearings are that there should be a minimal number of people present and that the witness should have the opportunity to speak freely outside the highly-charged confrontational atmosphere of a public trial. For this reason we suggest that, as with child witnesses, the parties present should be disrobed and that judges should control cross-examination with especial care.

3.11 Evidence in such proceedings should, we think, be given under oath or affirmation. Where no video-recorded interview is put in evidence the witness should be taken through his or her evidence-in-chief first and then cross-examined. A recording of the hearing would be played at the appropriate place during the subsequent trial.

(iii) The live television link

3.12 It seems to us that the live television link now used to take children's evidence from outside the courtroom is most effective where a witness is likely to be intimidated by the presence of a particular person or persons in the court or by the courtroom ambience. If a witness suffers from an inherent disadvantage caused by age, handicap or trauma it is likely to be less successful than a preliminary hearing for relieving the stress of the occasion by altering the pace, tone and context. Nonetheless we think there will be occasions when an adult witness will feel confident of testifying successfully if the link can be used or when the judge might decide that use of the link alone would, in the circumstances of the case, be sufficient to ensure that the witness did not suffer an unusual or unreasonable degree of mental stress from giving evidence. We therefore favour making the link available to adult vulnerable witnesses subject to judicial discretion.

3.13 At this juncture we should say that the failure to include mentally disordered witnesses with children under 14 as persons eligible to use the live television link has been presented to us as a serious omission. Whatever the outcome of our proposals generally we are strongly convinced that special consideration should be given to the needs of this group, members of which seem, sadly, to be particularly subject to sexual and violent crime. All too often the circumstances under which they are now required to testify are neither decent nor humane.

Conclusions

3.14 We have concluded that in a small number of serious cases elderly, handicapped, badly traumatised and similarly affected witnesses should, eventually, be able to give evidence on the same general terms as we have proposed for child witnesses. We think that judges should enjoy a substantial discretion in this area, both in determining the eligibility of vulnerable witnesses to testify in this way and in deciding which particular techniques should be allowable in an individual case.

3.15 Once our recommendations in relation to child witnesses are implemented and working successfully we believe a high priority must then attach to extending the new measures to vulnerable adults. If changes of the sort which we have suggested cannot be introduced reasonably soon in respect of all adult vulnerable witnesses we would propose that the earliest provision should be made for victims of serious sexual offences, who face special and generally recognised difficulties.

CHAPTER 4

THE VIDEO-RECORDED INTERVIEW

Introduction

4.1 In this chapter we explain our conclusions about how video-recorded interviews should be made. We begin with some particular observations about the investigation of offences against children and we then indicate those matters we believe should be addressed by a Code of Practice and the policy we think such a code should embody. The code, we suggest, should provide authoritative guidance to responsible agencies about best practice and guarantee some uniformity of judicial approach to video-recorded evidence. Most of the matters which we discuss relate solely to children but some references are made to older vulnerable witnesses and the way in which these provisions might eventually be extended to them.

The investigation of offences against children

4.2 When the Report of the Inquiry into Child Abuse in Cleveland was published in July 1988 the Home Office issued a circular which gave guidance to chief officers of police about the investigation of child sexual abuse (Annex B). This broadly follows recommendations made in the Cleveland Report for improving inter-agency co-operation, principally between the police and social services, and endorses the approach pioneered in the London Borough of Bexley, which is being successfully adopted throughout the Metropolitan Police area where a detailed statement of principles and practice, The Force Response to Child Abuse within the Family, has been drawn up. Subsequent Home Office circulars have provided more detailed guidance about the training of those engaged in such investigations.

4.3 In summary the procedures commended by the Home Office require recognition by all the agencies involved of the overriding importance of the welfare of the child. They require early consultation and coordination between the police and social services, extensive information sharing, joint investigations and joint interviews. They are underpinned by joint training schemes and where available the use of joint interviewing facilities. The nature and extent of the inter-agency co-operation necessary naturally depends upon the circumstances surrounding a particular inquiry. In some cases where child protection and welfare is a central issue the whole investigation will effectively be a joint operation between police officers and social workers. Characteristically such cases will involve inter-familial abuse. In other circumstances, for instance where a child has suffered an isolated experience at the hands of a stranger, the role of the police is likely to be dominant.

4.4 We would make two principal points about these procedures. First, while we recognise that the investigation of offences is an operational matter for which Chief Constables must be responsible, we do not believe that the investigation of many offences against children can take place successfully, with proper consideration for the welfare of children, unless effective joint working arrangements are in place. This is especially important if video-recorded interviews with child witnesses are to be made generally because one of the principal purposes of this is to spare children the ordeal of repeatedly recounting traumatic experiences. This aim can be defeated by inadequate cooperation between the police and social services.

4.5 Second, we are concerned that the Home Office guidance to police forces only applies in cases of sexual abuse. It seems to us that the approach which it outlines is just as appropriate in cases of physical abuse, cruelty and neglect. Clearly the sort of measures which we have described will not be necessary or desirable in every case, but we do think that the joint working machinery should always be available for the responsible police officers and social workers to employ by agreement in cases which involve children and that the agencies should always consult, however briefly, where a child appears to have been the victim of an offence or a witness to a serious violent crime.

4.6 A separate working group has considered the question of how the training of police officers and social workers engaged in child abuse work should be developed. In this report we only look in detail at aspects of training which relate directly to the interviewing of children and other vulnerable witnesses. Nevertheless we do think it important to strongly endorse joint training and the deployment of specialist joint investigation teams. As we have seen already this is a highly sensitive area. Rigid definition of the roles of police and social workers is not always possible or desirable and much must be decided locally by comparatively junior officers. Obviously this requires a high degree of flexibility and responsiveness. This need will be increased if video-recorded interviews with child witnesses become a standard feature of such investigations. For this reason we think that every opportunity should be taken to promote mutual understanding on a professional and personal level between those members of the two agencies who will undertake this work in a particular area. This will be enhanced by joint training.

4.7 Social workers and police officers selected for the investigation of child abuse cases must necessarily be personally suitable, have a strong commitment to the work and good communication skills. Their training should include elements of child psychology and cognitive development and of the law which relates to children and violent crime generally. We think that making video-recorded interviews admissible in court should increase the value placed upon communication skills and broaden the specialist legal training necessary. Because it is intended that recorded interviews will substantially replace examination-in-chief at trial, interviewers must receive training in the law of evidence, especially as it relates to rules and procedures for the examination of witnesses in court.

Towards a Code of Practice

4.8 We recommend that a code for the conduct of video-recorded interviews should contain general guidance about best practice and some obligatory features which guarantee the rights of accused persons and protect the welfare of witnesses. It cannot, and should not, bind the courts so that an interview which complies with it is automatically allowed in evidence and one which does not is always excluded. Nevertheless, we propose that courts should always have regard to the Code of Practice in making this decision and that, as we have already explained, where a recording which complies with the code is excluded the court should give reasons for this. We hope that the existence of a code will create a climate in which video-recorded interviews will be recognised by the courts as a safe and acceptable source of evidence and will not be rejected for technical reasons which do not bear directly on the fairness of the proceedings. In the paragraphs which follow we list the matters to which the code should apply and explain our conclusions about each.

(i) Timing

4.9 The video-recorded interview which is to be admissible in court should, we believe, broadly equate with a witness statement in which the first detailed account of a complaint is given to the police. It should be clear that the aim of the interview is to establish what happened and that it does not have a therapeutic or other purpose. It should be conducted as soon as practicable after an offence has been reported, but allowing sufficient time or inter-agency consultation and consideration of the circumstances surrounding the case, as well as for prior medical examination where that is appropriate. There are several reasons for this recommendation. The agencies concerned must have an opportunity to consider the legal context and implications of the interview before it takes place. Interviews conducted in advance of this are likely to be of limited evidential value. Once a plan of action has been agreed by the agencies it is important to proceed quickly. This will minimise the stress experienced by witnesses, reduce the opportunity for them to be influenced by others or forget important details and enable the accused person to be acquainted with the allegations made against him at an early stage.

4.10 We recognise that several days may elapse after the initial complaint before an interview can be arranged but we do not think longer delays should be tolerated. In some exceptional cases it may be necessary for the police to carry out an interview immediately if the initial complaint suggests that deferment might result in the escape of an offender or the destruction of evidence.

4.11 Once a witness has been interviewed we do not think further questioning should take place until the prosecutor has had the opportunity to view the recording and consider the papers in the case. At this stage it *may* be necessary to elicit further information. This should normally be done by holding a supplementary video-recorded interview, but if the questions are unlikely to be prolonged or distressing a written statement *may* be taken. In either case the person who conducted the initial interview should, if practicable, conduct the supplementary one. It must be remembered that where it is proposed to rely upon material which is only in a written statement the witness may be required to repeat it at a preliminary hearing or, exceptionally, at trial.

(ii) Location

4.12 In some areas purpose-built interview suites are already available at hospitals and similar places away from the police station where children and other vulnerable witnesses such as rape victims may be interviewed. In principle, however, we see no objection to interviews taking place within police stations where suitable facilities are available. The suitability of available locations should be considered by the police officers and social workers engaged in an investigation together. The only prescription we would make is that the room chosen should be capable of accommodating the equipment, the interviewer and the subject comfortably, should be free from noise and other distractions and should be attractively decorated. Sometimes it may be necessary to record an interview with a badly injured, traumatised or elderly witness. We see no objection to this taking place in the subject's own home if suitable arrangements can be made.

(iii) Equipment

4.13 The video equipment used should be of high quality and should be capable of clearly recording the words, gestures and facial expressions of all the parties present in the room where the interview is conducted. We strongly recommend the use of two cameras: a static camera giving a general view of the room and a moving camera. We also recommend the use of film and equipment which automatically records the time and date of the interview. This provides a guarantee of continuity and a useful means of indexing the tape so that key passages can be located later. A principal justification for allowing video recordings to be put in evidence rather than other forms of out-of-court statement is the faithfulness to life of the record which they provide. This must not be jeopardised by the use of inadequate equipment.

(iv) Participants

4.14 If the subject of an interview is a vulnerable adult we think that no person should ordinarily be present in the room where it takes place except for the witness, the interviewer (usually a police officer) and, if it is unavoidable, a technician. Rather different additional considerations apply to child witnesses, especially the very young. We think that it may sometimes be necessary for a police officer and a social worker to conduct the interview together. This can be ineffective, however, and we suggest that the agencies should consider nominating a single interviewer who is professionally briefed beforehand about the needs of the agency to which he or she does not belong. Our experience of video-recorded interviews suggests that the presence of parents or other friendly parties can be a distraction and should be discouraged. With very small children, however, this may be essential to reassure the child. It is obviously necessary that where a third party is present he or she should not take part in the discussion of issues material to the alleged offence. It is important to minimise the number of people present so that the recording provides an accurate record of what transpired. The court will wish to be assured that the witness was not prompted or encouraged during the interview and to provide a comprehensive record of the words, gestures and expressions of more than two people can be technically demanding.

4.15 The interviewer will usually be a social worker or police officer who has been who has been trained in the handling of abuse cases if the subject is a child. We think that in some circumstances other people who have a responsibility for the health, care or welfare of children should be permitted to conduct interviews, provided that they are thoroughly briefed beforehand about the agencies' requirements and legal considerations. Particularly where sexual abuse is concerned children may choose to put their confidence in an individual adult such as a doctor, nurse, teacher or health worker and be reluctant or unwilling to explain what happened to anyone else in detail at first. Provided that the person in question is prepared to cooperate and is properly instructed by specialists in advance about how to conduct the interview we see no objection to their doing so. We do not think this will happen often, but we believe that in some conditions it may be essential for the protection of children and the detection of crime.

(v) Consent

4.16 Existing Home Office guidelines to the police on the investigation of sexual offences against children contain a specimen consent form for parents to complete where it is proposed to video-record an interview with a child. We think this may be unnecessary. It seems to us that the consent of witnesses, child witnesses or parents to the making of a video-recorded interview should only be sought where consent would be necessary if the interview were not recorded. The fullest possible information should always be given to interested parties and the witness would, from a practical point of view, always have the option of withholding testimony. But we do not think that written consent should be sought specifically to conduct an interview in this particular way. If a parent's preference for an interview not to be recorded is to be overridden there is little point in seeking consent in the first place. If it is to be respected the only outcome is likely to be that if the case proceeds to court the child will suffer greater stress than necessary. We believe that where serious offences have been committed against children video recording should be the standard and accepted way in which their evidence is given to the police and the courts. If subsequently a tape is to be used for training purposes we think that specific consent should then be sought.

(vi) Conducting the interview

4.17 At the start of any interview the interviewer should state the names of the people present and the time and location. Explanations should also be given for any interruptions in the proceedings.

4.18 The structure and content of interviews with children should be carefully considered by all those involved in advance. We have no wish to change existing practices simply because of the introduction of video recording and its proposed admissibility as evidence. We should, though, record our endorsement of the 'step-wise' approach to the interview proposed by Professor Yuille of the University of British Columbia, although we do not think it necessary to assess here the techniques which he has developed for analysing the content of the interview subsequently. Essentially this approach requires the interviewer to proceed from the most general, open aspects of the interview to the more specific. The first exchanges are designed to build rapport between the child and the interviewer, the seriousness of the context and the importance of giving a truthful account are then established. After this the child is allowed to speak as freely and fully as possible about his or her experience. Where further questioning is necessary it should graduate from the open to the specific.

4.19 The advantage of employing this sort of method is that it seems most likely to achieve a truthful account from the child and one given in a way acceptable to the courts. If a detailed protocol for interviewing is to be included in a Code of Practice we think that the 'step-wise' approach should be carefully examined before it is drawn up.

(vii) Leading questions

4.20 Because it is proposed that video-recorded interviews should replace the examination-in-chief of witnesses in court they ought to be conducted as far as possible in accordance with the rules which govern that procedure. This means that when issues are addressed which relate to the commission of an offence the interviewer should avoid asking questions which suggest the answer and should not assume that facts are established which are likely to be in dispute. Where children are concerned the courts already allow some latitude in this area depending upon the child's age and understanding. We think the important point is that interviewers should never be the first to suggest that a particular offence was committed or that a particular person was the perpetrator. We do not believe that the courts will exclude fairly-conducted interviews for purely technical reasons or because of the inclusion of occasional insignificant leading questions. Nevertheless it should be remembered that crucial leading questions which relate to the central facts of a case must be avoided wherever possible. They may well result in the exclusion of the interview at court.

4.21 Sometimes it will become clear after an interview has been recorded that it is flawed for evidential purposes. We do not think that an unsuccessful interview of this sort should necessarily preclude a successful prosecution. If, having finally disclosed what happened, the child is prepared to give further details and adhere to his or her account, we see no objection to the preparation of a statement based upon it. At this point the prosecutor would have to decide whether to call the child for examination-in-chief at a preliminary hearing, or if exceptionally the child so wished, in court. If this were done the defence would, of course, be able to produce the recording and argue that the child's complaint had been manufactured by the interviewer. We do not anticipate that this would occur often.

(viii) Anatomically-correct dolls

4.22 The use of anatomically-correct dolls and other aids such as drawings or diagrams in the investigation of child sexual abuse has been a subject of considerable controversy. We have no doubt that unless these are approached with caution their use will be regarded by the courts as suggestive and prejudicial. We propose that the Code of Practice should make clear that such aids should only be used to help a child establish details with which he or she may have verbal difficulties once the general substance of a complaint is clear.

(ix) Showing the recording to the accused

4.23 We think that the Code of Practice should provide for the video-recorded interview to be shown to the accused person as soon as practicably possible, although he may choose not to comment or reserve his comments until his solicitor is present. This should take place within the framework set out by the Police and Criminal Evidence Act 1984.

(x) Ownership, copies and storage

4.24 We suggest that ownership of the recording should be vested in the responsible police force. Copies may be sent to the prosecuting authority and to the social services only. These copies should be returned to the police when they are no longer required. When an accused person or his legal representatives wish to view a recording they should be allowed reasonable facilities to do so at a police station or prison establishment but should never be able to borrow the tape. This may cause some inconvenience, but we think that wider circulation of such recordings would be so undesirable that measures to prevent it are justified.

4.25 We have concluded that the police should destroy all copies of video-recorded interviews once their continued existence serves no further purpose. We anticipate that it may be necessary to store tapes for periods of twenty years or longer.

CHAPTER 5

OTHER LEGAL ISSUES

COMPETENCE

Introduction

5.1 We have already seen that the reason why video-recorded interviews cannot be given as evidence is the rule against hearsay. But even if this were to be abnegated, either in general or in the specific way which we have proposed, many video recordings could still not be used. This is because in England and Wales most very young children are simply not regarded as competent witnesses at all and their testimony cannot ever be lawful evidence. Obviously so long as this situation persists the benefits to be gained from the use of video recording, which we have already explained, will in practice be severely limited. In this chapter we consider how the courts decide whether a child is competent to give evidence and we set out our proposals for reform.

The competence requirement

5.2 As a general rule anyone who can give relevant evidence in a case, except for a person of unsound mind or a child of tender years, is presumed to be a competent witness. For practical purposes a person under fourteen years of age is a child of tender years. Under both common law and statute such a child may give sworn evidence if he or she understands the nature of the oath and the obligation of speaking the truth. If a child does not understand the oath he or she may nevertheless give unsworn evidence by reason of section 38 of the Children and Young Persons Act 1933 if "in the opinion of the court, he [or she] is possessed of sufficient intelligence to justify reception of the evidence, and understands the duty of speaking the truth".

5.3 It is the responsibility of the trial judge to examine potential child witnesses in court to ascertain whether they have the necessary understanding of the oath or of the concepts of truth and duty. The burden of proving this rests upon the party which has chosen to call the witness, so that if the judge is not satisfied beyond reasonable doubt that a potential witness for the prosecution has the requisite understanding he or she will not be allowed to give evidence. Section 34 of the Criminal Justice Act 1988 effectively abolished the legal distinction between the evidence of sworn and unsworn child witnesses and it is now of little significance whether a child qualifies as competent witness by understanding the oath or by understanding the duty of speaking the truth.

5.4 Obviously children with differing levels of intelligence and at various developmental stages entertain notions of quite varying sophistication and accuracy about the oath and concepts like truth and duty. The task of establishing whether a particular witness has reached an adequate standard can be an extremely difficult one and some judges find the procedure very unsatisfactory. Guidance has, however, been provided by the higher courts and this, we believe, helps to explain why young child witnesses are more rarely called in England and Wales than in other similar jurisdictions.

The case of *Wallwork*

5.5 In the case of *Wallwork* (1958)[4] a witness of five years of age was called to give evidence, although she did not actually do so. The Court of Criminal Appeal deprecated this and the Lord Chief Justice, Lord Goddard, observed that it was 'ridiculous' to suppose that any value could have been attached to the evidence of such a witness. The effect of *Wallwork*, it appears to us, is that prosecutors will not generally adduce, or courts receive, evidence from young children unless they seem to have the understanding normally to be expected of a child of about eight. In a more recent unreported case *Wright and Ormerod* (1987), the Court of Appeal Criminal Division reiterated the policy of *Wallwork*. Mr Justice Ognall said that the validity and good sense of the judgment remained 'untrammelled' and that "it must require quite exceptional circumstances to justify the reception of this kind of evidence".

5.6 This contrasts sharply with the position in practice in Scotland where there is a similar formal competence requirement but where it is not unusual for children of four, five and six to give evidence and where witnesses as young as three have testified. The Scottish authority on evidence, Dickson[5], suggests that this more open attitude is long standing. In this connection we also think that a further consequence of the policy of *Wallwork* is that our courts have proved far slower than some others to adopt measures which produce an informal 'child-friendly' atmosphere before and during proceedings precisely because the very young children who would benefit most from this hardly ever appear.

Conclusions

5.7 The present situation was heavily criticised by a number of those who gave evidence to us. Police witnesses in particular felt that *Wallwork* made it

[4] 42 Cr. App. R. 153.
[5] W G Dickson, *A Treatise on the Law of Evidence in Scotland*, 3rd edition 1887, 1543–1548.

virtually impossible to convict offenders who molest very young children in private. Some social workers were puzzled by cases in which child victims who seemed to be able to give perfectly clear accounts of offences committed against them were not permitted to do so in court. They were aware of the stress produced by a court appearance under present conditions, however, and were not altogether sure that the prosecuting authorities had taken the wrong decisions from the point of view of the children's welfare.

5.8 It seems clear to us that the competence requirement interpreted in the light of *Wallwork* does lead to the abandonment of prosecutions for a large number of serious violent and sexual offences against children with all the attendant unfortunate consequences which we have already discussed in relation to the admissibility of video-recorded interviews. We conclude that in view of these considerations the present requirement is only justifiable if it operates to exclude particularly unreliable evidence and therefore to prevent an unusual danger of miscarriages of justice.

5.9 We do not think that the influence of *Wallwork* can be justified in principle at all since its effect has been to substitute a sort of age limit for witnesses where Parliament plainly intended there to be a test of understanding in each case. It has persisted despite modern thought about the rights and psychology of children, we suggest, because the traditional courtroom experience is so obviously an inappropriate one for the very young. Legal conservatism about practices and procedures and concern about the immediate welfare of child witnesses have both helped to ensure that our courts do not hear evidence which would be heard in other jurisdictions.

5.10 The weight of recent research indicates that young children are no more likely to give inaccurate or untruthful evidence than other witnesses. Indeed the Government accepted the general force of this argument during the passage of the Criminal Justice Act 1988 in relation to the proposal which was to become section 34. This abolished the requirement that the unsworn evidence of children should be corroborated—or confirmed in material particulars by other evidence—before the court could act upon it. In proposing this measure Ministers took account of a survey of modern research about child witnesses which concluded that children as young as five were likely to provide reliable evidence.

5.11 A competence requirement is evidently only useful if by reference to the test which it imposes it is possible to ascertain whether a child is likely to subsequently give a truthful and accurate account. We have failed to find any evidence that the existing requirement achieves this. Indeed it seems logical to suppose that a child who is not able to explain what the oath signifies, or what concepts like truth and duty mean, is rather less likely to be sophisticated enough to invent and consistently and successfully sustain falsehoods than other witnesses. Alternative formulations of the requirement are open to the same objection. We do not think for example that the test proposed in the Eleventh Report of the Criminal Law

Revision Committee[6], that the child should understand the importance of telling the truth in the proceedings, would be any more likely to provide a dependable touchstone.

5.12 In principle it seems wrong to us that our courts should refuse to consider any relevant understandable evidence. If a child's account is available it should be heard. We have already looked at ways in which video recording could be used to obtain such evidence where this might now present insuperable difficulties. Once this evidence is admitted juries will obviously weigh matters such as the demeanour of the witness, his or her maturity and understanding and the coherence and consistency of the testimony, in deciding how much reliance to place upon it. We think that this would be a much more satisfactory proceeding and one far better attuned to the principle of trial by jury, modern psychological research and the practice in other jurisdictions than the present approach which appears to us to be founded upon the archaic belief that children below a certain age or level of understanding are either too senseless or too morally delinquent to be worth listening to at all.

Our proposals

5.13 It follows that we believe the competence requirement which is applied to potential child witnesses should be dispensed with and that it should not be replaced. Once any witness has begun to testify he or she may appear to be of unsound mind, become incoherent or fail to communicate in a way that makes sense. The judge is already able to rule such a witness incompetent and to advise the jury to ignore any evidence that may have been given. We think that this power, applied where necessary at the preliminary hearing or trial, is all that is needed. We should hasten to add that is a power which should only be exercised after considerable thought and perseverance and that this is especially important in the case of young children.

5.14 If it is accepted that children who are capable of giving an account should be permitted to do so the question of whether they should give evidence sworn or unsworn arises. As we have seen there is no longer any effective legal distinction to be made between sworn and unsworn evience. It does, however, seem possible that some jurors may be inclined to draw an inference and also that it might become customary for small children with no appreciation of the divine sanction to take the oath. Neither of these possibilities seems desirable. For this reason we propose that all witnesses under the age of 14 should give evidence unsworn and that those who are older should be able to take the oath or affirm, as the Criminal Law Revision Committee recommended in its eleventh report.

[6] Cmnd 4991 paragraphs 204–08.

5.15 Although we do not believe that there should be a formal requirement in this respect, we think that judges may find it helpful to admonish child witnesses to give a full and truthful account of what occurred in terms suitable to their age and understanding. This could be to the effect of "Tell us all you can remember of what happened. Don't make anything up or leave anything out. This is very important". We feel bound to make the point that in the circumstances children will hardly be unaware of the significance of the occasion which, it seems to us, they will mostly necessarily have been made to understand to the best of their ability.

5.16 When we heard evidence it was put to us that it would be desirable if the jury were always to be warned that unsworn child witnesses could not be prosecuted for perjury. We are inclined to reject this suggestion. Section 38(2) of the Children and Young Persons Act 1933 does in fact provide that a child witness is liable to be punished if he or she wilfully gives false evidence where, had the evidence been sworn, he or she would have been guilty of perjury. In any case we hardly think that jurors can actually suppose that in modern conditions it is likely that penal sanctions will be employed against small children under the age of eight who will be principally affected by our proposals.

THE CORROBORATION WARNING

Introduction

5.17 Another legal matter which the group thought itself bound to consider is the warning which the judge must give the jury in trials for sexual offences that it is always dangerous to convict on the uncorroborated evidence of the complainant. In this chapter we consider the nature of the rule, its purpose and practical consequences. We believe that this issue is of direct relevance to the question of video-recorded evidence because we think that unless the rule is altered our proposals for facilitating the testimony of children and of other vulnerable witnesses may, at any rate in so far as sexual offences are concerned, have a much more limited effect than we intend. We therefore also set out recommendations for reform in what we recognise as a controversial area which is now being considered by the Law Commission.

The warning

5.18 In England and Wales it is generally for the jury to decide whether to convict an accused upon the evidence of a single witness if, in all the circumstances, it is persuaded of his guilt beyond reasonable doubt. Where the witness is alleged to be the victim of a sexual offence, however, the jury must be warned that this would be perilous. The position was explained by Lord Justice Salmon in *R v Henry* (1969):[7]

> "What the judge has to do is to use clear and simple language that will without any doubt convey to the jury that in cases of alleged sexual offences it is really dangerous to convict on the evidence of the woman or girl alone. This is dangerous because human experience has shown that in these courts girls and women do sometimes tell an entirely false story which is very easy to fabricate and very difficult to refute. Such stories are fabricated for all sorts of reasons, which I need not now enumerate, and sometimes for no reason at all".

At this point it should be said that the rule also applies to male complainants.

5.19 The specific dangers of a conviction in these circumstances were identified in the Eleventh Report of the Criminal Law Revision Committee. These are said to be that "the complainant may have made a false accusation owing to sexual neurosis, jealousy, fantasy, spite or a girl's refusal to admit that she consented to an act of which she is now ashamed".[8] The dangers must always be identified and the warning given whatever the actual state of the evidence, otherwise a conviction is liable to be subsequently overturned.

5.20 In making his direction to the jury the judge should explain what is meant by corroboration (although the word need not be used) and point out any evidence which is capable of amounting to corroboration. It is then for the jury to decide as a matter of fact whether the evidence of a single witness is actually corroborated, or confirmed according to the criteria which the judge has set out. It remains open to the jury to convict in spite of the absence of such confirmatory evidence if they are prepared to ignore the danger suggested to them. They may also of course, disregard any corroborative evidence if they do not believe the witness in the first place.

Corroboration

5.21 Corroborative evidence must be independent of the source of the evidence to be corroborated and must confirm in some material particular both that the crime in question was committed and that the defendant committed it. In a rape case for example this means that there must be specific evidence other than that of the complainant that intercourse took place, and that the accused was responsible, and that consent was not given.

5.22 Whether a particular piece of evidence is capable of providing corroboration is, in England and Wales, often a complex technical question. It is clear

[7] 53 Cr. App. R. 150.
[8] Cmnd 4991 paragraph 186.

however that an accumulation of pieces of strong circumstantial evidence, each of which is in itself incapable of amounting to corroborative evidence, is not sufficient. For example on a complaint of rape the accused and the complainant might have been seen together at an isolated spot, the complainant might then have been seen in a distraught state shortly afterwards and have alleged that the offence took place, a doctor might have confirmed that rape had occurred after a medical examination and the accused might have refused to make a statement to the police or give evidence. In such a case there would be insufficient independent evidence relating each of the material particulars of the offence to the defendant and the complainant would not be corroborated. On hearing the evidence and considering all the circumstances the jury might very well conclude that the accused was guilty beyond reasonable doubt. They should nevertheless be warned that returning such a verdict would be dangerous.

The effects of the warning

5.23 Because the issue of corroboration has become a narrow and complicated one and because misdirections to the effect that particular pieces of evidence might be corroborative can prove fatal we think that judges must be disinclined to give such directions unless they are absolutely convinced that their reasoning is unassailable. One result of this is that summings-up may read extremely oddly to the layman. Here a formal warning on the lines described that conviction would be 'dangerous' may sometimes be set in the context of a recapitulation of the evidence which makes it clear that on a general consideration of the case the judge takes rather a different view.

5.24 We suspect that many jurors find the whole exercise quite impenetrable. For them consideration of the probity of evidence and the reliability of witnesses is all of a piece. In looking at the case they will have already employed the knowledge suggested by their own experiences of life in assessing possible motives like sexual neurosis, jealousy, fantasy and the rest. What does the warning and the narrow corroboration requirement mean to them? Does it perhaps suggest to some that there is official information to the effect that women who claim to have been raped and children who say they have been abused are far more likely to be untruthful than their own knowledge and experience might indicate? The rigour and particularity of the corroboration requirement and the weight of the warning certainly could seem to suggest that this is the case.

Conclusions

5.25 It can only be supposed that in court the warning is either disregarded or that it actually leads to the acquittal of defendants who, had the jury evaluated all the evidence in the usual way, would have been convicted. Clearly many of the witnesses most likely to benefit from our proposals will be the victims of sexual offences. They cannot usually be corroborated. We think that it would be questionable in principle and undesirable in practice to introduce quite radical measures for facilitating their evidence, as well as unfair to them, if, once admitted, it were to continue to be invariably characterised as 'dangerous' by judges.

5.26 We have concluded that the elaborate technical approach to corroboration which has grown up in England and Wales over the last seventy years or so has proved confusing and counterproductive and that, at least in respect of sexual offences, it has tended to cause injustice. The warning which must be given in sexual cases seems to us to be a crude and indiscriminate measure which is particularly ill-suited to a class of offences which take place in such widely varying circumstances.

5.27 We especially question the reasons which are usually given for the warning. It is true that complainants in sexual cases, like their counterparts in other cases, do sometimes tell entirely false stories. But we know of no evidence whatever which suggests that this takes place on such a scale and in a way so calculated to successfully deceive the jury that a special measure designed to enhance the normal standard of proof is necessary. On the contrary all the evidence which we received suggests that the stress, trauma and public humiliation so often experienced by the victims of sexual offences in court, and the intimidation to which they are sometimes subjected out of court, deter many from testifying at all and certainly militate strongly against the bringing of false evidence.

5.28 In all this it must also be remembered that a crucial function of the law is the protection of the community. In recent years substantial and apparently unremitting rises in the number of sexual crimes committed against women and children have been recorded. In such a context it is clearly of the utmost importance that rules and practices which can deflect the course of justice in these cases should be abandoned. To us this seems especially relevant to a rule which is not only highly questionable in itself but in its practical effect is arguably sexually discriminatory.

Our proposals

5.29 There are several possible approaches to reform. The Criminal Law Revision Committee's Eleventh report suggested that the jury should be warned of the 'special need for caution' rather than the 'danger' of convicting upon uncorroborated evidence, although they also suggested that as a matter of law conviction upon the uncorroborated evidence of a witness under 14 years of age should not be possible. Neither of these courses recommends itself to us. The first proposal would leave the central problem of what constitutes corroboration untouched and the second is plainly inimical to recent scientific thought and legislative developments in relation to child witnesses which we have wholly endorsed.

5.30 A more promising line was developed by the Canadian courts. For some years, perhaps beginning with the case of *Warkentin* (1977),[9] they showed signs of adopting a less restrictive and specific approach to what constitutes corroboration and of accepting 'cumulative corroboration' of the sort already described in paragraph 5.6 above. Now, by an amendment to the Canadian Criminal Code and the Canada Evidence Act, the corroboration warning in cases involving sexual offences has simply been abolished.

5.31 We believe that the conclusion reached by the Canadian legislature is right in principle. Existing safeguards which apply in all criminal cases are, we think, sufficient in those which involve sexual offences. If a case depends on the evidence of a single witness and this is so unsatisfactory that the judge thinks a conviction would be unsafe he may remind the jury of its right to return a not guilty verdict without hearing further evidence. Additional rules which relate only to this class of cases seem to us neither necessary nor desirable.

[9] 2 SCR 355.

CHAPTER 6

THE MAGISTRATES' COURTS

Introduction

6.1 In this chapter we consider the implications of our main recommendations for the conduct of summary proceedings. We have already indicated our view that it is essential for the participation of child witnesses in court proceedings for serious offences to be minimised and to take place as speedily as is consonant with the interests of justice. We explain here why we believe the achievement of this aim requires major changes which will affect the conduct of the magistrates' courts, and we make consequential recommendations.

Summary trials

6.2 Although violent and sexual offences against children are much more likely to be tried on indictment in the Crown Court than similar offences against older victims, many such cases are heard in the magistrates' courts, although it is not clear what proportion of these is resolved by guilty pleas. We have not proposed that our recommendations in relation to the admissibility of video-recorded interviews and the holding of preliminary hearings should apply there because we are not certain that this would be immediately practicable or affordable. We have, however already recommended that video recorded interviews should be admissible at trials for serious violent and sexual offences in the juvenile courts. If a workable system for taking children's evidence on the lines which we have suggested is brought into operation, we propose that the question of its possible application to summary trials should be reviewed at an early stage. We have also concluded that magistrates should receive clear guidance about the use of measures to prevent the intimidation of witnesses and that screens and other necessary equipment should always be readily available for this purpose. This subject should be addressed in their training programmes.

Committal proceedings

6.3 At present before an accused may be tried on indictment in the Crown Court he must be committed for trial by examining justices. At this stage it is necessary for the prosecution to establish that there is sufficient evidence to justify trial by jury, a prima facie case. Despite recent changes to facilitate the use of documentary evidence in the form of written statements for this purpose, it remains possible for the defence to insist upon the calling of witnesses to give evidence in person. Where this is done the witness may be cross-examined. In such cases the evidence given is written down and rendered into deposition form. A committal hearing at which the principal prosecution witnesses appear in person occurs in about 10% of cases. This is sometimes called an 'old-style' committal.

6.4 These procedures have been strongly criticised. Reform was recommended by the James Committee (1975)[10] and the Royal Commission on Criminal Procedure (1981)[11], as well as by a number of interested professional bodies. It has been argued that committal hearings, whether in the 'old style' or paper form, do not result in the weeding-out of ill-founded prosecutions as often as they should, that they are cumbersome, expensive, time-consuming and that on occasions they are abused by the defence to deter witnesses from appearing at the subsequent trial or to undermine their confidence. The Criminal Justice Act 1987, following the recommendations of the Roskill Committee, provided for the bypassing of committal hearings in cases which involve serious or complex fraud, although in such cases the issue of whether there is a case to answer may be taken at a preliminary stage in the Crown Court, and, where there is insufficient evidence, the defendant may be discharged.

6.5 At the time of writing the Home Office and the Lord Chancellor's Department had recently issued a consultation paper on the future of committal hearings which makes it clear that radical change is contemplated. Essentially the paper identifies two likely options. Both would entail enabling the prosecutor to decide whether an offence which was triable in the Crown Court should in fact be dealt with there, although where a defendant has a right to opt for trial by jury in respect of an offence which is triable summarily this is unaffected. Both options also allow the defendant to argue that there is insufficient evidence to justify a jury trial. In one case this must be done before a Crown Court judge and in the other before a magistrates' court, although the matter would be decided on the papers and on legal representations and witnesses would not have to give oral evidence. The Government is inclined to favour the option of a magistrates' court hearing. Although it is acknowledged that the advantages of a hearing before a Crown Court judge "would be a reduction in pre-trial delays and an authoritative decision by a judge on the merits of any application for discharge, as well as greater influence over the state of preparedness of the case".[12] It is argued that there would also be an unacceptable reduction in the number of judges actually available to hear cases.

---

[10] Cmnd 6323.

[11] Cmnd 8092.

[12] *Committal Proceedings: A Consultation Paper*, 1989, paragraph 8.

6.6 It seems to us that in cases which involve children existing committal proceedings are irredeemably flawed. They enable defendants to subject child witnesses to all of the burdens which we have already discussed: delay, appearance in open court, cross-examination in open court, face-to-face confrontation with an alleged perpetrator and repeated unnecessary worry about matters which may be extremely distressing or even traumatic. Measures designed to protect children in the Crown Court only seem likely to increase the frequency of such abuses. Naturally we welcome proposals for change.

6.7 Of the options offered in the consultation document we strongly favour a system which would allow those accused of offences against children, at least, to apply for discharge in the Crown Court. The advantages of this, identified by the Government's consultation paper, seem especially important in cases which involve children. It is obvious that a procedure which enables pre-trial delays to be reduced and which exerts greater authority over the preparation of cases is, for the reasons which we have already explained, much to be preferred to one which is less likely to do so. Moreover, we think that judges would probably be better equipped to filter out prosecutions which were flawed than magistrates. As we have seen one criticism of the present arrangements is that justices sometimes fail in this regard. Clearly if a case which involves child witnesses is allowed to proceed to trial when there is no prospect of success this will unnecessarily prolong the stress and uncertainty which they experience. In the next part of this chapter we explain how we think a procedure which provided for the question of whether there is a case to answer to be heard in the Crown Court might operate in relation to the recommendations which we have already made in respect of child witnesses. As far as older vulnerable witnesses are concerned, we have concluded that to reduce stress and avoid the possible duplication of effort inherent in two different courts viewing video-recorded evidence a Crown Court hearing would at least be preferable.

Our proposals

6.8 Where an offence against a child is alleged which comes within the scope of our recommendations and is triable on indictment only we propose that the question of whether there is sufficient evidence to justify a trial by jury should be determined by a Crown Court judge at the pre-trial application at which the admissibility of video-recorded evidence is determined or, exceptionally where there is no such application, at a pre-trial application for the purpose. After viewing any video recording put in evidence and ruling upon its admissibility the judge would consider an application from the accused to be discharged. In taking this decision he would also have regard to any additional evidence in documentary form put in by the prosecutor. Where an offence was triable either on indictment or summarily, the prosecutor would decide how to proceed and, if he determined that the case would be heard in the Crown Court, the accused would have the same opportunity to apply for discharge as if the offence were only triable on indictment.

6.9 In a magistrates' court we think that no child witness should be required to give evidence unless it is established that the case in which he or she is involved will be tried summarily. If, for example, an offence is triable either summarily or on indictment, or if a child is witness to the commission of an offence but not the victim, the court should rely upon the child's video-recorded evidence or written statement in deciding whether there is a case to answer or determining mode of trial. This seems to be consistent with both of the options which the Home Office and the Lord Chancellor's Department are now considering.

6.10 It will be necessary to develop these proposals in the light of the decisions which are eventually taken about committal proceedings generally. Plainly arrangements for serving evidence and the question of time-limits will have to be addressed in some detail. For obvious reasons these are not matters which we have chosen to consider in depth here.

Conclusions

6.11 Improvements to the position of the child witness at trials for serious offences in the Crown Court are not possible without radical reform to the present system of committal hearings. Unless this takes place changes to Crown Court procedures will be increasingly frustrated in the magistrates' courts. We have already had cases drawn to our attention in which defendants accused of child abuse have sought to confront the principal prosecution witness there, apparently because they are conscious that this can be prevented at trial by the use of the live television link. This is likely to occur more frequently. The provision in the Criminal Justice Act 1988 which allows an accused to be convicted on the uncorroborated evidence of an unsworn child witness has the effect of introducing a new class of young child witness. In the past the corroborative evidence which was required to confirm a young child's complaint was sometimes sufficient to establish a prima facie case and it was not necessary for the child to testify in person until trial. Where there is no such evidence the young child will always be vulnerable at an 'old-style' committal.

6.12 The best solution is one which is calculated to reduce delay, maximise the number of occasions on which flawed prosecutions do not proceed and ensure that the preparation of cases which are to go to trial is accelerated. This can be achieved by providing that the pre-trial application in the Crown Court, at which we have already proposed that a ruling shall be made about the admissibility of video-recorded evidence, shall, where an offence is alleged to have been committed against a child, also provide an opportunity for the accused to apply for discharge. This would have the incidental but important advantage of ensuring that evidence was not considered twice before trial.

CHAPTER 7

FINAL CONCLUSIONS

Introduction

7.1 In this last chapter we briefly consider the practical and resource implications of the proposals which we have made, we say something about the priority which reform of the law relating to the protection and status of child witnesses should enjoy and we end by making some general observations and mentioning suggestions for further change which were made to us in the course of our enquiry but which, although relevant, were clearly outside the particular scope of this exercise.

The cost of reform

7.2 At the investigative stage it seems to us that in principle our recommendations could be implemented without incurring any extra cost through the use of existing facilities. However it would in practice be necessary for the police and social services teams responsible for investigating abuse which are not already suitably equipped to be furnished with adequate video recording equipment. Teams should also be trained to conduct interviews with children in ways which are both effective and forensically acceptable. We found that even comparatively sophisticated video equipment of the sort we have recommended is now available relatively inexpensively and can be operated without extensive technical knowledge. Home Office Circular 52/1988 gives clear guidance about the basic joint investigative structure within which we believe the necessary additional training about legal issues which is contingent upon the admissibility of video recordings may be accommodated and developed in the light of court decisions. We have concluded that provided these arrangements are in place recording interviews with child witnesses can be made practicable and affordable for police forces and social services departments through some modest but essential extra financial provision, careful planning and administrative cooperation.

7.3 Where the courts and the prosecution process are concerned our proposals are likely to result in some increase in legal aid costs arising from the need to remunerate lawyers for the extra time spent in viewing recordings, an overall rise in costs caused by abolition of the competence requirement and the prosecution of cases which, but for more facilitative procedures for taking children's evidence would not come to court, the additional expenditure required to equip courts for preliminary hearings, and some constraints on the availability of judges who are engaged in pre-trial hearings.

7.4 On the other hand the availability and admissibility of video recordings, authoritative pre-trial judicial decisions about whether there is a case to answer and preliminary hearings are all innovations which are likely to reduce both the number of contested cases which result in a full trial and the number of trials which are aborted. The potential savings are considerable.

7.5 In the absence of statistics about the number of children who appear as witnesses in the Crown Court we are unable to price our proposals, even on a speculative basis. We are certain that if our ideas are accepted in principle it will be necessary to carry out a quite detailed analysis of court business so that adequate provision for implementation can be made. We were not equipped to do this.

7.6 Despite these difficulties we should draw attention to a calculation made by the Home Office statistics branch from figures collected in the courts for a single month in 1988. This suggests that about 2,500 persons are dealt with in the Crown Court for violent and sexual offences against children under 16 each year. This figure relates to defendants rather than victims, includes uncontested cases and, does not, of course, take account of the increase in prosecutions which might result from our recommendations. Nonetheless it seems to us that a caseload of this general order could well be dealt with by a limited number of Crown Court centres which were specially equipped for preliminary hearings and were staffed by judges with experience of child abuse cases. The actual cost of furnishing a court centre with the closed circuit television and audio links necessary is, we understand, likely to be in the region of £50,000.

7.7 Our proposal that the competence requirement for child witnesses should be abolished offers no prospective compensating savings. Experienced prosecutors suggested that this might by itself produce an increase of some 5% in the number of prosecutions for offences against children which are brought. We think this probably represents a small proportion of the number of offences actually committed against very young victims and that removing the near certainty of immunity from prosecution for those who abuse small children in private fully justifies incurring additional legal and other costs.

Priorities

7.8 We recognise that the resources which are directed to the implementation of our proposals will not be available for other projects of improvement and reform within the criminal justice system and that giving special consideration to cases which involve children may mean that other cases are delayed longer than might otherwise be the case. Assigning priorities is a political matter and we do not propose to rank our recommendations in relation to competing demands. Nevertheless we should point out that an overwhelming preponderance of those who have responsibility for child witnesses believe that the need for change is extremely pressing. We think that the parents, carers, social workers, medical workers and police officers who see the effects of court appearances upon children at first hand are uniquely qualified to gauge the urgency which should attach to reform.

The future

7.9 Measures to expedite trials for offences against children, to enable child witnesses to give an early account of their experiences and to undergo cross-examination out-of-court are, we think, only part of the solution to the question of how abuse cases should be handled. We suggest that a fundamental change of attitude towards children in the legal context is now required. The professional training of judges and lawyers could usefully address some issues in child psychology and cognitive development. Lawyers should understand how to speak to children and should appreciate the consequences of misleading or oppressive questioning.

7.10 The courts should be more receptive to children. Where children do appear in a public court they should be informed, in so far as they are able to understand, about the purpose of the proceedings and the functions of the people present. Visits to courts and suitably written booklets are useful ways of achieving this. Child victims are sometimes still placed in the same waiting areas as defendants. Arrangements to prevent this must be improved.

7.11 When a child is to appear in open court judges should always consider whether wigs, gowns and other regalia should be removed. We are of the opinion that child abuse cases should only be tried by experienced and approved judges.

7.12 It also seems to us that the measures which we have proposed might be used to relieve the stress upon child witnesses in wardship and custody proceedings. Rules could ensure that recordings of evidence given by child witnesses in the criminal courts were subsequently made available in such cases. In addition video recordings might be made of evidence given by child witnesses through the live television link. Such material would be available on a retrial and in wardship or custody proceedings. These measures would further reduce the number of occasions on which children were called upon to repeat distressing evidence.

7.13 Several other matters were put to us which seemed to us beyond our terms of reference and which we were unable to consider in detail. In child sexual abuse cases where the only issue is the identity of the defendant it is sometimes suggested that there is an argument for allowing any previous convictions for similar offences against children to be put in evidence. Where it is clear that one of two parents or carers has abused a child and there is no evidence pointing to either directly it is sometimes argued that the law should be changed to create a rebuttable presumption, which prevents the withholding of evidence, that both are responsible in law. The disposal of offenders is another area in which a range of new ideas might be explored.

7.14 We think the guarantee which we have proposed that children need not appear in the Crown Court against their wishes is an important first step. There are very many other practical, legal and penal issues bearing upon child abuse cases which require careful re-examination in the light of modern conditions and research. We hope our report will focus public and political attention on this vital subject and that improvements will not be long delayed.

SUMMARY OF RECOMMENDATIONS

1. We recommend that at trials on indictment for violent and sexual offences and offences of cruelty and neglect and at comparable trials in the juvenile courts, video-recorded interviews with children under the age of 14 conducted by police officers, social workers or those whose duties include the investigation of crime or the protection of the welfare of children should be admissible as evidence. Where the offence charged is of a sexual nature this provision should extend to child witnesses under the age of 17 (paragraphs 2.25 and 2.36–37).

2. When such a case comes within the jurisdiction of the Crown Court we recommend that the court should determine whether a particular video-recorded interview is to be admitted in whole or part at a pre-trial application. In making this decision the court should have regard to the Code of Practice for the conduct of such interviews. A recording should only be excluded if, in the court's opinion, including it would be contrary to the interests of justice. Where a court rules that no part of a recording is to be admitted in evidence reasons for its decision should be given in writing (paragraphs 2.27–28).

3. Once any application for video-recorded evidence to be admitted has been determined we recommend that at the request of the prosecution arrangements should be made to hold a preliminary hearing in informal surroundings out of court as soon as practicable. No child witness to whom our proposals apply should be required to appear in open court during a trial unless he or she wishes to do so (paragraphs 2.25–26).

4. At the preliminary hearing we recommend that any video recording which has been allowed in evidence should be shown to the child witness and that he or she should be asked to adopt the account which it contains and expand upon any aspects which the prosecution wishes to explore. The defence should then have the opportunity to cross-examine the child. The preliminary hearing should take place outside the courtroom in informal surroundings and should video-recorded. Nobody should be present in the same room as the child except the judge, advocates and a parent or supporter, but the accused should be able to hear and view the proceedings through closed circuit television or a two way mirror and communicate with his legal representatives (paragraphs 2.29 and 2.31).

5. We recommend that defendants who are charged with sexual or violent offences and offences of cruelty or neglect should be prohibited by statute from carrying out in person the cross-examination of witnesses who are under the age of 14 or, in the case of sexual offences, under 17, whether at a preliminary hearing or at a trial on indictment in open court (paragraph 2.30).

6. A majority of us recommend that the court should have discretion to order exceptionally that questions advocates wish to put to a child should be relayed

through a person approved by the court who enjoys the child's confidence (paragraph 2.32).

7. We recommend that any video recording of an interview with a child witness which is admitted in evidence should be shown at that point in the 'live' trial at which the child would normally give evidence-in-chief and that the video recording of any preliminary hearing should be shown subsequently (paragraph 2.35).

8. We recommend that whenever it is necessary to recall a child witness who was cross-examined at a preliminary hearing a further out-of-court hearing should be held under the same conditions as the preliminary hearing (paragraph 2.31).

9. We recommend that extension of the measures described above to adult vulnerable witnesses, under the conditions we set out below, should enjoy a high priority once changes in respect of child witnesses have been made (paragraph 3.15).

10. At trials on indictment for sexual and violent offences, and trials for comparable offences in juvenile court, we recommend that on application, and after considering all relevant matters, a court may direct that an adult person who is likely to suffer an unusual and unreasonable degree of mental stress by giving evidence in open court should be treated as a vulnerable witness. There should be a rebuttable presumption that victims of serious sexual offences are vulnerable witnesses (paragraph 3.5).

11. Where a person is to be treated as a vulnerable witness the court may direct that a video-recorded interview in which that person has made statements relevant to the commission of an offence shall be admissible in evidence, that the person may be examined and cross-examined at a preliminary hearing or that the person may give evidence by live television link from outside the courtroom (paragraph 3.7).

12. We recommend that the guidance issued to police forces about the investigation of child sexual abuse should apply also to cases of physical abuse, cruelty and neglect (paragraph 4.5).

13. We recommend that the training of police officers and social workers responsible for interviewing child witnesses should include a component concerning the rules which govern the examination of witnesses in court (paragraph 4.7).

14. We recommend that there should be a Code of Practice for the conduct of video-recorded interviews with children and other vulnerable witnesses designed to protect the rights of accused persons and the welfare of witnesses and containing guidance about best practice. The court should have regard to the Code of Practice in determining whether a particular recording should be admitted in evidence in whole or part (paragraph 4.8).

15. We recommend that the Code of Practice shall contain guidance relating to the location, style and structure of interviews (paragraph 4.12 and 4.17–21).

16. We recommend that the Code of Practice shall contain directions relating to the timing of interviews and supplementary interviews, the standard of equipment to be used, the persons permitted to be present during a recording, the use of interviewing aids, the circumstances under which a recording is to be shown to an accused and the custody, copying, storage and destruction of tapes (paragraphs 4.9–11, 4.13–15 and 4.22–25).

17. We recommend that all children should be presumed to be competent witnesses (paragraph 5.13).

18. We recommend that all children under the age of 14 should give evidence unsworn, whether at a preliminary hearing or during a trial (paragraph 5.14).

19. We recommend that at trials on indictment for sexual offences any rule or practice which makes it obligatory for the court to give a direction to the jury about the danger of convicting the accused on the uncorroborated evidence of the complainant should be abolished (paragraphs 5.30–5.31).

20. We recommend that guidance should be given to magistrates' courts about the use of screens and other measures for the protection of children and other vulnerable witnesses (paragraph 6.2).

21. We recommend that the possible application of our general proposals to magistrates' courts should be reviewed at an early stage after their introduction in the Crown Court (paragraph 6.2).

22. We recommend that where an offence against a child which comes within the ambit of our general recommendations is triable on indictment or summarily the question of whether the offence is to be tried on indictment should be determined by the prosecutor (paragraphs 6.5–6).

23. We recommend that where the prosecutor determines that such an offence is to be tried on indictment the question of whether there is in fact sufficient evidence to justify a trial should be determined on application by a Crown Court judge at the same time as an application to admit any video-recorded evidence is determined or, if no such application is made, that a pre-trial hearing should be held for the purpose (paragraph 6.8).

24. We recommend that where a violent offence is alleged no child witness under the age of 14, or, if the offence is of a sexual character, no child witness under the age of 17, shall be required to give evidence in person at a magistrates' court hearing unless the offence is to be tried summarily and the child's evidence is given during the summary trial (paragraph 6.9).

ANNEX A

EVIDENCE

The group received oral* or written evidence or both** from the following:

Dr Jan Aldridge, Psychologist, Leeds University*

The Association of Chief Police Officers

The Association of County Councils

The Association of Metropolitan Authorities

The Association of Police Surgeons of England and Wales

The Association of Police Superintendents

Barnardo's

Dr Arnon Bentovim, Consultant Psychiatrist**

The London Borough of Bexley, Social Services Department*

The British Association for the Study and Prevention of Child Abuse and Neglect

The Rt Hon Lord Justice Butler-Sloss DBE*

Childline

The Children's Legal Centre

The Council of Her Majesty's Circuit Judges

The Criminal Bar Association**

The Baroness Faithfull OBE**

The Guild of British Newspaper Editors

Dr H G Hanks, St James' University Hospital, Leeds**

Dr C J Hobbs, St James' University Hospital, Leeds**

Dr D P H Jones, The Park Hospital for Sick Children, Oxford*

The Justices' Clerks' Society

The Law Society**

Leeds Social Services Department

The Magistrates' Association

Metropolitan Police, Bexleyheath*

The National Children's Bureau

The National Society for the Prevention of Cruelty to Children**

Sheriff Gordon Nicholson QC

The Scottish Law Commission*

The Police Federation of England and Wales**

Esther Rantzen, BBC Television

The Royal College of Psychiatrists

Sybil Sharpe, Wolverhampton Polytechnic

John Spencer, Selwyn College, University of Cambridge**

Dr Eileen Vizard, Consultant Psychiatrist**

West Yorkshire Police**

Dr Jane Wynne, Consultant Paediatrician, Leeds General Infirmary**

ANNEX B

The Chief Officer of Police

Copy to: Chief Crown Prosecutor
Chief Clerk to Crown Court
Clerk to the Justices
Clerk to the Police Authority
Director of Education
Director of Social Services
Chief Executive, Regional
Health Authority

6 July 1988

Dear Chief Officer

HOME OFFICE CIRCULAR 52/1988
THE INVESTIGATION OF CHILD SEXUAL ABUSE

1. Chief Officers will be aware of growing public concern about the incidence of child sexual abuse and of the need to take effective action to safeguard the welfare of the victims. The purpose of this Circular is to provide guidance to the police on the procedures they adopt in the investigation of allegations of child sexual abuse. It has been agreed with the Association of Chief Police Officers and the Association of Directors of Social Services, and is based on the recommendations of a working group including members from the police, medical profession, social services, forensic science service, the Home Office and DHSS. It is intended to supplement existing local procedures for handling cases of non-accidental injury and neglect. For the purposes of this circular children are people aged 17 or under.

2. The report of Lord Justice Butler-Sloss' Inquiry into child sexual abuse in Cleveland is being published simultaneously with the issue of this circular. The report makes a number of recommendations about the investigation of child sexual abuse and emphasises that the key to effective action is a close working relationship between the agencies concerned, the NSPCC and health authorities. A shortened version of the report is enclosed and the guidance contained in this circular takes its recommendations into account. The Department of Health and Social security is also publishing its guide to inter-agency procedures "Working Together". Copies of the guide and covering DHSS circular LAC/S8/10 and HC (8S) 38 are being sent to chief officers with this circular. Finally, chief officers are also being sent a copy of a circular from the Department of Education and Science which provides guidance on procedures within the education service.

GENERAL CONSIDERATIONS

3. The investigation of allegations of the sexual abuse of children by a member of the family can raise sensitive issues. Family relationships may make it more difficult for the investigators in gathering evidence to establish what has happened and in deciding whether the public interest requires the bringing of a prosecution. It is also necessary to ensure that effective arrangements are made for the protection, support and care of the child in situations where this may not be adequately provided by the family, although each case must be considered carefully before action is taken to separate a child from a parent in view of the serious consequences of such action. In all these areas, decision making can be improved through consultation between the agencies involved in the case.

INVESTIGATION ARRANGEMENTS

Joint investigations with the social services

4. Although the police will wish to ensure that all appropriate steps are taken for the protection of the child, the primary responsibility for this will fall to the social services department. A number of police forces have established joint investigation arrangements with their local social services departments, and all chief officers will wish to consider establishing such arrangements in their own force areas. The aim of these arrangements should be to utilise the respective skills of police officers, social workers and the medical services in the investigation of the allegations, while providing for the welfare of the child and ensuring that the stress which victims may experience as a consequence of the investigative process is reduced to a minimum. They will also help to minimise effort, develop better lines of communication and co-operation, and increase public confidence.

5. The lead in co-ordinating the arrangements for considering the child's welfare should be taken by a senior officer of the social services department, who should liaise with an equivalent police officer in initiating an investigation. The senior social work officer will provide a point which all agencies can approach in cases of concern. He can then make arrangements to secure the appointment of investigating officers who will agree together on the handling of the case, and the co-ordinator will subsequently convene a case conference when appropriate.

6. Chief officers will wish to ensure that officers involved in the investigation receive training to enable them to deal effectively and sympathetically with child victims, to handle the difficult and emotional issues which may arise in child abuse cases, and to help them to establish close working relations with their social work colleagues. While it will be desirable to ensure that the police team is co-ordinated by a middle ranking officer at Detective Inspector or Detective Chief Inspector level, the investigating police officers themselves may be Constables

or Sergeants who have been trained for the purpose, and it will normally be appropriate for the investigating officers to take part in the case conferences.

7. It may be in the best interests of the victim if the investigation of cases of child sexual abuse is based on the place where the child lives. The social services department in the home area will be responsible for the child's welfare, and there is advantage in their being able to work with the local police in the investigation, rather than with police officers from another area, if the suspected offence takes place away from the home. This may pose some difficulties for established police procedures, and there may be cases which require speedy intervention by the police in the area where an offence is committed away from the child's home. Each case must be treated on its merits. However, chief officers are asked to ensure they develop between local forces, as well as within their own force, working arrangements which will enable investigations to be based on the place where the victim lives in appropriate cases.

Action on receipt of referral

8. Instances of child sexual abuse may come to notice in a number of ways. There may not be any allegation in the normal sense as children will rarely make a formal claim of abuse. Police officers may find that they will be considering cases referred to them by others, such as teachers, parents, or doctors, who have recognised behavioural changes or physical symptoms in children which arouse their concern. Such referrals should be regarded as allegations or potential allegations of abuse.

9. Where there is a suspicion of sexual abuse because of minor behavioural manifestations or inconclusive physical findings where there has been no allegation or complaint of abuse by the child or a third party, there is a particular need for multidisciplinary assessment using the best skills available in the area, in order to determine whether there is any cause for concern which would require further investigation or other action. "Working Together" recommends that agencies should consider carefully the conclusions and recommendations of the report of the Inquiry on Child Abuse in Cleveland 1987 where Lord Justice Butler-Sloss recommends that the need for such an assessment will best be met by a specialist assessment team of social worker, doctor and police officer who would jointly undertake an initial assessment and advise on the need for further action, if any. Lord Justice Butler-Sloss envisages that the team would be drawn from three local lists of suitably qualified and experienced professionals identified by the local authority, the health authority and the police respectively.

10. Chief officers will wish to consider, through the medium of Area Child Protection Committees, whether the arrangements in their area are providing this specialist multi-disciplinary assessment. In areas where there are properly defined procedures for inter-agency collaboration involving the police, social workers and

medical practitioners, such may be the case. In other areas, chief officers will wish to participate in the drawing up of appropriate procedures under the auspices of the Area Child Protection Committee. In either case, there is no objection to a police officer participating both in the specialist assessment and the investigation of any offence, provided that he has received the necessary training and has been designated for child sexual abuse work.

11. Where, following a specialist multi-disciplinary assessment or otherwise, an investigation into a criminal offence is initiated, the investigators should work on the principle of interviewing together the source of referral, the victim and, where appropriate, members of his or her family, the lead in the interview being taken by whichever officer is felt to be best qualified in the circumstances. It is important to ensure that information, including that relating to the relevant criminal records of suspects, is fully shared between both agencies, subject to any statutory requirements on confidentiality. This information should be made available to both the police officer and social work investigators so that they are in a position to discuss openly each case together and reach an agreed view on how to take the investigation forward.

12. In cases of non accidental injury to children, speed is often essential to prevent further harm to the victim. This may not always be necessary in child sexual abuse cases if there is reason to believe the child is not at immediate risk of further abuse—the information may, for example, have come to notice after the abuse has stopped, or the abuse may be only occasional (e.g. where the risk is from a family member who visits the home). There may, therefore, be more time for the investigating team and their senior officers to consider how best to investigate the case and how to approach the victim and his or her family before making a direct intervention. The team will also wish to consider whether there are grounds to believe that any of the victim's siblings may also be victims or be at risk. Once the team has made its enquiries, it will be necessary for its members to report back to their own supervising officers, and ultimately to a case conference, arranged by the social services department, which will consider what action is necessary to protect the welfare of the victim.

13. In exceptional cases, urgent action may be needed before the appointment of the joint team. Where unilateral action is desirable, this should be taken only as far as is necessary to protect the child, to preserve evidence (for care or criminal proceedings), or to prevent the escape of the suspect. As soon as possible contact should be made with the other investigator to review the action that has been taken and to enable the investigation to proceed from then onward on a joint basis.

Interviewing the victim

14. The principal aim of the interview with the victim is to establish what has happened, thus enabling the police and social services to reach an informed decision on what further action is necessary, and the gathering of evidence on

which to base a prosecution will arise naturally from this. The investigators should agree in advance how the interview with the child should be conducted. They will wish to consider, in the light of the circumstances of each case, who should be present. Both the police officer and the social workers will normally attend at the outset, and it may assist the child if a trusted adult is present (such as a parent not involved, or who has not colluded, in the abuse, or a teacher, or a doctor, such as a child psychiatrist), although it may be that the presence of a parent may in some cases have an inhibiting effect on the child.

15. The lead in conducting the interview should be taken by whichever investigator is best able to communicate with the child. Because of the difficulty that may in some cases be experienced in communicating with children, whose vocabulary may not be fully developed, or who may be reluctant to talk about their experiences, it may not always be possible to conduct the interview without prompting the child or asking leading questions. This should be done with caution as, from the point of view of evidence in criminal proceedings, this may not be satisfactory. The investigators must be conscious of the need to be objective in establishing the truth, and not to influence the child to tell them what he or she believes they want to hear.

The use of video recording equipment

16. The use of video recording equipment to make a record of the investigators' interview with the victim may be helpful to the police and social workers. It can play a significant role in reducing the stress caused for victims resulting from repeated questioning about their experiences, since the video film can be seen by other professionals who need to know of the child's experiences—for example, doctors, social workers involved with other members of the family, or more senior police officers or social workers concerned to review the case. The video recording should be made as unobtrusively as possible. It will usually be important to explain the procedures to the child so that he or she is aware of what is happening. It is unlikely that sophisticated video filming equipment will be necessary to meet the needs of the police and social work investigators, although staff who operate the equipment should be trained in its use.

17. The primary purpose of making a video recording of the interview will be to assist the investigating officers and the professional agencies concerned with the child's welfare. Under the present law the video recording will be admissible evidence in criminal proceedings only in exceptional circumstances. The possibility of change in the law has been raised in debates on the Criminal Justice Bill which is now before Parliament. The Government has indicated that it is not yet persuaded that there is a case for the ready admissibility of video recordings. Were there to be any change in the law, however, further guidance will be issued to chief officers.

18. Chief officers should reach agreement locally through the Area Child Abuse Committee with the Director of Social Services on arrangements for the provision of video equipment and the safe keeping of video recordings,

taking account of the needs of the police to have access for the purposes of the investigation and any subsequent prosecution, and the needs of the social services and other professional agencies to have access as required. Such access is permissible only within the scope of the parent's written authority, and proper arrangements should be made for storing the tape securely and maintaining confidentiality. In cases which lead to prosecution the police may be best placed to look after the video tape, while in other cases it may prove more satisfactory for this to be undertaken by the social services department. In establishing local arrangements the police and social services will wish to bear in mind the requirements of the rules of discovery in civil court proceedings.

Medical examination

19. In cases where the alleged abuse is recent, the need for a medical examination should be considered. It will only normally be desirable to hold the forensic medical examination immediately after the investigators' interview with the victim if very recent abuse is revealed; in cases which come to light some time after the incidents have occurred or, in cases involving known minor touching, forensic medical examination may serve no useful purpose. The victim and parents should be given a choice as to whether the examination will be conducted by a male or female doctor. In addition, medical examination to determine whether treatment for the victim is necessary is always an important consideration at an early stage. It is good practice to keep the number of medical examinations to a minimum to reduce the stress on the child and consequently, wherever possible, any forensic medical examination should be carried out at the same time that the victim is examined by a doctor who is considering the need for medical treatment. This may be achieved by providing for joint examinations by a police surgeon and a paediatrician or by a paediatrician with forensic training. But some flexibility may be required in areas where no paediatrician is readily available. This might involve giving forensic training to other members of the medical profession. Further guidance on these issues is contained in Annex A, which is the text of a joint statement by the British Paediatric Association and the Association of Police Surgeons. Advice on the medical examination of sexually abused children is also available from the Forensic Science Service.

Consent

20. As a matter of good practice the police and social services should obtain consent to an interview being carried out and recorded on video. The consent should be sought from the victim or, where the child is not of sufficient age and understanding, from the person who is in law responsible for the child normally a parent or guardian—and a specimen consent form is attached at Annex B. If consent is refused by a parent or guardian (if, for example, a parent may be a

suspect), the investigators may need to decide whether to interview the child without parental consent, and to record the interview on video. It may also be necessary, where the statutory requirements are satisfied, to consider the child's removal to a place of safety under s.28 of the Children and Young Persons Act 1969 or s.40 of the 1933 Act. Particular care will be necessary in any subsequent use which is made of the video in view of the nature of the information recorded on it.

21. In carrying out a medical examination a doctor should seek consent either from the child or a parent or guardian, where a child is not of sufficient age and understanding. In such cases where consent is refused by the parent or guardian, the decision as to whether it is medically necessary to proceed is for the doctor's professional judgement. If consent is refused (for example, where a parent may be the suspect) it may be necessary to consider applying to a magistrates' court for the child to be taken into the care of the local authority on an interim care order, or to the Family Division of the High Court for the child to be made a ward of court.

Interviews with suspects

22. The conduct of the interview will be the responsibility of the police officer, but he will find it helpful to discuss the interview in advance with his social work colleague. The investigating police officer may consider inviting the social worker, who has been working with him in the case, to sit in on any interview which takes place with the suspect. There is no objection to the video film or appropriate parts of it, being shown to the suspect, if it is thought this would make a useful contribution to the conduct of the investigation.

TRAINING

23. Training has an important role in equipping police officers, social workers and doctors to deal with the important professional and personal issues raised by cases of child sexual abuse. General awareness training for all police officers will be desirable to enable them to appreciate the nature and extent of the problem and to know of their force's investigation arrangements. Chief officers will also wish to discuss with their local Directors of Social Services the establishment of joint training arrangements for members of the investigation teams and for senior officers who will be responsible for the management of the teams, so that they may consider together the problems they will face both in their treatment of victims and in carrying out joint investigations. Such training should be aimed at enabling the investigators to develop an understanding of, and respect for, each others' functions, the role of the police in investigating criminal offences and of social workers in child care, and the consequences for day-to-day practice. Joint

training can also provide a useful forum for the consideration of the criminal and civil law in relation to child sexual abuse and the complex legal issues that can arise during the course of an investigation. Chief officers will, in particular, recognise the difficulties that surround traditional methods of police interviews with victims, including the taking of written statements. It will be important for investigators to be able to establish a rapport with the child, but transposing the child's words into an acceptable form of written statement raises obvious evidential problems particularly where the child's vocabulary does not extend to recognised terminology. The training should pay particular attention to the development of interviewing skills and an understanding of the child's behaviour and response to the experiences of the interview. Training should also sensitively address the personal issues for investigators that can surface when working with sexually abused children and their families.

FACILITIES

24. A guiding principle is to provide facilities for interviewing the child in surroundings which are not likely to threaten or intimidate, and to ensure the child is not obliged to face repeated questioning about his or her experiences by the various professional agencies which may need to know about them. The nature of the facilities which should be used will vary according to local circumstances and should be considered in consultation with other agencies, including social services departments and health authorities. In most cases it is unlikely that police stations or the victim's family home will prove suitable. It may be desirable to seek arrangements with a local hospital to use rooms in its paediatric department. Alternatively, where there are special child care facilities available, or where special examination suites have been established for rape victims, these might be suitable. In other areas, where cases are likely to be infrequent and centralised facilities in hospital could cause unnecessarily long journeys for the child, it may prove satisfactory to make suitable arrangements with a local medical practice to use a doctor's surgery or group clinic. The principal aim is to provide the victim with reassuring, therapeutic surroundings, where medical and, wherever possible, child psychiatric assistance is close to hand.

CRIMINAL PROCEEDINGS

25. When a case of child sexual abuse has been investigated and it is established there is sufficient evidence to justify prosecution, the police should consider whether there is an acceptable alternative to the prosecution in the interests of the child and the family, such as a caution. In reaching this decision the police will wish to take full account of the views of other agencies concerned with the case, in particular the social services department, on how a prosecution might affect the victim and others in the family. The Crown Prosecution Service will also be

ready to offer advice on the sufficiency of evidence in any case and the balance of the public interest. In cases where a prosecution is brought, guidance on the provisions of sections 42 and 43 of the Children and Young Persons Act 1933, which relate to the admissibility of depositions by child victims in place of their appearance in court to give evidence, is contained in Annex C to this Circular. Chief officers will wish to bear in mind the need to deal expeditiously with such cases in the interests of the child, and so help to minimise the time before the case comes to court. The Director of Public Prosecutions is issuing similar guidance to the Crown Prosecution Service.

Civil Proceedings

26. Whether or not it is possible to secure sufficient evidence on which to base a prosecution it will be necessary to consider action to protect the welfare of the child, such as care proceedings, and the police will wish to consider what assistance they can provide the social services department in gathering evidence for use in civil proceedings. Both police and social services will wish to consider the need for the child to be removed to a place of safety. They will also wish to consider whether action is appropriate to seek authority to have the victim taken into the care of the local authority, or made a ward of court. An outline of these procedures is attached at Annex D.

Summary

27. Chief officers are asked to consider with their local Director of Social services the arrangements that are made for the investigation of cases of child sexual abuse, taking account of the desirability of:

i. ensuring that the *welfare of the child* is recognised as the overriding concern of all the professional agencies, who should work together to protect children from abuse and assist in their future safety (paragraph 2);

ii. *conducting investigations jointly* with social service departments and sharing each other's expertise (paragraph 4);

iii. *sharing all relevant information* between the police officers and social workers involved in investigations, and taking decisions jointly (paragraph 11);

iv. holding *joint interviews* with victims to reduce the number of occasions in which children are asked to explain what happened to them (paragraphs 14–15). To this end the *video-recording* of interviews is recommended to assist the investigators and their professional colleagues (paragraph 16–18);

v. making arrangements for the *medical examination* of victims by a paediatrician with forensic training, or jointly by a paediatrician and police surgeon, and ensuring the victim and parents have a choice as to whether the examination will be carried out by a male or female doctor (paragraph 19);

vi. arranging *specialist training* for police and social work investigators (paragraph 23);

vii. providing *facilities* which help to put children at ease, such as rooms in hospital or social services buildings rather than in police stations (paragraph 24);

Conclusion

28. It is essential that all the professional agencies concerned with the protection and welfare of children work together in harmony and towards a common goal. The lead in establishing effective arrangements for the child's welfare will rest with the social services department. The police's concern will be to ensure the safety of the child and to work with the social workers and medical staff to investigate any suspected offence, to ensure the family is treated sensitively and justly, and to gather evidence for use in criminal or civil proceedings. It is likely that, in many cases, criminal proceedings will not be possible. The success of the police intervention, however, is not to be measured in terms of the prosecutions which are brought, but of the protection which their actions bring to children at risk.

Yours faithfully

E SODEN

BRITISH PAEDIATRIC ASSOCIATION

ASSOCIATION OF POLICE SURGEONS OF GREAT BRITAIN

AGREED JOINT STATEMENT:
from a Working Party of the Association of Police Surgeons of Great Britain and the British Paediatric Association

Child Sexual Abuse

1. Child Sexual abuse may present to professionals either as:

   a) a "crisis"

   or:

   b) as an incidental finding with:

      i. an allegation by a parent or "third party", or disclosure by a child

      ii. a pattern of physical features

      iii. behavioural, developmental or psychiatric problems in a child

2. As part of the initial full assessment of the child, where there is a need for a forensic examination, there should only be one such examination. It may be appropriate to delay this examination until further information is obtained and the child interviewed. It should be carried out in a paediatric environment by an appropriately trained doctor. There are advantages in a joint consultation being carried out eg between a paediatrician and an experienced police surgeon.

3. The medical examination, although providing corroboration, may in many cases neither support nor contradict the diagnosis of sexual abuse.

4. Any examining doctor(s) should provide a written report for the medical and statutory agencies responsible for the care of the child including police statements when requested.

5. The diagnosis thus necessitates full and continuing consultation with other professionals involved with each child, eg family doctor, social worker, child psychiatrist, clinical psychologist and an experienced police officer.

6. These views need to be coordinated in a case conference which should be attended by examining doctor(s) who should be prepared to attend any court hearing to present and be cross-examined on the forensic evidence.

7. Each Health District has a multi-disciplinary Child Protection Committee, (previously known as the Area Review Committee), concerned with the management of child abuse. A working party of this committee should establish local procedures and utilise the available experience and skills for the development of child sexual abuse teams. These multi-disciplinary child sexual abuse teams should include inter alia: consultant paediatricians, including those with a special interest in community child health, and/or senior clinical medical officers (SCMOs) and police surgeons.

8. The continuing paediatric care of the child should be supervised by a consultant paediatrician who should attend further case conferences and support the Social Services Department and the family doctor, health visitor and other members of the primary health care team. Apart from any emergency treatment, police surgeons are not responsible for continuing care of the child who should be referred to the GP.

9. Both Associations recognise the need for further training and research.

10. The British Paediatric Association and the Association of Police Surgeons of Great Britain are available to provide joint advice on any difficulties between members of our two Associations arising out of these agreed procedures.

ANNEX B

____________________ county council
____________________ police

Please read this carefully and feel free to cross out any statements you do not agree with.

I the undersigned give my consent for:

(1) .... to be medically examined
(2) .... to be interviewed by a Social Worker and a Police Officer
(3) the recording of the interview on videotape
(4) the videotape recording to be made available to other professionals directly responsible for or concerned in the investigation or the provision of physical or medical care.
(5) the videotape recording to be shown for training of professionals. Where this occurs, I understand that any surnames or other identifying words will be deleted from the recording.

You may add any special conditions here:-

Signing this document does not remove any rights to take legal action should you ever feel the videotape has been shown or used irresponsibly.

Signed ....

Name (capitals) ....

Witnessed by ....

Name (capitals) ....

Date ....

ANNEX C

CHILDREN AND YOUNG PERSONS ACT 1933

Sections 42 and 43: Depositions by Child Victims

1. If it is decided that a criminal prosecution should be brought but there is concern that a court appearance may seriously damage the health of the child, chief officers will wish to consider with the Crown Prosecution Service whether the provisions of sections 42 and 43 of the Children and Young Persons Act 1933 should be used. These provide for a written deposition of the child to be admissible in evidence in certain circumstances without the child having to appear before the court. First, a medical practitioner must notify the magistrate, who is to take the deposition, and subsequently the court of trial, by sworn evidence that attendance before a court would involve serious danger to the child's life or health. While the Home Secretary has no authority to interpret the law this would seem to apply to either the child's physical or mental health. Second, the magistrate is empowered to take, and the court of trial to admit, only a *sworn* deposition. Third, the child must be the alleged victim of an offence listed in Schedule 1 to the Act. This covers most offences involving sexual or physical assault on children. Fourth, the accused must be given reasonable notice of the intention to take the deposition and he, his counsel, or his solicitor, must be given the opportunity to be present and to cross-examine the child. If the accused chooses not to be present this does not affect the admissibility of the deposition.

2. Provided these conditions are met, section 42 authorises a magistrate to take a sworn deposition from the child and to transmit it to the court of trial. The magistrate must add to the deposition a statement of his reason for taking it, the date and place it was taken and the names of those present. The Act is silent on venue and there seems no reason why the deposition should not be taken at a place convenient for the child, for example her home or a hospital, provided the magistrate agrees and the accused is given a reasonable opportunity to be present. Under section 43, once the court of trial is satisfied by the medical practitioner that the child's appearance would involve serious damage to her life or health, such a deposition is admissible in evidence without further proof.

ANNEX D

CIVIL PROCEEDINGS

The Legal Framework[1]

This annex sets out the content of the main legislative provisions relating to civil proceedings: responsibility for taking action in civil proceedings will normally fall to social services departments, but the police may find this outline of current procedures helpful.

A. Duty to Investigate

1. The duty of the local authority to investigate information received suggesting that a child may need protection is described in Section 2 of the Children and Young Persons Act 1969 in relation to the possible need for care proceedings

> "(1) If a local authority receives information suggesting that there are grounds for bringing care proceedings in respect of a child or young person who resides or is found in their area, it shall be the duty of the authority to cause inquiries to be made into the case unless they are satisfied that such inquiries are unnecessary."

and is implicit in the Child Care Act 1980, Section 2

> "Where it appears to a local authority with respect to a child in their area appearing to them to be under the age of seventeen
>
> (a) that he has neither parent nor guardian or has been and remains abandoned by his parents or guardian or is lost;
>
> (b) that his parents or guardian are, for the time being or permanently, prevented by reason of mental or bodily disease or infirmity or other incapacity or any other circumstances from providing for his proper accommodation, maintenance and upbringing: and
>
> (c) in either case, that the intervention of the local authority under this section is necessary in the interests of the welfare of the child.
>
> it shall be the duty of the local authority to receive the child into their care under this section."

---

[1] Editors' note. As readers familiar with the English legal system will immediately recognise, this summary is now very out of date. This area of the law was reshaped by the Children Act 1989.

B. Prevention

2. The general duty of the local authority to promote the welfare of children and to take preventive action is described in Section 1 (1, of the Child Care Act 1980 as follows:

> "It shall be the duty of every local authority to make available such advice, guidance and assistance as may promote the welfare of children by diminishing the need to receive children into or keep them in care under this Act or to bring children before a juvenile court; and any provisions made by a local authority under this sub-section may, if the local authority think fit, include provision for giving assistance in kind or, in exceptional circumstances, in cash."

C. Reception into Care—Voluntary Care

3. The grounds for receiving children into voluntary care are described in Section 2(1) of the Child Care Act 1980 as follows:

> "Where it appears to a local authority with respect to a child in their area appearing to them to be under the age of 17:
>
> (a) that he has neither parent nor guardian or has been and remains abandoned by his parents or guardian or is lost; or
>
> (b) that his parents or guardian are, for the time being or permanently, prevented by reason of mental or bodily disease or infirmity or other incapacity or any other circumstances from providing for his proper accommodation, maintenance and upbringing: and
>
> (c) in either case, that the intervention of the local authority under this section is necessary in the interests of the welfare of the child,

it shall be the duty of the local authority to receive the child into their care under this section."

D. Care Proceedings

4. The grounds, some of which are specifically related to child abuse, which have to be satisfied in care proceedings before a court can make a care order under Section 1 of the Children and Young Persons Act 1969 (as amended) are set out in Section 1(2) as follows

> "(2) If the court before which a child or young person is brought under this section is of the opinion that any of the following conditions is satisfied with respect to him, that is to say—
>
> (a) his proper development is being avoidably prevented or neglected or his health is being avoidably impaired or neglected or he is being ill-treated: or

(b) it is probable that the condition set out in the preceding paragraph would be satisfied in his case, having regard to the fact that the court or another court has found that that condition is or was satisfied in the case of another child or young person who is or was a member of the household to which he belongs; or

(bb) it is probable that the condition set out in paragraph (a) of this sub-section will be satisfied in his case, having regard to the fact that a person who has been convicted of an offence mentioned in Schedule 1 to the Act of 1933 is, or may become, a member of the same household as the child or young person

(c) he is exposed to moral danger; or

(d) he is beyond the control of his parent or guardian; or

(e) he is of compulsory school age within the meaning of the Education Act 1944 and is not receiving sufficient full-time education suitable to his age, ability and aptitude; or

(f) he is guilty of an offence, excluding homicide,

and also that he is in need of care of control which he is unlikely to receive unless the court makes an order under this section in respect of him, then, subject to the following provisions of this section and sections 2 and 3 of this Act, the court may if it thinks fit make such an order."

E. Emergency Situations

5. Under Section 28(1) of the Children and Young Persons Act 1969 a child or young person may be removed to a place of safety for not more than 28 days on application by any person to a justice. The Section provides:

"If, upon application to a justice by any person for authority to detain a child or young person and take him to a place of safety, the justice is satisfied that the applicant has reasonable cause to believe that—

(a) any of the conditions set out in Section (2) (a) to (e) of this Act is satisfied in respect of the child or young person; or

(b) an appropriate court would find the conditions set out in section 1(2) (b) of this Act satisfied in respect of him, or;

(c) the child or young person is about to leave the United Kingdom in contravention of section 25 of the Act of 1933 (which regulates the sending abroad of juvenile entertainers),

the justice may grant the application; and the child or young person in respect of whom an authorisation is issued under this sub-section may be detained in a place of safety by virtue of the authorisation of 28 days beginning with the date of authorisation, or such short period beginning with that date as may be specified in the authorisation".

The conditions mentioned in paragraph (a) and (b) are those which may be grounds for seeking a care order, and are set out at paragraph 4.

6. Section 28(2) of the 1969 Act authorises a constable to detain a child or young person without application to a justice for not more than 8 days on similar grounds except the conditions set out in Section 1(2) (e) (or if he is satisfied that an offence is being committed under Section 10(1) of the Children and Young Persons Act, 1933 which penalises a vagrant for taking a juvenile from place to place).

7. Under *section 40 of the Children and Young persons Act 1933* a warrant to search for or remove a child or young person may be obtained:

1. If it appears to a justice of the peace on information on oath laid by a person who, in the opinion of the justice, is acting in the interests of a child or young person, that there is reasonable cause to suspect

    a. that the child or young person has been or is being assaulted, ill-treated, or neglected in any place within the jurisdiction of the justice, in a manner likely to cause him unnecessary suffering, or injury to health; or

    b. that any offence mentioned in the First Schedule to this Act has been or is being committed in respect of the child or young person,

    the justice may issue a warrant authorising any constable named therein to search for the child or young person, and, if it is found that he has been or is being assaulted, ill-treated, or neglected in manner aforesaid, or that any such offence as aforesaid has been or is being committed in respect of him, to take him to a place of safety, or authorising any constable to remove him with or without search to a place of safety, and a child or young person taken to a place of safety in pursuance of such a warrant may be detained there until he can be brought before a juvenile court.

2. A justice issuing a warrant under this section may by the same warrant cause any person accused of any offence in respect of the child or young person to be apprehended and brought before a court of summary jurisdiction, and proceedings to be taken against him according to law.

3. Any constable authorised by warrant under this section to search for any child or young person, or to remove any child or young person with or without search, may enter (if need be by force) any house,

building, or other place specified in the warrant, and may remove him therefrom.

4. Every warrant issued under this section shall be addressed to and executed by a constable, who shall be accompanied by the person laying the information, if that person so desires, unless the justice by whom the warrant is issued otherwise directs, and may also, if the justice by whom the warrant is issued so directs, be accompanied by a duly qualified medical practitioner.

5. It shall not be necessary in any information or warrant under this section to name the child or young person.

8. Section 14 of the Armed Forces Act 1981 (as amended by the 1986 Act) provides for the temporary removal to and detention in a place of safety abroad of children of service families in need of care or control.

(1) "This section applies to a child who—

(a) forms part of the family of a person subject to service law serving in a country or territory outside the United Kingdom or of a civilian in a corresponding position;

(b) resides outside the united Kingdom with that family or another such family; and

(c) is under seventeen years of age and unmarried.

(2) This section also applies to a child who is staying (for however short a time) with a family other than the family to which he belongs but otherwise satisfies the conditions specified in subsection (1) above and so applies to him as if he resided with that family.

(3) If an officer having jurisdiction in relation to a child to whom this section applies thinks fit, he may, on being satisfied on one or more of the grounds specified in subsection (4) below that the child is in need of care or control, order the child to be removed to and detained in a place of safety.

(4) The grounds which justify the making of such an order in relation to a child to whom this section applies are—

(a) that his proper development is being avoidably prevented or neglected or his health is being avoidably impaired or neglected or he is being or is likely to be ill-treated;

(b) that he is exposed to moral danger;

(c) that he is beyond the control of his parent or guardian or, in a case where the child resides for the time being with the family of another person, of that person.

(4A) A place of safety in which a child is required to be detained under this section may be situated either in the country or territory where the child resides or elsewhere (including in the United Kingdom); and an officer having jurisdiction in relation to a child detained in a place of safety outside the United Kingdom may make an order (including an order involving the return of the child to the United Kingdom) modifying the order by which the child is detained so as to require the child to be removed to and detained in another place of safety.

(5) The officers having jurisdiction in relation to a child to whom this section applies or a child detained in a place of safety are—

(a) the commanding officer of the person to whose family the child belongs;

(b) the commanding officer of the person with whose family the child resides or, as the case may be, was residing when he was removed to a place of safety."

F. Supervision orders

9. *Sections 11–19 of the Children and Young Persons Act 1969* set out provisions relating to supervision orders:—

Section 11 states

"Any provision of this Act authorising a court to make a supervision order in respect of any person shall be construed as authorising the court to make an order placing him under the supervision of a local authority designated by the order or of a probation officer; and in this Act "supervised person" shall be construed accordingly and "supervised person" and "supervisor", in relation to a supervision order, mean respectively the person placed or to be placed under supervision by the order and the person under whose supervision he is placed or to be placed by order.

The power to include requirements in supervision orders is set out in section 12:—

1. "A supervision order may require the supervised person to reside with an individual named in the order who agrees to the requirement, but a requirement imposed by a supervision order in pursuance of this subsection shall be subject to any such requirement of the order as is authorised by the following provisions of this section.

2. Subject to section 19(6) of this Act, a supervision order may require the supervised person to comply with such directions of the

supervisor as are mentioned in paragraph (a) or (b) or paragraphs (a) and (b) of this subsection, that is to say

a. directions requiring the supervised person to live for a single period specified in the directions at a place so specified;

b. directions given from time to time requiring him to do all or any of the following things

    i. to live at a place or places specified in the directions for a period or periods so specified.

    ii. to present himself to a person or persons specified in the directions at a place or places and on a day or days so specified;

but it shall be for the supervisor to decide whether and to what extent he exercises any power to give directions conferred on him by virtue of the preceding provisions of this subsection and to decide the form of any directions; and a requirement imposed by a supervision order in pursuance of this subsection shall be subject to any such requirement of the order as is authorised by subsection (4) of this section".

[requirement subsections 3–5 not quoted]

Section 14 sets out the duties of a supervisor

"While a supervision order is in force it shall be the duty of the supervisor to advise, assist and befriend the supervised person".

Section 15 allows for the variation and discharge of a supervision order and the substitution of a care order:—

"If while a supervision order is in force in respect of a supervised person who has not attained the age of eighteen it appears to a juvenile court, on the application of the supervisor or the supervised person, that it is appropriate to make an order under this subsection, the court may make an order discharging the supervision order or varying it by

a. cancelling any requirement included in it in pursuance of section 12 or section 18(2) (b) of this Act; or

b. inserting in it (either in addition to or in substitution for any of its provisions) any provision which could have been included in the order if the court had then had power to make it and were exercising the power,

and may on discharging the supervision order make a care order (other than an interim order) in respect of the supervised person;"

G. Care Orders

10. Section 1(2) of the Children and Young Persons Act 1969 sets out the grounds which need to be satisfied before a court will grant a care order. This section is quoted at D.

Section 1(3) of the same Act sets out the type of order which the court may make under section 1:—

a. an order requiring his parent or guardian to enter in a recognisance to take proper care of him and exercise proper control over him; or

b. a supervision order; or

c. a care order (other than an interim order); or

d. a hospital order within the meaning of Part V of the Mental Health Act 1959; or

e. a guardianship order within the meaning of that Act.

11. Section 10 of the Child Care Act 1980 sets out the powers and duties of local authorities with respect to children committed to their care—

"(1) It shall be the duty of a local authority to whose care a child is committed by a care order or by a warrant under section 23(1) of the Children and Young Persons Act 1969 (which relates to remands in the care of local authorities) to receive the child into their care and, notwithstanding any claim by his parent or guardian, to keep him in their care while the order of warrant is in force.

(2) A local authority shall, subject to the following provisions of this section, have the same powers and duties with respect to a person in their care by virtue of a care order or such a warrant as his parent or guardian would have apart from the order or warrant and may (without prejudice to the foregoing provisions of this subsection but subject to regulations made in pursuance of section 39 of this Act) restrict his liberty to such extent as the authority consider appropriate.

(3) A local authority shall not cause a child in their care by virtue of a care order to be brought up in any religious creed other than that in which he would have been brought up apart from the order.

(4) It shall be the duty of a local authority to comply with any provision included in an interim order in pursuance of section 22(2) of the Children and Young Persons Act 1969 and, in the case of a person in their care by virtue of section 23 of that Act, to permit him to be removed from their care in due course of law."

H. Responsibility of Local Authority for Children in Care

12. In discharging its responsibilities for children in care, whether they have been received voluntarily into care, or committed into care by a court order, the local authority must act in accordance with its duty under Section 18(1) of the Child Care Act 1980, which sets out the so-called 'welfare principle'. That sub-section states:

> "In reaching any decision relating to a child in their care, a local authority shall give first consideration to the need to safeguard and promote the welfare of the child throughout his childhood; and shall so far as practicable ascertain the wishes and feelings of the child regarding the decision and give due consideration to them, having regard to his age and understanding."

I. Children and Young Persons (Amendment) Act 1986

13. The Children and Young Persons (Amendment) Act 1987 contains four provisions:

i. *A power for the Secretary of State to make regulations* (Section 1) to cover the children in the care of a local authority who go to live with their parents or guardians, relatives or friends while still in care. Regulations made under this new power would apply to all children in care who are not living with foster parents or in a childrens home;

ii. *A new right for parents or guardians to be made full parties to care proceedings when the court believes that their interests are different from the child's* (Section 3). The main difference in giving such parents party status is to clarify their right to take part fully in proceedings and as a consequence to have a right of appeal;

iii. *A new right for grandparents to apply to the court or to a single magistrate to be joined as parties to the proceedings* (Section 3). Rules have been made setting out the criteria which the court (or magistrates) must apply when considering applications from grandparents to become parties;

iv. *A new right for parents and guardians who were made parties to care and related proceedings* (ie those relating to a child's removal from home and subsequent care) *to appeal to the Crown Court against an order made in those proceedings* (Section 2). This allows such parents (or guardians) to appeal on their own behalf against all forms of court order in such cases.

14. The Act will apply only to proceedings which begin after it is brought into force. Sections 2 and 3 of the Act will be implemented on 1 August 1988 and section 1 at a later date, yet to be announced.

Index

Introductory Note

References such as '178–9' indicate (not necessarily continuous) discussion of a topic across a range of pages. Wherever possible in the case of topics with many references, these have either been divided into sub-topics or only the most significant discussions of the topic are listed. Because the entire work is about 'child witnesses' the use of this term (and certain others which occur constantly throughout the book) as an entry point has been restricted. Information will be found under the corresponding detailed topics.